Defense Relations Between
the United States and Vietnam

ALSO BY LEWIS M. STERN

*The Vietnamese Communist Party's Agenda for Reform:
A Study of the Eighth National Party Congress*
(McFarland, 1998)

*Imprisoned or Missing in Vietnam:
Policies of the Vietnamese Government Concerning
Captured and Unaccounted for United States Soldiers, 1969–1994*
(McFarland, 1995)

Defense Relations Between the United States and Vietnam

The Process of Normalization, 1977–2003

Lewis M. Stern

McFarland & Company, Inc., Publishers
Jefferson, North Carolina, and London

The views expressed in this book are those of the author alone and do not represent the position of the Department of Defense or any part of the United States government.

LIBRARY OF CONGRESS CATALOGUING-IN-PUBLICATION DATA

Stern, Lewis M.
   Defense relations between the United States and Vietnam : the process of normalization, 1977–2003 / by Lewis M. Stern.
      p.   cm.
   Includes bibliographical references and index.

   ISBN 0-7864-2168-1 (softcover : 50# alkaline paper)

   1. United States — Foreign relations — Vietnam.
2. Vietnam — Foreign relations — United States.   3. United States — Military relations — Vietman.   4. Vietnam — Military relations — United States.   5. United States — Foreign relations — 1945–1989.   6. United States — Foreign relations — 1989–
I. Title.
E183.8.V5S74   2005
327.730597'09'049 — dc22   2005007355

British Library cataloguing data are available

©2005 Lewis M. Stern. All rights reserved

No part of this book may be reproduced or transmitted in any form or by any means, electronic or mechanical, including photocopying or recording, or by any information storage and retrieval system, without permission in writing from the publisher.

Cover images ©2005 Corbis

Manufactured in the United States of America

McFarland & Company, Inc., Publishers
  Box 611, Jefferson, North Carolina 28640
    www.mcfarlandpub.com

Contents

Preface	1
1 — Exploring New Foundations, 1977–1993	7
2 — Stumbling Toward a Relationship, 1994–1995	36
3 — Building Defense Ties, 1995	69
4 — Making Military Contacts, 1996	93
5 — Ground Floor Military Relations, 1997	124
6 — Making Defense Relations Work, 1998	161
7 — Nudging Things Along, Muddling Towards Dénouement, 1999–2000	189
8 — Conclusions, Observations, Musings	221
Notes	245
Bibliography	271
Index	287

Preface

In November 2003, bundled against a cold and misty morning, a group of senior Vietnamese gentlemen dressed in winter parkas and blending with the small groups of other tourists, stood with their heads bowed before the grave of America's first president, George Washington, at the founding father's Mount Vernon estate in Fairfax County, Virginia. A modest man at the head of this cluster offered some words of respect to those within earshot. Americans in the crowd, selling flowers in honor of Veterans' Day, offered the Vietnamese bouquets and red poppies for their lapels. Washington was a great man, the most senior gentleman said. Because of his vision, his love of peace, and his personal commitment to national freedom and independence, he belonged, not just to the United States, but to the world. The group would later inscribe such words in the guest books of the estate, signing them on behalf of their leader, Major General Pham Van Tra, the Minister of Defense of the Socialist Republic of Vietnam.

Tra, a highly decorated officer in the People's Army and a veteran of major combat engagements dating from his enlistment in 1953, had met with Secretary of Defense Donald Rumsfeld the day before this outing, on 10 November, becoming the first Defense Minister of the Socialist Republic to grace the halls of the Pentagon. Over lunch, the Secretary told Tra and his delegation that there had been improvements in the bilateral defense relationship. The Vietnamese and the U.S. had found ways to cooperate on demining, humanitarian disaster assistance, search and rescue, and medical assistance. Defense Minister Tra noted that previous visits to the United States, including a trip by former vice minister of defense Tran Hanh in October 1998, had brought about positive results for relations between the two defense departments and the two militaries. Mr. Rumsfeld stated that this visit should hopefully help define additional ways the militaries could work together, possibly on counter terrorism and counter narcotics efforts. Minister Tra replied that he hoped to discuss ways to improve military relations, and to encourage increased exchanges of military delegations not only at the highest levels but also at middle ranks in a way that would improve mutual understanding.

The minister told Secretary Rumsfeld that a U.S. Navy ship would be welcomed in Ho Chi Minh City port during 19–22 November, and that he hoped his own visit to Washington would be followed by visits to Vietnam by each of the commanders of the U.S. armed services. Tra was pleased by Rumsfeld's comments that the U.S. and the Vietnamese shared the same goals: preserving independence, protecting the citizenry, and preserving sovereignty, and by the secretary's willingness to share the Vietnamese view that we "should not allow the future to repeat the past."

This book is the story of how the relationship between the United States and Vietnam progressed from the first efforts to press forward with initiatives aimed at developing rudimentary defense relations, to the point at which a visit to the U.S. by the Vietnamese defense minister was possible.

In the late 1980s, during his tenure as deputy assistant secretary of defense for Asia and the Pacific, Professor Karl Jackson described policymakers at work as the equivalent of a clutch of beagles aggressively pursuing a lone rabbit. The rabbit lurches forward, feinting left and then right, and darts ahead at breakneck speed. In a noisy cloud of dust the predators stumble after the hare, barking, churning up earth, fixated on their target. At some point, one lone head juts up from that scrambling crowd of dogs, notices that the prey has run off at a tangent, and stumbles to get the forward-moving mass of hunters to change course. The resulting comic book image of dogs plowing into one another, blundering to regain their footing as they individually realize the situation has changed, is a fair depiction of the less elegant dimensions of the policy-making process.

This book is an attempt to clear away some of the dust stirred up by the process of developing a defense relationship between the United States and Vietnam during the period from 1990 to 2000. It is a personal account of Department of Defense policy toward Vietnam gleaned from my involvement as the director for Indochina, Thailand and Burma in the Office of the Assistant Secretary of Defense for International Security Affairs from 1988 to 2001. And it is my own effort to unscramble the Vietnamese side of the equation.

During the years 1988–2001, I served as the policy focal point for the Pentagon on defense policy issues concerning Vietnam. My responsibilities were distinct from the Defense Department offices concerned with sustaining the U.S. government's efforts to account for service personnel missing as a result of the war in Indochina. From 1994 to 1996, I focused on the question of when and how the Department of Defense should establish bilateral defense relations with the Socialist Republic of Vietnam (SRV). From 1996 to 2000, I managed the process of coordinating U.S. defense policy toward Vietnam, and conducted the effort to nudge the Vietnamese Defense Ministry to enter into a ground-floor level military relationship with the United States. I had the support of senior Defense Department officials during 1993-94 when I first broached the idea of a "military-to-military" relationship with Vietnam, and the assistance of colleagues on the Joint Staff and at the Pacific Command, and very able cooperation from the first U.S. defense attaché assigned to Hanoi in 1995, U.S. army colonel Edward O'Dowd, now retired. Simply put, I managed what was, in relationship to other burning issues, a minor policy initiative for a selection of busy Pentagon decision-makers (the "E Ring") who, when they turned their attention to my area of interest, relied on my views and their instincts, and the good sense and opinions of their colleagues in other agencies, to formulate positions in response to my recommendations.

This book begins with a review of the attempts under President Jimmy Carter to normalize relations with Vietnam in 1978, and progresses to a brief examination of POW/MIA-related developments in the early 1990s. The book then looks at the process of normalizing relations with Vietnam begun under President Clinton, focusing on first discussions of the prospects for defense relations during the period from the February 1994 lifting of the embargo through the July 1995 decision to normalize relations. The larger part of this story revolves around policy decisions that initiated formal military-to-military contacts between the U.S. and Vietnam during the 1995-96 period; the first steps toward interaction between Hanoi and Washington on defense issues, beginning with the November 1996 visit to Vietnam by an interagency delegation headed by the deputy assistant secretary of defense for Asia and the Pacific; and the working level discussions over the design and management of the annual calendar of events in the military-to-military relationship during 1997 to 1998. Finally, this study looks at increasingly higher level contacts in the bilateral defense relationship during the period 1998–2000, as well as the effort to develop a "strategic dialogue" (doi thoai chien luoc) during that period.

In the course of managing this policy, I developed close, continuous relationships with a wide range of senior and middle departmental level officials in the Vietnamese defense and foreign ministries. I had the opportunity to speak with National Assembly officials, staffers from various

Vietnamese Communist Party (VNCP) departments, and representatives from other ministries. I owe a great intellectual debt to many of these Vietnamese who helped me clarify what were daunting aspects of the history of Vietnamese foreign policy decisions, and who shared their perspectives in ways that made the Vietnamese angle on this story much more accessible to me. Deputy Foreign Minister Tran Quang Co; Ambassador Le Van Bang; the first deputy chief of the Vietnamese Mission in Washington, Ha Huy Thong, and his successor, Pham Van Que; the director of the Foreign Ministry's Americas Department, Nguyen Xuan Phong, and his successor, Nguyen Manh Hung; Ministry of Interior advisor Le Minh Tran; and countless others provided extremely useful insights and personal views that helped me interpret Vietnamese decisions and actions. I owe a special gratitude to Senior Colonel Vo Dinh Quang, the first SRV defense attaché in Washington (1997–2000), for both his friendship and his sage guidance of my efforts to fathom Vietnamese policy and politics. I owe a similar debt to Senior Colonel Nguyen Ngoc Giao, who replaced Senior Colonel Quang, for his patient willingness to work together to sustain bilateral defense relations. The observations of many other Vietnamese are recorded in this book under the shroud of anonymity.

I am grateful for the assistance, guidance and criticisms offered by many friends and colleagues. General John W. Vessey, Jr., the presidential emissary from 1987 to 1992, set an example with his unerringly logical, even-handed and sensible approach to problems that dogged the earliest effort to engage the Vietnamese on the POW/MIA issue. Hershel Gober, the deputy secretary of Veterans Affairs and the head of four presidential delegations that traveled to Vietnam on the instructions of President William Clinton, encouraged me to think about Vietnamese negotiating tactics, policy planning, and implementation strategies. Robert Jones, who served as the deputy assistant secretary of defense for POW/MIA Affairs from 1998 to 2001, urged continued contemplation of the larger problems involved in this new relationship, beyond the day to day management of issues, and politely tolerated many test drives of the observations and theories that became the core of this book. Stanley Roth and Kurt Campbell, respectively the assistant secretary of state and the deputy assistant secretary of defense for Asia and the Pacific during President Clinton's tenure, patiently considered many lengthy treatises on the nuances of the U.S.–Vietnamese relationship that were put before them. Dennis Harter, the deputy chief of the U.S. Mission in Hanoi from 1997 to 2000, was a friendly and critical sounding board, and a thoughtful observer on whose experience in diplomacy and knowledge of Southeast Asia I could rely for tough measures of the perspective articulated in this book. Virginia Foote encouraged my efforts to continue looking for ways to unlock the Vietnamese puzzle, and went far on her own toward clarifying this murky, frustrating and complex relationship. Tran Van Ca and Pham Duc Kien were generous with their time, and extremely helpful in my efforts to understand leadership behavior in Vietnam.

Edward O'Dowd, Colonel, U.S. Army (retired), served as the first U.S. defense attaché in Hanoi from 1995 to 1999, during which time we cemented a fast friendship, galvanized by a shared interest in Vietnam's history. His contribution to the development of normal military ties with Vietnam is inestimable, and I am immensely grateful for his help in my attempt to write about this process.

Fred Brown, William Turley, and Joseph Zasloff were constructive critics through the gestation of this writing project. I also owe my gratitude to a procession of Joint Staff and Pacific Command colleagues whose hard work, keen insights, and dedication to the U.S. national defense made the difference between success and failure for this policy.

Many people contributed to my understanding of this thing called policy, shaped my thinking about defense and security issues, or helped me comprehend strategic matters. I owe great quantities of thanks to Richard Armitage, Dorothy Avery, Jacques Bekaert, Robert Bergin, Amy Blagg, Nayan Chanda, Kenneth Conboy, Robert Destatte, Chuck Downs, Michael Eiland, Carl Ford, Charles and Cecelia Gillin, Fred Groth, Murray Hiebert, Karl Jackson, Joseph Kinder, Douglas Kinnard, Sandy Kristoff, John McAuliffe, Robert Manning, Chau Kim Nhan, Douglas Peterson, Merle Pribbenow, Kenneth Quinn, Paul and Sophie Quinn-Judge, Niyom Rathimarit, Patricia Ravalgi, David Reuther, Jean Andre Sauvageot, Mark Sidel, George Thomas, Khuc Minh Thu, Stephen Young, and Francis Zwenik. I absolve them all of any responsibility for my failure to master the lessons they tried to teach me.

I was honored by the decision by the Office of the Under Secretary of Defense for Policy to select me for a year-long "academic assignment" from September 2001 to September 2002. I deeply appreciate the hospitality afforded me by the Paul H. Nitze School of Advance International Studies (SAIS), Johns Hopkins University, which offered me status as a visiting scholar during the year I took to write this book. I gratefully acknowledge the special efforts of Fred Brown and Karl Jackson to welcome me into an impressive community of scholars working at SAIS.

My wife, Mary, and my children, Ethan and Anna, learned to live with the inconvenience of a mid-career "at home Dad." Anna and Ethan struggled over how to describe my sudden departure from a normal routine, suggesting at various times that I had been assigned, "undercover," to Johns Hopkins, or that I had simply been fired. Somehow, that sounded more feasible to them than the explanation that I had returned to school and taken it upon myself to write another book. I enjoyed the opportunity to greet Anna at the end of her high school day, to pack Mary's lunch for a change, to count on surprise visits from Ethan in between his college classes, and to have the solitude of our home in which to complete my writing project.

My friend and colleague Douglas Pike passed away in May 2002, about a week after I finished writing the conclusion to this study. I always counted on Doug's critical readings to set me right, and I will miss his counsel, guidance, and friendship. There are thousands of "Vietnam Watchers," as he used to call this ragtag analytic army, who profited as I did from Doug's consistent willingness to spend hours talking about a country that fascinated him. He made an enduring contribution to the effort to understand Vietnam. In a humble effort to remember my friend, I dedicate this book to Douglas Pike's intellectual energy, his academic accomplishments, and his endless capacity for collegiality.

1
EXPLORING NEW FOUNDATIONS, 1977–1993

The Normalization of U.S.–Vietnamese Relations:
  First Efforts

From the late 1970s, when the Administration of President Jimmy Carter briefly and unsuccessfully explored normalization of relations with the Socialist Republic of Vietnam (SRV), through the last days of the administration of President George Bush, when the first steps toward lifting portions of the U.S.–imposed embargo were taken, the Vietnamese viewed normalization as a means of ending isolation, eliminating the embargo, opening up trade opportunities, and reaching closure on some of the more nettlesome bilateral issues (especially the POW/MIA issue and refugee related matters) that had dominated relations with the U.S. since the end of the war in 1975. In late 1978, Vietnam approached the possibility of normalization with the U.S. as an opportunity to demonstrate its sovereign strength and diplomatic prowess. From Hanoi's perspective, entering into relations with Washington would enhance Vietnam's reputation as a powerful, confident Southeast Asian country, and drive home the point that Hanoi could hold its own in direct negotiations with the United States. Though there were clear advantages that would accrue to Vietnam from an early normalization with the United States, Hanoi continued to press for American aid as part of the normalization package deal, well beyond the point at which this issue ceased to be an effective bargaining chip, thus driving the U.S. to conclude that the Vietnamese price for normal bilateral relations was too high. Vietnam approached the prospect for normalization with the United States in the mid– and late–1980s with a similar series of non-negotiable starting points that essentially demanded the complete cessation of the embargo, a substantial contribution from the U.S. to "healing the wounds of war," and instant and complete recognition of Hanoi's parity with other nations in trade and diplomacy.

The strategic meaning of normalization to the Vietnamese during these two periods is suggested by Hanoi's decision to pursue negotiating tactics that ultimately spoiled any chance of early normalization. In 1978, as Hanoi tenaciously stuck to its initial demand for U.S. reconstruction assistance, the Vietnamese were bracing themselves for a confrontation with China and a long-term military investment in Cambodia. Vietnam acknowledged that these realities would plunge the Socialist Republic deeper into Moscow's debt as Hanoi sought the military assistance necessary to cope with the security requirements that would spring from the situation in Cambodia, and the Chinese threat along the northern border. It seemed to some observers that Vietnam's flirtation with normalization during December 1977–September 1978 was an effort to "balance" its increased reliance on the Soviet Union with a more cordial, potentially lucrative new relationship with the U.S., Moscow's chief rival. At the same time, in this analysis, Hanoi probably calculated that a normal relationship with the U.S. would at least telegraph the message to Beijing that American interests were now part of the equation, so that any attempt by China to bring pressure to bear on Vietnam would have to take into account the possibility of an American reaction that could be inimical to Beijing's interests.[1]

It is possible that some elements of the Vietnamese leadership believed that the Carter Administration would have been delighted to resume its role as the key balancing force in the region, and to re-energize Washington's efforts to prevent China from isolating Southeast Asia. It seems more likely, though, that the Vietnamese leadership consensus was that a relationship with Washington would not bring anything of strategic value to Vietnam, and could only offer some minor tactical opportunities to offset China's plans for isolating Vietnam. Indeed, there were similarities between Vietnam's thinking in 1977–78 about the strategic relevance of a relationship with the U.S. and Hanoi's reasoning about normalization in the late 1980s and early 1990s. In both periods, Vietnam was decidedly unwilling to place any credence in the argument that formal, proper relations with the U.S. would redound to Hanoi's favor in immediate terms, and especially where security and defense issues were concerned. Thus, in 1978, as in the late 1980s and early 1990s, Vietnam calculated that "casting the net widely" to find new friends in many areas of the globe was the Socialist

Republic's best bet. In the mid 1970s this was referred to as "consolidating the international rear," and involved a commitment to winning friends, reducing foes, and developing sympathy and support in both the "revolutionary" and the "progressive" forces of the world.[2]

To U.S. supporters of normalization during 1977–78, the process represented an opportunity to unfreeze the dialogue over a myriad of bilateral issues, especially POW/MIA–related matters. Moreover, U.S. supporters of normalization saw the development of positive bilateral relations as one strategic option among many that would remind China of the rules of behavior, and communicate U.S. willingness to resume its leadership role in Asia in the aftermath of the war.[3] That, however, was not the most widely shared thinking on the strategic meaning and value of a relationship with Hanoi. The House of Representatives had thought enough about the issue, and about Vietnam's terms for entering into a bilateral relationship, to prompt the passage of an amendment to the State Department Authorization Bill in mid–1978 prohibiting any form of reparations. A later Senate amendment required the U.S. government to oppose International Financial Institution (IFI) loans to Vietnam. The legislation effectively prohibited any agreement to postwar reconstruction assistance, and preemptively eliminated the possibility of relations on terms that would have worked for Hanoi. The amendments signaled congressional disagreement with the conclusions of the Presidential Commission, headed by Leonard Woodcock, which visited Vietnam in 1977, and reported that "improved relations with the governments of Vietnam and Laos" were the "best hope for obtaining a proper accounting for our MIAs."[4] The amendments underscored Congressional consensus that Vietnam's price for normalization was too high for a commodity that would not result in a quick accounting for America's MIAs, and would not yield a strategic dividend for the U.S. In the end, Congress seemed to have shared the Administration's view of the inconsequential impact that U.S.–Vietnamese normalization would have on the equation of regional power.[5]

Hanoi may have believed that the Carter administration was committed to achieving normalization quickly, and that the Administration was therefore prepared to strike some arrangement regarding the issue of reconstruction assistance. The Vietnamese clearly miscalculated the extent to which normalization would be a quick and easy decision by the U.S. government, especially following the initial disappointing contacts in mid–1977. Even in the midst of a flurry of congressional and constituency concern over the POW/MIA issue, Hanoi seems to have misunderstood the profound impact this issue exerted on American policy-makers. Hanoi miscalculated the influence of organized non-governmental interests in the

U.S. committed to seeking answers to questions about the fate of missing American service personnel, and misjudged the willingness of elected U.S. officials to make decisions regarding foreign policy issues on the basis of domestic political calculations.

By the mid- and late-1980s, the U.S. regarded normalization as the key bargaining chip in accelerating resolution of the POW/MIA issue, and as an important lever in the international effort to resolve the conflict in Cambodia. In Washington, the process of normalization itself was governed by a thick net of existing laws and established diplomatic positions. However, the decision to enter into a dialogue leading to normalization was a policy matter. Thus, the timing of that decision was a function of practical and political considerations.

United States Policy Toward Vietnam During the Early 1990s

During the administration of President Ronald Reagan, the U.S. and Vietnam resumed MIA discussions and initiated dialogue about the emigration of Amerasian children, the Orderly Departure Program, and the legal exit of former inmates of Vietnamese reeducation camps.[6] However, during both the Reagan and the Bush Administrations, the U.S. continued to refuse to consider normalization of relations as long as Vietnam occupied Cambodia and played a destabilizing role in the region. Washington's position was that once a political settlement of the Cambodian problem was achieved in accordance with the principles of the International Conference on Kampuchea, the U.S. would consider normalization with Vietnam, which would proceed at a pace conditioned by the progress of efforts to account for missing American service personnel.

By agreeing to expanded POW/MIA discussions, Vietnam hoped to make a slight dent in its diplomatic isolation, and to sustain U.S. interest in the refinement of Orderly Departure Program procedures. Additionally, Hanoi hoped to engage Washington in efforts to develop a system for managing the migration of children of American servicemen and Vietnamese mothers. Hanoi also hoped to get Washington to allow continued mailing of remittances and commercial items by Vietnamese residents of the U.S. to relatives in Vietnam.

Hanoi's mantra during 1990-91 was that Vietnam had been more cooperative and forthcoming on the POW/MIA issue during those years than ever before; that support for Washington's policy toward Indochina was dwindling; and that increasing pressure from U.S. businesses would render Washington's position untenable. Washington criticized Hanoi for allowing the momentum on POW/MIA cooperation to diminish, and warned that the failure to resolve the POW/MIA issue would pose a significant obstacle to improving relations once a comprehensive settlement was reached in Cambodia. A September 1990 meeting between Richard Solomon, Assistant Secretary of State for East Asia and the Pacific, and Deputy Foreign Minister Le Mai, a subsequent September discussion in New York between Secretary of State James Baker and Foreign Minister Nguyen Co Thach, and an October meeting in Washington between Thach and Presidential Emissary John Vessey pressed things forward slightly, and led to Vietnamese acceptance of U.S. proposals for several significant POW/MIA initiatives.[7] The Vietnamese media hailed the Vessey-Thach meeting as a "breakthrough" in bilateral relations, and stressed the importance of lifting the embargo and establishing diplomatic relations.

In early April 1991 Assistant Secretary of State Solomon presented the Vietnamese Permanent Representative to the United Nations with a description of the four-phased process through which bilateral U.S.–Vietnamese relations would develop in the aftermath of Hanoi's signing the international agreement for a peaceful settlement of the Cambodian conflict. The document described how cooperation on the POW/MIA issue would influence the pace and scope of the normalization of relations. Phase One was to begin with the signing of the Paris Agreement on Cambodia, which took place on 23 October 1991. Phase Two was to begin with the establishment of the United Nations Transitional Authority in Cambodian (UNTAC), and the initial steps toward a United Nations–supervised election in Cambodia. Phase Three was to begin once Vietnam and the authorities in Phnom Penh had supported the implementation of the Paris Agreement for six months. Phase Four, the final phase, was to begin following a free and democratic election in Cambodia, the establishment of a new National Assembly, and the demobilization of the four Cambodian factions. Foreign Minister Nguyen Co Thach reacted negatively to the Roadmap, as the outline of the future of U.S.–Vietnamese relations came to be called. In Hanoi's view, the U.S. government had set conditions that Vietnam would be unable to satisfy as a result of diminishing influence over the Phnom Penh government and trends beyond Vietnam's control. Nevertheless, Thach promised continued cooperation on the POW/MIA issue, while neither accepting nor rejecting the Roadmap.[8]

From the start, the Vietnamese argued that the Roadmap was a unilateral document dictating a course of action, not a negotiating position, and was therefore an affront to their sovereignty. The Roadmap, Hanoi averred, was seriously out of date, given trends toward reconciliation in the region and progress in implementing the peace agreement in Cambodia. Moreover, from Vietnam's perspective, rapid normalization between Washington and Hanoi would be the best means of guaranteeing the fullest possible accounting for missing Americans. The Vietnamese sought to proceed with MIA cooperation without making formal references to the Roadmap.

Throughout most of 1991, Hanoi argued that it had contributed to the resolution of the Cambodian conflict by withdrawing its troops, and participated in the efforts to formulate a peace plan. Hanoi claimed it had committed itself to respect the decisions of Cambodia's Supreme National Council, the body created to represent Cambodia in the peacekeeping process, and had agreed to accept international supervision and control of a ceasefire and support an enhanced role for the United Nations in administering a free election in Cambodia.[9] Hanoi rejected the charge that it continued to obstruct efforts to resolve the conflict in Cambodia, and asserted that Washington's condition for normalization — that is, the peaceful settlement of the situation in Cambodia — demonstrated a less than earnest interest in normalization on the part of the U.S. government, because normalization itself would be a key catalyst for the rapid resolution of the conflict in Cambodia.

Vietnam's position on U.S. relations would not change appreciably during 1991. A mid-year shift in leadership, and changes in the style and substance of foreign policy making, resulting from the June 1991 7th National Congress of the Vietnamese Communist Party (VNCP), clarified Vietnam's regional goals and diplomatic priorities.

The Shifting Locus of Foreign Policy Decisions

The 7th National Party Congress convened on 24 June 1991. The resulting new lineup of the Politburo, Secretariat and Central Committee, and Do Muoi's election to the position of General Secretary, represented a net gain for the cautious reformers, and a boost for the military. Muoi was widely regarded as an action-oriented leader with considerable experience in untangling Byzantine state bureaucracies. There was some confidence among Vietnamese officials that Muoi would continue the reforms. Though at first a lukewarm subscriber to the reformist line in the mid–1980s, Muoi quickly became an important voice for sustained economic change and policy flexibility.

Foreign Minister Nguyen Co Thach, the architect of Vietnam's policy toward the United States, lost his Politburo seat. He stepped down from his ministerial post at the National Assembly session in August. Minister of Defense Le Duc Anh became the second ranking Politburo member, and Doan Khue moved to the number five slot, replacing Anh as Defense Minister at the August National Assembly session. Together, the positioning of Anh and Khue represented an important advance in influence for the People's Army, which had been burdened with the need to slim down fast in the face of severe budget constraints, and had become embroiled in a debate over new national security requirements, Cambodia, and the role of the peacetime army.

The new Politburo and Central Committee left the Foreign Ministry without Politburo-level representation. Four foreign ministry officials— one ambassador and three vice ministers—were elected to the 7th Central Committee. Vice Foreign Minister Tran Quang Co was elevated to full membership from alternate status. Four Ministry of National Defense (MND) officials, all incumbents, were elected to the Central Committee. The two Ministry of Interior (MOI) vice ministers elected to the 7th Congress were incumbents. Though the Ministry of Foreign Affairs (MFA) had the same number of seats on the Central Committee as the more conservative MND, the MND officials were experienced second term members. Additionally, the four MND incumbents coupled with the two incumbent MOI members of the Central Committee gave those ministries a slight voting edge over the MFA. Altogether, this was a net gain for the two ministries that had been engaged in frontal combat with Foreign Minister Thach over the mending of the relationship with China, expanding Vietnam's network of foreign relations, and managing the U.S.–Vietnamese relationship. The new Politburo was a clear victory for the views espoused by Le Duc Anh in favor of a rapid normalization with Beijing, as well as a negative comment on Thach's approach to Cambodia and the United States.

In the aftermath of the Party Congress, potentially important changes in the manner in which Vietnam made and implemented foreign policy began to take place. General Secretary Do Muoi became involved in the management of important foreign relations in a manner that distinguished him from his predecessor. Muoi worked to clarify policy goals on a range of critical issues, including bilateral relations with China, relations with the U.S., and POW/MIA cooperation. He utilized a talented advisory staff, and urged Central Executive Committee leaders involved in foreign policy to travel, improve their educational level, and become more effective diplomats. Foreign policy professionals began to play more important roles within the system, conducting foreign policy in accordance with rules, and engaging in actions intended to shape and influence policy formulation.

With Nguyen Manh Cam's elevation to the Politburo at the January 1994 interim party conference, foreign policy issues were debated with increased rigor. The External Relations Department of the Vietnamese Communist Party's Central Committee gradually became more involved in the foreign policy-making process, assuming responsibility for thoroughly coordinating position papers intended to galvanize discussion throughout the party and the government. The National Assembly had begun to demand greater responsiveness from the Foreign Ministry, which in turn caused the External Relations Department of the VNCP to focus more closely on reviewing policies and answering the questions of legislators in coordination with the Foreign Ministry.

Recalibrating the Roadmap

By the end of 1991, the Administration's view was that the Vietnamese had not complied with the several specific requirements spelled out as Phase One benchmarks. The Vietnamese had not satisfactorily accounted for the remaining Last Known Alive discrepancy cases. They had not responded to the U.S. request that a mechanism to investigate live sighting reports be established. Additionally, Vietnam had not been responsive to proposals for a 24-month concept of operations that would enable continued joint field investigations. Hanoi indicated that the most it was prepared to do was sustain the current level of activity.

The Administration's thinking was that the Roadmap was intended to demonstrate that the U.S. was prepared to move forward with alacrity matching Vietnamese responsiveness to U.S. requests for cooperation on the POW/MIA issue. The four phases of the Roadmap were keyed to specific Vietnamese actions on this issue. Washington did not envision an automatic shift from one phase to the next. The U.S. did make it clear that Phase One would begin with the signing of the Paris Agreement, and that Phase Two could begin with the deployment of UNTAC, ambodia. However, faced with the desultory performance of the Vietnamese on the Phase One POW/MIA matters, the Administration was not prepared to move to the next step in this process until Hanoi cooperated in a manner that led to real accounting results.

While the specificity of the Roadmap may have been attractive to elements of the Vietnamese foreign policy establishment, if only because it represented a complete and authoritative inventory of precisely what the U.S. wanted from Vietnam, in the end the document did not fit with Hanoi's assessment of the potential for a constructive U.S.–Vietnamese relationship, and the price that Hanoi should have to pay to achieve that goal. During the tenure of the 6th VNCP Congress (1986–91), Vietnam was prepared to seek broader, friendlier relations with all countries, including the U.S. But there were limits to Hanoi's forbearance, and clear limits to what Hanoi was prepared to do to secure a normal relationship with Washington. Hanoi was prepared to support plans to bring a peaceful end to the conflict of Cambodia, but only in a manner that avoided casting Vietnam in the role of the country that abandoned support for Phnom Penh. What looked like lukewarm Vietnamese support for a United Nations presence was probably Hanoi's concern for embracing the peace plan at the expense of its long relationship with its client regime in Phnom Penh.

Moreover, Hanoi had a sense that the dividends that would ultimately become available as a result of normalization with the U.S. were limited, and probably not worth struggling over. Hanoi felt sure that Congress would not accept the Administration's policy toward Indochina. If Vietnam saw any utility to the Roadmap, it was the clarity with which the document articulated the steps necessary to get to the stage where U.S. objections to loans by the IFIs would be dropped. This represented a clear-cut indication of what it would take to improve the bilateral and multilateral economic environment, an issue of central importance to Vietnam.

In early 1992 Vietnam became more direct in urging the "model" for normalization with the U.S. that stood in contrast to the Roadmap. Hanoi's stance on normalization started with support for bilateral talks which took into consideration "the viewpoints of each side." Hanoi suggested that there was high-level agreement to separate the POW/MIA problem from other political issues. Vietnam would strive to solve the MIA issue regardless of whether or not relations with the U.S. were normalized.

Hanoi's "model" for normalization was the process of Sino-Vietnamese *rapprochement*, in which Beijing and Hanoi set aside difficult problems, normalized relations, and allowed the existence of all this newfound good will to provide the energy necessary to solve intractable problems. Hanoi proposed that Washington do the same, reasoning that "as long as the United States did not realize its interests in its relations with Vietnam there would be obstacles in the process toward normalization."

On 13 April 1992 the Department of State announced that the U.S. would grant an exception to the economic embargo with Vietnam that would allow the establishment of telecommunications links with Vietnam. On 29 April, the Department of State announced the lifting of all embargo restrictions on the activities of non-governmental humanitarian and non-profit organizations, and the decision to grant exceptions to the embargo that would permit commercial sales to meet basic human needs. These decisions were taken in recognition of Vietnam's cooperation on the POW/MIA issue. Though certain of the actions fell into Phase Two of the Roadmap, the Administration made it clear that it would be wrong to say that Phase Two had begun because Washington still expected more cooperation from Hanoi on the question of U.S. remains and access to wartime archival information on the fate of missing Americans.

Vietnam's Foreign Policy Priorities

In mid–1992, the Vietnamese Communist Party articulated a complex foreign policy approach integrating a concern for the domestic consequences of regional and international economic trends with recognition that, beyond sustaining economic momentum, there was a pressing need to focus on preserving political stability. The VNCP third plenary, convened from 18 to 29 June 1992, endorsed establishing new diplomatic and economic relations as a foreign policy priority, and emphasized the importance of national defense and security, calling on the country and the armed forces to "resolutely fight back those peaceful evolution schemes and tricks of hostile forces and their sabotage activities." In his 18 June speech to the plenary session, General Secretary Do Muoi stressed that national defense considerations needed to be taken into account in formulating steps toward an open door foreign policy by improving the quality of the armed forces and assuring party control over the military.

Muoi argued that isolation was not a possibility for any nation, even developed countries. He endorsed a comprehensive expansion of foreign relations along political, economic, cultural, technological and scientific dimensions with the active involvement of the party, state, mass organizations and all non-governmental entities. He placed a priority on regional relations and economic links aimed at strengthening markets. Muoi restated the importance of conducting this expansion of relations with an eye toward the relationship between external policies and national issues, party activities, and security and defense. To the General Secretary, the most effective way to combat plots to undermine reform was to satisfy the socioeconomic needs of the population. Success in consolidating the nation's defense and security would entail increasing the party's leadership over the armed forces. Elevating the quality of the military and the public security service would guarantee security. That would require attention to the living standard of cadres and officers, and to the quality of military training.[10]

It appears that during this plenary session the Central Committee discussed a wide range of foreign policy issues, from the health of socialism in the aftermath of the breakup of the Soviet Union to the conditions for regional stability, the meaning of Vietnam's integration into the Association of Southeast Asian Nations (ASEAN), and the fundamental policy assumptions behind the effort to broaden bilateral relations on a global basis.

The plenary session may have formulated a series of concept papers on the world situation, and on the ideological underpinnings and the economic dimension of foreign policy, defense and security issues. Summaries of these key issues appeared as part of a controlled Defense Ministry document issued to propagate the substance of the third plenary resolution two months after the Central Committee session.[11]

That document echoed forecasts suggesting that Asia would become the world's most important region by the 21st century, owing to its untapped resources, its rate of economic development, and its strategic importance. The Central Committee, according to the Defense Ministry synopsis, concerned itself with the contradictions that could exert potentially destabilizing influence in the region, including the emergence of tensions involving economic and political competition between the region's larger players and the world's key capitalist markets; between socialist and imperialist powers; and between developing countries and the U.S. as well as Japan. The Central Committee also focused on the complexity of the fluid situation in Cambodia, and differences of views within ASEAN.

The Defense Ministry document captured the evolution of ASEAN-Vietnam relations, and the central role played by trade and economic forces in the process of regional change that made it possible for Vietnam to sign the Bali Treaty and become a member of ASEAN. The synopsis drew out four global trends: the trend toward independence and self-strengthening on the part of all people; undiminished support for socialist ideals and resistance toward imperialism on the part of all socialist countries, communist and workers' parties, and all revolutionary forces; the trend toward diversifying and expanding relations between nations to improve regional links; and cooperation between different political and social systems with the goal of creating a durable peace. These trends, the document stated, had critical impact on Vietnam's domestic and foreign policies.[12]

Foreign policy principles must preserve independence, unity and socialism, the synopsis asserted, but at the same time they must allow for creativity and flexibility, and must respond to current conditions and "concrete circumstances." Nationalism and internationalism must be fused. International duties must be fulfilled, not because of the advantage accrued to the Vietnamese people by sustaining such commitments to revolutionary movements throughout the world, but for the good of people everywhere. Diversified, expanded foreign relations would serve to protect independence and national wealth.

Vietnam's foreign policy goal, according to the Defense Ministry synopsis, should be to achieve cooperative participation in regional affairs, and to expand relations with every nation. The synopsis concluded that Vietnam should understand the challenges and opportunities regarding economic development, and should pursue the development of foreign economic relations in accordance with the precepts set down by the party and the state in an attentive, cautious manner, because a foreign policy strategy based on widened relations presented any number of emerging forces with the opportunity to undermine political security, social order, and culture.[13]

These conservative principles introduced a discourse on the responsibilities of national defense and the protection of national security, and a call for increased vigilance and efforts to defeat the trickery of "peaceful transformation" schemes aimed at ending the VNCP's grip on power and circumventing socialism in Vietnam. That section of the synopsis stressed the need to confront Western propaganda aimed at undermining popular confidence in the party, discrediting the regime's standing and preventing the government from doing its job. The document pointed to the use of espionage nets, armed counter-revolutionary groups of exiles, and overseas Vietnamese associations to oppose the regime and threaten Vietnam's stability.[14]

This was a fairly bleak atmosphere in which to explore the potential for the normalization of relations with the U.S. The diminished influence of the foreign policy leadership, and the more conservative views of the defense establishment, combined to yield a circumspect, distrustful leadership that was ill-prepared to negotiate in the context of the Roadmap, concerned about long term consequences for Vietnam's regional standing that might be brought on by changes wrought by an internationally brokered solution to the Cambodian conflict, and preoccupied with threats to sovereignty and security.

Bush Presidency End Game Approach on Vietnam

In the aftermath of the 7th Party Congress, and through the end of 1992, Hanoi accorded normalization a fairly low priority, and held relatively low expectations regarding what might be expected of a relationship with the U.S. In Hanoi's view, Vietnam's participation in the resolution of the Cambodian conflict had removed a major obstacle to improving relations with many countries. Vietnam had restored friendly relations with Beijing, and improved the tone of relations with the ASEAN countries, hoping to establish the conditions for the resumption of development aid, attract foreign investment, and develop more effective, efficient trade ties with many countries. These were precisely the areas in which Vietnam saw little prospect for rapid progress in a relationship with the U.S.[15]

In the months leading up to the November 1992 elections in the U.S., Hanoi demonstrated a serious interest in addressing a wide range of bilateral problems and improving overall relations with important friends, partners and neighbors, such as Russia and Thailand.[16] Hanoi also made it clear that it was prepared to sustain cooperation with the U.S. on the POW/MIA issue, but was not going to tolerate allegations that the Socialist Republic continued to hold live U.S. prisoners.[17] At the same time Vietnam began to draw attention to what it described as the expanding consensus among U.S. non-governmental organizations and interest groups favoring normalization.[18] Vietnam sought to suggest that popular sentiment in favor of upgrading U.S.–Vietnamese ties was far ahead of official Washington's thinking. Vietnam restated its perception that organized U.S. interests, with government collusion, continued to conspire against Vietnam by challenging socialist precepts, propounding anti-government ideas, and mobilizing overseas Vietnamese against the Socialist Republic, in concert with far flung, like-minded organizations in France, England and Russia.[19]

Through the end of 1992, the key interagency focus in Washington remained fixed on the question of when and how quickly the U.S. should take the remaining steps left in Phase Two of the Roadmap: allowing American businesses to set up offices and negotiate contracts for execution in Phase Three; and initiating U.S. government participation in international efforts to eliminate Vietnam's IMF arrears. A central argument in favor of moving forward was that a new Vietnamese decision-making team had been put in place, and that leadership appeared inclined to be less confrontational about the POW/MIA issue. The fulcrum of this argument was the assumption that moving to Phase Two was a relatively cost-free way of acknowledging that there were new possibilities, and that Vietnam's cooperation, evident by the end of the year, was one of the results of this new leadership's first policy decisions.

However, senior Pentagon officials preferred to signal that the U.S.

would not take any of the remaining steps in Phase Two until Washington had a chance to evaluate the Vietnamese response to U.S. requirements regarding archival research, including Hanoi's cooperation with the first U.S. archival team, deployed to Vietnam in late October 1992 to initiate cooperation in uncovering Vietnamese wartime archival evidence that might shed light on the fates of U.S. service personnel. Many senior U.S. officials at State and Defense believed that the Vietnamese had not actually given the U.S. anything new in terms of historical documents and relevant photography from wartime archives that could help provide answers about on the fate of American MIAs.[20] Other senior U.S. government officials in the interagency working group made the case that Vietnam's agreement to cooperate should not be regarded as different from any of the other SRV promises to enhance POW/MIA cooperation made during the tenure of Foreign Minister Thach. In short, at the working level, members of the interagency group continued to discuss different viewpoints regarding Vietnamese intentions, the Foreign Ministry's negotiating posture, Hanoi's cooperative spirit and the POW/MIA results that derived from that cooperation.

Though most of the interagency dialogue that took place revolved around the POW/MIA issue, there was incrementally more room for addressing the question of U.S.–Vietnamese relations on the basis of larger foreign policy interests. So, in the aftermath of the 1992 election, the office of the Deputy Assistant Secretary of Defense for Asia and the Pacific (DASD/AP) made the case that ceremoniously moving to Phase Two of the Roadmap would not reward Hanoi with the single most important incentive — the lifting of the embargo — but it would allow Washington to telegraph its willingness to follow up on President Bush's Rose Garden promise to examine ways to move the process forward. Moving to Phase Two would eliminate the feeling, shared by major aid donors and trading partners such as Japan and South Korea, that the U.S. was dragging its feet. It would also press beyond the assumptions that underpinned the view that the Vietnamese were still withholding POW/MIA information, a position that did not adequately take into account the changes in the way the new Vietnamese leadership was prepared to manage the POW/MIA issue, and their initial steps to be responsive to U.S. requests for wartime information bearing on missing U.S. service personnel.

In the end, this argument had little resonance in the interagency group. Interestingly, on 2 December Senator John Kerry talked to President Bush about the extent to which the Vietnamese had been responsive to U.S. requests related to missing Americans, stressing the need for a major U.S. government step recognizing this new cooperation. Secretary of Defense Richard Cheney, who was present at the meeting, spoke of the need to fulfill obligations to the families, and the necessity for Vietnam to provide remains before the Department of Defense would agree to move forward. Secretary Cheney believed that while the U.S. should not rush forward, there was a need for flexibility. Cheney requested that then Principal Deputy Assistant Secretary of Defense for International Security Affairs, Carl Ford, and Under Secretary of Defense for Policy, Paul Wolfowitz, determine what could be given up from Phase Two. The Office of the Deputy Assistant Secretary of Defense for POW/MIA Affairs drafted a memo, in accordance with Ford's instructions, stating that the Defense Department could "give up" one of the three steps remaining in Phase Two, specifically the step relating to joining with other countries to help clear up Vietnam's arrears with the IMF.[21]

In the midst of these discussions in Washington, Hanoi signaled that moving to empower businessmen to agree to contracts that would be executed following the lifting of the embargo, and lifting the restrictions that prohibited such activities without agreeing to help Vietnam eliminate its IMF arrears, would be regarded as insufficient. A senior Foreign Ministry official privately made it clear that in the event the U.S. decided to move on all of the remaining Phase Two steps except the arrears issue, Hanoi would interpret this to mean that Washington was not serious about taking any real constructive actions before 20 January 1993.[22]

On 14 December, the White House announced that the U.S. government would begin to permit U.S. firms to sign contracts that could be executed following the lifting of the embargo. To facilitate this step, the White House announced the U.S. would begin implementing further exceptions to the embargo, including the establishment of liberal licensing policies to permit U.S. firms to open offices in Vietnam, hire staffs, write and design plans, and carry out preliminary feasibility and engineering studies, and technical surveys. The Vietnamese reacted in a 15 December Foreign Ministry statement which pointed out that though positive, this step fell short of "creating favorable conditions" for U.S. companies to engage in business in the Vietnamese market. According to the Foreign Ministry spokesperson, Vietnamese companies would still find it difficult to "have real relations" with American companies under circumstances that mandated deferring the execution of contracts.

The Foreign Ministry statement studiously avoided drawing a link between progress on the POW/MIA issue and further steps toward normalization. Departing from the usual formulaic expressions, the Vietnamese emphasized the mutual economic and business advantages of taking steps that would allow U.S. businesses to "truly engage in business" in Vietnam.

A commentary broadcast by the Voice of Vietnam on 16 December was more blunt about the practical difficulties of establishing business dealings with American companies prohibited from executing contracts. The commentary avoided drawing any relationship between the steps announced by the U.S. and progress on the POW/MIA issue. The 16 December broadcast cited positive comments by the former Australian Prime Minister, who was in Vietnam in mid–December, and unidentified American businessmen in Asia who supported the moves, lamented the continued existence of restrictions governing business, and urged lifting the embargo by 20 January.

Senators John Kerry and Bob Smith visited Vietnam in mid–December. Smith told the foreign media that he had extracted an "expanded commitment" from Hanoi to conduct live sighting investigations, and that Vietnam had committed itself, in a memorandum, to search for information in Vietnamese files relating to pilots downed on the Ho Chi Minh Trail, on Lao territory, and to cooperate more closely with Laos to solve the Border Cases.

The visit by these two key members of the Senate Select Committee on POW/MIA Affairs may have narrowed the differences that threatened to complicate the writing of the Committee's final report, and which could have resulted in the an explosive minority response that would have reintroduced the most inflammatory POW/MIA rhetoric at an inopportune moment. Smith hailed the Vietnamese pledge to "further facilitate" live sighting investigations as one of the more significant results of the visit. He pressed the Vietnamese to allow U.S. specialists to investigate all reports as they came in, rather than just those in the docket at the time, or those judged to have merit according to undefined Vietnamese standards of evidence. That meant Hanoi had moved away from the position of the Foreign Ministry's Vietnamese Office for Seeking Missing Personnel (VNOSMP), articulated in late 1991 and early 1992, to the effect that the U.S. should provide the Vietnamese with synopses of live sighting cases requiring investigation so that Vietnam could evaluate the efficacy of actually conducting such investigations. The departure from the previously held position marked a subtle change in Vietnamese attitudes toward the issue, made possible by the retirement of more conservative senior officials who were replaced by officials decidedly more interested in resolving problems and making new policy than repeating long-standing boilerplate on the POW/MIA issue.

Vietnamese Views Following President Clinton's Inauguration

Following the 20 January 1993 inauguration of President William Clinton, Vietnamese officials privately expressed serious concern over the prospect that the new administration would either (a) launch a prolonged reevaluation of POW/MIA policy, which would certainly cause a suspension of activities, or (b) take a strong position requiring a "full accounting" instead of the "fullest possible accounting" of American soldiers missing in Indochina or mandating a thorough reexamination of each and every MIA case.

Clinton's decision to leave the remaining elements of the embargo in place was a great source of frustration for the Foreign Ministry and the senior leadership of Vietnam. The Politburo was concerned because there was no real acknowledgement from the new Administration in Washington that the process was working effectively. In its January 1993 monthly internal review of current events, the Defense Ministry's General Political Department noted that Washington believed that Vietnam had still not put forth sufficient effort and had not achieved "tangible results" on the POW/MIA problem. By then, Clinton had emphasized the importance of actively pursuing the issue on behalf of the families of missing American service personnel. The General Political Department's review suggested that the Ministry of Defense was prepared for a long period of inaction as the new administration in Washington coped with the domestic dimensions of the normalization issue. Moreover, the assessment indicated that Washington's critical view of Vietnamese cooperation on the POW/MIA issue would probably complicate progress toward normalization, though without necessarily interrupting activities aimed at accounting for missing Americans.[23]

Senior Vietnamese officials privately stated their concern that a lengthy U.S. review of POW/MIA policy, especially if it entailed a barrage of new requirements, would weaken support for normalization in Hanoi. Foreign Ministry officials, through February and March, noted their reluctance to go back to their leadership with recommendations that Vietnam comply with additional "confidence building" steps. Pro-normalization officials felt they would be seriously vulnerable if they tried to make the case, yet one more time, that normalization was just around the corner if only Hanoi could find a way to satisfy Washington's latest POW/MIA-related request. These officials believed that they'd be unable to make any headway against the view, strongly held by the Defense Ministry, that there had never been an inclination in Washington, from the end of the Bush administration to the first months following the inauguration of the new American leadership, to lift the embargo against Vietnam.[24]

The View from Washington: Clinton's Approach to Vietnam

The Clinton Administration was especially cautious about the POW/MIA issue, and not at all adverse to offering extreme formulations about the importance of accounting for all missing service personnel, departing from the more nuanced "fullest possible accounting" language, perhaps as a nod to the active conservative groups that had strongly supported Bush's candidacy. During his first weeks in office, Clinton was rumored to have told a group of staffers that he would not allow himself to be ambushed on this issue by getting too far ahead of the most vocal critics of the U.S. government on the more controversial elements of the POW/MIA problem. The implication of this rumor, and the image of the new president foreclosing on the possibility that he would open himself to a politically costly moment on this problem, suggested that the Vietnamese expectation of a long period of inaction was not far off the mark.

Many of the earliest policy options considered by the new administration were aimed at postponing a decision on lifting of the embargo and establishing normal relations with Vietnam. Through February, it appeared that the interagency working group agreed that while the argument could be made that the 1993 Roadmap had been overtaken by events, it made sense to reaffirm the relevance of that document to Washington as a means of reminding Hanoi that progress toward normalization would be conditioned by the pace and scope of POW/MIA cooperation. The interagency group was divided over the suggestion that taking the remaining step in phase two of the Roadmap — settling Vietnam's arrears — was a relatively inexpensive way of sustaining momentum, introducing the new Administration's policies in a positive way, and signaling that the next move was up to Hanoi. Pentagon officials responsible for POW/MIA affairs argued that moving quickly to erase Hanoi's arrears in the IMF without additional Vietnamese concessions on the remains issue would leave the U.S. open to criticism by vocal families and veterans groups that could argue the U.S. unnecessarily gave up its leverage.

By mid-March, the State Department was mulling over the utility of dispatching General Vessey to Vietnam to "sustain momentum." However, the Vietnamese were looking for earnest answers on the arrears issue, and an end to the embargo. In-country archival research, preparations for scheduled joint field activities, consultations between the VNOSMP and the U.S. Pacific Command's Joint Task Force Full Accounting (JTFFA) continued, and did not require the intervention of a presidential-level delegation to jump start activities. Clearly, the Vietnamese had a very different expectation of the next high-level step required to propel the relationship forward. In fact, it seemed that Hanoi was looking for some indication that the entire POW/MIA accounting venture would be brought to an end in the context of establishing formal relations, proclaiming the dawn of a new era, and closing out accounts from the war in at least figurative terms.

More than anything else, the Vietnamese wanted some indication that Washington still intended to follow the path toward normalization plotted by the U.S. in the Roadmap. The Vietnamese anxiously sought reassurances that the existing level of POW/MIA activity would continue to receive U.S. acknowledgement that the results of joint fieldwork and live sighting investigations were positive, thus paving the way for the end of the embargo.

Since Washington had not yet gotten to that point, it seemed to some in the interagency working group that the U.S. would be just as well served by muddling along until a policy was defined, rather than ceremoniously dispatching a presidential delegation. That is, the Vietnamese were probably more inclined to accept the notion that the new administration had gone into a deep huddle on the question of policy toward Vietnam than to agree to an empty gesture in the form of a high level U.S. government delegation intended to string things along until Washington had sorted through the issue and made up its mind.

On 1 April, Winston Lord, Assistant Secretary of State for East Asia and the Pacific, told the Senate Foreign Relations Committee that the Clinton Administration could make a rapid decision on the establishment of normal relations with Vietnam. During 3–8 April, former Secretary of State Edmund Muskie led a Center for National Policy delegation to Vietnam. He told Foreign Minister Nguyen Manh Cam and General Secretary Do Muoi that the Clinton administration was "closely reviewing" the embargo. In early April, Senator Frank Murkowski submitted a bill urging the end to the embargo. Hanoi attached a great deal of significance to these events, highlighting them in the party-controlled media, and emphasizing the extent to which they demonstrated that support for the embargo within the U.S., as well as from Washington's traditional friends, continued to wither away. In Washington, this string of activities was the beginning of the search for "top cover," the Administration's effort to guarantee that it had iron clad support for the lifting of the embargo and the eventual establishment of normal relations from a broad band of organizations, elected officials, prominent businessmen, national level veterans organizations, active duty military officers, and former senior U.S. government officials.[25]

In early April Clinton asked Vessey to travel to Vietnam to inform the Vietnamese leadership about the results of the U.S. assessment of work conducted on the discrepancy cases through the early part of 1993, and to detail U.S. government requirements in four areas: joint investigations, remains repatriations, archival access, and trilateral activities regarding Lao Border Cases.

At roughly the same time, an Australian academic conducting research in Moscow archives gained access to a Soviet military intelligence document which claimed that in the early 1970s Vietnam held hundreds of more American POWs than U.S. intelligence reporting at the time had concluded were in Vietnamese custody. The Soviet intelligence report was based on a document that was identified as a report to the Vietnamese Communist Party's Politburo by General Tran Van Quang. The President instructed Vessey to raise this report with his Vietnamese hosts, and request access to General Quang.[26] The Soviet document, and the controversy it generated, eliminated the possibility of moving quickly toward normalization.

Slouching Toward Normalization

The Vietnamese strained to extract every public relations advantage in May, returning to the practice of characterizing the relative success of joint work and the accomplishments of technical sessions with the Joint Task Force.[27] However, by mid–1993 the Politburo was greatly frustrated by the U.S. government's failure to move forward. Senior Vietnamese leaders felt the U.S. was out to humiliate Vietnam. Middle level Foreign Ministry officials privately argued that Washington was not serious about the POW/MIA issue, and merely sought to heap demand upon demand, without any indication of a commitment to entering into a normal bilateral relationship with Hanoi. The more strident tone of Vietnamese comments was the result of increasingly strong criticisms of the Foreign Ministry's management of the POW/MIA issue by National Assembly delegates, who had begun to express their chagrin that Vietnam's cooperation went unrewarded, and that Hanoi's own humanitarian woes continued to be ignored by the U.S.

Senator John Kerry visited Hanoi in mid–May. He delivered a letter from Clinton to President Le Duc Anh expressing the view that strengthened humanitarian cooperation would create the conditions that would lead to normalization.[28] Kerry candidly told his primary interlocutor, Acting Foreign Minister Tran Quang Co, a Central Committee member, that domestic political realities in the U.S. exerted real constraints on the kind of decisions that could be taken regarding normalization. In a private session, Kerry gave Co his firm assurances that if Vietnam complied with his requests for additional cooperation on specific POW/MIA matters, then Kerry would be prepared to return to Hanoi in late May to early June with Senator John McCain and other legislators, representatives of the national-level veterans organizations, and the media in order to demonstrate to the American people the extent to which cooperation had increased, and the ways in which Vietnam's helpfulness had resulted in significant progress toward establishing a mechanism capable of achieving the fullest possible accounting.

According to a senior Vietnamese official, in late May, following Kerry's visit, General Secretary Do Muoi summoned members of the Foreign Ministry and the VNOSMP to a meeting. Muoi told those present that he would receive the second Kerry delegation, but that would be the last delegation he would meet from the U.S. on the POW/MIA issue. Muoi reportedly said that when Vietnam came forward with documents, the U.S. denounced the government for withholding information. This, Muoi charged, was not a helpful approach. According to a VNOSMP official, Muoi stated that Vietnam was prepared to stop looking for information on missing Americans if Washington persisted in responding to Hanoi's efforts in this manner. Additionally, Muoi told those present at the meeting that the U.S. government should not believe that Vietnam felt compelled to respond to each and every request as a means of hastening the lifting of the embargo. The U.S. government, Muoi argued, was mistaken if it believed that Vietnam was in a precarious position, and that it therefore must comply with U.S. requirements on the POW/MIA issue.[29]

On 2 July the White House announced the decision to refrain from opposing the efforts of other countries to settle Vietnam's arrears with the IMF. The White House also announced that a high level delegation would visit Hanoi in July to review progress and to inform the Vietnamese of Washington's decision to cease objecting to the settlement of Vietnam's arrears. The White House made it clear that no additional steps would be taken toward normalization until the Vietnamese were responsive to U.S. government requests for further action regarding the recovery and repatriation of remains, continued field investigations of the discrepancy cases and live sightings, trilateral cooperation on the Lao Border cases, and access to wartime information in Defense Ministry archives.[30]

The Foreign Ministry was cordial in its public response to Washington's 2 July announcement. The Ministry's statement noted that the decision was a "significant step" in line with "the world trend," and one that would be beneficial to the process of normalization. The decision would help build "mutual trust," and "accelerate resolution of the remaining issues between the two countries." The Vietnamese military was less inclined to see this as a major step forward. The military continued to believe that the domestic political implications of the POW/MIA issue in the U.S. would prevent the Clinton Administration from moving quickly toward lifting the embargo, which they saw as the ultimate dividend of Hanoi's policy of cooperation. The military viewed the interim steps, such as those spelled out in Phase Two and Three of the Roadmap, as being of minor importance.

Privately, Foreign Ministry officials long involved in the POW/MIA issue were ecstatic. Washington's decision represented the culmination of considerable investments by the Foreign Ministry. Middle and senior foreign ministry officials calculated that a negative U.S. government decision would have had a consequential impact on their credibility, and in turn on the Foreign Ministry's ability to sustain cooperation. To a certain extent, Cam and his Ministry labored under the same pressures that ultimately compromised former Foreign Minister Nguyen Co Thach's position: the inability to argue convincingly that responding to U.S. government requests for additional cooperation would lead to significant steps by Washington toward ending the embargo.[31]

In mid–July, a U.S. presidential delegation, headed by Deputy Secretary for Veterans Affairs Hershel Gober and Assistant Secretary of State Winston Lord, met with SRV government counterparts in Hanoi. The Vietnamese side agree to the proposed assignment to Hanoi of three State Department officials who would be responsible for assisting U.S. POW/MIA families that had been invited by the Vietnamese Government in order to "accelerate efforts to account for POWs and MIAs." The Vietnamese agreed to step up the efforts to locate documents relevant to missing U.S. service personnel, and to make such documents available to the U.S. Hanoi agreed to aggressively pursue the remaining 92 discrepancy cases, and to continue their cooperation on live sighting investigations and joint field investigations. The Vietnamese side also agreed to attend a 9 August trilateral meeting on the Lao Border Cases.

On the troublesome issue of consular access to Americans detained for violating Vietnamese laws, Minister of Interior Bui Thien Ngo told Assistant Secretary Lord that he would take into account "the improving relations between our two countries" in handling cases of detained or incarcerated Americans, and that he was "willing to go beyond the law" to achieve that goal. Vice Minister for Foreign Affairs Le Mai accepted the proposal for a dialogue on human rights "on a permanent basis." The manner in which Vietnam received the delegation demonstrated that, in spite of his earlier frustration, Muoi remained engaged in the POW/MIA issue, and focused on the broader question of overall U.S.–Vietnamese ties. He was clearly prepared to take the necessary steps to respond to the U.S. government's requests. He told the delegation that Hanoi was committed to creating "favorable conditions for the U.S. side to finish resolving the outstanding issues of American MIAs," a message that was repeated by senior Vietnamese officials to visiting U.S. lawmakers in August.[32]

By the last quarter of 1993, the Vietnamese sensed a change in the tone of dialogue with the U.S., a willingness to edge forward in frustratingly incremental ways that, nevertheless, represented a signal from Washington. Vietnamese officials believed that the United States had begun to look for ways to solve problems using new instruments, new vocabulary, and new approaches to lingering bilateral problems. Widening the areas in which the U.S. and Vietnam engaged in formal dialogue on issues such as human rights struck Hanoi as Washington's attempt to identify problems that could be solved and progress that could be made in a new relationship. In its August report, the General Political Department made the case that a proliferation of congressional delegations, the assignment of three State Department officials to Hanoi, and continued POW/MIA work (especially on the border cases involving trilateral cooperation between Washington, Vientiane and Hanoi), as well as the interests of large American companies, reflected the broadening of government, state and commercial relations between the U.S. and Vietnam. These circumstances, the report argued, would increase the pressure on President Clinton to lift the embargo.[33]

To the American side, though these decisions represented departures from the way of doing business with Vietnam, they were intended to spur progress in the priority POW/MIA area, not to water down national attention to this issue. The hope was that by generating some forward movement on a range of issues, the resulting energy and enthusiasm would be translated into momentum in the POW/MIA area. And, by introducing bilateral issues beyond the POW/MIA problem, Washington acknowledged the range of problems that would have to be managed en route to normalization.

Hanoi expressed particular concern with a 1 September statement by Assistant Secretary Lord in which he explained that the President's authority to conduct embargos against certain countries would lapse unless he decided to renew that authority following the mid–September review. Lord said that though Vietnam had been cooperating on the MIA matter, Vietnam's record on human rights, highlighted by the government's refusal to allow Senator Chuck Robb to visit an imprisoned dissident, was "discouraging."[34]

Just days before Clinton was to review the Trading With The Enemy Act, a second document from the Soviet military intelligence archives was revealed, and again captured headlines in U.S. papers in a way that threatened to derail progress on the MIA issue. The document, which stated that Vietnam held 735 U.S. aviators as POWs in 1971 instead of the 368 whose names the Vietnamese had publicly released, was said to be a translation of a report to the 20th plenary session of the Central Committee, which according to the document ran from the end of December 1970 to the beginning of 1971.[35]

The Vietnamese denounced the document as an "ill intentioned fabrication" designed to halt progress towards the lifting of the embargo and bilateral normalization. Station commentaries between 10 and 11 September drew links between the disclosure of the first "Soviet document" and the second, and quoted State Department and congressional officials who portrayed the second document as a fabrication. Vietnamese radio broadcasts criticized "ultra rightist" forces in the U.S. determined to "block or undermine any positive developments in U.S.–Vietnamese relations. In early October, according to Russian radio broadcasts, Foreign Minister Nguyen Manh Cam and Andre Kozyrev, head of the Russian Federation's Foreign Policy Department, met in Moscow and agreed that the Federation would no longer release such documents until there had been time enough to confer with the Vietnamese on any new items unearthed in archives.[36]

Trading with the Enemy Act

On 13 September, the White House announced the President's decision to sign a determination renewing his authority under the Trading With The Enemy Act, thus extending the President's authority to impose and maintain central control over certain trade assets and funds affecting Vietnam, Cambodia, Cuba, North Korea and the Baltic Nations. Regarding Vietnam, the presidential determination maintained the embargo with an adjustment permitting U.S. firms to bid on projects financed by the IFIs. In explaining the decision, the White House noted that some progress had been made toward obtaining the remains of missing U.S. service personnel, resolution of the discrepancy cases, trilateral investigations of the Lao Border Cases, and access to POW/MIA–related documents. However, the "tangible results" of these efforts were "not yet sufficient."[37]

The Vietnamese reacted strongly against the decision to keep the embargo in place, but with an eye toward avoiding any possibility of jeopardizing the modest progress toward normalization. The Foreign Ministry spokesperson expressed "regret" that Washington had maintained the embargo, a decision that "ran counter to international and regional development trends and was against the aspiration and interest of Vietnamese and American peoples." At the same time, the Foreign Ministry made it clear that Vietnam would continue to cooperate with the U.S. to resolve the MIA issue.[38] Deputy Foreign Minister Le Mai argued that the decision to extend the embargo ran "counter to the trends of negotiation and cooperation as well as freedom in doing business and trade in the current world situation." Mai suggested that Washington and Hanoi should "continue their negotiations and that differences between the two sides should be frankly discussed while efforts should be made to continue cooperation." He stressed the importance of freeing U.S. businesses to compete equally in Vietnam.[39]

Vietnamese press and radio commentary was less restrained. A 17 September article in *Nhan Dan* denounced the decision as "absurd and outdated." U.S. "actions do not match its words," the article continued, because the "United States itself has many times issued statements praising Vietnam's cooperation in the MIA issue." An 18 September Voice of Vietnam Network commentary doubted Washington's professed interest in turning a new page in U.S.–Vietnamese relations. The commentary argued that Washington was not prepared to stand by its stated intention to keep the POW/MIA issue a humanitarian one, free from politics and separate from other issues.[40]

One Step Forward, One Step Backward: Motion but No Movement

In the last months of 1993, Vietnamese officials privately expressed their wariness regarding the Clinton Administration's intentions toward the Socialist Republic, and publicly noted their willingness to continue humanitarian cooperation, even in the face of unfavorable political decisions regarding the embargo and normalization.[41] Vietnamese media accounts played up the significance of the 4 October meeting between Secretary of State Warren Christopher and Deputy Prime Minister Phan Van Khai in New York, during which Khai "affirmed" Vietnam's commitment to "build a new relationship" between Vietnam and the United States "conforming to the fundamental and long term interests of the two peoples and the trend of history."[42]

Assistant Secretary Lord visited Hanoi during 13 to 15 December 1993 to restate the importance of tangible progress in the four areas of POW/MIA cooperation specified by Clinton in his July 1993 statement. Lord told Prime Minister Vo Van Kiet, Foreign Minister Cam, and Deputy Foreign Minister Nguyen Duy Nien that the U.S. expected concrete results from Vietnamese government efforts to recover American remains, continued efforts to resolve the remaining discrepancy cases and live sighting reports, further assistance in implementing trilateral investigations, and accelerated efforts to provide the U.S. with access to wartime archival documents that could help shed light on the fate of American MIAs.

The Vietnamese media stated that the meetings took place in a "frank and constructive" atmosphere. Kiet acknowledged the "contribution to the promotion of mutual understanding" made by the visit, reaffirmed Vietnam's pledge to cooperate on humanitarian issues, and noted the "positive developments" in bilateral relations that would hopefully lead to the normalization of relations.[43] According to Vietnamese media accounts, Kiet told Lord that Vietnam sympathized with the U.S. on its "internal difficulties, which have resulted in a setback in the normalization process and have not met the aspirations of the two peoples," an indication that the senior-most Vietnamese leadership believed that the Administration was still reluctant to incur the wrath of veterans organizations and POW/MIA family and activist groups by lifting the embargo against Vietnam. Kiet told Lord that "we should not leave the impression that the MIA issue blocks normalization of relations...."[44] Echoing that sentiment in December, middle level Vietnamese officials pointed out that national assembly delegates and the senior leadership of the Vietnamese Communist Party, which was preparing for a mid-term Central Committee conference that would assess foreign and domestic policies, were debating Hanoi's policies toward the U.S., which had become the target of strong domestic criticism. The Vietnamese sought to telegraph the view that continued equivocation by the U.S. government on the decision to lift the embargo represented a problem that could result in a scaling back of the vastly improved Vietnamese POW/MIA cooperation.

For Washington, by the fourth quarter of the year, it had become increasingly difficult to manage the POW/MIA issue with an eye to how to handle the remaining portions of the embargo. The contradiction was between (1) the pressure to horse trade in order to achieve U.S. government objectives and (2) the desire to sustain momentum by lifting elements of the embargo in order to encouraged continued Vietnamese cooperation. The Administration had modified the embargo to permit U.S.

firms to carry out IFI-funded projects. The remaining options were to modify the embargo to permit U.S. firms to carry out projects in the communications and the aviation sector, to vote "yes" on all IFI loans which met normal financial development and other usual criteria in the IFIs, and to voice support for General Agreement on Tariffs and Trade (GATT) observer status for Vietnam.

There was not a great deal left with which the U.S. could reward Vietnam for progress toward accomplishing the goals defined by the President in his 2 July statement. Although Washington sliced the last stages of the embargo thinly, moving forward with the remaining increments would mean that the U.S. would lose the leverage that the Trading With The Enemy Act afforded. Additionally, the U.S. government had not clarified implementing guidelines in a manner that specified what activities companies could undertake in Vietnam. There was still a good deal of confusion in the business community regarding how to move forward as a result of the 13 September decision to allow U.S. firms to bid on IFI-financed projects.

During this period, Hanoi expressed its frustration by working hard to independently develop relations with the World Bank and the Asian Development Bank. The Vietnamese received the IMF director in late September, headlined the creation of the "Friends of Vietnam" group that was to clear Hanoi's arrears, and highlighted the fact that the Asian Development Bank was poised to approve its first loan to Vietnam in over two decades in spite of the U.S. trade embargo. The Vietnamese paid an inordinate amount of media attention to the IMF's October clearance of Vietnam's arrears. Hanoi's message was that the Vietnamese were prepared to take the more difficult path toward modernization and integration into the world economy in the face of stubborn Washington refusal to lift the embargo, and that the U.S. policies would lose support as the international community grew weary of this game.

The State Department looked to a December date, at which point an ongoing JTFFA field investigation was scheduled to be completed, as the right time for pressing forward with another "assessment," and a decision memorandum on lifting the embargo.

Through the end of 1993, the dynamic that drove the fledgling bilateral relationship forward was powered by Hanoi's motivation to free itself from the U.S.-imposed embargo, and Washington's desire to keep the POW/MIA issue center stage.

Hanoi tended to focus its efforts to be responsive in the area of establishing mechanisms that could help shed light on missing Americans, such as the standing up of a repository for wartime archival items or the agreement to devise a mutually satisfying way of addressing live sighting reports in a manner that was transparent, quick and immediately responsive to such potentially detrimental reports of Americans still hidden in secret prisons.

Though the U.S. government was prepared to acknowledge the utility of such "mechanisms," congressional critics and veterans organizations, as well as family organization groups, pressured Washington into looking at these exercises as empty bureaucratic gestures. The U.S. government had to ask for "tangible progress," which meant progress in the area of accounting for missing servicemen. That meant either the return of a live American, the repatriation of remains, or a credible explanation of what became of the missing American (and why that individual's remains could not be located, identified and repatriated). Internal debates within the interagency group regarding the logic and likelihood of such an accounting did not alter the political reality for the government: to the active, vocal constituencies, accounting meant getting answers, not gesturing in the direction of responsiveness.

So, while Vietnam might earn credit for a cooperative spirit strong enough to consent to the establishment of a southern branch of the VNOSMP based in Ho Chi Minh City, or the staffing of an office focused on locating wartime documents with defense and interior officials, those acts were insufficient if they did not lead to the accounting for missing Americans.

That meant the Vietnamese had to edge toward responsiveness to U.S. requirements if they were to earn any points toward normalization. This required Hanoi to make difficult decisions within a bureaucracy increasingly divided over how to respond to U.S. requests for additional information or cooperation on practical field investigations. On the one hand, some in the Foreign Ministry, and possibly the Office of the Prime Minister, felt that the U.S. was headed inexorably to normalization, if only as a result of regional and global trends and trading realities, business pressure, and other regional equities that would overshadow the importance of the MIA issue. On the other hand, the Defense Ministry, elements of the Interior Ministry, and probably senior Central Committee departmental level officials appeared to believe that the U.S. had no real desire to normalize quickly, no strategic motivation to move down that road, and no real worries about how long normalization — including the signing of a trade agreement — would actually take.

This meant that, for the Hanoi decision-making process, hard choices had to be made about doing things for the U.S. that the defense establishment and security ministry viewed as invasive and troublesome. Thus, agreeing to "amnesty" for citizens who might have artifacts from crash sites, or information about Americans last known alive in the custody of Vietnamese military entities, or Americans who were placed in the prison system, plunged elements of the Vietnamese government responsible for managing relations with the U.S. into discussions regarding what Hanoi could do for the Americans without going to far toward violating the Socialist Republic's sense of propriety, sovereign dignity, or security and defense requirements.

For the U.S. government, this involved making tough political decisions about exactly how to reward Vietnamese cooperation, and how to credibly certify Vietnamese activities to comply with legislation mandating serious interagency assessments of Vietnam's responsiveness. For the State Department, that meant figuring out a means of avoiding public language that might minimize Vietnam's cooperation, and thus result in the thorough and complete alienation of elements of the Foreign Ministry that were prepared to accept positive U.S. government statements and use them as the core of an argument intended to press the SRV leadership to move forward. And it meant doing this without jeopardizing the coherence of the interagency consensus, in a way that kept the more conservative U.S. players (at Defense, the Joint Staff, and the Pacific Command [PACOM]) engaged, or at least prepared to concede that it was important to avoid shutting down channels of communication and risking the closing of all POW/MIA work.

2
STUMBLING TOWARD A RELATIONSHIP, 1994–1995

Lifting the Embargo

On 3 February 1994, President Clinton announced the decision to remove the provisions of the Trading With The Enemy Act that prohibited Americans from doing business in Vietnam, and to expand the official U.S. presence in Vietnam by establishing a liaison office. The establishment of a liaison office in Hanoi would enable the U.S. to "provide services for Americans" in Vietnam and facilitate U.S. efforts to "pursue a human rights dialogue with the Vietnamese government." Clinton underscored the limited nature of the decision. These actions, he said, "do not constitute a normalization of our relationship. Before that happens, we must have more progress, more cooperation, and more answers."[1]

The government in Hanoi spoke of the decision as a "step forward," but in restrained tones using measured words, recognizing that the practical economic impact would be minor until Vietnamese access to U.S. markets was granted in the form of Most Favored Nation (MFN) trading status, a step that Washington had made clear would take place as part of a future agenda, following efforts to more fully resolve the POW/MIA issue, and deal with claims and consular matters, and human rights issues.[2]

The February 1994 issue of the General Political Department's (GDP) monthly report contained a straightforward description of the decision to lift the embargo and expand the U.S. presence in Vietnam to the level of a liaison office. The report noted that after 19 years of an "anti–Vietnamese embargo," America had not attained its aims and must as a consequence "regularize" (dieu chinh) its policy along the direction of improving the relationship with Vietnam. The GDP report did not acknowledge that the most important aspect of U.S. policy toward Vietnam remained obtaining information about missing Americans. The military view, as expressed in the report, was that this would be a long and very difficult process that would require Vietnam to struggle against Washington's efforts to "profit" from all the problems of democracy and human rights.[3]

Vietnamese officials quickly sought to establish the parameters for this new relationship. Hanoi reiterated that if the U.S. wanted the benefit of a normal relationship with Vietnam "it must treat Vietnam equally, with respect for independence and sovereignty, and then the prospects for a U.S.–Vietnamese relationship would develop." Additionally, Hanoi precluded the possibility that U.S. firms would be accorded a priority or unfair advantage over firms from other countries in bids to engage in business in Vietnam. The Vietnamese acknowledged that this first step was important to them, and that they understood considerable work on the modalities of a future relationship would have to be tackled, beginning with questions concerning frozen assets, property claims, and human rights matters. However, for the moment, a critical hurdle had been overcome and, as the Vietnamese media put it, America and Vietnam could begin to regard one another as friends.[4]

First Thoughts on Defense Relations

On the eve of the Presidential decision to lift the embargo, Under Secretary of Defense for Policy Walter Slocombe asked the Office of the Assistant Secretary of Defense for International Security Affairs (ISA) for some first thoughts on U.S.–Vietnamese relations.[5] ISA responded with a "think piece" which began by noting that while Vietnam did not represent a vital strategic interest to the U.S. Government, there was significant strategic value to lifting the embargo, and ultimately entering into a relationship with Vietnam, which represented a growing market of potential interest to U.S. businesses as well as an increasingly significant part of Southeast Asia.

Two exploratory efforts to develop support for a modest military relationship with Vietnam, one in early 1993 and the second in early 1994, failed to generate much interest within the interagency working group looking at U.S.–Vietnamese relations. As part of an early 1993 interagency review of policy toward Vietnam, ISA contributed a paper which made the case that a relationship with Vietnam would allow the U.S. to influence and nurture the trend toward reduced military activity in Southeast Asia, and would present an opportunity to further blunt China's ability to preempt U.S. influence in Southeast Asia. The paper concluded that even as the People's Army of Vietnam (PAVN) downsized, the Vietnamese Armed Forces remained one of the largest defense establishments in the region. PAVN was a central player in both domestic and foreign policies. For that reason alone it would make sense to develop relations with the Vietnamese military leadership, and to seek to influence the future of the military in a society that was becoming increasingly complex in character.

However, the positions taken in the paper did not resonate with the interagency working group, did not get much of a hearing within the Office of the Assistant Secretary of Defense for International Security Affairs, and received no support from senior officials in the Pentagon. The Defense Department remained focused on facilitating POW/MIA activities. There was certainly no sense at the working level in the Defense Department that a formal relationship between Hanoi and Washington would contribute to enhancing cooperation. Nor was there a dialogue within the interagency group on the extent to which normalization might establish an environment in which a more rapid pace and wider scope of activities could encourage more effective efforts to account for America's missing service personnel.

In December 1993, ISA restated the argument concerning the strategic imperatives lurking in the future of the U.S.–Vietnamese relationship. At that point, the White House, the Departments of State and Treasury, and other members of the interagency group were still focused on managing policy in accordance with the Roadmap, keeping the priority fixed on resolving the POW/MIA issue, settling arrears, determining the trajectory for future commercial policies, and gauging Congressional sentiment on embargo-related issues, U.S. policy toward international financial assistance, and a host of other issues including consular matters, human rights problems, and the resolution of the conflict in Cambodia. This version of the mid–1993 pitch fell flat within the interagency working group.

A second ISA pitch in early 1994 on the subject of bilateral defense relations included a strong humanitarian component. A relationship with Vietnam, in this argument, would afford the U.S. military the opportunity to lend a hand to efforts to reconstruct a country victimized by its own policies, leadership, and aggressive strategic goals over the last two decades. A humanitarian starting point would be a good one for the U.S. military, one with which it was familiar and one which could be most easily explained to hesitant Vietnamese military officers, provincial officials, and middle level government cadre who were likely to remain somewhat skittish about military-to-military relations with Washington.

However, Washington was acutely sensitive to the political liabilities of moving too quickly toward normalization. The argument that there were security equities at stake was not uncontroversial, and did not figure in Defense Department thinking about the relationship with Vietnam during the period just before the 1994 decision to lift the embargo and normalize relations.

ISA showed that ASEAN believed economic ties were the integrating force that would reintroduce Vietnam, and Cambodia, into the Southeast Asian community of nations. A normalized U.S.–Vietnamese relationship would recognize existing ASEAN perceptions of the economic and diplomatic reality of a changing Indochina, and confront China with a new constellation of forces that could not easily be manipulated for Beijing's purposes.

The ISA paper was careful to avoid suggesting that a U.S.–Vietnamese relationship would afford Washington any strategic leverage in future confrontations with China, or that a U.S.–Vietnamese relationship would be construed by Beijing as a threat to its interests. The earliest observations by knowledgeable academics, commentators and government officials did in fact point to the potential strategic value of preempting a Vietnamese–Chinese condominium, as though establishing a relationship with the U.S. government might preclude the possibility of Vietnam's sustaining relations with Beijing. Moreover, comments from senior Pentagon officials on the earliest efforts to attract attention to the possibility of a U.S.–Vietnamese relationship focused on the importance of selling the concept by arguing that normalization would have an impact on Chinese efforts to offset America's presence in the region. However, though zero sum concepts of politics and diplomacy might offer some explanatory value in sorting out U.S. plans, intentions and foreign policy priorities, they brought nothing to attempts to understand Vietnamese thinking about foreign relationships, and seemed to offer similarly minimal dividends in efforts to analyze China's thinking. Indeed, the Chinese would later signal that a U.S.–Vietnamese relationship, and specifically U.S.–Vietnamese military relations, would contribute in a positive way to regional stability and peace.

ISA argued that there was a compelling economic basis to the case that a military-to-military relationship with Vietnam would serve U.S. interests, and provide a sound humanitarian foundation for the relationship. The economic part of the argument was intended to underscore what was new in Hanoi's orientation toward the world. The rush to economic advantage that many suspected would follow the lifting of the embargo was not only a measure of the riches to be made in Vietnam, but an indication that the businesses and governments of Southeast Asia, Europe and the United States saw Vietnam as part of the fabric of a stable, vibrant and thriving group of Southeast Asian countries, where economic progress was increasingly matched by maturing democratic structures and social development. Moreover, Vietnam's receptivity to new trading partners, its willingness to accommodate the scramble for contracts and business opportunities by writing new investment laws, rationalizing the banking system, and building new hotels and office spaces, suggested that Vietnam was prepared to think of itself as a potential member of overarching economic and security associations. Further, it demonstrated that Vietnam was keen on making new friends and was willing to abide by the rules that guided the conduct of world affairs in the post Cold War period.

The humanitarian component of this argument was that the first normal contacts between the U.S. and Vietnamese defense establishments should build on the kinds of humanitarian projects that had been underway from the late 1980s as part of the U.S. government effort to develop a level of Vietnamese cooperation on the POW/MIA issue. Most of those initiatives, including the work of the U.S. Navy malarial research team and prosthetics and child care assistance were aimed at responding to Vietnam's humanitarian needs in order to keep Hanoi focused on resolving MIA cases. However, some humanitarian activities authorized in the early 1990s as additions to the expanded Vessey Initiative were sustained because of their connections to international health initiatives managed by, for example, the World Health Organization; their relationship to work of the U.S. Armed Forces Research Institute of Medical Science (AFRIMS), which began operating in Vietnam during the Paris Peace process in Cambodia, focusing on research into specific tropical diseases; or because they could be rationalized as strictly humanitarian efforts that did not go beyond the Vessey Initiative, and supplemented the expanded list of possibilities agreed to by the several working level humanitarian delegations that traveled to Vietnam between August 1987 and 1992.[6]

Thus, ISA argued that it would make sense to give positive consideration to requests for the cooperation of U.S. military specialists, such as the Army Corps of Engineers, in projects relating to Vietnam that were conducted as humanitarian undertakings under the auspices of, for example, the United Nations Development Program and the World Food Program. ISA advised that it would be appropriate to begin doing so in April, when the U.S. liaison office in Hanoi was scheduled to open. Such activities could create good will, and have a positive impact on the work of the Joint Task Force-Full Accounting. Such undertakings could also familiarize the Vietnamese with the capabilities of the U.S. military, and allow U.S. personnel involved in humanitarian programs to learn more about conditions on the ground in Vietnam. In short, since it was already part of the relationship, humanitarian undertakings could be a natural bridge toward normal defense relations.

ISA offered two additional proposals in early 1994 aimed at identifying areas where quick, uncontroversial policy agreement could be secured within DoD to initiatives aimed at making some headway toward military-to-military contacts with Vietnam. The first proposal urged support for visits to Vietnam by the U.S. Army Center of Military History (CMH) to begin the process of writing the military's history of battles and campaigns, complementing already published Service histories. That proposal elicited in-principal support, but generated no real interest in using this as a wedge to pry open Vietnamese attitudes toward normalized defense relations.

The second proposal urged DoD policy-level approval for "reasonable requests" for first visits to Vietnam by appropriate DoD officials and service personnel beyond those connected to the POW/MIA mission. The goal was to accomplish this in a manner that would not do harm to the U.S. government desire to keep all eyes focused on extracting continued POW/MIA cooperation from Vietnam. Familiarization visits would guarantee that service personnel and DoD officials who would be involved in some dimension of the future security relationship would have at least some understanding of on-the-ground realities. While this proposal was benign enough to earn in-principal agreement, it butted heads with the idea that all DoD interaction with Vietnam should be focused on POW/MIA activities. Consequently, there were no U.S. military representatives who were prepared to articulate an interest in official travel as long as such proposed visits were not POW/MIA mission essential.[7]

The core of ISA's thinking continued to be that U.S. concerns with access to port facilities in Vietnam, non-proliferation of conventional weapons in the region, counter narcotics cooperation in Southeast Asia, and democratization in the region could all be served by lifting the embargo, proceeding toward the establishment of formal relations, and exploring military-to-military relations in that context. The addition of the human rights part of this argument was an attempt to recognize the importance accorded this issue by U.S. lawmakers.

The ISA paper emphasized that what DoD stood to gain from a limited approach to defense relations was confined to such intangibles as credibility and bankable good will, which would make it easier in the future to move forward with military-to-military initiatives that could benefit the overall relationship, and improve POW/MIA cooperation. The first steps toward a defense relationship with Vietnam would be small ones taken in a humanitarian spirit, with potentially minimal initial returns to labor. One possibility discussed was the revival of aerial mapping agreements that the U.S. Defense Mapping Agency had with the South Vietnamese government dating from the 1950s. Evaluating the legal validity and practical utility of earlier agreements had been one of the first steps taken in the U.S. approach to the Cambodian military, and the possibility of doing this with Vietnam held wide attraction for military operators, humanitarian affairs program specialists, and JTFFA personnel who labored with seriously outdated U.S. military maps and inferior Vietnamese cartographic products.

However, through the first two months of 1994, there was still little in the way of enthusiastic support for the idea of reaching out to the Vietnamese defense establishment. That matched Vietnam's continued downplaying of the strategic importance of relations with Washington. Hanoi placed the task of achieving normalization at the lower end of its inventory of diplomatic goals, and stressed the importance of efforts to compensate for the economic disadvantages imposed by the embargo.[8] The Vietnamese senior leadership publicly displayed an unambiguous disinterest in the relationship with the U.S. The top leadership in Hanoi strongly supported old school non-alignment and self-reliance in terms that sounded out of touch with global trends, the regionalization of markets, and the creation of world scale economies.

The Post-Embargo Atmosphere

The Vietnamese media spoke approvingly of Clinton's decision in the weeks following the lifting of the embargo, hinting broadly at potential dividends for Vietnam, the U.S., and the international community.[9] The Vietnamese noted that POW/MIA cooperation had proceeded apace, unaffected by the decision to lift the embargo, which senior and middle level Vietnamese diplomats had long suggested, privately, would be the case. Media pieces highlighted local efforts to provide artifacts and information to U.S. teams; the implied message was that such cooperation was an example of the willingness of the people of Vietnam to be helpful, a willingness that was stimulated by the lifting of the embargo.[10] The Vietnamese rhetoric on the POW/MIA issue leveled off, and the sharp edge of arguments was replaced by a reasoned approach to the overall relationship.[11]

For example, a delegation representing the National League of POW/MIA Families visited Vietnam in late March 1994, and criticized the U.S. Government's statements commending Hanoi for its cooperation. The

National League of Families delegation also criticized the Administration for telegraphing the message that requests for "unilateral actions" by Vietnam to resolve cases would not be allowed to complicate the achievement of a normal relationship between Vietnam and the United States. Vietnam's response set the pace for future reactions to criticisms from domestic constituencies in the U.S. that objected to Clinton's handling of normalization. Vietnamese officials told the League representatives that steps taken by Washington through the first quarter of 1994 had improved the climate of the relationship between the U.S. and Vietnam, a fact which would help assure continued cooperation. The Vietnamese repeated familiar refrains regarding the difficulty associated with the remaining cases, and reiterated their commitment to continue to search for relevant archival documents.[12] Hanoi promised to repatriate remains as they were discovered, and stressed their own concern for the approximately 300,000 Vietnamese MIAs.[13]

Though Vietnam continued to be responsive to the U.S. regarding POW/MIA-related matters, the fact was that Vietnam had begun to formulate a more complex picture of the relationship. Shortly after Clinton announced the lifting of the embargo, the VNCP-controlled daily newspaper published a taxonomy of the Vietnamese–American relationship from 1987 to 1994. The inventory of steps toward the elimination of the economic embargo began, according to this article, with the first visit to Vietnam by President Reagan's Presidential Emissary to discuss humanitarian issues independently of matters such as the modalities of normalization and economic assistance. The article suggested that the "MIA Problem" was only one dimension of the relationship, and not a particularly critical element in the mix of bilateral issues that included Cambodia, refugees, and reeducation camp inmates. In fact, only ten items of the 54 chronological points explicitly mentioned the POW/MIA issue, suggesting that Hanoi preferred to depict the relationship as having unfolded with minimal reference to the issue of missing Americans, and with a more even focus on a range of other problem areas including Vietnam's military presence in Cambodia.[14]

In March 1994, State, Justice and Treasury specialists and their Vietnamese counterparts met for the first time to discuss the disposition of seized U.S. property. The Vietnamese acknowledged that there was much work ahead, spoke of the "positive results" from the first session, and noted that for the immediate future the working level would be occupied with discussions of a range of "concrete issues" including claims regarding more than 500 million dollars in seized or frozen assets.[15] On 26 May the Foreign Ministry announced the establishment of U.S. and Vietnamese liaison offices in the respective capitals in accordance with the framework of the 1963 Vienna Convention on Consular Relations.[16] Among the issues that lay ahead were Most Favored Nations (MFN) status, the timing of a bilateral trade agreement, Generalized System of Preferences (GSP) issues, Overseas Private Investment Corporation (OPIC) and Export-Import (EXIM) bank matters, World Trade Organization (WTO) membership, aviation agreement issues, export licensing and matters relating to IFI loans. For Vietnam, as for China, Washington would have to determine whether or not the freedom of emigration objectives of the Jackson-Vanik Amendment could best be fulfilled via a Presidential Determination that waived the requirements of the amendment. Intellectual property rights issues would also play a key part in the process of negotiating a bilateral trade agreement. It was clear that Hanoi had only the most rudimentary understanding of the means of achieving a trade agreement, securing MFN status, and accomplishing the establishment of normal economic relations.

In its March 1994 internal report, the Defense Ministry's General Political Department highlighted the relationship between Vietnam and the U.S. after the lifting of the embargo, and called attention to the difficulties for Vietnam of managing bilateral financial and commercial relations in the absence of MFN status. The report stated that following the loosening (noi long) of the embargo, the United States introduced the issues of democracy and human rights into the agenda with Vietnam. The emphasis shifted to some of the very practical dimensions of managing the entry-level relationship with the U.S., and working out the problematic details of engaging with Washington on sensitive international issues including human rights matters. However, as it became increasingly apparent that normalization would not be achieved rapidly or automatically, without additional exertions in the POW/MIA realm, the GPD returned to earlier expressions of exasperation with the U.S. view of Vietnam.[17]

Through mid–1994, the Vietnamese very deliberately noted the dividends that lifting the embargo offered in terms of enhanced cooperation and sustained attention to POW/MIA work. Senior leaders, such as Prime Minister Vo Van Kiet, argued that it was in Washington's interest to move quickly through the requisite motions to achieve full normalization.[18] The Vietnamese made much of the early June repatriation of remains collected during the 29th joint POW/MIA field activities, hailing the hand-over of remains in 1994 as further evidence of Vietnam's sincere humanitarian approach to the issue.[19] In similar terms, on the occasion of the late June commencement of the 30th joint field activities, Vietnamese media reports gave prominent play to U.S. statements portraying Hanoi's cooperation in a positive light, and emphasized the significance of trilateral cooperation on the Lao border cases which Clinton had singled out as one of the four most important areas of POW/MIA work by which Vietnamese seriousness about resolving this issue would be judged.[20] In a step meant to reinforce Hanoi's message that it was serious about resolving the POW/MIA issue, General Tran Van Quang, head of the Vietnam Veterans Association, visited California in June in conjunction with activities of the International Committee for Fund Raising for the Construction of Vietnam's Van Canh Friendship Village, and met with veterans groups and non governmental organizations to discuss humanitarian issues.[21]

Hanoi approached the new phase of U.S.–Vietnamese relations cautiously, and with an eye to both the likely economic advantages and the potential consequences of the lifting of the embargo. The Vietnamese recognized the opportunities that would emerge from empowering U.S. companies to compete for Vietnamese business in terms of jobs that would be created, technology that would become available to Vietnam, and access to capital that would result from the activism of the international financial and monetary institutions and the competition between American and foreign companies for Vietnamese markets. Hanoi also recognized that Vietnamese companies and the country's economy in general stood to lose in this competition unless Vietnamese players could form large enough economic groupings with significant financial strength that would enable them to stand a chance in this competition. Finally, the Vietnamese recognized that their country was sadly bereft of trained managers who understood professional business practices and could take advantage of opportunities as they emerged. These, and other arguments concerning the impact of modernization on the environment and the social costs of rapid marketization, stood behind the conservative reaction to the lifting of the embargo that stressed the continued and preeminent role of the state in the economic realm.

Hanoi characterized the early March discussions prefatory to the opening of the liaison offices, and the first session of bilateral discussions on human rights, as positive, but reiterated the refrain that no single issue should be allowed to become an obstacle to normalization, a message intended to have direct bearing on the future of the POW/MIA issue. The most strongly stated version of this conservative perspective was articulated by Do Muoi at the 7th Plenum of the Vietnamese Communist Party in July 1994. Muoi's opening speech placed the goals of industrialization and modernization in the context of regional and global development, and urged focused efforts to "catch up with world progress" by employing strategies that built upon Vietnamese economic strengths by forging good foreign economic relations, and developing appropriate aid and cooperation relationships. However, Muoi stressed that it would be wrong "to place too much hope in outside sources of capital" as the basis for efforts to develop manpower, natural resources and other starting points for industrialization. Muoi strongly advocated limiting the extent to which foreign capital was utilized as the engine for modernization in order to "firmly maintain economic independence and sovereignty and avoid the state of growing debts and serious consequences in other respects." Muoi defended a much more cautious approach to economic relations with foreign countries, and sought to tamp down the expectations that had grown in anticipation of the lifting of the embargo, and the enthusiasm for normal trade and economic relations with the U.S. Muoi did not link this part of the argument with the abiding concern within the Politburo over "peaceful transformation" schemes that Vietnam alleged were supported by the U.S. Government, though there was no reason to assume that the case he made did not grow out of the preoccupation with American efforts to destabilize the Socialist Republic. Muoi was more immediately concerned with the consequences of mortgaging Vietnam's future economic independence to a vision of Hanoi's role in emerging global markets and relations that depended on the establishment of normal trade protocols with the U.S. as a catalyst for all future economic improvements for Vietnam.[22]

The Presidential Delegation and Its Aftermath

In July 1994 Deputy Secretary for Veterans Affairs Hershel Gober, Assistant Secretary of State for East Asia and the Pacific Winston Lord, and Deputy Secretary of Defense for POW/MIA Affairs James Wold, accompanied by veterans service organization representatives and the Executive Director of the National League of Families, visited Hanoi for talks with senior government officials.

General Secretary Muoi reminded the U.S. visitors of Vietnam's record of accomplishments on this issue, and called for continued humanitarian POW/MIA cooperation. He emphasized that the POW/MIA matter should not be allowed to become an obstacle to normalization. All the Vietnamese leaders with whom the delegation met signaled their willingness to improve POW/MIA cooperation. The Vietnamese received, but did not comment on, the long-term plan for JTFFA field activities. The Vietnamese agreed to facilitate live sighting investigations involving visits to Vietnamese prisons, and to cooperate in JTFFA efforts to conduct field work in "sensitive areas," including Cam Ranh and Haiphong. Bui Thien Ngo, the Minister of Interior, agreed to establish a "special team" to facilitate POW/MIA work by his ministry, and accepted the delegation's request that the Interior Ministry search its records for wartime information and documents bearing on missing American service personnel. For the first time, the Ministry of Labor, War Invalids and Social Affairs was represented at the plenary session, though this may have been more to underscore Vietnam's humanitarian needs than to suggest that the Ministry was to be a part of the POW/MIA case resolution process. Nevertheless, the U.S. delegation leadership took this as an indication that there was broadened ministerial involvement in the POW/MIA issue. Deputy Defense Minister Nguyen Thoi Bung reiterated Vietnam's willingness to stick with the effort, and expressed frustration over being asked to go beyond what Vietnam considered to be its extraordinary efforts to date. Bung emphasized several times that Vietnam had willingly done what no other country had ever done before by opening its prisons to investigations by special U.S. teams, handing over sensitive documents, and facilitating intrusive field investigations.

Throughout the visit Vietnam's impatience with the U.S. Government's deliberately slow, cautious approach to normalization was apparent. The Vietnamese leadership demonstrated its appreciation of the complexities of the legal and technical process involved in planning for an exchange of offices and ambassadors. However, the Vietnamese side very clearly telegraphed its unwillingness to abide by the rules that tied normalization to the POW/MIA issue in a roadmap-like fashion. The Vietnamese placed a primacy on real dialogue, evidenced by the manner in which Vice Foreign Minister Le Mai conducted the government-only meeting on issues that ranged over regional security matters, the question of a continuing U.S. presence in Asia, the future of Cambodia, counternarcotics issues, as well as bilateral issues including property claims, consular access, and human rights issues.[23] The visit to Ho Chi Minh City revealed a stronger, well-led southern office of the VNOSMP than had existed only one year before, perhaps largely as a result of assigning some serious-minded, talented foreign service officers to the southern office of the Foreign Ministry. Their comprehensive presentation on the work of the VNOSMP suggested an orderliness and professionalism that had not been evident in earlier meetings.

The Vietnamese were strikingly more concerned about their own MIAs, and intent on discussing their humanitarian needs. Those issues were given strong voice by Nguyen Thoi Bung, and echoed by Nguyen Thi Hanh in her presentation on behalf of the Ministry of Labor. Vietnamese media coverage of the visit highlighted the delegation's "reaffirmation" that Washington was committed to a course that would result in the normalization of U.S.–Vietnamese relations, and noted the delegation's expression of appreciation for Vietnam's consistent goodwill and cooperation on the POW/MIA issue that had brought about "concrete results" (ket qua cu the) in resolving the issue. Articles carried in the party's authoritative daily newspaper and Vietnamese news agency broadcasts quoted Hanoi's statements welcoming the Presidential decision to lift the embargo and establish liaison offices, emphasizing that this represented a step toward ushering in a new era of bilateral relations.

Vietnamese media coverage fastidiously avoided characterizing the visit, though the Voice of Vietnam text of 4 July noted that the U.S. side "appraised this visit as a splendid success." The earlier English language broadcast of 4 July quoted extensively from the pre-departure press conference held by the U.S. delegation in Hanoi, and spoke of the delegation's "high appreciation" for Vietnam's cooperation, a decidedly more tentative description of the U.S. side's view of the visit.

Indeed, by the time the delegation had returned to Washington, the Vietnamese were privately expressing concern over the manner in which the U.S. Government leaders has described the results of the visit. Senior Vietnamese diplomats asked serious questions about the meaning of press reports that quoted senior State Department officials as having said that Vietnamese cooperation had lagged behind expectations. Subsequent U.S. Government press conferences that sought to correct this view probably did little to assuage Vietnamese concerns.[24]

Hanoi was very attentive to mid–July statements by administration officials on areas in which Vietnamese cooperation was partial and unsatisfactory. For example, on 15 July Deputy Assistant Secretary of Defense for POW/MIA Affairs James Wold told the annual meeting of the League of Families that:

> Despite this tangible cooperation in the President's four key areas, we believe there are still additional ways Hanoi can cooperate. I have just returned from Vietnam and Laos with the delegation led by Deputy Secretary for Veterans Affairs Gober and Assistant Secretary Lord. There, we told the Vietnamese that although we have seen steady, constructive progress in the President's four key areas, there was more work to be done. We underscored the view that Vietnam can shoulder responsibility for undertaking more work in these four areas on a unilateral basis. In particular, we pointed to some key areas where improvements could be made, including: sustained efforts to unilaterally comb archives and ministerial repositories for information; more active efforts by the Vietnamese government to assist our Task Force in gaining control of remains that may be in the hands of private Vietnamese citizens reluctant to relinquish them; and efforts to have provincial authorities urge that local citizens who have knowledge of grave or crash sites come forward.[25]

In his remarks to the same audience, Deputy National Security Advisor Sandy Berger stated:

> Frankly, we have been disappointed with the Vietnamese Government's failure to follow up on our request for further information on the 84 special remains cases. The presidential delegation clearly expressed this disappointment to the Vietnamese Government. We are watching closely to see if they will move forward on this issue. In addition, we continue to press the Vietnamese to provide the documents that the League first requested during its March mission, and that the Presidential delegation laid on the table again last week. Although we recognize that the Vietnamese Government may not possess every single item on the list, we believe that we have made clear the types of documents we are seeking. We await their response. These are the kinds of issues—issues where we demand results, not just promises—that stand in the way of progress on the POW/MIA issue and, in turn, on closer ties between the United States and Vietnam.... Any steps toward normalization will depend directly on further progress on the POW/MIA issue.[26]

Vietnamese diplomats stationed overseas and senior Foreign Ministry personnel winced at these comments. Linkage was troublesome to the Vietnamese, and even a certain amount of understanding of the political context and the domestic motivations that prompted the administration to speak these views did not soften the private reaction by Vietnamese diplomats to these words.[27]

In August 1994, the Foreign Operations Appropriations Act removed two legal obstacles to extending bilateral assistance to Vietnam (Section 507 of the 1994 Act and Section 13 of the State Department Appropriations Act of 1973), in effect enabling the President to exercise discretionary authority to initiate direct aid. However, foreign assistance was still subject to legislation that imposed limits on providing aid, including (1) critical parts of Section 620 of the Foreign Assistance Act of 1961 which prohibited the U.S. government from providing assistance to any communist country and to any country in default on a foreign assistance loan, and (2) Section 512 of the Foreign Operations Appropriations Act of 1994 which prohibited assistance to any country in default of a foreign assistance loan.[28] In spite of the fact that the step was a modest one, the Vietnamese media noted that the U.S. Senate had lifted the ban on aid for Vietnam, and thereby "annulled a two-decade long anti–Vietnamese policy."[29]

POW/MIA Progress, September–December

From mid–September to late October, the Vietnamese received a string of U.S. visitors, beginning with Deputy Assistant Secretary of State Peter Tomsen. The Commander in Chief of the Pacific, Admiral R.C. Macke, visited Hanoi and toured several excavation sites in late September. Deputy Assistant Secretary of Defense for POW/MIA Affairs, James Wold, returned to Vietnam in late October. The three visitors stressed the importance of productive cooperation in remains repatriations, joint field work, trilateral activities regarding the Lao Border Cases, and archival research.[30] The U.S. officials acknowledged Vietnam's cooperation, and thanked Hanoi for the access granted to joint teams to conduct investigations of unresolved cases in areas around Cam Ranh Bay and Co To Island in Quang Ninh Province, and Hon Me in Thanh Hoa Province. The U.S. visitors stressed the importance of efforts to resolve priority discrepancy cases and live sighting cases, and urged that sustained attention be paid to the special remains cases. Finally, the U.S. officials acknowledged the positive steps taken by the Defense and Interior ministries in establishing special teams to search for documents in the archives of the ministries and within provinces. They urged continued efforts to locate provincial shoot down records and specific command chronologies, in addition to witnesses with wartime recollections of shoot downs involving U.S. pilots or the capture of U.S. service personnel. In mid–October, during the annual United Nations General Assembly session, Foreign Minister Nguyen Manh Cam told Secretary of State Warren Christopher that Vietnam resolved to continue providing assistance to efforts to account for missing personnel.[31] Christopher reiterated the need for "tangible progress" on the POW/MIA effort before the U.S. could move toward full normalization.

The Vietnamese media accorded attention to an early October turnover of seven sets of remains and articles recovered during the 31st joint field investigations.[32] Two of the sets of remains were thought to represent individuals on the list of the 84 special remains cases, a fact highlighted by the Vietnamese accounts.[33] In early October, the family of Colonel Charles Shelton, the last combatant in the Vietnam War officially listed as a prisoner to symbolize U.S. commitment to account for American MIAs, requested a change in status for Colonel Shelton to killed in action.[34] Many middle and senior-level Vietnamese Defense and Foreign Ministry officials regarded this as a gesture of closure, and cited it frequently as an indication that the POW/MIA issue had entered an "endgame" phase. In late October, the Defense Department officially announced that 13 MIA cases had been resolved. The year 1994 saw the third highest number of remains repatriated since 1987.

In mid–November, General Secretary Muoi received Senator Kerry in Hanoi. Muoi reaffirmed Vietnam's "close cooperation in resolving remaining cases of MIAs," and restated Hanoi's "readiness to promote multifaceted cooperation" with the U.S. to help achieve a normal bilateral relationship. Also in mid–November, Prime Minister Kiet met with a delegation of Senators led by Christopher Bond. Kiet stressed Vietnam's "consistent policy" of cooperation on POW/MIA matters. He told the lawmakers that normalization would "create more favorable conditions for bilateral POW/MIA cooperation."[35] At about the same time, the Vietnamese media highlighted the fact that more than 50 boxes of remains had been returned to the U.S. for forensic examination as a result of the last several cycles of joint excavations.[36] Importantly, in early December the Vietnamese and the Lao agreed to facilitate the use of Vietnamese witnesses in joint field activities on Lao soil, an arrangement that had been a sensitive point for Vientiane.[37] Finally, in an initiative that built upon the trilateral agreement with Laos, in early December a Cambodian government delegation prepared to travel to Hanoi to discuss MIAs on the Vietnamese–Cambodian border, and to explore how Phnom Penh might exploit Vietnamese archival holdings to uncover information regarding U.S. personnel missing in Cambodia.[38]

The National Defense Authorization Act for fiscal year 1995, which was signed into law by President Clinton on 5 October 1994, included six sections requiring the administration to take specific steps regarding POW/MIA policy or to provide status reports on various aspects of the issue to Congress. Section 1034 required the Secretary of Defense to provide Congress with two lists regarding unaccounted for U.S. personnel from the Vietnam conflict within 45 days of the enactment of the Act. Specifically, this act required "a complete listing by name of all such personnel about whom it is possible that officials of the Socialist Republic of Vietnam can produce additional information or remains that could lead to the maximum possible accounting for those personnel, as determined on the basis of all information available to the U.S. Government."[39]

The Vietnamese were acutely aware of the reporting requirement imposed on the Administration by this law. They were familiar with the views and influence of its author, Senator Robert Smith. Hanoi calculated that Smith's alliance with several members of Congress, and support for his view from the American Legion and the National League of Families, would not be sufficient to undermine the ability of pro-normalization legislators such as John McCain and John Kerry to counteract the conservatives.[40]

"Lightning and Thunder, Progress and Results": Vietnamese End-of-Year Perspectives in 1994

In late 1994, senior Foreign Ministry officials acknowledged that the POW/MIA issue was still a hard one for U.S. policy makers, and remained an emotionally charged issue for the American public. However, these officials sensed that there had been some shifts in attitudes in the U.S. that suggested the content of the emotions was becoming somewhat more muted. One diplomat stated that while in the past the League of Families had stressed the importance of repatriating remains which were assumed to be "readily available" in a purported Vietnamese warehouse, in the last months of 1994 that call had been replaced with language urging that Vietnam do more "unilaterally," a trend that suggested, to some Vietnamese, movement away from the troublesome issue of warehoused remains. The diplomat did not suggest that this meant the repatriation of remains had become any less important to the United States than it had been when the Roadmap was first presented to Hanoi. However, the diplomat did take this as an indication that there was some willingness among U.S. POW/MIA "activists" to cool down the rhetoric on the POW/MIA issue. Interestingly, in October 1994 Vice Foreign Minister Tran Quang Co repeated the refrain that Vietnam recognized the emotionally charged character of the POW/MIA issue, and voiced confidence that the problems were in fact being solved. He discussed the trend toward more open lines of U.S.–Vietnamese communications on the issue, and the emergence of more effective forms of cooperation. He traced the changes to the retirement of some of the Foreign Ministry's veterans and the active and effective leadership of Nguyen Manh Cam.

By the last quarter of 1994 Hanoi calculated that the POW/MIA issue was less and less likely to exert a negative impact on the direction, tone and content of the overall bilateral relationship because other matters, such as preserving the agreement allowing consular access to Americans detained by Vietnamese authorities, were at least as important to the U.S. Government as sustaining progress on the POW/MIA front. Hanoi began to act on the presumption that the POW/MIA issue was increasingly part of a larger package of bilateral issues, each of which involved important equities from the perspective of the U.S. government agencies and interest groups involved. For that reason, Hanoi approached the POW/MIA issue as more and more of a routine government-to-government problem requiring management and care, but not having the same sort of potentially disruptive impact on relations as the MIA issue had exerted over the prior decade. As part of this effort to signal that the POW/MIA issue was a manageable one requiring routines rather than intensive policy-level intervention, Hanoi sought to establish more clear-cut means of utilizing available diplomatic representation in the U.S. to systematically handle POW/MIA discussions. Additionally, comments on the POW/MIA issue from senior Vietnamese leaders more and more tended to be more positive, encouraging, less loaded with political freight, and indicative of the view that the structures and working-level contacts that ran this issue were on track, seeing eye-to-eye, and accomplishing the goals of both Washington and Hanoi.

Further, newspaper articles in the Vietnamese press began to avoid the argument that U.S. neglect of Vietnam's humanitarian needs, and Washington's failure to give credit where credit was due for expanded Vietnamese cooperation, had polarized the two sides. Additionally, Vietnamese media accounts of senior level contacts on other issues, such as claims and properties, and publicity for ministerial-level meetings on the status of prenormalization discussions, were generally positive, suggesting balance in all facets of the relationship.

Some Vietnamese analysts and officials observed that in the U.S., many foreign policy commentators had offered variations of the argument that for Washington, a normal and proper relationship with Hanoi represented a means of leveraging China into more civilized behavior in the region. Those Vietnamese observers were also attentive to a second line of thought which argued that in view of Hanoi's fears of Beijing's plans and intentions, Washington was in a better position to attract Vietnam into a relationship on terms favorable to U.S. interests. These arguments convinced the Vietnamese that their country had been accorded some importance in the strategic thinking of American policy makers, if only in terms of the impact on Washington's equities in Southeast Asia. On that basis, it seemed increasingly unlikely to Hanoi that normalization could be held hostage to the POW/MIA issue. In that view, Washington had recognized the strategic gamble involved in squandering an opportunity to normalize relations with Vietnam, and was not inclined to pass up a chance to offset Beijing's influence in Southeast Asia. Vietnamese observers believed that in the U.S., issues with exclusively domestic resonance would have a decreasing relevance to the calculus of strategic interests.

Yet, the Vietnamese remained concerned with the possibility that each visit by a U.S. Government representative could erect additional roadblocks to progress, stipulate additional requirements, and result in the yet another shift in the location of the goal posts. Given those concerns, the Vietnamese wanted to know precisely what dividends they would reap from agreeing to interview one more Vietnamese witness, locate one more member of a particular military unit involved in wartime incidents associated with the fate of missing Americans, or undertake further archival searches in pursuit of files that were presumed to exist and imagined to hold answers to questions about the disposition of the remains of American soldiers. To Vietnamese familiar with the issue, the U.S. had made it excruciatingly clear what was required from Hanoi in terms of joint field operations, live sighting investigations, trilateral border case cooperation, remains repatriation, and archival research. However, the U.S. had still not defined closure for this issue. The Vietnamese were not quite comfortable with the knowledge that Washington envisioned the effort to account for MIAs as a process that could take a generation or more to complete. Hanoi wanted to know when the job would be done. Would Vietnam have to agree to reinvestigate these cases, and would refusal to do so risk seeing the issue escalate once more into a political frenzy in the US? As one senior Vietnamese official privately put it shortly after a U.S. presidential delegation visit, having spelled out what the United States wanted, could Washington now tell Vietnam what it really wanted?

Washington's policy remained unambiguously focused on accounting for missing service personnel, the "highest national priority." A slight change in the tone and intensity of public statements on the issue, and a less combative vocabulary, may have suggested a sea change to the Vietnamese. U.S. government recognition that Hanoi had made strides toward a more cooperative atmosphere, defined practical ways of addressing specific case-related questions, and continued to assign serious personnel to new mechanisms focused on the problem full time may have also hinted at a new way of thinking about the bilateral issue.

At its core, though, the issue remained the starting point for all official discussions with Vietnamese government officials, and an earnest priority matter driven by congressional attention, executive office sensitivity to the potential for a political backlash, and continued family and veteran service organization attention to the issue. It had become more manageable, and its goals more easily translated into quantifiable indicators of success and failure. The presidential focus on joint field investigations and live sighting investigations, trilateral work on the Lao border cases, repatriation of remains, and archival research offered four stable and consistent indications of progress toward the fullest possible accounting.

The key point was that the presidential decision to lift the embargo was predicated on achieving the fullest possible accounting. While the Vietnamese reasoned that the global irrelevance of this issue would prod the U.S., in the face of real economic opportunities and strategic possibilities, to abandon this "obstacle" to normalization, in Washington the calculation was that the political consequences of walking away from the POW/MIA issues could be crippling. However, it was not for political reasons only that the focus remained fixed on accomplishing the fullest possible accounting. The slightest diminishment of commitment would represent yet another division between civilian leadership and the military. The Administration, acutely aware of the need to tread carefully on armed services issues, would not risk breaking faith over an article of such importance to the Pentagon.

Through the end of 1994, there was support in the Pentagon for internal discussions about moving the relationship with Vietnam from the single-issue focus on the POW/MIA problem to a level of normal communications and initial interactions between the U.S. and Vietnamese defense establishments. Initial, informal feelers suggested the possibility that Vietnam would accept the notion that normal contacts between the two militaries should be a component of full normalization, but there was no constituency in DoD prepared to support approaching Vietnam directly at that time.[41]

Similarly, the Vietnamese military leadership was not inclined to spend much time hypothesizing over the potential utility of a defense relationship with the U.S. During most of the year, senior Vietnamese military officials looked at their country as a "key point" targeted by "imperialists," utilizing "peaceful transformation" as a multifaceted means of undermining the Socialist Republic. In this way of thinking, the unspoken dividend from the Cambodian peacekeeping process would be a weakened Vietnam. Chinese–Vietnamese relations were being kept off balance by "interests" intent on spoiling the possibility of rapprochement. Vietnam's economic development plans were being quietly ruined by this broad and sweeping challenge to the Socialist Republic. In this context, normalization with the U.S. was viewed with suspicion, and specific efforts to draw the Vietnamese military into dialogue with its American counterpart were regarded with a jaundiced eye. The entire atmosphere disposed PAVN toward a guarded approach to foreign relations.

Establishing Normal Relations with Vietnam

On 28 January 1995, the U.S. and Vietnam opened liaison offices in Hanoi and Washington under the Vienna Convention for Consular Relations, signed an agreement resolving the dispute over diplomatic properties, and settled outstanding claims issues. According to the Vietnamese media, these decisions marked "an important step on the path to normalization of relations, creating favorable conditions for the two governments to develop relations and continue solving problems of mutual interest."[42] At the time, some Vietnamese diplomats posted abroad privately expressed concern that the new Administration had not accorded priority attention to the issue of normalization. They believed that the anti–Vietnamese views of some U.S. legislators would be neutralized by Senators McCain, Kerry, and other congressional members who supported normal relations with Vietnam. These senior diplomats described a "new stage" in the POW/MIA issue, and argued that the cases of missing Americans that had not yet been resolved should be recognized as the hard ones where evidence would be sparse, witnesses to loss incidents would be few and far between, and skeletal remains would more than likely be unrecoverable or insufficient to build an argument for case resolution.

The U.S. message to Vietnam was familiar: Hanoi must do more. Vietnam must take "unilateral" steps that would "yield results" and have an appreciable impact on the accounting process. The Vietnamese response to these points resembled their answers to the Roadmap during April–December 1991. Bilateral exchanges became a rehearsed set of answers based on canned talking points. The Vietnamese argued that they were cooperating wholeheartedly, and were prepared to sustain this cooperation. The Vietnamese told visiting American lawmakers and administration representatives that their government would be responsive to "reasonable" requests from the U.S. Government, such as forming special teams to review historical archives in various ministries. Hanoi warned that it would not be able to satisfy requests for wartime archival documents that would resolve the POW/MIA issue because such materials did not exist. Additionally, senior Vietnamese officials argued that Hanoi would not be able to answer questions about "live prisoners" because they, too, did not exist.

In comments to Veterans of Foreign War (VFW) representatives in early 1995, General Secretary Muoi suggested that both Vietnamese and U.S. MIA namelists were inconsistent, and possibly simply wrong. Muoi's remarks to the VFW were uttered in a difficult foreign policy environment. Hanoi's efforts to cultivate relations with China had yielded no real improvements in that bilateral tie. Muoi was facing a long period of preparations for the 1996 Party Congress with a leadership that was split over basic national-level policy questions concerning the course of economic reforms, methods of dealing with corruption, the approach to take with Buddhist and Catholic dissent, and unfinished legislative business concerning foreign investment regulations. With all this, normalization of relations with the U.S., which might have otherwise struck Muoi as a relatively easy problem to solve, instead represented an intractable puzzle. In short, the Vietnamese had come to see each additional set of specific POW/MIA "requirements" as a "test" of their will, patience and strength. Senior Vietnamese Foreign Ministry officials privately implied that POW/MIA undertakings should be regarded as largely symbolic in nature, and stressed that the symbolism should flow two ways. Some were more direct in their argument that the U.S. must do more to help Vietnam with its MIA problem.[43]

During the first several months of 1995, Vietnam sought to gauge the intensity of Washington's POW/MIA focus. Senior Vietnamese Foreign Ministry officials informally stated that the U.S. Liaison Office (USLO) should subsume the JTFFA Detachment, and argued that joint field activities were no longer necessary given the degree of difficulty that characterized the remaining cases and the increasingly remote possibility of locating remains as the result of excavations. Foreign Ministry officials told Americans that the U.S. should consider closing the JTFFA or merging it with the USLO to increase efficiency and minimize costs. The Administration communicated its opposition to closing down field activities; no matter how costly, they represented a means of investigating individual cases and were therefore crucial to case resolution efforts. Washington also made it clear that the Joint Task Force Detachment in Hanoi represented a mission-oriented task force under the operational control of the Pacific Command, rather than a part of the diplomatic apparatus that was being established within the USLO. Combining the two under the roof of the Liaison Office was not a viable alternative.

Defense Relations: First Discussions

In late February 1995, the Vietnamese responded cautiously to informal discussions with senior State Department officials regarding the possibility of exchanging defense attachés at some future date. At that time, in the words of a senior SRV diplomat, the Vietnamese military was not an "open" military, and it would take considerable work to establish a basic, entry level relationship with PAVN. In the interim period the Vietnamese Ambassador to Washington, Le Van Bang, a respected Foreign Ministry insider, would serve as the point of contact with the Pentagon. Bang had played a role in the long history of the POW/MIA issue, and was predisposed to meet with middle and senior Pentagon officials for discussions aimed at broadening relationships and teasing out the idea of military contacts.

During March and April 1995, the Pacific Command reacted negatively to the idea of opening a defense liaison office (DLO) in Hanoi, a precursor to a Defense Attaché Office (DAO) that would exist until normalization. Putting a defense liaison office in Hanoi, Pacific Command representatives argued, would send the wrong signal to Vietnam. It would confuse the government of the Socialist Republic as to which U.S. government entity had cognizance over the POW/MIA issue, especially since the defense liaison officer, who would most likely be an Army colonel, would outrank the JTFFA Detachment Commander. The Commander in Chief of the Pacific was able to convince the Director of the Defense Intelligence Agency, who was responsible for the defense attaché system, to postpone plans to establish a DLO in Hanoi. In June, though, the DIA Director retired. With all indications pointing to an early decision on normalization, ISA pressed for a policy decision on opening a Defense Liaison Office, recommending support for placing a Defense Attaché in Hanoi as soon as the U.S. government upgraded its mission to ambassadorial level representation in order to insure that the Chief of the U.S. Liaison Office would have the benefit of a U.S. advisor on security and defense issues, and in order to encourage the U.S. mission to begin to build the kinds of contacts through normal liaison work that would serve U.S. interests once normalization took place. An active defense attaché presence would contribute to a better understanding of evolving Vietnamese views on fundamental security issues, threat perceptions, and intentions following integration into ASEAN in a way that would improve the content of a basic U.S.–Vietnamese defense relationship. There was every reason to believe that these goals could be pursued without compromising the priority placed on the POW/MIA issue. An effective institutional division of labor between the JTFFA and the DLO would help avoid "confusing" the Vietnamese about who was in charge.

Throughout the first quarter of 1995, the Administration in Washington sought to make clear that normalization was linked to progress on the POW/MIA issue, and that economics and the interests of U.S. businesses were extraneous to the decision process regarding normalization. National Security Advisor Anthony Lake refused to talk trade issues or meet with representatives of U.S. companies seeking business opportunities in Vietnam.[44] Hanoi responded to this policy by underscoring what it characterized as Vietnam's unprecedented cooperative response to Washington's requests for assistance, and restating its humanitarian approach to the POW/MIA issue. For example, during a 10–13 April visit to Hanoi by the Junior Vice Commander in Chief of the VFW, Deputy Foreign Minister Le Mai stressed Hanoi's intensification of "unilateral efforts" to investigate POW/MIA leads. Mai told the VFW that the provinces had been instructed to coax people to share information they might have on missing Americans. A Ministry of Interior representative told the VFW that provincial and municipal public security services were still under instructions to actively search for documents and to attempt to locate wartime security cadre who might recollect information on gravesites of American MIAs.[45] Vice Minister of Defense Nguyen Thoi Bung reiterated the Defense Ministry's record of cooperation in turning over archival holdings bearing on U.S. losses, and explained the limitations and gaps that characterized wartime records.[46] In early May, Le Mai drove these points home, telling a journalist that "in no war in history has there been so much cooperation between former enemies on accounting for MIAs as in this war." Mai acknowledged that the question of unaccounted for Americans was still a very emotional one in the U.S., but held forth that good will, "current realities," and Vietnam's cooperation could help get beyond these lingering problems. In an optimistic moment, Foreign Ministry official Nguyen Xuan Phong noted that the Clinton Administration had confronted the difficult job of tamping down emotions that had been purposely stirred by previous administrations.[47]

Congressional Activity Through Mid-Year

Senator Robert Smith's resolution on the normalization of relations with Vietnam, introduced in May, was aimed at prohibiting the appropriation of funds for the establishment or maintenance of an embassy, and prohibiting the granting of Most Favored Nations status to Vietnam, unless and until the President could certify three things: (1) that the Department of Defense had completed the compiling of a list of all personnel about whom it was possible that SRV officials could produce additional information or remains that could lead to the "maximum possible accounting" for those personnel"; (2) that the Vietnamese were cooperating fully in the four areas specified by the President; and (3) that Vietnam was being forthcoming regarding access to wartime documents and Central Committee records pertaining to missing American service personnel.[48]

Smith may have intended to attach these conditions to the Defense Department Authorization Act. The resolution accelerated Administration efforts to respond to the original reporting requirement articulated in Section 1034 of the National Defense Authorization Act for Fiscal Year 1995, in the form of a "comprehensive review" of POW/MIA cases under the auspices of the Defense POW/MIA Office. The Vietnamese closely monitored these congressional developments, presumably with the same basic confidence that informed Hanoi's view that rational voices would overcome the efforts of the few strident lawmakers.

In early May, the U.S.–Russian Joint Commission on POW/MIAs signed an "interim report," intended for presentation to Presidents Clinton and Boris Yeltsin in Moscow during early June. The report reviewed three years worth of work on a range of POW/MIA accounting issues. Senator Smith, a member of the Commission, challenged the reports conclusion that "no credible evidence" had been uncovered to support the contention that the Soviets transferred American POWs to the former Soviet Union, or that the Soviets had direct contact with American POWs in North Vietnam.[49] The Vietnamese media disposed of this issue in a brief, bland transmission on 4 May which highlighted the Commission's statement that there was "no reliable evidence to affirm that American prisoners of the Vietnam War" were transferred to the former Soviet Union.[50] The Vietnamese may have been consulted by the Russians prior to the planned signing of the report as the result of an agreement struck between Hanoi and Moscow in late 1993, following the public release of the second Soviet archival document that Hanoi felt had a potentially serious and negative impact on efforts to achieve the lifting of the embargo. That would explain the terse public acknowledgement of the Commission's report, and the apparent lack of concern over its impact on U.S.–Vietnamese normalization, in contrast with their response to the two "Soviet documents" that made headlines in American newspapers in 1993.[51]

The Third Presidential Delegation

The third Presidential Delegation since 1993 visited Vietnam during 15–17 May, and was headed by Deputy Secretary of Veterans Affairs Hershel Gober, Assistant Secretary of State Winston Lord, and DASD/POW-MIA James Wold. The delegation met with General Secretary Do Muoi, Prime Minister Vo Van Kiet, and senior Foreign Ministry officials, all of whom stressed Vietnam's commitment to remain responsive to U.S. requests for POW/MIA cooperation, to continue cooperation with the JTFFA, and to work to uncover documents and witnesses to help shed light on unresolved cases.[52]

The Vietnamese provided the Presidential Delegation with three main reports. The VNOSMP turned over a detailed account of unilateral Vietnamese actions related to efforts to investigate the 84 Special Remains cases.⁵³ The Defense Ministry turned over a report on the activities of the Special Information Team established in direct response to the a June 1994 request from a Presidential Delegation.⁵⁴ That team searched central and provincial archival holdings of the Ministry of Defense for information bearing on U.S. MIAs. The Interior Ministry turned over a similar report. Both the defense and interior ministries reports included documents, sketches of gravesites, and other information gleaned from provincial file searches. The Vietnamese gave every reason to believe that they had established a routine means of facilitating these inter-ministerial actions, that they had developed the mechanisms required to respond to "reasonable" requests from the U.S. side for relevant information, and that all the players from the ministries to the provinces were earnestly working to achieve a level of responsiveness that could contribute to resolving cases.⁵⁵

The visit indicated that the Vietnamese had made a broad commitment to look for provincial-level documentation bearing on missing U.S. personnel, and demonstrated a willingness and capacity to conduct fruitful file searches. Hanoi offered assurances that they were prepared to continue the work of the two ministerial-level special information teams, and to continue working with U.S. casualty resolution specialists.

According to senior Vietnamese diplomats, Hanoi was very pleased with the visit by the Presidential Delegation, and anxiously monitored developments in Washington, especially the draft Congressional Resolution and McCain's support for normalization, to determine the impact of the visit. The Vietnamese were particularly taken by McCain's *Washington Times* article, in which he argued that those who disagreed with the U.S. government assessments concerning the level of Vietnam's POW/MIA cooperation were not directly involved in the accounting process. Those on the ground, McCain stated, had all noted Vietnam's high level of cooperation.⁵⁶

By mid-year, Vietnam was looking for ways to minimize the extent to which the POW/MIA issue entered into arguments justifying rapid and complete normalization. Media commentaries in May quoted senior Vietnamese leaders acknowledging that the timing of normalization required a decisive act before the November elections in the U.S. so that the issue would not become bogged down in electoral tactics of the conservative factions of the Republican Party, mimicking arguments penned by American pundits. Other Vietnamese officials seemed to suggest that the publication of former Secretary of Defense Robert McNamara's memoirs, in which he stated that pursuing the war in Vietnam was a mistake, and a rancor-free celebration of the 20th anniversary of the fall of Saigon, had created conditions for a reconciliation between Washington and Hanoi. The economic reality of steadily growing American investment in Vietnam, and the realization that failing to normalize at this juncture would repeat the train of events that led to the missed opportunity of 1978, were reference points in the Vietnamese case for full diplomatic and economic normalization.[57]

Fully aware that it would be held to a stringent test of "tangible results," Vietnam sought to move the process along in noticeable increments. In late May, Hanoi authorized the first underwater recovery of a B-52 that crashed in southern Vietnam in 1967. Also in late May, the VNOSMP turned over additional reports from the Ministry of Interior's special research team that was formed to research ministerial and provincial archival holdings. President Le Duc Anh drove home the predictable points concerning Vietnam's cooperation, and the mutual advantages of normalization, in a late May meeting with U.S. Representative William Richardson. In early June the Vietnamese approached the Executive Director of the National League of Families, whose brother's plane that had crashed at sea was the subject of another underwater search operation, on the assumption that a modest gesture of friendship might contribute to alleviating tensions and blunting the offensive taken by conservative American legislators in alliance with veterans groups and family organizations. More often than not, though, the Vietnamese stuck to tried and true arguments in making their case: Vietnam had hewed to a humanitarian approach, had returned more than 500 remains to the U.S., and had turned over tens of thousands of documents.[58]

In early June, the U.S. government continued to review the documents released to the May 1995 Delegation. The President acknowledged that he could not conclude that Hanoi had met Washington's criteria for the establishment of a normal relationship with the SRV until the review of the documents had been completed. In this context, the Vietnamese media stated that during the second week of June Secretary of State Christopher had recommended that the President establish full diplomatic relations with Vietnam. In a unique twist to the usual Vietnamese rhetoric, a mid–June radio station commentary made the case that since early 1990 the U.S. had readjusted its strategy, and the MIA issue had become only one of many factors defining the relationship, alongside of economic interests.[59]

Another POW/MIA Interlude

In early July, former Representative Billy Hendon, an outspoken POW/MIA activist from North Carolina, traveled to Vietnam and attempted to get the JTFFA and the U.S. Liaison Office to accompany him to a "secret military jail" in Vinh Phuc Province where, he claimed, live Americans were being held. Hendon chained himself to the gate outside the JTFFA Detachment facility in Hanoi twice on 4 June. After being cut loose by the JTFFA he moved into a local hotel and proposed a meeting in the lobby of the Liaison Office, to which the USLO Chief consented. However, on the day of that meeting Hendon moved into the street in front of the Liaison Office, amidst a throng of reporters, and demanded that the USLO Chief meet him there, produce a four-wheel drive vehicle for travel to Vinh Phu, and accompany him to the Hung Hoa site in question.

Washington sought to assure the Vietnamese that the U.S. side would not bend to the whims of activists who were prepared to travel to Vietnam to draw attention to their own personal theories. Administration officials were concerned that if the U.S. government could not say that U.S. specialists had gone to Vinh Phu to investigate Hendon's claims, Washington would find it increasingly difficult to press forward with upgrading the relationship with Vietnam, especially given congressional attention to the issue of normalization and the question of Vietnamese cooperation with the JTFFA. Ultimately, after Hendon repeatedly refused to provide the specific coordinates of the prison in question, the JTFFA traveled to the general area but could not locate the facility that Hendon claimed housed live Americans.[60]

The Vietnamese reacted by reiterating their commitment to facilitate visits to any point in the country in the conduct of live sighting investigations; visits to military-controlled facilities would take somewhat longer, but would not be impossible to arrange. The Vietnamese stipulated that though they would not object to having a journalist join a U.S. government team that would travel to an area to conduct such an investigation, they did not want Hendon to join any such event, suggesting the extent to which the Vietnamese were concerned that the issue could be highjacked by "extremists" and anti-regime activists who would embarrass the Vietnamese government and set back the cause of U.S.–Vietnamese relations in significant ways.

The Vietnamese media's handling of Hendon's actions was non-confrontational and terse. The Vietnamese media reported the events surrounding Hendon's public claims, relying on Reuter's wire service reporting to describe the former representative's statements and activities, and avoiding the dramatic moments of Hendon's visit.[61] However, the Vietnamese were apparently uncertain as to whether the antic by Hendon could derail a decision on normalization, and similarly unsure of Clinton's willingness to overcome the impact of Hendon's actions.[62] Hanoi appeared to be aware that a late June congressional hearing on the casualty resolution process could become a bully pulpit for anti-normal-ization forces.

Between mid–June and mid–July, the U.S. government undertook several assessments of the status of POW/MIA cooperation, some in response to congressional inquiries. Washington sought to defend the argument that normal, proper relations would facilitate increased cooperation, not a slackening off of the Vietnamese incentive to work with the JTFFA. The Administration argued that a bilateral relationship allowed to develop across the customary spectrum of diplomatic interaction would add depth to Vietnamese cooperation, and create routines and mechanisms supported by both governments that would facilitate the resolution of cases.[63]

The Vietnamese position was that the Socialist Republic had already demonstrated its good faith commitment to cooperation with years of hard work and a stated readiness to continue such efforts. The U.S. government view was that the energy expended to date demonstrated resolve to continue to enhance cooperation in the future. Conservative congressional interests, POW/MIA family organizations and some veterans groups sought to show that not enough had been done. That was a position that most of the national level veterans organizations, conservative congressional members, and the POW/MIA activists held firmly through the eve of normalization.

On 15 June 1995, the Veterans of Foreign Wars announced that it had ceased opposing normalization of relations, and would support that step if it would promote further progress toward the fullest possible accounting. Five days later, the National Commander of AmVets acknowledged "substantial progress" in Vietnam's cooperation, and concluded that normalization "must be part of a reciprocal process aimed at achieving the fullest possible accounting." The American Legion remained strongly opposed to normalization.[64]

Senate Resolution 34, introduced by Robert Dole and Bob Smith in late June, sought to deny the President the funds necessary to establish an embassy in Vietnam. In response, McCain and Kerry introduced an amendment to the State Department Authorization Act that called for unconditional establishment of full diplomatic relations with Vietnam. In early July, Senator Tom Harken led a delegation to Hanoi, where he met with Prime Minister Kiet and Vice Foreign Minister Le Mai, among other SRV leaders, all of whom reaffirmed Vietnam's commitment to continued cooperation with the U.S. in efforts to account for missing Americans, regardless of the decision taken in Washington on normalization.[65] By early

July, senators inclined to be supportive of normalization found it difficult to take a strong public position in the absence of any indication that the White House had made up its mind. The Hill was aware that the assessment of the documents Vietnam provided to the Presidential Delegation in mid–May, and to the JTFFA in late May, had been circulated for interagency comment.[66] Senators were not convinced that the Administration had decided to act, and made it clear that they would be more comfortable waiting until the administration had reached a decision before they formulated a strong resolution of support. This represented a very different situation than that which obtained in January 1994, in advance of the lifting of the embargo, when there was a steady stream of congressional delegations traveling to Hanoi that were fairly confident the President would lift the embargo, and that wanted to provide "top cover" for the Administration in this visible way.

Administration witnesses speaking before congressional hearings in June and July reiterated the importance attached to achieving the fullest possible accounting, and described all decisions concerning U.S.–Vietnamese relations as having been "motivated by and directed toward" that goal.[67] In hearings before the House International Relations Committee on 12 July, one day after the President announced normalization, government witnesses gave the Vietnamese credit for undiminished cooperation on joint field investigations, effective unilateral steps to solicit assistance from the Vietnamese people with evidence bearing on missing Americans, positive actions on trilateral investigations that had led to the productive use of Vietnamese eyewitnesses on Lao soil, and sustained efforts to locate and provide to the U.S. archival documents containing new leads on individual cases.[68] The 7 July invitation to Administration witnesses to testify before the Committee on International Relations noted that the Administration had not yet provided a complete response to Section 1034 of the National Defense Authorization Act for Fiscal Year 1995, which required a list of all personnel about whom it was possible, in the judgment of the U.S. Government, that Vietnamese officials could produce additional information or remains that "could lead to the maximum possible accounting for those personnel." The 12 July hearing focused in part on the Administration's plans for pursuing further progress in the four areas emphasized by the president as the criteria for measuring POW/MIA progress.

Hanoi did not react directly and publicly to the critical views expressed by some organizations and congressional interests. Hanoi retained a residual confidence that the more sober voices of elected officials would drown out the more extreme views, in part based on the confidence of pro-normalization U.S. organizations that held this view themselves.

There was some real frustration on the part of the Vietnamese that years of demonstrating a willing spirit and an accommodating, "humanitarian" attitude had not contributed to tamping down anti–Vietnamese tendencies held by veterans groups and family associations. Finally, Foreign Ministry officials suspected that these harsher views of Vietnam's performance in the realm of POW/MIA cooperation would convince more conservative Vietnamese government, party and military officials that their own more extreme evaluations of Washington's motive for pursuing the POW/MIA issue were on the mark: the U.S. government continued to press the Vietnamese to cooperate in this area out of a mean-spirited attitude toward Vietnam, with the goal of fomenting trouble for the country, discrediting the SRV leadership, and undermining Vietnamese diplomacy.

Normalization and the Vietnamese Response

President Clinton announced his decision to normalize relations with Vietnam on 11 July on the basis of the assessment that Vietnam had made progress on a number of issues, including efforts to account for missing American service personnel. Clinton made it clear that he expected that normalization would lead to further "tangible progress." He firmly communicated the point that continued progress toward the fullest possible accounting must be understood by the Vietnamese as the highest national priority for the United States, and the most important issue in the U.S.–Vietnamese relationship. Clinton also stated that in order to "facilitate continued progress," a "full Presidential delegation," including veterans and family organization representatives, would return to Vietnam in 1995.[69]

The President, National Security Council officials, and State and Defense spokespersons stressed that the core of the normalized relationship would revolve around effort to focus Vietnam's attention on joint field activities, live sighting investigations, trilateral cooperation on the Lao Border cases, the repatriation of remains, and the search for archival information bearing on the fate of U.S. MIAs. The Administration argued that Vietnamese cooperation in the areas of joint field activities and trilateral work on the Border Cases had been excellent. Vietnam had unilaterally provided a significant proportion of the total remains repatriated. The turnovers of documents in 1995 represented the positive impact of Vietnamese initiatives undertaken during the twelve prior months, including the utilization of defense and interior documents search teams, and SRV efforts to seek information from war veterans. Administration spokespersons said that the highest levels of the Vietnamese government had offered their assurances that full cooperation would continue, and noted that normalization would enable the U.S. Government to sustain discussions at the highest levels and to keep the Vietnamese focused on the assurances of continued cooperation that Hanoi had offered.

Through late July, senators who opposed the decision to normalize U.S.–Vietnamese relations considered attaching the three preconditions on the funding for the new embassy in Hanoi to the Fiscal Year 1996 Defense Authorization Bill that Senator Smith had first offered in May. In response, the Administration committed to providing Congress with the results of the Comprehensive Review for all unaccounted for Americans in Southeast Asia, and reiterated its on-the-record statement regarding the level of Vietnamese cooperation. In response to questions from legislators on access to Central Committee-level records pertaining to captured Americans, the Administration restated its commitment to continuing efforts to pursue wartime documents of potential value to the accounting process. Department of Defense officials felt that the bill would prohibit the U.S. government from moving forward in a way that would allow the use of normal diplomatic discourse to sustain high-level Vietnamese attention to the POW/MIA issue, and would lock the Administration into a continuous battle with certain members of Congress who gave every indication that they would keep levying new requirements for certifications on various aspects of Vietnam's cooperation.

The Vietnamese were privately elated but publicly restrained in their response to the President's announcement of the U.S. government decision to normalize relations with Hanoi. The Vietnamese press reported positive worldwide responses to normalization, stressed the advantages to the region of U.S.–Vietnamese normalization in terms of stability and the potential for expanded economic intercourse, and downplayed the POW/MIA side of the equation.[70] Vietnam leaders looked beyond the moment of normalization, and envisioned the hard work that would be necessary to deal diplomatically with important bilateral issues such as human rights problems, economic and trade issues, and scientific and technological cooperation.[71] In the assessment of senior Foreign Ministry officials, Vietnam accomplished the establishment of bilateral links with the U.S. without succumbing to "prerequisites" or conditions (dieu kien tien quyet) to normalization that were set out by the U.S. The immediate future of the relationship with Washington would revolve around the negotiation of a trade agreement and normalization of economic relations.

To the Vietnamese, normalization represented an important decision marking the beginning of a new stage in U.S.–Vietnamese relations and a new period of reconciliation between Vietnamese and Americans, as well as between all Americans over the issue of the Vietnam War. To get to that point, Vietnamese officials believed that serious exertions on the part of both the U.S. and the SRV would be required, especially after the conditions put forth by the U.S. Department of State in the form of the "Roadmap" of April 1991. That document had slowed the process down, according to the views of a range of Vietnamese officials, and left a legacy of suspicion and a tradition of measuring Vietnamese compliance with U.S. government requirements in exacting, public ways that put Vietnam in a difficult, untenable position.

According to one of the first lengthy treatments of this issue following the 11 July decision to normalize, carried in the August issue of the party's monthly journal, "many people" in the U.S. hindered normalization by making the POW/MIA issue an obstacle to progress. The article pointed to Dole and Smith as the key figures behind a Senate resolution freezing the funding for the establishment of an embassy in Hanoi. It also blamed the two senators for blocking a U.S. decision to grant Most Favored Nations status to Vietnam until the President could certify (1) that Vietnam had attained a level of acceptable cooperation on the POW/MIA issue, and (2) that Vietnam was prepared to work with the U.S. to compile a list of all missing U.S. service personnel. The article argued that the activities of many organizations, including all the associations of Vietnamese refugees in the U.S., opposed further steps toward developing bilateral relations in a way that was consonant with the views expressed by the Senate resolution. The article recognized the extent to which the POW/MIA issue had become a sensitive matter in American society, and stated Vietnam's sympathy for the families of the missing service personnel, drawing a clear distinction between the legitimate interest of MIA families and all other organizations that had fixed on this problem as a means of achieving their own political goals.[72]

3
BUILDING DEFENSE TIES, 1995

Introduction: The Working Level Process Begins

In mid–June, ISA convened a working group consisting of representatives from the Joint Staff (J-5) and the armed services for a first discussion of DoD policy regarding military relations with Vietnam. The proposals that were discussed at the meeting were intended to be modest starting points for the effort to develop defense relations with Vietnam. They focused on humanitarian undertakings, such as demining, cooperation between the U.S. Army Corps of Engineers and the Ministry of Water Resources on the rehabilitation of river and sea dikes, and continued military medical cooperation.

ISA laid out a host of other possibilities, including using DoD resources to show PAVN how it might convert its assets and capabilities to civilian use, a program that had met with some success among countries that had formerly been Soviet Bloc states. ISA supported placing a Defense Attaché in Hanoi, and proposing to the Vietnamese that a senior DoD delegation, headed by the Assistant Secretary of Defense for International Security Affairs, travel to Vietnam in August 1995.

Finally, ISA supported exchanges between Vietnamese and U.S. military historians, the development of a schedule of regular visits to Vietnam by the National Defense University and the U.S. Air War College, visits to the U.S. by counterpart organizations in the Vietnamese military, a direct relationship between the Defense Mapping Agency and the Vietnamese military's mapping institute, and reciprocal visits by officials representing the military service academies.

The goal was to keep the framework for the first steps toward defense relations focused initially on building Vietnamese confidence in U.S. plans and intentions, and aimed at developing familiarity between the two military establishments.

ISA's desire was to keep this a low-keyed approach, "under the radar scope," with a modest scope and a deliberately slow pace. Indeed, at the outset, and through at least 1998, ISA spoke of "military to military contacts," avoiding the use of broader terms that would describe the proposed interaction as the basis for a "defense relationship," as a means to avoid galvanizing the opposition of POW/MIA interests, suggesting to U.S. legislators that the Pentagon had embarked on an attempt to develop a profound new security alliance without appropriate prior consultations with lawmakers, and as a way to blunt the possibility that Hanoi would shy away from initiatives intended to draw them out for fear of moving too quickly toward the embrace of the U.S.

The service responses to these proposals were polite and correct, and unenthusiastic. The Army appeared to believe it had the most at stake, as the service that would contribute the first defense attaché, and that it had the most experience in Vietnam. The Navy was ambivalent, and viewed its role as revolving around the ultimate question of ship visits and port calls, acts of military diplomacy that were deliberately not part of the ISA picture of what the first stage relationship might look like, largely as a result of indications that the Vietnamese would not be comfortable with a set of first steps that included such visible U.S. military activity. The Air Force was prepared to formulate a generic, entry-level program revolving around airport safety, senior officer visits, and Air War College trips. The U.S. Marine Corps (USMC) was inclined to think out of the box, to look for strategic meaning in a relationship, and to express concern with the deliberately cautious nature of this attempt to form defense links with Vietnam. Part of that might have been the clear investment the USMC may have been contemplating at that time, in terms of developing a cadre of foreign area specialists through assigning field grade officers to defense attaché offices. Another part may have been the sense that there was a real absence of long-term thinking, and planning, about the evolution of the American commitment to Asia's security and the resources it would take to accomplish such goals. Marine interest in identifying future training areas in Asia may have, in at least small part, motivated inventive thinking from the Corps on the issue of future U.S.–Vietnamese defense relations.[1]

The ISA initiatives concerning defense links with Vietnam were formulated, and injected into the policy system, in a slightly different manner than the usual process, in part because of the delicate controversies that continued to swirl about Hanoi's POW/MIA cooperation, in part because of internal differences over the appropriateness of formulating such plans before the Defense POW/MIA Office (DPMO) ruled on the extent to which a U.S.–Vietnamese military relationship would impact on its work, and in part because of the minimal attention consistently given to Vietnam on matters other than the fullest possible accounting.

Though the first drafts for a program of entry-level interaction with the Vietnamese military were drawn up by ISA during June and July 1995, it was not until mid–September that the issue was conveyed, in formal memoranda seeking decisions, to the Assistant Secretary of Defense for International Security Affairs. That represented an extraordinarily long time for gestation of a policy recommendation. The ISA draft memorandum to the Assistant Secretary was subjected to a lengthy review intended to resolve disagreements at the working level between ISA, DPMO and PACOM on the extent to which a fledgling defense relationship would shift Vietnam's focus from the POW/MIA issue. The coordination process required of ISA was more exacting, and broader, than that generally required. Formal, leadership-level coordination was required from parallel offices, such as the Humanitarian Assistance Program office within the Office of the Assistant Secretary of Defense for Special Operations and Low Intensity Conflict, because of the "humanitarian" content involved in the proposal, whereas desk level coordination might have been satisfactory in more typical circumstances.[2] Between 13 June and 7 July, at least five drafts of the memo for the DASD/AP configured the start up program in various ways, and embroidered on the basic approach defined in 1993. The Pentagon's middle level policy leadership flirted with the idea of defense relations with Hanoi. In anticipation of political problems they experimented with various repackaging strategies aimed at finding the least objectionable language and a structure that would not ignite opposition, would blend well with existing regional initiatives, and not get too far out in front of the instincts of senior Pentagon decision makers.

A policy decision did not emerge from the process begun in June–July 1995 until well into 1996. The process of coordination clarified the views of the working level counterparts of ISA at the Department of State and the National Security Council, and provided helpful indications of how the policy should be shaped to insure continued support at that level.

The lengthy period of introspection also allowed a certain leeway in testing hypotheses about the issue of U.S.–Vietnamese defense relations with groups and individuals outside the government capable of speaking for, or commenting intelligently about, the views of the constituencies and interests most likely to offer strong and public objections to this contemplated course of action. Working level discussions with conservative think tank analysts, non-governmental supporters of normalization, ethnic Vietnamese political activists, and POW/MIA interests enabled ISA to articulate the subtleties of the argument on behalf of bilateral defense relations with Vietnam, to confront some of the concerns spoken by such interest groups, and to gauge the possible intensity of blowback from taking steps toward establishing first contacts with the Vietnamese military.[3] Extraordinary attention was paid to the views of individuals associated with nongovernmental POW/MIA groups, and to the potential for veterans group criticism, and Congressional objections, before senior defense officials were prepared to rule on the question of whether to draw the Vietnamese military into a dialogue on a future defense relationship.

Normalization and the Changing Vocabulary of the POW/MIA Issue

From the perspective of the Department of Defense, during the period leading up to and in the immediate aftermath of normalization, the single most important issue in the U.S.–Vietnamese relationship, the proverbial "national priority," remained the POW/MIA issue. That changed in slow and subtle ways after normalization. When the president announced the normalization of relations with Vietnam on 11 July, he firmly communicated that continued progress toward the fullest possible accounting must be understood by the Vietnamese as the highest national priority of the U.S., and the most important issue in the bilateral relationship. At the same time the President described a relationship that must begin to grow and develop in areas including trade, commerce, culture and other areas that characterized customary normal relations between sovereign states. Similarly, during his August 1995 visit to Hanoi, Secretary of State Warren Christopher told his interlocutors that the relationship should grow and develop in other areas, even as the fullest possible accounting remained the highest priority.[4]

The Department of Defense thinking shifted subtly away from the position that normalization should not take place until the fullest possible accounting had been rendered, moving toward the view that normalization would enable the U.S. to get to the core of the POW/MIA issue expeditiously, using tools of diplomacy, and the complete set of channels of communication that formal and proper relationships made available to governments. The POW/MIA rhetoric was reshaped in a manner intended to convey flexibility sufficient enough to support the development of the overall relationship in a variety of dimensions. For example, in mid–1995 public affairs guidance drafts specified that "DoD supports normalization as a means of sustaining Vietnam's high level attention to the POW/MIA issue, and as a means of providing a firmer foundation for addressing a wide range of issues with Vietnam." Draft public affairs guidance language moved away from the language of "linkage" according to which full normalization would in some manner still be a function of POW/MIA cooperation and progress, and closer to a more open-ended statement to the effect that "DoD supports moving forward in the relationship with Vietnam, with the provision that continued progress toward the fullest possible accounting be understood by the Vietnamese as our highest national priority, and the most important issue in our bilateral relationship."[5]

Pentagon thinking was that moving to the next level of representation as soon as possible would have the effect of sustaining Vietnam's high level attention to the issue, and providing a firmer foundation for addressing a wide range of issues with Vietnam. Normalization, according to this thinking, would increase U.S. leverage in the context of the POW/MIA issue by involving a higher level of government officials from both sides in sustaining cooperation, and by introducing a proliferation of interests with an investment in the issue (veterans, families, congressional delegations) that would keep Hanoi focused. Normalization would allow more frequent, routine opportunities to remind Vietnam of the central importance of this issue, and would arm the U.S. government with more consequential diplomatic means of expressing concern for lapses in cooperation.

By mid–July, there was basic inter-agency agreement in Washington that the relationship with Vietnam should continue to feature the importance of the POW/MIA issue, and that accounting for missing American service personnel would remain the most important issue in the bilateral relationship, "which must grow and develop in other areas." It was this last phrase, harking back to the Presidential language describing the decision to normalize, that was crucial to framing the argument in favor of proceeding with initiatives in other areas of the relationship, such as defense relations. At the outset, though, the argument in favor of the development of defense relations had to continue to feature the prominence of the POW/MIA issue, or risk having no traction at all. As the case was framed in the period following the President's decision to normalize relations, military-to-military contacts could have a positive impact on POW/MIA progress. The relationship, however, should be pursued in order to establish a solid basis for institutional dialogue while supporting the efforts of the Joint Task Force in Vietnam. Visits to Vietnam by DoD personnel should emphasize the priority importance accorded to the POW/MIA effort, in a manner that paralleled the message being delivered by other U.S. delegations.

The practical dimensions of complex policy issues sometimes emerge as matters for decision in the simplest of forms. So, while ISA was formulating positions on enduring questions regarding the impact of normalization on regional stability, the strategic dividends of developing defense relations with Vietnam, and the political consequences of the policy choices involved, the first manifestation of the issue was in the realm of ordinary and routine bureaucratic procedures. In short, it was a housekeeping issue, a question concerning the kinds of official DoD visits that should take place in the initial period of military contacts, that first captured center stage, and required an assistant secretary-level decision to resolve.

On the eve of normalization, ISA recommended that the Defense Department should limit visits to Vietnam by Pentagon officials, especially senior ones, so that there would be no possibility of interpreting proposals for official U.S. military travel to Vietnam as a sign that the Pentagon was rushing into courtship with Hanoi. A quick and uncontrolled flurry of senior level visits to Vietnam could have telegraphed unintended messages to China and the region, and overloaded Vietnamese circuits at a moment that called for cautious, deliberately low-keyed overtures.

ISA endorsed a CINCPAC visit, and recommended that it be billed as a visit to review JTFFA troops, noting that Admiral Larson traveled to Vietnam in January 1994, meaning that Admiral Macke would not be breaking new ground. DoD would, however, want to avoid telegraphing the message that the U.S. was approaching Vietnam right off the bat to ask for access to facilities or agreement to ship visits. ISA therefore took the view that Macke should not travel to Vietnam before a visit by a DoD policy level representative.

In the aftermath of Secretary of State Christopher's visit to Hanoi, there was a constituency in the Pentagon for a Secretary of Defense visit. However, ISA wanted to avoid sending the message to China that Dr. William Perry had shifted his strategic attention to Vietnam. ISA recommended that the Department think in terms of bringing Vietnamese military officials to the U.S., perhaps through non governmental agencies, for working-level discussions of issues of mutual interest that would help define some baselines for dialogue and activities for a military-to-military relationship.

DoD policy approval for travel to Vietnam by senior personnel of flag rank or equivalent and senior level visitors from DoD became one of the first tests of wills over the POW/MIA issue. ISA made the case that authority for such travel should be sought from the Under Secretary of Defense for Policy through the Assistant Secretary of Defense for International Security Affairs, following interagency coordination. PACOM made the counter argument that high level visits should be ruled on by the JTFFA because their mission remained the primary one. The compromise formula yielded an ad hoc arrangement according to which PACOM and the U.S. Defense Attaché's Office in Hanoi, which was to be established in December 1995, were to be asked to evaluate all proposed visits to ensure that such activities did not interfere with the capabilities of the U.S. Embassy and the JTFFA Detachment in Hanoi to support ongoing POW/MIA activities. Thus, the engine driving the Pentagon's thinking about relations with Vietnam remained the POW/MIA issue. Only subtle, virtually invisible steps to shift U.S. rhetoric on this matter had taken place, but in ways that did not impact on policy, or make the Defense establishment any more receptive to the argument that the U.S. needed to begin to think about developing contacts with the Vietnamese military.

Vietnam's Views of Post-Normalization Possibilities

Vietnam viewed the meaning of normalization with the United States in the context of its commitment to broadened, "diversified" relations, and sought to retain balance in all its foreign relationships. Following President Clinton's announcement of normalization, Deputy Foreign Minister Le Mai remarked that for the first time since the end of World War II, Vietnam enjoyed full diplomatic relations with all the "superpowers." This was a critical fact for Hanoi, meaning not only that Vietnam was able to construct relations with over 150 countries, and gain admission to ASEAN and other regional organizations, but that Hanoi had managed to establish its relevance and importance to the foreign and trade policies of the largest, most powerful countries in the world.[6] Though normal relations with the U.S. was a welcome breakthrough that brought with it the potential for meaningful bilateral cooperation, and significant opportunities to enhance regional stability, Vietnam was intent on avoiding dependence on a single relationship. Hanoi was intent on guarding against looking at the new link with Washington as the solution to all its foreign and trade problems. The relationship with the U.S. would not be allowed to become the only foreign relationship with value and meaning for Hanoi. Normalization's impact would derive from Hanoi's broader commitment to careful, balanced foreign policy attentive to all the countries with which Vietnam had diplomatic connections. Senior Vietnamese officials who hailed the accomplishment of U.S.–Vietnamese normalization emphasized the need to recognize the limits of that new relationship, the global realities that set the parameters for diplomacy with the U.S., and the internal U.S. equities that would shape the nature of the new friendship.[7]

That thinking was reflected in the Vietnamese military's views about normalization, and about the prospects for post-normalization relations with the U.S. military establishment. To the Ministry of Defense, as Deputy Defense Minister Nguyen Thoi Bung argued in a July 1995 article in the Army's monthly journal, the expanding military relations that developed as Vietnam's diplomatic ties with foreign countries multiplied were an important evolution in Hanoi's relationships; Vietnam needed to approach these relationships carefully. Foreign schemes and malevolent intentions had to be taken into account in assessing the potential risks and dividends for each military relationship. Defense relationships had to be evaluated effectively and quickly in a rapidly changing world. The military needed to become proficient in making judgments regarding the likely impact of any course of action on Vietnam's foreign policy priorities and national interests. Bung favored immediate steps to train military personnel who could play a role in foreign and security policy management, and to equip MND personnel with language skills and an awareness of global political issues. His inventory of basic skill deficits in the MND suggested significant research, staff and development gaps in the Defense Ministry's international relations bureaucracy.[8] The implication was that Vietnam's military might not be up to managing these complex, multifaceted relations, including the new link with the U.S.

The important thing about Bung's article was that the Vice Minister acknowledged the military's role in Vietnam's effort to expand and diversify its foreign relations. While he did not explicitly single out the possibility of a future military-to-military relationship between the U.S. and Vietnam, he offered less rigid definitions of the kinds of bilateral relations into which Hanoi could safely enter, and fewer cautionary notes, suggesting that defense relations between Hanoi and Washington were not out of the realm of possibility.

According to media commentary in the weeks after normalization, the Vietnamese military believed that a formal and proper relationship with the U.S. would continue to enhance Vietnam's role and prestige in the international arena, not because of the intrinsic value and importance of that bilateral relationship, but because of the constellation of favorable, positive foreign policy advances, including accession to ASEAN membership, and increased cooperation with the European Union.[9] The military appeared skeptical about the future of U.S.–Vietnamese relations. Through the end of 1995, military commentary continued to warn of the "antagonistic forces" promoting "peaceful transformation" that sought to foment disorder in the Socialist Republic and end the Party's leadership. Military officials urged a careful approach to U.S. relations, and suggested that the best guarantee for Vietnam's future was still vigilant attention to national development and economic reform. Finally, public statements by military officials continued to remind the country of the threats to the country's sovereignty posed by representations from outsiders regarding human rights, labor issues, and democratization.[10]

The Vietnamese military had staked out a position on normalized relations with the U.S. based on foreign policy priorities, and broad party guidance on global trends, but the military had not given much thought to the practical ramifications of normalization for the Vietnamese defense establishment. The Defense Ministry had developed an in-principal approach to normalization that fit seamlessly with larger foreign policy orientations, and had generated a set of talking points that referenced the commitment to "diversified" relationships. The armed forces had carved out some generalized precepts intended to govern a larger role for military diplomacy in the development of new friendships in the region and beyond. However, the Vietnamese military had not coined a response to overtures in the arena of bilateral military relations. Senior Vietnamese military officials appear to have concluded that little would come from normalization beyond U.S. blandishments regarding human rights, intellectual property rights issues, market access, democratization, and labor issues.[11] Additionally, Vietnamese military officers and other officials made it clear that, short of steps that would enrich PAVN's arms inventory, or provide some quick and enduring remedy to Vietnam's angst over Chinese positions regarding disputed territories, there was little that would be attractive to the PAVN leadership in terms of the modest, exploratory initiative contemplated by DoD as the first step toward defense relations.

As Bung suggested in his *Tap Chi Cong San* article, there may not have been much in the way of a foreign policy apparatus within the Defense Ministry capable of preparing the leadership to confront such possibilities, equipping the top MND decision-makers with the background and options necessary to shape a policy position, and respond to U.S. initiatives. In 1995, the major general who presided over policy level talks regarding bilateral military relations was promoted into the job of Director for the MND's External Relations Department. That may have coincided with Vice Minister Bung's mid-year inventory of personnel needs and organization requirements necessary to ramp up the office responsible for managing the military dimension of foreign policy.[12] However, that promotion, and the suggestive thinking about personnel and training needs for the ERD, did not represent a sea change in the way the Defense Ministry went about the business of managing defense relations, and contributing to government thinking about the military element in the development of foreign relationships. Even with the MND's endorsement of an upgrade in personnel for the ERD, little appreciable progress appears to have been made toward developing a cadre of U.S. specialists in this period.

It is not clear whether U.S. working-level interest in military-to-military contacts took the Vietnamese military by surprise. It is clear that, through the last quarter of the year, none of the steps taken by the U.S. formally or informally evoked much interest from the Vietnamese, or provoked any attempt to organize MND resources to confront the challenge of thinking about the defense dimension of the normalization process.

Economics in Command: Developing Bilateral Relations, August–December 1995

Secretary of State Christopher traveled to Hanoi in August to mark the opening of the U.S. Embassy. In his meetings with the SRV leadership, and in remarks to students at the Foreign Ministry's Institute for International Relations, Christopher restated the priority commitment to determining the fate of unaccounted for Americans.[13] The Secretary of State noted that the first step in the process of establishing normal economic ties would be the negotiation of a bilateral trade agreement that would facilitate granting Vietnam Most Favored Nation's trading status. Christopher observed that the U.S. and Vietnam could cooperate through the ASEAN Regional Forum to assure stability in Southeast Asia by working together to preserve freedom of navigation in the South China Sea, by encouraging the peaceful resolution of competing claims to resources in the area, and by devising means to fight narcotics trafficking in the region. Christopher also emphasized the extent to which a bilateral dialogue on human rights issues would contribute to deepening U.S.–Vietnamese ties.[14]

The Vietnamese response to Christopher's statements ranged from a polite and proper acknowledgement that both new opportunities and challenges would be part of the landscape of continuous efforts to shape the future of this relationship, to more rigorous cautionary notes that pointed out the sustained efforts of "The West" to rid the world of socialism.[15] More issue-specific commentary focused on the U.S. government's human rights policies, and reflected Hanoi's readiness to continue to hold talks on the issue as long as the dialogue was focused on the global dimensions of the problem rather than issues specific to Vietnam's policies regarding citizen rights. Media pieces registered the SRV's refusal to accept U.S.

stipulations regarding human rights practices as conditions for the pursuit of economic and trade relations between the two countries.[16]

During the last quarter of 1995 the U.S. government was consumed with questions concerning the implementation of economic measures in the relationship with Vietnam, the management of existing legislative restrictions on interactions with and assistance to Vietnam, and the steps necessary to remove or mitigate such restrictions. The Jackson-Vanik Amendment, regarding compliance with freedom of emigration standards, required a presidential determination of full compliance, or a waiver of such compliance based on a determination that a waiver would promote the amendment's objectives. Under Title IV of the 1974 Trade Act, the granting of Most Favored Nations status required compliance with freedom of emigration requirements and the conclusion of a bilateral trade agreement, which itself would require the approval of both houses of Congress. Related trade act provisions required that MFN status be denied to "non-market economy countries" which the president determined were not cooperating with the U.S. in accounting for, repatriating, or returning the remains of MIAs.[17]

Additionally, Vietnam, which had been denied the status of a "beneficiary developing country" (BDC) under the U.S. Generalized System of Preferences, could not qualify for duty free treatment. Before Vietnam could be granted the designation that would entitle it to trade preferences, Hanoi would have to settle expropriation or nationalization claims made by U.S. citizens, demonstrate that it did not aid or grant sanctuary to terrorists, show that it afforded internationally recognized rights to its workers, secure MFN status, and become a party to the General Agreement on Tariffs and Trade.[18] Countries that were communist were generally denied BDC status, as were countries that failed to measure up to "discretionary criteria" which the President was required to take into account, including the level of U.S. access to markets, adequate and effective intellectual property rights protection, and the existence of barriers to investment and trade in services.

Beyond this, before the Overseas Private Investment Corporation (OPIC) could insure, reinsure, guarantee or finance projects by U.S. private companies, Vietnam had to conclude an agreement with OPIC on country specific programs, but before a country specific agreement could be signed Vietnam had to comply with fair labor requirements and Jackson-Vanik free emigration criteria. Moreover, before the Trade and Development Agency could conduct any work in a country, such as providing grants for feasibility studies and other activities related to projects to promote U.S. private sector participation in such projects, and before

EXIM Bank financing could be deployed in Vietnam, basic Foreign Assistance Act restrictions would have to be confronted.[19]

Thus, economics and trade became the engine that began to drive the process of normalization. It was not until mid–September that the NSC Director for Asian Affairs supported convening an interagency meeting on the development of the U.S.–Vietnamese relationship in areas separate from economic relations. In early October, Foreign Minister Cam met with Christopher in Washington, and the two reviewed the operation of embassies in Hanoi and Washington, discussed the pace of trade activities and U.S. investments in Vietnam, as well as "humanitarian" issues including the mission of the JTFFA.[20] The meeting made it clear that, from the first halting steps following the lifting of the embargo, through the establishment of liaison offices, and the first steps toward a bilateral trade agreement, Vietnam had not yet begun to fathom the complexities of the process of normalization.[21]

POW/MIA Interlude

In mid–November, the Department of Defense completed the assessment of cases of unaccounted for Americans that was triggered by legislation requiring the Pentagon to compile a listing by name of all personnel "about whom it is possible that officials of the SRV (and the Lao People's Democratic Republic) can produce additional information or remains that could lead to the maximum possible accounting for those personnel, as determined on the basis of all information available to the U.S. Government...."[22]

The initial Vietnamese media response indicated a great deal of confusion over the report. Vietnamese newspapers appeared to have inverted the statistics. One *Vietnam News* story, for example, stated that the Defense Department had concluded that 1,476 cases of the total of 2,202 unresolved losses reviewed required no further action. The Comprehensive Review actually concluded that 1,475 cases would require some form of additional investigative work. At first, the Vietnamese were at a loss as to how to respond to the report. They appeared to have consulted with a range of close friends and non-governmental organizations for advice in a manner that suggested they were no more confident about how to proceed in this instance than they were when faced with the Senate Select Committee's final report.

Following the public release of the review, the Vietnamese reacted to U.S. attempts to schedule a late November–early December visit to Hanoi by a Presidential Delegation by expressing concern that the success of the delegation could only be assured by good advance work aimed at facilitating a thorough review of the key points the delegation would deliver to the Vietnamese leadership. In some ways that suggested a desire on the part of the Vietnamese side to get a better picture of what would drive the delegation's visit to Vietnam, and in other ways that reflected Hanoi's sense that early warning of key requests the delegation intended to make would be the best way to guarantee a productive visit. Either way, the Vietnamese had become a lot more sensitive to the optics of such visits, and placed no small emphasis on managing these contacts effectively in a way that left little to chance. Hanoi accepted the cancellation of the delegation, and the attempt to reschedule the fourth Presidential Delegation for late January, without comment and without despairing of the meaning of the postponement. However, there was every reason to believe that the Vietnamese were aware of the extent to which the veterans and the National League of Families representative had come to loggerheads with Administration representatives over the core issues to be raised by the delegation in its talks with Vietnamese leaders.

End-of-Year Congressional Actions and Vietnamese Reactions

On 13 November, the Under Secretary of Defense for Policy, Walter B. Slocombe, updated the February 1995 report to Congress that responded to Section 1034 of the National Defense Authorization Act on missing U.S. service personnel about whom it was judged possible that Vietnamese officials could produce additional information or remains that could lead to the maximum possible accounting for these individuals. The Defense Department update noted that the Comprehensive Review of cases had been completed. Based on those results the Department was able to say that the conclusions transmitted to Congress in the February 1995 report, signed by the Secretary of Defense, remained unchanged: there was no evidence that either Vietnam or Laos were deliberately withholding information about any of the cases of missing U.S. personnel.

On 14 November, the House Committee on National Security chaired a hearing on the POW/MIA issue to review the Administration's reiteration of the Defense Secretary's February report. The hearing featured nongovernmental witnesses representing family and veterans' interests who issued extremely critical comments on the Administration's decision to normalize relations with Vietnam. Carl Ford, the former Principal Deputy Assistant Secretary of Defense for International Security Affairs, argued that the level of Vietnamese cooperation had not improved. Rather, he stated, the "range of activities this administration uses to calculate Vietnam's efforts" had altered in a manner that devalued the tough measures of progress used under the Bush Administration and its predecessors. Richard Childress, former Director of Asian Affairs in the National Security Council, said "accountability through unilateral action by Vietnam has been at a virtual halt for over three years, and the cases of greatest concern can never be resolved through joint field operations."

On 29 November, the House-Senate Appropriations Conference voted for an amendment to appropriations legislation that effectively froze funding for an expanded American diplomatic presence in Vietnam until the President certified that the Vietnamese were fully cooperative in efforts to account for missing U.S. personnel. In the specific language added by the House to the version of Section 609 of the appropriations law, the President was required to certify within 60 days," based upon all information available to the U.S. Government, that the Government of the Socialist Republic of Vietnam was fully cooperating with the United States in the following four areas: (1) resolving discrepancy cases, live sightings and field activities; (2) recovering and repatriating remains; (3) accelerating efforts to provide documents that will help lead to the fullest possible accounting of POW/MIAs; and (4) providing further assistance in implementing trilateral investigations with Laos." The Administration urged a veto of the legislation for several reasons that had nothing to do with the POW/MIA issue, but rather focused criticism on legislative efforts to eviscerate departmental budgets, and sought to have the negative ramifications of this POW/MIA provision singled out in the proposed veto language.

On 30 November, Representative Robert Dornan chaired a hearing on the subject of "US and Vietnamese Government Accountability for POW/MIAs" in his capacity as chairman of the Military Personnel Subcommittee of the National Security Committee. In his opening remarks he described the successful effort to press the amendment to the appropriations act into law as a "historic vote," and a victory for the families of American POWs and MIAs. Dornan stated that the provisions of the amendment required presidential certification "that the Communist war criminals who control Vietnam 'fully cooperate' in providing the fullest possible accounting for our 2,170 POW/MIAs." He asserted that the legislation in combination with the Defense Department's Comprehensive Review sent a strong message to Vietnam that the U.S. Congress "will no longer tolerate their cynical manipulation of the families of our missing heros."

Dornan argued that the Vietnamese could "easily resolve between 300 and 600 cases," and that Hanoi continued to warehouse the remains of more than 250 men. He stated that the Vietnamese government continued to withhold valuable documents, including records of the Politburo and the Central Committee, "hundreds of original records that provided the basis for the hastily prepared 'Unit 559' document that chronologically lists the shootdown of American aircraft in Laos by North Vietnamese forces," and the "original records of the mortuary section of the Military Law Division of the Ministry of Defense, which was reportedly the primary organization for the collection, processing and warehousing of the bodily remains of deceased Americans in North Vietnam and areas of Laos." Dornan also questioned why the Vietnamese had not moved with dispatch to resolve the remaining discrepancy cases. Finally, on 15 December Dornan convened another hearing on the Administration's intentions regarding the rescheduled January 1996 Presidential Delegation, and covered the same points articulated in the earlier hearing.

From July through December, the Vietnamese press was silent on the congressional hearings and the Administration's reports to the Hill on specific POW/MIA issues. Senior Vietnamese government officials argued that the actions and statements of individual American lawmakers no longer caused consternation in Hanoi. The Vietnamese government was confident that it was managing relations correctly and effectively. One diplomat stated privately that Hanoi's efforts to pursue discussions that would lead to a trade agreement, as well as efforts to continue the human rights dialogue and to conduct all official contacts in an open and frank manner, had created a momentum that would sustain the relationship through rough periods occasioned by the attacks of a few vocal U.S. legislators whose words had less and less resonance within their own chambers.

However, the U.S.–Vietnamese relationship came under increasingly critical scrutiny in Hanoi as various government agencies prepared their positions in anticipation of the Eighth National Congress of the Vietnamese Communist Party, scheduled to convene in July 1996. A senior Ministry of Interior official privately stated that the policy question being considered was whether or not the relationship with Washington could advance beyond the stage it had attained by late 1995 without politically costly investments by the Vietnamese, and whether or not to "write off" the possibility of achieving a trade agreement and Most Favored Nations trading status in a reasonable period of time. Influential elements of the Interior Ministry calculated that the Clinton Administration would not be able to get beyond the POW/MIA issue as a result of strong congressional voices and the White House's reluctance to alienate families and the military.

Those officials also concluded that American investment would not begin pouring in at a rapid and consequential rate, suggesting that there was little that could be jeopardized by revising foreign policy to reflect that the Washington-Hanoi relationship would probably not advance in any significant way over the next several years. Similar conservative inclinations on national security issues were articulated during the course of the preparatory party committee conferences that were responsible for reviewing the key documents to be put before the National Congress.[23] An October editorial in the Military Party Committee's monthly journal stressed the "internal and external threats" facing the country, paying particular attention to "peaceful transformation" strategies. This was not an environment conducive to the more optimistic views articulated by the Foreign Ministry, which had argued that progress on the range of U.S. concerns-- economic, human rights, regional security-- had in effect developed a dialectic of its own that argued for undiminished efforts to prod the U.S.–Vietnamese relationship forward, in spite of negative indicators from the U.S. Congress.

Last Quarter Developments in the Military Relationship

During the last months of 1995, ISA's goal was to keep attention focused on the issue of defense relations with Vietnam, and to insure that the potential for military-to-military relations was part of the post-normalization dialogue within the interagency group and inside the Pentagon. Within the interagency forum, the matter of defense relations was not a center stage item. State Department officials designated to serve in senior U.S. embassy staff positions had given only passing consideration to the question of bilateral defense relations. The question of U.S.–Vietnamese military relations had not yet been factored into the equation of post-normalization policy issues.

At DoD, no decisions had been made, apart from the designation by DIA of the Army colonel who would become the first U.S. Defense Attaché in Hanoi. The energy necessary to sustain a policy initiative toward defense relations was not yet present, in part because of the continued discomfort by senior officials who felt that exploring relations with the Vietnamese military might dislodge Hanoi's commitment to the fullest possible accounting, and in part because the idea of a bilateral military relationship with Hanoi had not yet matured in the Pentagon's policy crucible. It remained a working-level property, an idea in play between ISA, the Joint Staff, PACOM, and the State Department. It also continued to be a work in progress within ISA; initial formulations of policy proposals had several times been reviewed and referred back to the action level by the DASD/AP.

For the Pentagon's policy leadership, the question of relations with Vietnam in the post-normalization period remained an issue of how to keep the U.S. government's eye on the POW/MIA mission. Beyond that was the tradition of thinking about Vietnam in particular, and Southeast Asian defense policy matters in general, as a subset of defense and security interests revolving around U.S.–China relations. The challenge was convincing the DoD leadership that the U.S. could vigorously pursue the commitment to accounting for U.S. service personnel while defining the parameters for a formal U.S.–Vietnamese defense relationship. The challenge regarding larger regional defense and security issues was more complex and subtle, and involved convincing the leadership that there was an intrinsic value to pursing dialogue with the Vietnamese military separate and distinct from any dividends that might accrue to the U.S. in the context of its relationship with Beijing. However, through the end of 1995, none of the working level formulations regarding a ground floor level relationship between the U.S. and the Vietnamese militaries had attained the traction necessary to convince senior officials to move forward with formal proposals addressed to the Assistant Secretary of Defense for International Security Affairs.

The chances of driving the system to a decision point were remote, so "visit diplomacy" presented itself as one means of engendering senior level interest in the subject of U.S.–Vietnamese defense relations. ISA sought ASD/ISA-level agreement to meet with visiting Vietnamese dignitaries, arguing that such meetings represented one more means of emphasizing the importance to the Pentagon of the POW/MIA issue, and that such sessions presented an opportunity to gauge Vietnamese thinking about a wide range of security issues of importance to the U.S. The first such meeting was a mid–August visit to the Pentagon by Hong Ha, Chairman of the Vietnamese Communist Party Central Committee's External Relations Department.

The meeting between Hong Ha and his host, ASD/ISA Joseph Nye, Jr., was the first attempt to broker a dialogue between senior Pentagon officials and visiting SRV leaders. As with subsequent first efforts to put DoD and SRV officials in contact, the good offices of a non-governmental organization, in this instance the American Council of Learned Societies, was an essential part of the process.[24] The initiative was taken by ISA. The SRV Embassy had no real role in formulating the plan, although at the request of ISA the Vietnamese Ambassador joined the meeting between

Ha and Nye. The meeting was designed as a "courtesy call," meaning that it was intended as a brief act of protocol, not a chance to delve into issues of policy and substance. Additionally, it was intended primarily as an opportunity for DoD to underscore that the fullest possible accounting was the most important issue in the U.S.–SRV relationship. However, this particular meeting clearly promised several bonus dividends.

First, by securing a meeting with the ASD/ISA for Ha, the Pentagon continued to build a reputation as a part of the U.S. government to which all manner of Vietnamese could come during visits to Washington to hear frank views on critical issues. Meetings, even courtesy calls, were an important commodity, the currency that fueled the workings of any bilateral relationship. Securing agreement to conducting this session at the ASD level demonstrated DoD's seriousness about the relationship, and readiness to accord traveling Vietnamese diplomats the courtesies and access befitting a normal relationship.

Second, by according Hong Ha some attention, DoD placed itself in a position to enhance the relationship with the Central Committee's External Relations Department, which had an important role in the foreign policy-making process, acting as the party's conscience on foreign affairs and providing foreign policy advice to the Central Committee. The VNCP's External Relations Department had assumed responsibility for coordinating position papers intended to galvanize policy discussion throughout the system. The Department farmed out assignments to its various sections, which consulted with the network of external relations sections in provinces, ministries and mass organizations, drafted reports which were read first by the Secretariat before they went to the Politburo, which reviewed the drafts and passed them on to the Central Committee. This was important because it suggested that the machinery running foreign policy had become somewhat more complex and institutional, and had come to involve efforts to represent inter-ministerial interests in formal policy making in a manner that seemed unique to the foreign policy establishment under Nguyen Manh Cam.

Finally, Ha appeared to have a close personal relationship with VNCP Secretary General Do Muoi, who had been involved in the management of important foreign relations, including bilateral links with ASEAN members, in a manner that exceeded the level of his predecessor's intervention in foreign relations. Muoi had taken this role seriously, and had done much to clarify policy goals on a range of critical issues, including bilateral relations with China, relations with the U.S., and the POW/MIA issue. He had utilized a particularly talented advisory staff to the greatest advantage, including Hong Ha. A courtesy call with Ha would help the Pentagon begin to build the kinds of personal connections necessary to sustain a meaningful dialogue in the future.

The event itself was a polite and undistinguished exchange of views.[25] Nye emphasized the importance of the fullest possible accounting to the Congress and the American people and urged continued cooperation. Ha spoke warmly of President Clinton's decision to normalize relations and of the Secretary of State's visit to Hanoi. He underscored Hanoi's determination to sustain POW/MIA cooperation and develop firm and productive relations with the U.S. Ha noted that Vietnam's cooperation with a former adversary to answer questions about the fate of missing service personnel was "unprecedented" in the annals of modern warfare. He referred briefly to the magnitude of Vietnam's own problem of accounting for missing personnel, and asked for American assistance in this area. He concluded by saying that Hanoi was hopeful the U.S.–Vietnamese relationship would expand in a "spirited" way in various areas, and referred to the potential for trade relations as particularly important. Nye replied that the U.S. looked forward to progress on POW/MIA issues, as well as improvements in the overall relationship, and was pleased that Vietnam had joined ASEAN and would hopefully play a constructive role in the region.

Importantly, Ha and Nye delved into regional security issues, making the visit one of the first such opportunities to share thinking at this level on defense issues. Ha observed that his delegation had traveled through Southeast Asia en route to the U.S., and that his impression was that the Asian Pacific region was the most dynamic region in terms of economic development, essentially stable in political terms, and a strategically important region. In spite of this economic success and basic stability, Ha said that there were still potentially destabilizing influences at work in the region. Nye echoed Ha's view of East Asia as a dynamic region, and emphasized that the U.S. continued to view itself as a "Pacific country." The forward presence of the U.S. was an important means of reassuring the region and guaranteeing stability, which in turn allowed the area to preserve its high level of economic development. The U.S., Nye stressed, was committed to remaining engaged with China, and faced some difficult problems in managing Korean Peninsula security matters. Ha and Nye discussed the U.S. position on conflicting claims to territories and the importance of free passage on the high seas to regional economic development and well being. The exchange was the first set piece dialogue involving a senior Pentagon official. Though the meeting broke no new ground, it demonstrated that such exchanges could take place in a friendly atmosphere, could serve to remind Hanoi of the continued importance of

POW/MIA cooperation, and could afford a means of clarifying positions on regional security issues of mutual importance. Finally, the meeting showed that Hanoi itself was sensitive to the optics of a formal relationship between the military establishments. Though willing to discuss a wide range of security issues, Ha did not raise the prospect of beginning a relationship between the two militaries. Moreover, the Vietnamese media accounts of Ha's visit to the U.S. omitted references to the meetings at the Pentagon.[26]

The Origin of "Stages"

In late September 1995, ISA reconfigured earlier proposals for bilateral defense relations into a three-stage plan, beginning with a short term phase intended to establish first contacts. According to this plan, the first step in the relationship should be the opening of a Defense Attaché Office in the U.S. Embassy in Hanoi. DIA had selected a candidate. By October 1995, the Vietnamese had signaled that before they granted a visa to the U.S. Defense Attaché-designate, the U.S. should agree that Vietnam could open a Defense Attaché office in Washington. That promised to delay the dispatch of the U.S. candidate.[27] In the event, the U.S. Defense Attaché Office opened in December 1995, three months before the Vietnamese dispatched their military representative to serve in their embassy in Washington.

The second step in the ISA plan was DASD/AP participation in a Presidential Delegation planned for late November–early December. The precedent had been set, in the last three visits to Hanoi, for a separate dialogue on regional issues. The planned late November trip to Hanoi struck ISA as a good opportunity to insert a senior DoD official into this dialogue, and to turn attention to issues of special interest to the Department of Defense, including the main message of the East Asia Strategy Review, the U.S.–Japan Initiative, and freedom on navigation issues. The Vietnamese were eager for dialogue, and it appeared that they would welcome the opportunity to renew discussions on Cambodia, the Korean peninsula, and the Spratly Islands, as well as ASEAN's plans for the Regional Forum on security issues.

ISA envisioned the second stage as a collection of practical actions necessary to establish ground floor contacts between DoD entities and the Vietnamese; explain the U.S. government's regional interests, humanitarian programs, and health-related initiatives; and integrate Vietnam into specialized regional training opportunities offered to friends and allies.

This stage was designed to be a twelve-month long process of making contacts aimed at increasing mutual understanding, establishing a solid basis for appropriate military dialogues between institutions, while supporting JTFFA's efforts in Vietnam. The first round of initiatives in this mid-term stage involved a visit to Vietnam by the regional officer of the Defense Mapping Agency (December–January), the dispatch of a working level DoD policy team aimed at briefing the Vietnamese on freedom of navigation issues (January–February); and a conference involving the PAVN Military History Institute and DoD military historians affiliated with the U.S. Army Center for Military History, the Office of the Naval Historian, and the USAF Historian's Office (July–August 1995).

The third stage, focused on the longer term future, was to involve DoD humanitarian assistance for various prosthetics projects in Vietnam aimed at serving the veterans population, support which originated as part of the Vessey Initiative; invitations to Vietnamese military medical institutions to participate in the Association of Medical Surgeons of the U.S. (AMSUS) annual meeting; expanded support for the malarial research initiative of the Naval Medical Research Institute (Bethesda, Maryland); assistance to the Defense Ministry's AIDS prevention committee, established in late 1991; and the dispatch of a DoD health survey team to collect information in Vietnam using experienced health workers associated with the Uniformed Services University of Health Sciences. ISA anticipated that Hanoi would have an interest in demining training and in cooperation between the U.S. Army Corps of Engineers and the Ministry of Water Resources aimed at advising the UNDP-funded rehabilitation of river and sea dikes. Future efforts could, in this plan, involve Vietnamese participation in Title 10 funded Section 1051 Bilateral/Regional Cooperation programs and USN assistance to anti-piracy initiatives, including evaluation of equipment and training of the People's Navy.

The policy level consensus was that the first stages of U.S.–Vietnamese military-to-military contacts should remain scrupulously humanitarian and focused on establishing benign contacts aimed at enhancing mutual understanding. These first efforts would require considerable confidence building in order to get beyond lingering suspicions and to establish a solid basis for formal institutional dialogue. In these first steps, the U.S. side could build on the POW/MIA-related humanitarian undertakings of the late 1980s and early 1990s. ISA's view was that Hanoi would value the relationship with the U.S., but seek to move cautiously in order to maximize its credibility in the region as a non-aligned force, to convince ASEAN that it would not drag fellow members along with it in some crusade against Beijing, and to demonstrate to the region that Hanoi saw its future lying in the cultivation of close and profitable ties with Southeast Asia.

PACOM, with Joint Staff concurrence, argued that the pace and scope of military contacts with Vietnam should be gauged according to the level of progress in POW/MIA work. The work of the Joint Task Force should override any imperative to make ground floor level contacts between the U.S. and the Vietnamese militaries. The central U.S. government equity in developing military contacts should continue to be providing support to the JTFFA mission in Vietnam. All visits to Vietnam by DoD officials should revolve around the POW/MIA issue, and all contacts should be cleared with PACOM to insure compatibility with the JTFFA mission. In the near term, contacts should be expanded but only if the Vietnamese continued to cooperate and make progress on POW/MIA-related matters. Longer-term initiatives such as participation in USPACOM-sponsored conferences, humanitarian projects, and demining training should be a function of continued POW/MIA progress at the discretion of CINCPAC.

That formulation sought to enshrine a "pace and scope" linkage that characterized the bilateral relationship before Vietnam improved POW/MIA cooperation, established the mechanisms necessary to transact business with the Joint Task Force, and shifted responsibilities for managing POW/MIA cooperation upwards in its own hierarchy. At a point in time when the U.S. government had committed itself to retaining the priority focus on POW/MIA matters while broadening the relationship in many areas (economic, consular affairs, political relations, counter narcotics cooperation), the Joint Staff/PACOM formulation promised to work to the disadvantage of military-to-military contacts while other dimensions of the relationship moved ahead with a natural and mutually advantageous momentum. ISA took the view that deferring any military contacts, humanitarian undertakings or regional security dialogue with the Vietnamese for one or two years would compromise DoD's ability to register views on regional issues of significance to the U.S. government. The PACOM approach called into question several rounds of regional security dialogue conducted at the Assistant Secretary level, in which DoD had participated. Finally, it jeopardized opportunities to weigh in directly with the Vietnamese military on POW/MIA issues in a manner that could have positive impact on Vietnamese cooperation.

In the ISA formulation, the POW/MIA issue would remain the most important issue in the bilateral relationship. Military-to-military contacts would be recognized as one way of exerting positive impact on POW/MIA progress. The relationship, however, would be pursued in order to establish a solid basis for institutional dialogue, while supporting the Joint Task

Force's efforts. Visits to Vietnam by DoD personnel would be expected to emphasize the priority importance accorded to the POW/MIA effort, in a manner that paralleled the message that delegations from other U.S. government departments would be expected to deliver. Approval for travel to Vietnam by senior personnel of flag rank or equivalent and senior level visitors from DoD or the armed services would be sought from the Under Secretary of Defense for Policy through the ASD/ISA. All DoD visitors would preface discussions with appropriate, coordinated talking points emphasizing the importance of POW/MIA cooperation. Later initiatives involving CINCPAC funds would be a function of progress in the overall relationship, sustained POW/MIA cooperation, and the availability of CINCPAC resources. Decisions regarding long-term steps would be presented to the Interagency Working Group for discussion and coordination.

Interestingly, in coordinating the ISA paper, retired Air Force General James Wold, in his capacity as DASD/POW-MIA, emphasized that his central concern was in guaranteeing that POW/MIA issues continued to receive priority attention, and that high level U.S. government emphasis continued to be placed on the importance of sustained and improved cooperation in a consistent manner. This represented a shift on the part of DPMO which had argued, in 1994 and early 1995, that any initiative toward establishing even the most modest of contacts with the Vietnamese military had to be opposed by the Pentagon because it would suggest that the U.S. government had allowed the priority accorded to the POW/MIA issue to slip downward, because it would distract the Vietnamese government from its commitment to cooperate with the JTFFA, and because it would risk interrupting on-the-ground activities of the Joint Task Force as the Vietnamese began shifting their resources to the work of developing defense relations with the U.S. In other words, this time the Pentagon's primary entity responsible for managing POW/MIA policy was a lot less concerned with the fine tuning of the proposed military to-military contacts than was PACOM. In the end, by October 1995, Pentagon policy makers were prepared to argue that the U.S. needed to move ahead, but not as rapidly as recommended by ISA, and not as slowly as proposed by PACOM.

By the end of the year there was some support in the Administration for moving forward on a Jackson-Vanik amendment waiver for Vietnam. By December, the State Department and the NSC believed that the benefits to Vietnam of a waiver in the form of EXIM, OPIC, TDA and PL 480 assistance would afford the U.S. government leverage in coaxing Hanoi toward progress in the area of emigration policy. The State Department had confidence that Hanoi would provide the U.S. government with the assurances required by the Jackson-Vanik amendment to the effect that exit permit regulations would not be used to bar certain types of people from legally departing Vietnam.

Hanoi expressed frustration that there had not been more forward movement toward the normalization of economic relations. The State Department appeared to believe that taking steps necessary to obtain the Jackson-Vanik waiver would assure Vietnam that Washington remained serious about pursing a course toward a normal economic relationship. The State Department supported notifying Congress of the Administration's intent to move forward on the waiver before the annual notification was due in June 1996. The National Security Council was inclined to support State's desire to seek assurances from Vietnam regarding emigration policy. If the Vietnamese were prepared to offer those assurances, the State Department would then consult with Congress prior to issuing the waiver.[28]

The waiver, however, did not have to be approved by Congress. Eight Senators, including McCain, Harkins, Kerrey, and Kerry, had urged that a waiver be granted and that the U.S. government begin programs to support U.S. businesses operating in Vietnam. The steps that could be taken after granting the waiver were incremental, and were likely to be spread out over time in a manner that would satisfy those who did not want to move too quickly. At the time, it appeared that EXIM programs could probably begin before the end of the year. OPIC insurance and reinsurance and investment guarantees would follow, but not before Vietnam implemented laws to extend internationally recognized worker rights to its population. MFN status would have to await the completion of a trade agreement, which would have to be blessed by Congress.

The slightly more positive attitude about taking concrete steps forward in the relationship with Vietnam, and a diminished concern that Congress would simply react negatively to anything concerning Vietnam, probably contributed to eliminating some of the barriers to pressing ahead on the proposal for modest military contacts with Vietnam. However, by the year's end, the Pentagon had not yet made a decision on the most basic proposals regarding military relations with Vietnam, leaving the Department in an awkward posture as other parts of the relationship moved forward.

4

MAKING MILITARY CONTACTS, 1996

The Foreign Policy Context

The draft Political Report prepared for the 8th Congress of the Vietnamese Communist Party, and publicly mentioned for the first time in mid–January 1996 broadcasts, singled out foreign policy accomplishments. The draft document heralded the importance of the restoration of relations with China, the strengthening of "relations of special solidarity and friendship" with Laos, entry into ASEAN and other international and regional organizations, the normalization of relations with the U.S., the establishment of ties with the countries in the Commonwealth of Independent States, and broadening of links with South Asia, the Middle East, Africa and Latin America.

Vietnam, the draft document showed, looked at relations with Washington as one of several initiatives aimed at widening market opportunities for Vietnam, and cultivating friendships. By thinking about foreign policy in such terms, Hanoi was able to speak about the potential for normal relations with the United States as though it were but one of several new opportunities for the Socialist Republic that sprung from the wisdom of Hanoi's foreign policy clairvoyance. By "diversifying" its relationships, Hanoi was able to hedge its bets so that if any single bilateral link faltered, Vietnam would not confront an insurmountable foreign policy crisis. In Hanoi's thinking, no single foreign policy issue was important enough to require that Vietnam make inordinate investments of political capital in managing that issue, and no single foreign relationship merited disproportionate attention in a way that would torque Vietnam's diplomacy in one direction or another at the expense of its national interests.

This meant that the leverage Washington once possessed as a result of the allure of normalization had diminished. It also appeared to mean that Vietnam's strong commitment to an even-keeled diplomacy, to transacting foreign policy business in normal ways through routine channels, and to playing in accordance with broadly accepted rules, would contribute to minimizing the risks that Hanoi would look at the POW/MIA issue as a means of achieving leverage in the relationship with the U.S.

U.S.–Vietnamese Economic Relations

In the first months of 1996 Hanoi was preoccupied with securing a trade agreement and Most Favored Nation Status, and a waiver of the provisions of the Jackson-Vanik amendment.

The Administration believed that the benefits to the Vietnamese of a waiver would be attractive enough to Hanoi to provide the U.S. government with leverage that could be useful in prodding Hanoi toward compliance with emigration concerns.[1] The State Department's starting point was that Vietnamese emigration policy was not completely out of line with the Jackson-Vanik requirements, but was not sufficiently "liberal" to allow certification. State remained confident that Hanoi would provide the U.S. with the assurances required by the Jackson-Vanik amendment to the effect that exit permit regulations would not be used to bar certain people from legally departing Vietnam, and on that basis was prepared to proceed with a waiver. In early 1996, the White House was inclined to go forward in the manner recommended by the State Department.

Much of the strategizing in Washington on this approach was undertaken with an eye to how the game plan would play with American's veterans and the active national-level veterans organizations, the organizations speaking for the interests of families of MIAs, and the congressional opponents of normalization. Accordingly, the Administration selected a slow pace, and a program of incremental steps that would follow the granting of a Jackson-Vanik waiver. At the time, Administration thinking was that EXIM programs could probably begin before the end of the year, and OPIC guarantees could follow before the New Year, but not before Vietnam implemented laws to extend internationally recognized rights to workers. MFN status would have to wait until the completion of a trade agreement.

POW/MIA: The Measured Pace

Though not enthusiastic about the measured pace Washington preferred to take, Vietnam was prepared to act patiently, and quite sensibly kept the POW/MIA issue compartmentalized as a distinctly humanitarian matter that would not be affected by the pace and scope of progress in other areas of the relationship. This approach was evident during Assistant Secretary of State Winston Lord's January visit to Hanoi. Lord met with ministers from the trade, investment and foreign ministries, and engaged in talks on a broad range of issues including POW/MIA progress.[2] The same approach guided Deputy Prime Minister Nguyen Khanh's early February visit to the U.S. Khanh focused on scientific and educational dialogue and bilateral exchanges concerning social issues. He sought to articulate Vietnam's continuing interest in seeing the bilateral relationship unfold in many areas at once—in commercial, economic, cultural, scientific and educational areas—so that one single issue would not dominate the relationship.[3]

In late January, the Deputy Assistant Secretary of Defense for POW/MIA Affairs, James Wold, traveled to Hanoi, Phnom Penh and Vientiane to discuss the results of the Comprehensive Review of all cases of unaccounted for Americans in Southeast Asia, the year-long study conducted by the Defense POW/MIA Office, the JTFFA, and the U.S. Army's Central Identification Laboratory in Hawaii (CILHI). The Comprehensive Review, released in November 1995, had already been the source of some confused speculation and misunderstanding by the Vietnamese, who early on—in part as the result of some of the western press coverage focused on this report—had missed several key points and come away with an inverted understanding of the report's conclusions regarding unresolved cases.

The Comprehensive Review, Wold told the Vietnamese, placed unresolved cases in one of three groupings: cases for which specific next steps in the "investigative process" had been identified by the U.S. side; cases for which current leads had been exhausted, and further action would have to be deferred until additional information came to light; and cases for which no action by either the Vietnamese or the U.S. would result in the recovery of remains. The Review concluded that cases involving approximately 1,476 individuals (940 of whom were lost in Vietnam) required either further in-country investigation in the form of detailed "loss-site" surveys, excavations, archival research or witness interviews; U.S. conducted research and analysis, including forensic analysis of previously recovered remains, combat record searches, and interviews with American "observers"; or unilateral Vietnamese actions. In the case of 159 individuals, 142 of whom were losses associated with Vietnam, the Review concluded that no further work would yield results until additional information was brought to light. In the cases of 567 individual, accounting for 26 percent of the cases of U.S. personnel missing in Southeast Asia, the Review concluded that no amount of work would result in the repatriation of remains. Approximately 530 of those individuals were lost in Vietnam or off Vietnamese coasts. Finally, the Comprehensive Review attempted to clarify and update the Priority Discrepancy Case Lists and the Special Remains Lists.

The Vietnamese seemed to regard this as a clarifying moment, although they had looked on the exercise from its start in mid–1995 with some skepticism and concern that the goal posts were about to be moved yet one more time. Apart from initial confusion, and the need to study the POW/MIA arithmetic, senior Vietnamese agreed that the tasks had been narrowed down and more effectively defined in a manner that clarified exactly what was left for Vietnam to do on a case-by-case basis.[4]

In spite of the complicated technical issues implicit in the categorizations of cases, the potential for misunderstanding on the part of the Vietnamese, and the criticisms of the Review and DPMO within the Beltway, by early 1996 the POW/MIA issue had reached a comfortable moment in that there were no headline-grabbing dimensions to the issue. Domestic debate was confined to fairly specific disputes over aspects of the Comprehensive Review, or the performance and leadership of the DPMO. Additionally, at the time there were reasons to be confident in the plans for achieving a bilateral trade agreement. The touchy subjects including Vietnam's human rights practices and labor rights policies were being managed through dialogue between the State Department and the Foreign Ministry at the deputy assistant secretary level, and had settled down in a way that promised a hiatus from the tendency for shrill and public set piece exchanges on these issues during congressional busy seasons.

In late January, in response to continued ISA efforts to nudge the system toward a decision on military relations with Vietnam, the Under Secretary of Defense for Policy made the decision that the Department should not do anything with Vietnam in the way of new activities. In practical terms, that means the Defense Department could continue formal interaction between U.S. and Vietnamese military medical specialists, Vietnamese participation in multinational Title 10 funded conferences run by PACOM, and DoD interaction with visiting Vietnamese delegations. Senior DoD officials had accepted the argument regarding the dividends that would result from a more formal, proper and communicative relationship with

Hanoi — including positive implications for POW/MIA cooperation — and were thus prepared to allow these limited in an incremental way. However, the "E Ring" was not yet prepared to endorse an approach to Hanoi featuring the first steps toward military relations.

By February, the Under Secretary had become concerned that the White House's preoccupation with the political liabilities implicit in any new Vietnam-related initiatives would create discomfort with existing DoD activities. At about that time, Section 609 of the State Department Appropriations Bill for 1996, rolled into the 1996 fiscal year budget agreement, required that funds obligated could not be expended to pay for the cost incurred in opening or operating diplomatic or consular posts in Vietnam that were not operating on 11 July 1995, or the cost of expanding the U.S. diplomatic or consular presence in Vietnam, or any increase in personnel assigned to U.S. diplomatic of consular posts in Vietnam above the levels that existed as of 11 July 1995. Section 609 stated that those strictures could be removed by means of a presidential certification, submitted within 60 days of the passage of the bill, that stated Vietnam was "cooperating in full faith with the United States" in the four areas specified by the President in January 1994 as the key areas for bilateral POW/MIA cooperation. Congressman Robert Dornan and Senators Bob Smith and Craig Thomas sent a letter to the Secretary of State in which they argued that in accordance with the law, the U.S. Embassy should be closed and the liaison office, its predecessor, reestablished. Further, they made the case that the Charge D'Affairs, who was in Washington for routine consultations, should not be allowed to return to Vietnam, and that personnel assigned after 11 July 1995 should be withdrawn until the required presidential certification was submitted by the Administration.

Under Secretary of Defense Slocombe calculated that there would be little Congressional tolerance for an opening gambit in military relations with Vietnam.

The March 1996 Presidential Delegation

In March 1996, a Presidential Delegation of Administration officials, veterans service organization representatives, and the Executive Director of the National League of Families visited Hanoi, as well as Vientiane and Phnom Penh, and emphasized the continued importance placed on the resolution of the POW/MIA issue by the U.S. Government, the American people, Congress, the families of MIAs, and veterans. The trip, twice cancelled as the result of a U.S. government budget crisis and foul weather in

Washington, fulfilled President Clinton's July 1995 promise to the families and veterans that he would dispatch a delegation to remind the Vietnamese of the priority accorded to the POW/MIA issue.

The delegation met with General Secretary Do Muoi, Prime Minister Vo Van Kiet, Foreign Minister Nguyen Manh Cam, Vice Defense Minister Nguyen Thoi Bung, and representatives of the VNOSMP and Vietnam's Veterans Association. The Vietnamese side convened a plenary session chaired by Vice Foreign Minister Le Mai, who was joined by representatives of the VNOSMP, the Foreign, Defense and Interior Ministries, as well as an official from the Ministry of Labor, Social Affairs and Invalids. A senior Vietnamese diplomat made it clear that the decision to arrange meetings with Muoi and Kiet represented the Vietnamese government's desire to signal absolute commitment to continued cooperation on this issue, and the decision to place Le Mai in charge of the plenary session — even in the midst of his involvement in preparations for the Eighth Party Congress — signaled top level concern over managing this delegation's visit appropriately and effectively.

All of the Vietnamese officials who met with the U.S. delegation expressed their government's commitment to follow through on promises to cooperate in the four areas specified by President Clinton in July 1994 as the means by which the U.S. would measure progress. The Vietnamese officials echoed one another in citing their long tradition of treating the POW/MIA issue as a humanitarian issue, and reaffirming willingness to conduct joint fieldwork, investigations and other undertakings in accordance with the work plan and with reference to the priorities specified in the Comprehensive Review. Vice Foreign Minister Mai turned six reports over to the delegation detailing Vietnamese accomplishments in the four areas.

Two important positions emerged in the plenary session and the meetings conducted at the Defense Ministry's MIA Office. In the plenary meeting, Mai observed that "some" had suggested Vietnam should provide archival information that could be useful in assessing losses in Cambodia and Laos to the U.S. Mai very deliberately stressed that during the war, Vietnamese troops were deployed to Laos and Cambodia for "very short times," and did not place any of the territory of these two countries under the "permanent control" of Vietnamese troops, thus challenging the long-standing U.S. presumption that Lao losses could only be resolved using Vietnamese archives and witnesses since PAVN controlled the Lao territory where 80 percent of the Lao cases were said to have taken place, specifically along the Ho Chi Minh Trail. In his meeting with the U.S. delegation, Senior Colonel Tran Bien, head of the MND's MIA Office, stated that the Vietnamese MIA Office, constituted in 1973, and specifically the Defense Ministry's element of that office, began the work of "unilaterally" conducting operations to locate and take possession of remains following the U.S. Operation Homecoming, with the goal of organizing the repatriation of these remains to the U.S. In this way, Bien added some depth to an argument that Foreign Minister Cam offered to Presidential Emissary John Vessey in January 1992. At that time, Cam stated that after the war, Vietnamese military units policed remains from the battle sites and forwarded them to central authorities, which had to maintain and store them in some fashion until a bilateral channel for resolving the issue emerged in the 1980s. Cam's remarks on this dimension of the "warehouse" issue represented the first official acknowledgement that Vietnam did actively and in an organized fashion remove the remains of U.S. soldiers from combat sites and transfer custody of those remains and associated identification media to a central entity, which Cam did not identify. Cam's explanation that a "warehouse" existed, but had been emptied once the bilateral dialogue had begun in earnest in the 1980s, reflected similar expressions made on the margins of technical meetings as early as 1991. Bien's direct reference to this issue might have been an effort to tamp down what some Vietnamese may have perceived as a trend toward reopening this issue, deduced from statements made by both legislators and non-govern-mental witnesses at public hearings in late 1995 and early 1996.[5]

Le Mai pointedly raised U.S. humanitarian assistance for Vietnam in his discussions with White House, State and Defense officials in the delegation, saying that before normalization the U.S. had provided humanitarian aid to Vietnam as part of the process, but that since normalization there had been no new initiatives to address Vietnam's needs. In the plenary meeting, Mai noted that the consequences of the war remained severe, and that Vietnam was looking forward to the assistance from the U.S. government and the American people.

In his remarks to the Presidential Delegation, Do Muoi hooked the issue of Vietnam's MIA problem with Agent Orange's residual impact, arguing that both issues exerted an influence on Vietnam's capacity to pursue socioeconomic development and heal the wounds of war.[6] In short, the Vietnamese MIA issue was raised to drive home the contrasting proportionality of postwar problems under which Vietnam had labored and those issues that had affected the U.S., especially the MIA issue. The Vietnamese MIAs were also discussed in order to direct attention to an area where Vietnam felt its humanitarian needs had been repeatedly delegitimized, as well as to suggest the focus for the single most meaningful postwar gesture of reconciliation.

All the Vietnamese officials with whom the delegation met challenged the view that normalization would result in a diminishment of Vietnam's readiness to cooperate in accounting for American MIAs as economic interests and business concerns came to the fore. Foreign Minister Cam, Le Mai, and Vice Defense Minister Nguyen Thoi Bung forcefully stressed that this prediction of a downturn in Hanoi's interest in the MIA issue had been proven incorrect. Mai pointed to Hanoi's agreement to establish special teams to conduct priority investigations; locate wartime documents relevant to the MIA issue; energize local levels to assist in archival searches and other types of joint field work; and extend the time that joint field teams could spend at a field site as indication of Hanoi's flexibility and willingness to continue to work with the U.S. in ways that were not tied to normalization. Hanoi's willingness to pay sustained attention to the POW/MIA issue, coupled with Vietnam's positive contributions to multilateral meetings (including the ASEAN Regional Forum (ARF) Search and Rescue sessions), and concrete steps by Hanoi to select and train a Vietnamese military attaché for assignment to Washington were developments that made it easier for ISA to urge that DoD reconsider the decision to defer judgment regarding military relations with Vietnam.

Revisiting the Proposal for Military Relations

The relative success of the March visit to Vietnam by the Presidential Delegation was enough to generate DoD interest in revisiting the issue of defense relations with the SRV. Working level NSC and State Department willingness to support bilateral military contacts, and the public announcement of the nomination of Douglas "Pete" Peterson as Ambassador to Vietnam, had a positive impact on ISA proposal for military-to-military relations with Vietnam.[7]

The inhospitable environment appeared to have changed enough to warrant another look at the timing for such an approach. First, before mid–1996 the Vietnamese had selected a candidate for the position of military attaché in the SRV's Washington Embassy.[8] Second, in the first months of 1996 the Vietnamese officially spoke their interest in participating in bilateral discussions and multilateral dialogues that would advance mutual understanding, enhance "transparency," and contribute to Hanoi's familiarity with sea law, freedom of navigation issues, counter narcotics problems and other regional and global issues. Third, as early as the first quarter of 1996 Vietnamese military officials quietly stated the Defense Ministry's interest in a military-to-military relationship with the United States. Though concerned about the possibility that the region could misinterpret the intent of U.S.–Vietnamese defense relations, Vietnamese military officials were intent on signaling the desire to learn more about the PACOM Expanded Relations Program, the National Defense University's international fellows program, and U.S. practices and international conventions governing port calls and ship visits.

In April, ISA urged a reconsideration of the Under Secretary's decision of late January to defer action on bilateral military relations with Vietnam, and reiterated the proposal for an incremental program of "contacts." By late March–early April, the NSC Director for Asian Affairs and the Assistant Secretary of State for East Asia and the Pacific had stated their support for such an interim measure. Additionally, U.S. Chief of Mission Desaix Anderson had communicated his support for a bilateral military-to-military relationship calibrated to sustain the emphasis on POW/MIA cooperation, and aimed at keeping pace with the development of other dimensions of the U.S.–Vietnamese relationship. Anderson said that a modest military relationship between the U.S. and the Vietnamese would not arouse China, would signal the region that the U.S. intended to establish a broad relationship with a reforming Vietnam, and would serve U.S. interests by drawing the Vietnamese military into dialogue concerning regional issues of mutual interest. Anderson suggested several starting points, including support for visits by PAVN senior colonels to the U.S. for first discussions about policy issues, and a DASD/AP visit to Hanoi in mid-summer, followed by a CINCPAC visit to sustain attention to strategic issues of mutual interest.[9]

Anderson's proposals were well received at the State Department. In July, ISA restated support for a low-keyed approach to defense relations with Vietnam that would begin with a late September–early October visit to Hanoi by the DASD/AP, following by a CINCPAC visit which would serve as a well timed reminder of the priority the U.S. continued to attach to the POW/MIA issue. ISA endorsed expanding activities beyond the "multilateral" meetings of the sort allowed to by the Under Secretary of Defense in January 1996, exploring the potential for bilateral military cooperation, and getting Vietnamese agreement to a schedule of senior-level U.S. military visits to Vietnam.

During the period from April to July, the Under Secretary of Defense for Policy again expressed some concern regarding the potential for backlash from POW/MIA interests in response to any attempts to establish relations with the Vietnamese defense establishment. A brief surge in U.S. media attention to the esoteria of the POW/MIA issue, some Vietnamese media coverage that underscored Vietnam's diminishing tolerance for political combat over the POW/MIA issue, and initiatives by congressional opponents of normalization appeared to give the Under Secretary reason to pause. The work of the Joint Task Force continued apace, but Pentagon policy makers were not inclined to agree to proposals for the development of defense relations with Vietnam in the midst of momentarily renewed media attention to the issue, and while a few active and vocal lawmakers were still searching for legal means of derailing the Administration's Vietnam policy.

POW/MIA Events and Headlines

In early 1996, Representative Robert Dornan asked that the 1988 Special National Intelligence Estimate (SNIE) entitled "Hanoi and the POW/MIA Issue" be declassified. The 1988 SNIE concluded that Vietnam had "warehoused" the remains of U.S. MIAs. The text, based largely on the analytical positions formulated by the Defense Intelligence Agency's special office for POW/MIA Affairs, argued that there was "considerable evidence" that the Vietnamese had detailed information on the fates of several hundred personnel." According to the estimate, by the late 1980s the Vietnamese had already recovered and were warehousing between 400 and 600 remains." Discussions concerning the release of this document occupied the Under Secretary's attention during the year, and he frequently sought ISA assessments of the risks involved in agreeing to the request to declassify the SNIE.

The Vietnamese were sensitive to allegations that they maintained a warehouse of American remains; even after the work of the Senate Select Committee there was no shortage of rumors that the Vietnamese maintained a secret stock of "readily available" remains. However, there was little reason to assume that the declassification of the SNIE would harm U.S.–Vietnamese relations. The Vietnamese were not unfamiliar with the views expressed in the SNIE. They did not like the issue, and bridled at having to explain themselves, but they were not unfamiliar with the argument and the evidence. Between 1991 and 1993 DoD had briefed the sum and substance of the warehouse issue to senior Vietnamese. DoD had provided details about the "warehouse theory" at various public congressional hearings and during the course of the Senate Select Committee's hearings. In technical sessions with casualty resolution specialists during the late 1980s and early 1990s, the U.S. had reviewed above ground storage evidence with VNOSMP officials. There was ample reason to believe that it would be easier to explain to the Vietnamese why the U.S. declassified the document in question than to explain to the Hill (and especially Dornan's committee) why the U.S. decided to protect the document using Freedom of Information Act exemptions. The Administration had periodically touted President Clinton's decision to declassify POW/MIA information with speed and thoroughness in the interest of maximizing access to the record on this issue. Saying no to the request from Dornan had the potential to undermine this commitment to "openness." The issue percolated for the better part of the year. In the end, the release of the SNIE attracted little media attention, and had no appreciable impact on the calculus of forces arrayed on either side of the "Vietnam Issue," suggesting that major POW/MIA revelations had begun to have proportionately less impact on the process of bilateral relations than had been the case just one or two years earlier. However, in the early part of 1996 the Pentagon policy makers, and most of the interagency group, remained mindful of the potential domestic political consequences of decisions regarding the pace and scope of expanding the normalized relationship with Vietnam.[10]

In late April, several stories published in American newspapers criticized the Washington bureaucracies responsible for managing the POW/MIA issue, especially DPMO, for poor organization, ineffective management, and lingering inadequacies as the Pentagon's lead agency for this issue. One widely circulated report alleged that the Vietnamese government agencies that worked the POW/MIA issue in concert with the U.S. had earned a "multi-million dollar windfall" by diverting U.S. military vehicles provided for the purpose of supporting POW/MIA investigative efforts to tourist ventures cooked up by Vietnamese government officials assigned to work with the JTFFA. The story alleged that the Vietnamese made significant money by charging exorbitant fees for services undertaken during the conduct of joint field investigations, including helicopter transportation costs, compensation for farmland damaged during excavations, and per diem wages paid to Vietnamese workers who assisted U.S. personnel conducting excavations.[11]

The Vietnamese forcefully denied the allegations that government agencies had been featherbedding. Even though Hanoi was acutely sensitive to the content of these stories, the government in Hanoi responded in restrained ways, without allowing the news stories to drive policy or compromise working relations with U.S. agencies. Indeed, senior government officials in Hanoi privately made it plain that the VNOSMP had raised the question of how to achieve cost effectiveness in POW/MIA field work at technical meetings between the VNOSMP and the JTFFA in 1996, which "proved" that the Vietnamese were serious about looking for ways to hold down costs associated with POW/MIA work.

In mid–April, Vietnamese broadcast and print media highlighted U.S.

newspaper reports about a U.S. Army sergeant, carried on the records in "KIA/BNR" status beginning in 1970, whose existence came to light in 1996 when he formally requested welfare assistance through the social services bureaucracy of his home state. The Vietnamese media played the story as an example of the inconsistencies and inaccuracies that abounded in the U.S. side's list of unaccounted for troops. That story came out at roughly the same time as the revelation that the remains of two U.S. Marines killed in September 1967, and a third set of remains returned by the Vietnamese in 1986 and assumed to be the body of the single Marine who was listed as MIA following that 1967 firefight, had been misidentified, a fact which came to light in 1996 when the remains repatriated in 1986 were identified as those belonging to a Marine buried under the wrong identity in 1967.[12]

Another news item to which the Vietnamese paid close attention was the announcement that President Clinton had signed an order on 14 May that ended the classification of Vietnam as a combat zone. The order, which came into effect in late June, halted fixed allowances for troops attached to the JTFFA in Hanoi and temporary duty assignees participating in joint field activities. The Vietnamese saw this step as a symbolically important act of closure, a small but significant indication that the POW/MIA issue had come to the edge of extinction, since the order provided for the cessation of fixed allowances to the families of MIAs.[13]

In May, Representative Dornan, Senator Bob Smith, and Senator Craig Thomas sent a letter to the Secretary of State in which they argued that in accordance with Section 609 of the Omnibus Appropriations Act for fiscal year 1996, the U.S. Embassy in Hanoi should be closed and the liaison office, its predecessor, reestablished. The lawmakers argued that Charge D'Affairs Anderson, who coincidentally was in the United States, should not be allowed to return to Vietnam, and that personnel assigned after 11 July 1995 be withdrawn until a the President could certify that Vietnam was cooperating with the United States in the four key areas of POW/MIA investigative activities. On 29 May, Clinton signed Presidential Determination 96–28 which stated that based on all information available to the U.S. Government, the government of Vietnam was cooperating "in full faith" with the U.S. in the four areas mentioned in Section 609 of the Omnibus Appropriations Act.[14]

On 14 June, the Subcommittee for Military Personnel of the Committee on National Security, House of Representatives, held the first of a series of hearings on the POW/MIA issue, beginning with an examination of the "rational behind the Presidential Determination," featuring testimony from the Executive Director of the League of Families, the Chairperson of the

National Alliance of Families, and several "researchers" including the former director of the U.S. POW/MIA Office in Hanoi.[15]

Throughout this period, for ISA, the task of writing game plans for establishing relations with the Vietnamese military became an exercise in adjusting proposed schedules as windows of opportunity closed before the senior Pentagon leadership could rule on recommended courses of action. The proposed DASD/AP trip that was conceived of as the roll-out event kept getting pushed back, and was eventually separated from the series of events that ISA envisioned as the chain of activities that would represent DoD's opening gambit in the effort to develop relations with Vietnam's military. For example, early on, the follow-on CINCPAC visit was removed from the time line planned by ISA when it became clear that Pentagon policy makers would not make a decision in time enough to plan and get Vietnamese agreement to specific senior-level visits.

It also represented a debilitating confirmation of the suspicion that for every sound, reasoned and articulate "national interest" argument that ISA could offer in favor of establishing the basis for a relationship with the Vietnamese military, there was an endless inventory of counter arguments that would resonate positively with opponents of normalization who were convinced that each step toward a more complete relationship with the SRV represented a geometric increase in the likelihood that priority attention to the MIA issue would be downgraded, and that Administration commitment to the fullest possible accounting would be abandoned. Those counter-arguments, while not necessarily persuasive, were stated with a stridency sufficient to undermine the confidence of the Pentagon policy leadership in any argument on behalf of the idea of military-to-military relations with Vietnam.

This string of POW/MIA events did not dislodge U.S. policy toward Vietnam, did not elicit a massive backlash against the Administration's handling of the effort to account for missing personnel, and did not cause the Vietnamese to become unglued, vindictive or unhelpful to U.S. efforts to resolve this issue. In the end, that was comforting but not convincing evidence in favor of the argument that the DoD piece of the normalization puzzle could be moved into position.

Hanoi's Thinking About U.S. Relations

Though Vietnam was careful not to overreact to this escalation of POW/MIA rhetoric on the part of activist groups and the attendant press attention to the issue, Hanoi did telegraph the message that there were limits to its forbearance. Vietnam's military had clearly grown uncomfortable with the manner in which the POW/MIA issue continued to be the featured, center-stage priority in the bilateral relationship with the U.S. The military had demonstrated that it was prepared to urge a blunt, zero-sum approach to the question of U.S. willingness to proceed with normalization in a measured way, and was convinced that insidious political reasons were the only credible explanation of why Washington was not moving with dispatch toward a completely normal and proper relationship. In March, the Vietnamese military's daily newspaper published an article that was critical of the U.S. POW/MIA effort, and that alleged that Washington had used this effort to collect intelligence against Vietnamese targets. Interestingly, the first public statements by the SRV suggesting that the U.S. employed the POW/MIA apparatus as a means of spying in Vietnam must be credited to the Foreign Ministry. On 8 August 1992, Trinh Xuan Lang, Permanent Representative to the United Nations, told New York Times reporter Barbara Crosette that the U.S. had made "excessive demands" of Hanoi in its efforts to account for U.S. MIAs. Lang suggested that the ulterior motive for Washington's insistence on following through on live sighting reports by visiting prison sites and archives was to actively collect intelligence on the internal situation in Vietnam. While this argument was not given any further play by the Foreign Ministry, it reflected a view that had its origins in the earliest days of joint field investigations, when working-level Vietnamese officials from the Foreign Ministry were fairly open about their suspicions regarding U.S. officials engaged in POW/MIA field activities. The military's decision to spotlight those concerns in early 1996 showed that PAVN harbored serious reservations about the normalization process.[16]

The Foreign Ministry found itself in the uncomfortable position of having to bear the brunt of criticism for Vietnam's failure to take its own MIA issue seriously, a view that had been spoken by members of the National Assembly, veterans groups, and military units with increasing regularity since 1995. The Foreign Ministry also had to take on the lion's share of the responsibility for convincing provincial officials, National Assembly delegates and party leaders that staying the course would add up to real dividends in the bilateral relationship with the U.S. The Defense Ministry could portray its involvement as responsive to these constituencies, whereas the Foreign Ministry had to live with the reality that it had sought to be responsive to American requests for access to archives, an increased operational tempo for field activities, and more direct contact with witnesses to serve the goal of improving bilateral relations, accelerating access to international financial resources, and jump-starting the process of negotiating a trade agreement. Since none of those things had come to pass, the Foreign Ministry's track record was far less impressive than the military's, which had worked with the Ministry of Interior to locate and repatriate Vietnamese remains in Laos, and could therefore take credit for being attentive to Vietnam's MIA problem.

Through mid–1996, the Vietnamese continued to hope that the process of normalization would somehow result in a more clearcut end stage to the POW/MIA issue. In mid–1996, Vietnamese officials charged with working level responsibilities regarding the POW/MIA issue were actively posing questions about steps that might be taken jointly to reduce the expenditure of funds and energy involved in joint field work without diminishing the intensity of commitment to the fullest possible accounting.[17] This was a subtle variation of the earlier question posed by working level Foreign Ministry officials concerning the propriety of the "over representation" of official U.S. entities in Hanoi — with both a U.S. Liaison Office and the JTFFA — at a time when Vietnam's representation in the U.S. was limited to the presence of a liaison office. That question, at least in part, represented a Vietnamese effort to define what the relationship should look like in the aftermath of the decision to normalize.

There was little evidence, though, that the Vietnamese had entertained the notion of a military-to-military relationship in the 12 months following normalization. Though the Vietnamese had given thought to clearing the books on the POW/MIA issue, in a manner that demonstrated a failure to appreciate the seriousness and sensitivity for the U.S. of questions associated with the "end stage" of this issue, they had not given much thought to engaging with the U.S. on defense issues. In July 1993 and March 1996 the Vietnamese Defense Ministry joined Foreign Ministry representatives in discussions of regional security issues with U.S. State and Defense officials on the margins of POW/MIA delegations. However, according to senior SRV military officials, Vietnam did not turn its attention to the possibility of and prospects for a bilateral military relationship until late 1996, following the visit to Hanoi by Deputy Assistant Secretary of Defense Kurt Campbell.[18]

During roughly the same time, some senior Vietnamese foreign policy leaders appeared to see U.S.–Vietnamese normalization as the means by which Hanoi would be able to hedge its bets against a China that continued to pursue relations with Vietnam at a deliberately and frustratingly slow pace. That was not a universally shared view. Other senior Vietnamese officials made it clear that Vietnam wanted a relationship with the U.S. because that was in Vietnam's interests, not because a normal relationship with Washington would give Hanoi an advantage in its relations with Beijing. Vietnam could benefit from U.S. technology, markets and capital. Many senior officials stipulated that Vietnam would never again enter into a relationship with the express purpose of manipulating other bilateral links. Such officials maintained that relations between the two countries should be based on the respective national interests of the two countries, and that the relationship with Washington had evolved to the point where Vietnam could say that the two countries had consonant national interests that were well served by continued progress toward normalization. Different Vietnamese defined the strategic value of the relationship with Washington in different ways, suggesting that there was no firm consensus on the importance of working to sustain the trajectory of the bilateral tie with Washington.

Vietnam's Conservative Trend: Defense and Foreign Policy

By mid-year, a decidedly conservative frame of reference for defense and foreign policy emerged in the course of preparations for the 8th national congress of the Vietnamese Communist Party. The preoccupation with security, stability, the consequences of rapid change and unbridled reform, and the ideological price to be paid for departures from trusted Marxist principles, suffused discussion of regional issues, international economics, and foreign relationships.

Beginning in February, and lasting through April, the Party's theoretical journal, *Tap Chi Cong San*, ran three to four articles in each bimonthly issue in preparation for the national congress. The articles were written by academics associated with universities and research institutes, and middle-level government and party officials. They focused on the continued relevance of Marxism and Leninism, and the timeless strength of Ho Chi Minh's teachings, and offered a defense of Vietnam's strategic choices at various historic benchmarks. The articles paid homage to classical socialist theory, and restated the strong association the Communist Party drew between independence, development and national strength and "the socialist orientation." Other roads to development could not skirt poverty, and would not guarantee economic success and stability. Abandoning socialism meant condemning Vietnam to uncertainty, a perpetually primitive economy, unrelieved social distress, inequality, and class imbalances, reminiscent of the afflictions that characterized the American-supported Republic of South Vietnam.[19]

Though the articles did not touch on U.S.–Vietnamese relations, they revealed a decidedly conservative trend in thinking about foreign policy, and Vietnam's future, that remained a strong undercurrent for the rest of the year. A selection of the articles attributed the wavering convictions of a number of "doubters" about the wisdom of pursuing a socialist course to the collapse of the Soviet Union. The proverbial minority, "a number of people," argued that by electing to take a socialist course, Vietnam had chosen the wrong road, and needed to select another direction for the nation, namely the capitalist road to development, or a third course, the road to social democracy.[20] The articles did not take the threat of "peaceful transformation" as the most insidious form of anti-regime thinking, though they did not discount the challenge posed to the regime by such views. Rather, the articles suggested that a panicked post–Cold War view of Hanoi's options, and wrong thinking about the lessons of history and the realities of regional and global change, as well as the drift away from original Marxist standpoints, combined to prompt some quarters (in some instances with support from Overseas Vietnamese populations) to ask whether Vietnam had made the correct strategic choices.[21] Many of the writings portrayed a debate in which some people wondered whether a diluted version of socialism leavened by unalloyed market capitalism, or the Chinese course to development, or a softened socialism would meet Vietnam's developmental needs without the dislocations caused by pursuing the "socialist orientation."[22] The articles rejected those alternatives, urged a return to core Marxist-Leninist values, and a concerted attempt to reclaim the vision that drove Ho Chi Minh to dedicate his life to preserving Vietnam's independence and sovereignty.[23]

The military, and its party organizations, remained concerned with internal and external threat that came in the form of conspiracies of forces intent on transforming Vietnam through "peaceful evolution" schemes. The party organization for Military Region 7 conducted its congress in early April. In his speech to that meeting, Le Kha Phieu stressed very basic security themes, and the importance of concerted efforts to thwart "peaceful evolution."[24] Military Region 3's party organization conducted its session at roughly the same time, and echoed the concern with shoring up national defense capabilities, increasing educational efforts in that area, and remaining in a defensive posture against "peaceful evolution" conspiracies against Vietnam.[25] Do Muoi addressed the All-Army Party Organization Congress on 5 May, making the case for an integrated defense strategy that accomplished nation building tasks and fulfilled security responsibilities. Muoi repeated the admonition to defeat the schemes of "hostile forces" aimed at "spontaneous evolution," especially by preserving the party's preeminent political leadership role.[26]

Some unidentified elements in the party appear to have challenged the direction and content of foreign policy discussions, according to late

April articles in the military's daily newspaper. They argued that in the aftermath of the dissolution of the Soviet Union, Vietnam's foreign policy orientation should have changed, that Hanoi should have focused on a less selective broadening of relations, and expended more energy to define a foreign policy course that owed less to principles and was governed more by an imperative to survive by entering into alliances. That seemed to have been a veiled way of suggesting that relations with China had developed entirely too slowly for Vietnam's own good. The question of Vietnam's relationship with China was raised during the Third Military Region's party congress in late March. Delegates attending that meeting argued that geographic proximity posed a "complication" to an "open door policy," which itself — alongside of a market approach to economic development — made Vietnam vulnerable to forces favoring "peaceful evolution." Nevertheless, the shared border, China's commercial ports and its disposable capital made Beijing a real critical variable in Vietnam's economic strategy.[27]

In the end, the VNCP vigorously endorsed the broad contours of the foreign policy that had emerged as the domestic reform strategy began to evolve. The party underwrote the open door foreign policy, reiterated the importance of sustaining healthy economic relations with all countries, stressed the importance of normalization with China and continued efforts to shape a relationship with the United States, and emphasized the centrality of relations with ASEAN members and the international financial institutions. However, the more cautious, orthodox ideological instincts that informed debate during preparations for the party congress inclined foreign policy makers to a more careful view of possibilities, and a vocabulary that tied foreign policy to a proper Marxist world view.[28]

Making Policy Decisions

In mid–July, on the first anniversary of the establishment of normal relations between the United States and the Socialist Republic, National Security Advisor Anthony Lake traveled to Hanoi for talks about the next steps in the economic ties, refugee and emigration issues, and the development of the diplomatic relationship.[29] The Lake visit was a departure from the manner of doing business with Vietnam. From 1987 to 1992, at points at which the routines of the relationship were unable to develop enough momentum to overcome issue-oriented problems, Washington would dispatch the presidential emissary. After 1992, the U.S. government would send a presidential delegation to lend enough clout to the dialogue between the U.S. and Vietnam over the POW/MIA issue, or refugee-related matters, so as to press beyond the troublesome issues that could not be resolved by working level officials. In mid–1996, the bilateral relationship needed a jolt to get to the next level of discussions, to press beyond the comfort level that had enveloped both sides, and to energize discussions of bilateral issues impacting on normalization. A decision was made to have the National Security Advisor head a delegation to the SRV. With the opening of the embassy, and the imminent assignment of an ambassador to Hanoi, there was less of a reason to dispatch another presidential emissary, especially since one had just traveled to Hanoi in March 1996. The mid–1996 visit represented an opportunity for Lake to elevate the level of discussion between the U.S. and Vietnam.

Senior U.S. government officials privately suggested that Lake, who had probably calculated that he would not continue to serve as the National Security Advisor in a second Clinton term, wanted to make certain that the establishment of a normal, positive relationship with Vietnam was part of the "Clinton legacy," and wanted to assure that he had some official role in that effort. Others have suggested that it was an important personal journey, given his association with Vietnam and U.S. policy during the war that dated from the early 1960s. Lake himself remembers the issue slightly differently. He was scheduled to visit China to help launch a strategic dialogue at a vulnerable point in the U.S.–China relationship, and the decision to visit Thailand and Vietnam seemed logical since he had not been to Southeast Asia in his position as National Security Advisor. The primary purpose of the trip was related to China policy. The substance of the Vietnam trip revolved around the desire to make some progress on bilateral economic issues that would allow the Administration to move things along with Congress, and to deepen POW/MIA cooperation. Lake personally believed that stronger strategic cooperation with Vietnam would be helpful.[30]

In his meetings with key senior Vietnamese officials, the National Security Advisor praised Vietnam's cooperation with the JTFFA, and emphasized the importance of the POW/MIA issue to the United States. He discussed "important mutual interests" in the development of economic and trade relations. Lake urged Vietnam to agree to an extension of the 30 June deadline for the Resettlement Opportunities for Vietnamese Returnees (ROVR) Program. He also stressed the importance of obtaining Vietnam's assurances that exit permit regulations would not be used to bar certain types of people from legally departing Vietnam before the Administration could obtain a waiver to the provisions in the Jackson-Vanik Amendment. Lake discussed U.S. plans to open a consulate in Ho

Chi Minh City. Initially, the Administration's plan was to delay the opening of the consulate until after the November 1996 election, but the press of issues in South Vietnam, including refugee-related matters, and U.S. business interests in opportunities in the south, led Washington to seek to hasten the opening of a consulate.

Importantly, in his discussions with Party General Secretary Do Muoi, Lake stated that the militaries of the U.S. and Vietnam should begin to foster exchanges. Muoi agreed with this proposal, and expressed his confidence that patience and understanding would do much to bridge remaining gaps between Washington and Hanoi. Following that visit, Muoi's views were translated into instructions within the Defense Ministry, and senior officials from the MND's External Relations Department began actively soliciting the U.S. Defense Attaché's views regarding starting points for this venture in "dialogue" and "exchange."

Authoritative Vietnamese media credited Lake's visit with boosting the momentum of U.S.–Vietnamese relations. President Le Duc Anh stated that his meeting with the National Security Advisor on 13 July further accelerated bilateral ties. Prime Minister Vo Van Kiet applauded the visit as a "new effort" by Washington to "strengthen" bilateral ties. The Prime Minister praised "positive improvements" in the relationship in the year since diplomatic ties were established.[31] In July, shortly after Lake's visit to Vietnam, SRV media assessments commented that in the year that had passed since relations were normalized, Vietnam and the U.S. had built a "firm foundation" for the development of relations. Vietnamese media commentary pointed to the "declassification" of Vietnam as a war zone, and the recognition by Washington of Vietnam's "full cooperation in the MIA issue," as indications that American "attitudes and evaluation toward Vietnam" had changed. Pointing to rising U.S. investment levels, media commentary noted that Vietnam had become a "new partner" of the U.S., underscored the manner in which normalization exerted a positive impact in Asia, and emphasized the importance of planning for deliberate steps to enhance the relationship in the "post normalization stage."[32]

False Starts and Final Planning

In July, following Lake's visit to Vietnam, ISA approached the Deputy Chief of Mission (DCM) of the Vietnamese Embassy in Washington, Ha Huy Thong, to discuss the possibility of organizing a mid-year trip to Hanoi by a delegation headed by the Deputy Assistant Secretary of Defense for Asia and the Pacific. The meeting with the DCM was an informal, exploratory opportunity to talk about the shape of such an event. On ISA's part, it represented an attempt to probe the Embassy for what Hanoi's attitudes might be toward such an initiative, and an opportunity to enshrine the Lake visit as an authoritative marker on the importance of establishing dialogue between the U.S. and Vietnam's militaries. It also was a chance to signal DoD interest in an introductory meeting of defense officials, especially since the opportunities for formal, authoritative discussions on defense relations and security issues had been few and far between since the mid–1995 Presidential decision to normalize relations with Vietnam. But, the meeting took place ahead of a formal decision by the Pentagon policy bureaucracy on the course outlined in successive ISA decision memoranda, and ahead of any concrete indication that leadership above the level of the Deputy Assistant Secretary would authorize the travel of a DoD delegation to Vietnam to hammer out some sense of how to go about sculpting a relationship between the two militaries. At the same time, the meeting took place before the Vietnamese side had reached any decisions regarding the efficacy of proceeding with the military dimension of normalization.

So, on the U.S. side of things, the July meeting was based on working level confidence that the trajectory of policy would support such a first step in defense relations, and that the proposals still in the DoD policy pipeline continued to have the support and concurrence of staff-level State Department and National Security Council offices. Further, the meeting with the Vietnamese Deputy Chief of Mission was, from the ISA perspective, based on the assumption that some statement of interest, even at this rudimentary level, would be a helpful bit of encouragement to DoD leaders still contemplating the policy costs of the proposal to venture into modest contacts with the People's Army of Vietnam.

On the Vietnamese side, the Washington meeting between two old friends, each speaking in part for their respective offices, and in part on the basis of individual conviction that this was the right and sensible thing to do, represented a similar risk. The meeting did not take place on instructions from the Foreign Ministry, though it was hardly important enough to require that level of attention, and it did fall into the category of contacts conducted in the course of managing daily and routine embassy business. The meeting did require the DCM to make a judgment about the climate of opinion in Hanoi, and the extent to which the time was right to explore military relations, and it thus did require the Embassy to take a position that would be reported to senior DoD officials as an expression of polite, encouraging interest in this first step. On that basis, the DCM's positive tone, his own view that the U.S. proposal would be the right way to start the process of exploring the potential for bilateral defense relations, and his personal sense that such a proposal would probably be well received in Hanoi suggest that he was prepared to make a calculated bureaucratic gamble by communicating interest and striking a receptive tone, while not getting too far ahead of the system.

Meetings without formal instructions became an essential ingredient in the effort to press forward with policy-level decisions regarding the next steps in the normalization of defense relations. They occurred at the working level, on the margins of the flow of policy business, at a moment when one corner of that process was poised on the cusp of a decision it was not yet prepared to make. They did not represent daring, dramatic events, but were rather inconspicuous acts that sought to invigorate discussion that had ended inconclusively. Such working level meetings, conducted without instructions, played an role in the attempt to chart a unique course of relations between entities that had no frame of reference for this sort of dialogue. They represented an alternative to formal, technical-level meetings between defense bureaucracies that had little in the way of a track record of formal interaction on issues apart from the POW/MIA problem. The Pentagon and the Defense Ministry were creatures of habit that had no formal channels for dialogue, and no starting points for bureaucratic interaction. Vietnam had not yet dispatched a defense attaché to serve in Washington, and had not yet grown sufficiently accustomed to the presence of a U.S. defense attaché so that the assigned officer could take advantage of access to develop communication with appropriate MND points of contact. The Pentagon had not yet reached a decision on normalizing relations with the People's Army, was only vaguely conversant about the potential for such a relationship, and remained concerned with the consequences of any policy decision for the POW/MIA mission. Such meetings without formal instructions were a means of injecting new ideas into the system. For the U.S. side, they only worked if they were scrupulously and widely reported in normal interagency channels, and became part of the existing dialogue, adding a new perspective to the conventional wisdom, or a new piece of information to a system that was propelled along by pellets of data contained in information memos, preparatory briefs for meetings, and "weekly activity reports."

The concept for the proposed DAS-led delegation that ISA offered resonated with familiar priorities, such as the POW/MIA issue, and built on earlier meetings involving Vietnamese and American military representatives. ISA told Thong that the U.S. delegation would want to visit the JTFFA

Detachment in Hanoi and the Defense Ministry's MIA Office, under the leadership of Senior Colonel Tran Bien; the Presidential Delegation had visited Bien's office in March. ISA requested a call on Deputy Defense Minister Nguyen Thoi Bung, and reminded Thong that in the March meeting with the Presidential Delegation, Bung had raised some points about U.S.–Chinese relations. The intended head of the U.S. delegation, DASD/AP Campbell, would be the most appropriate individual to explain U.S. military relations with China. ISA told the DCM that the U.S. delegation would also be interested in meeting with Defense Ministry officials responsible for U.S.–Vietnamese relations, including representatives from the External Relations Department, and officials from the MND's Institute for Military Strategy and the National Defense Academy. ISA stated an interest in meeting with officials from the Institute for Military History, so as to propose the establishment of a formal working relationship with the U.S. Army Center for Military History that would bring U.S. and Vietnamese military historians together for frank discussions of a complex history. ISA also proposed meetings with representatives from the National Center for Social Sciences and Humanities, the Center for North American Studies, the Ho Chi Minh National Political Academy, the Foreign Ministry's Institute for International Relations, and the Vietnam-American Association.

ISA intended the hefty list of possible meetings with the U.S. delegation as an indication of the sort of initial contacts that should be accomplished during this visit to Hanoi, as a measure of the Pentagon's seriousness about military relations, and finally as an signal of the extent to which DoD was intent on building opportunities for dialogue.[33]

By mid–July it was clear that the Vietnamese were ill at ease with a DoD visit so close on the heels of the National Security Advisor's calls on the senior leadership. The Defense and Foreign Ministries felt as though a full court press was being made on them, and they reacted awkwardly to such intensive coverage, especially when they believed that there was the possibility that China would see something potentially unsettling in these U.S. initiatives toward Vietnam.

At roughly the same time, senior assistants to then Senior Colonel Vu Tan told the U.S. Defense Attaché—apparently on instructions—that the Defense Ministry had not had sufficient time to digest the substance of Lake's visit. The hurried attempt by DoD to assemble a trip to Vietnam did not make sense to the MND. Vu Tau made it clear that the MND would prefer the DASD-led Pentagon visit to take place at a decent interval following the Lake trip, instead of so soon after that visit. The Vietnamese were attentive to the fact that they were part of a much larger itinerary. At least one special assistant to Vu Tan suggested that the leadership would interpret this to mean that the stop in Hanoi, sandwiched between visits to other Southeast Asian countries, was a perfunctory visit, part of a regional swing, done more for convenience than for content. The Director of the Foreign Ministry's Americas Department, a close associate of the SRV Ambassador in Washington, and an official with a long history of responsibilities for the POW/MIA issue, told the U.S. Defense Attaché that his seniors believed the proposed DASD/AP visit was not a good idea, and that the Foreign Ministry questioned the necessity of a visit so soon after Lake's trip.

The Vietnamese needed to put the Lake visit behind them; process the implications of what the National Security Advisor said; formulate institutional responses to their leadership's agreement to military contacts; get through the ARF meeting; and get beyond their own National Assembly session at which they would name a new raft of ministers, including Defense and Foreign Affairs, as well as Interior, which were three portfolios intimately involved in shaping the U.S.–Vietnamese relationship. Finally, Vietnam had to have time enough to regain confidence in Washington's seriousness about normalization. At a minimum, Hanoi needed to see Ambassador-select Peterson go before the Senate for a confirmation hearing, and to see the first steps taken toward a Jackson-Vanik waiver on the basis of "emigration assurances."

In August, ISA told the Under Secretary of Defense for Policy that the DASD-level visit should be proposed to the Vietnamese for late September–early October. The rest of the plan involved a CINCPAC visit that would follow the DASD/AP visit, a two-person NDU delegation that would visit Hanoi in October 1996 to respond to Vietnam's desire to discuss the U.S. NDU system and the possibility of a first U.S. NDU visit to Vietnam in mid–1997, the expansion of multilateral activities accessible to the Vietnamese, formal bilateral activities and an increase in the tempo of visits to Vietnam by senior DoD officials.

On 8 August, the Under Secretary approved the plan for a last quarter visit to Hanoi by a delegation led by DASD Campbell, in part because he had grown more confident that the plan was sensitive to the potential political blowback that could come from a precipitous rush to a full relationship with the Vietnamese military, in part because he had become confident that the POW/MIA issue would still be the featured priority issue in the bilateral relationship, and in part because the potential for congressional backlash had in his estimate receded.

It is harder to trace the path that led to the Vietnamese decision. Several meetings between the DCM and ISA, following the July session at which ISA broached the possibility of a DASD/AP visit to Hanoi, and at least one session between the DCM and DASD Campbell probably provided the occasion for a cable from the Embassy to the Foreign Ministry reporting DoD views regarding the proposed trip, and describing ISA's efforts to address Vietnamese Defense Ministry concerns, which might have contributed to keeping the issue in play in Hanoi. The support of the Vietnamese chief of mission in Washington for basic steps toward dialogue between the two militaries probably counted for a great deal. Le Van Bang had a lot of credibility in the Foreign Ministry. He was an accomplished diplomat and a veteran of the Americas Department's, long responsible for managing the POW/MIA issue. He had close, working ties with the military that dated from his assignment in the VNOSMP. It appears that his cautious and optimistic approach to the U.S.–Vietnamese relationship, and his attentiveness to defense and security issues, might have been sufficient to convince the Defense Ministry to agree to a visit that Bang viewed as a potentially positive step forward in overall relations, a useful means of representing the high level of cooperation on the POW/MIA issue, and a chance worth taking to see what resources the Pentagon might bring to the table in an initial discussion of military-to-military relations.

The MND's initial hesitancy probably sprung from their preference for a calendar of military diplomacy that was balanced and in proportion, rather than crowded with events that suggested a tilt to one country or another. The Defense Ministry may very well have calculated that closely grouped visits, first by the National Security Advisor and then, only months later, by a senior Pentagon official, would have conveyed the wrong impression about the alacrity with which the Vietnamese military was prepared to move in shaping a plan for normalization between the two defense establishments. In terms of the timing of events, and planning for a year's worth of activities, the Defense Ministry's approach was "One Step Forward, Wait," reflecting reluctance to enthusiastically embrace the possibility of a defense relationship with the U.S. In the end, the Foreign Ministry's level of satisfaction with the relationship, the relative success of the first discussions on the opening of a U.S.–Vietnam air route, and the constructive nature of early talks on a bilateral trade agreement offered enough of a positive backdrop in the overall relationship to nudge the system to a decision that allowed a meeting with a Pentagon delegation to go forward during the last quarter of the year.[34]

Breaking the Ice: The October 1996 DoD-ERD Talks

Deputy Assistant Secretary of Defense Campbell led an interagency delegation to Vietnam from 3 to 6 October for discussions with representatives of the Vietnamese Defense Ministry on the first steps toward a bilateral defense relationship. As secondary goal, the delegation sought to begin a dialogue on regional security issues with representatives of the Defense Ministry. On the delegation's second day in Hanoi (4 October), the U.S. side, along with Charge Desaix Anderson, met with Vice Minister of Defense Nguyen Thoi Bung to discuss regional security issues and the first steps toward defense relations. The Vietnamese were genuinely appreciative of the run down on U.S. broad strategic interests in Asia, and acknowledged that they had studied the East Asia Strategy Review. Both sides dwelled on China for the majority of the plenary session, detailing current views, the reasoning behind U.S. actions during the Taiwan Straits Crisis, and future steps to sustaining engagement. The Vietnamese response placed a premium on preserving regional stability by avoiding provocative actions, under which they lumped both Chinese steps in the context of the South China Seas dispute and the U.S. response during the straits crisis. Both sides agreed that anything provocative that risked unhinging the peace in Asia is bad, and that Taiwan was an "internal matter" for China, and that when Chinese behavior neglected a peaceful approach in favor of one that undermined the "trend toward peace and stability," then Beijing's stance on Taiwan was no longer exclusively internal in nature.

The U.S. side proposed six modest initiatives that were intended to define the ground-floor level of activities between the two defense establishments through at least mid–1997: a CINCPAC visit to Hanoi in December, the assignment of an SRV Defense Attaché to Washington as soon as possible, a visit to the United States by a delegation of PAVN representatives in late 1996 or early 1997, a U.S. National Defense University visit to Vietnam as part of the annual Asian studies curriculum, a mid–1997 visit to Vietnam by the U.S. Air War College, and enhanced contacts between military specialists such as historians, program managers and legal experts. In the end, General Bung told the U.S. delegation that Defense Minister Doan Khue had stated his support for all six of these proposals.

The Vietnamese came to the early October talks in a manner that drew clear distinctions between this meeting and past official encounters, such as the meetings conducted with the Presidential Emissary and with Presidential POW/MIA Delegations. The October meeting was an exclusively Defense Ministry-managed event. The Vietnamese may have been mildly concerned with the multi-agency composition of the U.S. delegation, but they were not swayed from their intention to keep these talks in a strictly defense channel.[35]

The Defense Ministry seized control of the visit, managed its formalities via the U.S. Defense Attaché Office, and stacked their delegation with senior defense representatives.[36]

At the first meeting it became clear that the ERD had the confidence of the ministerial level, and the freedom to manage issues regarding bilateral military relations. The ERD was stocked with talented, multi-lingual, well-traveled officers. As time went on, it matured into the job and improved its standing with the Foreign Ministry and the VNCP's External Relations Department. At this first session, there was no reason to believe that there had been any effort to coordinate ERD positions with MFA colleagues.

The ERD blunted the importance of U.S.–proposed contacts with Vietnamese think tank and research institutions, turning aside requests for courtesy calls on such entities, and instead focused U.S. attention on department-level interlocutors who would shape the relationship. The ERD outranked and outnumbered the Foreign Ministry at its own meeting with Campbell's delegation, which featured Vice Foreign Minister Nguyen Dinh Bin, who studiously quoted the Defense Minister and repeated Vice Minister Bung's remarks at the plenary session on the subject of bilateral defense relations. Finally, the ERD exceeded all standards of hospitality demonstrated during all previous delegations, including the missions of the Presidential Emissary and the Presidential POW/MIA Delegations, a signal that the MND was in charge. On the first day of the U.S. delegation's visit to Hanoi, Vietnamese hosts from the MND gave every indication that the senior military leadership regarded the visit as a singularly important event. DASD/AP Campbell was met at the MND Guest House Reception Room by Vice Minister Bung, who emphasized his ministry's sincere hope for a mutually beneficial dialogue, and cited his government's resolution to sustain POW/MIA cooperation. A flock of Senior Colonels and a vice foreign minister attended the U.S. Chief of Mission's welcoming reception. The U.S. delegation was accommodated in the MND Guest House VIP suites, with no expense spared. On the margins of the first day's reception events, senior military officials expressed keen interest in frank exchanges regarding regional and global issues, while recognizing the continued importance of the POW/MIA issue. A recently promoted party central committee functionary attended the Chief of Mission's reception, and underscored the significance of these talks to the VNCP.

In his reply to DASD Campbell's presentation, Minister of Defense Doan Khue made several remarks that telegraphed his own perspective on defense relations with the United States, and defined the rules according to which Vietnam would proceed. First, Khue characterized the six proposals for the first stage of the defense relationship as "normal and necessary," a tag line in a sentence that communicated Vietnam's record of willingness to re-engage with countries that had returned to Vietnam at the end of the Indochina Wars. Without undermining the atmosphere in which the U.S. side had offered these first modest steps, and without minimizing the angst involved in arriving at this decision point in the Pentagon, Khue signaled Vietnam's familiarity with the road to establishing contacts with countries whose bilateral history with Vietnam was complicated by war.

Second, Khue stated that while accepting the package of six proposals, Vietnam would give serious thought to what the priorities should be in pursuing a start-up relationship with the U.S. military. He offered a very clear sense of where Vietnam wanted this all to lead, namely to a visit involving a "higher-ranking" delegation, a phrase that was to become the MND's shorthand reference to a Defense Minister's visit to the U.S., suggesting that Khue wanted to move beyond the U.S. vision of a process that would progress through a set of steps calibrated to keep pace with the slow, deliberate development of the overall relationship, and get to the point where the two senior-most representatives of the defense establishments could meet, and make headlines.[37]

Third, Khue spelled out his military's focus on standardization and modernization, the armed force's equivalent of "industrialization and modernization," the slogan summarizing Hanoi's economic and infrastructure development effort. The Defense Minister's dramatic pause, the proximity of the two thoughts, and the Vietnamese habit of speaking their thoughts through disconnected phrases, suggested that what he was getting at was the Defense Ministry's desire that the bilateral relationship serve those interests in unstated ways.

Fourth, the Vietnamese signaled their interest in contouring the relationship in a manner that was studiously reciprocal, and based on respect and mutual understanding. Khue made it clear that the relationship should progress through the normal steps required by both sides to maximize opportunities to become acquainted, but there should be a larger goal. For Vietnam, that was getting the relationship to a higher level of interaction at the earliest point in time, to accrue the dividends that such senior level interaction would bring in terms of legitimacy and recognition. The Vietnamese side was intent on getting assurances that the relationship would not be aimed at targeting any third country, and that Vietnam would not be drawn into a situation where it could be used as a lever against other countries.

The MND wanted the relationship to be governed by reciprocity, mutual respect, and mutual advantage. The matching U.S. points were, first, that caution must be exercised in thinking about the regional and global ramifications of the relationship, and that observers must not conceive of this bilateral relationship as a tool to be used against any third country. That principle was based on the safe assumption that the moment Washington sought to use the U.S.–Vietnamese defense relationship to achieve advantage against China was the moment Hanoi would cease to see any advantage to the bilateral defense relationship. Second, the military-to-military relationship would have to progress slowly, at a pace linked to the development of the overall relationship. The concern about the pace of the relationship was as much a reflection of preoccupation with the domestic consequences of this aspect of the U.S.–Vietnamese relationship as it was an acknowledgement that defense links with Hanoi needed to be shaped in a manner that did not move beyond the kinds of activities conducted with friends and allies in the region. A honeymoon that was too plush or characterized by excessive attention to Vietnam at the expense of relationships in the region would not do, and could exhaust the limitations on what was possible with the Vietnamese much too quickly. Third, in terms of defense activities, the U.S. should not shrink from doing the same sorts of things with the Vietnamese that the U.S. did with other ASEAN members. There was no reason that the Pentagon could not agree to "regional security consultations" with the Vietnamese, for example. Here, the idea was that if DoD were to enter into a defense relationship, it would have to involve meaningful activities. While these principles would develop, and be encapsulated in different vocabulary at different times, the three U.S. "rules of attention" stayed fairly stable throughout the first few years of the relationship: the U.S.–Vietnamese military tie should never be aimed at a third country, should progress in a modest and carefully calibrated pace that was attentive to progress in the overall bilateral relationship, and should be a two-way street involving matching commitments and involvement by both sides.

Following the DASD's trip, it became clear that the scheduling discussed during the October visit would not work. The CINCPAC plan for a trip to Hanoi was cancelled once between late October and early November. ISA believed that while a new time frame for that trip had not yet been defined, there was no reason to refrain from going ahead with planning for the Senior Colonel's delegation. The six initiatives spelled out by Campbell were not hinged together in a manner that would preclude moving forward with one event if agreement on the timing for another one of the initiatives proved to be difficult. Flexibility became the key to making the relationship work. For example, in November ISA told Ha Huy Thong, the SRV Embassy Deputy Chief of Mission, that DoD would not be adverse to pressing forward with the visit to the U.S. by an SRV Senior Colonels' delegation, even though the MND had not yet sent a Defense Attaché to Washington, and the U.S. side would be more than prepared to press forward with the NDU visit regardless of whether the first portion of the list of six initiatives had been completed.

In a November discussion with Thong, ISA stressed that getting a Defense Attaché from Vietnam into place quickly would make communications on the nuts and bolts of implementing the steps discussed during the Campbell visit that much easier, but it would also enhance military-to-military dialogue, and give us an opportunity to use the U.S. Defense Attaché to advance military contacts. ISA made the point that the Pentagon wanted the activities and opportunities available to the Vietnamese Defense Attaché in Washington to be a mirror of what the U.S. Defense Attaché would be able to do in Hanoi. While ISA would not seek to limit the Vietnamese Defense Attaché's opportunities or access until DoD had assured that the U.S. Defense representative in Hanoi would receive similar treatment, ISA would expect some reciprocity at the outset that would gradually improve and expand.

During this period, ISA relied on the "working group" of armed services representatives and Joint Staff officers to help shape thinking about the next steps after the six initiatives had been completed. The ISA view was that the process ought not to be dependent on a senior or mid-level delegation visit to Vietnam to jump-start planning for the next steps in the relationship. Instead, working level officials and military specialists from both the U.S. and the Vietnamese defense establishments should be brainstorming so as to sustain the momentum, rather than allowing it to trail off in the aftermath of the proposed NDU and Air War College visits to Vietnam.

In the same time frame, the ERD worked the issue for the Defense Ministry. In the absence of an SRV military representative in Washington, the Vietnamese Embassy's senior leadership played a key role in managing communications with ISA, and took a proprietary interest in offering recommendations intended to move the relationship forward. The Deputy Chief of Mission, for example, suggested that "educational visits" would be a fruitful area to explore in the early stage of the relationship. He pursued opportunities to dispatch MND personnel to CINCPAC's Asian and Pacific Center for Strategic Studies, and sought to nudge the MND to nominate a military official for the Atlantic Council's nine-month study visit, an arrangement tailored to attract military participation. Later, it became evident that the MND was not prepared to endorse a course that involved front-loading Vietnamese military officers into Defense Department-run training and educational opportunities.[38] It appeared that the Embassy was looking for ways in which the U.S. could be helpful to Vietnam's efforts to participate in conferences on regional security issues sponsored by the ASEAN Regional Forum, which led Vietnamese foreign service officers assigned to the Embassy in Washington to speak encouragingly about the prospects for such meetings. The fact that the MND's thinking about "next steps" remained ambiguous, and did not necessarily fit closely with the Foreign Ministry's views of what could be helpful to the process of developing military relations, suggested that the Vietnamese side, especially the Defense Ministry, did not spend a lot of time defining the channels of communication that would be used to flesh out the details with the U.S. Through late 1996, the ERD appears to have approached the issue through informal means, on the margins of multilateral events and through informal encounters with the U.S. Defense Attaché at representational events in Hanoi, indicating that the ERD did not see this as a labor intensive exercise requiring a lot of staffing work, preparatory time, and inter-agency coordination.

5

GROUND FLOOR MILITARY RELATIONS, 1997

U.S. Thinking About Defense Relations

The November 1996 visit to Hanoi by the U.S. delegation resulted in an agreement in principle to a modest set of proposals for first activities in a military-to-military relationship, but there was clearly a yawning gap between an agreement and an implementable plan. It took the first quarter of 1997 to press the program forward. That was less the result of the difficulties implicit in efforts to identify workable calendar days and devise mutually acceptable itineraries, and more a function of a difference between what it meant to have an agreement and to actually commit to staffing out the details of events.

For the U.S. side, the agreement signaled the need to set in motion a process that would achieve the goals that emerged from the November 1996 meeting. To the Vietnamese side, having an agreement was the result of a political act, separate from the discussion and decision required to move such agreements to fruition. Agreements had to be studied, considered, evaluated by progressively higher levels of leadership, and eventually transformed into a plan of action when official support for the proposals crystallized or external pressure to move forward reached a critical mass. Much of 1997, and successive years until 2001, were spent in consolidating the official understanding of what agreed upon programs meant, and ushering those agreements to points at which they could be translated into programmable events.

The Vietnamese were essentially in a reactive mode, distilling the proposals put on the table by the U.S. side and, in their own description, running them up the chain of command to the highest level of government for approval. This may have been an overstatement of the way the Defense Ministry handled the first U.S. salvos of ideas for military-to-military interaction, but it did suggest that the ERD was on the hook to seek the approval of the Minister of Defense for positions regarding these U.S. proposals.

The Ministry had already set the parameters within which U.S.–Vietnamese military relations would be possible, and there was clarity on the sorts of activities that would be judged acceptable. So, while the U.S. was urging military relations, dishing out the first ideas that would help fill out that concept, and presuming that senior MND-level decisions on each discreet activity would be required before plans could be put into effect, the Vietnamese were looking at the process somewhat differently. The Vietnamese were prepared to offer a philosophical agreement to the idea of "engagement," and to begin to think about the kinds of activities that would make the most sense to them as the basis for military relations. The question of the extent to which Vietnam was prepared to assent to any single activity was not relevant to the MND, which was not yet prepared to think in terms of scheduling events and moving into the business of implementation. It took from November to early March before the U.S. could move the Vietnamese system to accept an invitation for an orientation visit.

On the U.S. side, much of the period from December 1996 to March 1997 was spent in the Pentagon recalibrating starting points, assessing resources, and defining terms for a U.S.–Vietnamese defense relationship, explaining the extent to which the agreement struck in Hanoi during November 1996 fit with DoD policy interests, and consolidating support for the relationship.

Strategic Motivations

In the face of U.S. domestic focus on the POW/MIA issue, on Vietnamese political prisoners, on human and religious rights and other sensitive issues, and in light of Vietnam's own ambivalence on the issue of military relations with the U.S., it made no sense to take a dramatic and public step before the U.S. and Vietnam had begun to build the scaffolding on which a future relationship might hang. It was also clear that the opening gambit in the U.S.–Vietnamese relationship would be compared to the way in which the U.S. rolled out the relationship with the Chinese military. To the Pentagon, though, there were sharp differences between these relationships, and the reasons for reaching out to these two militaries.

The Department of Defense made the decision to develop a relationship with the People's Liberation Army because China had a real strategic impact as a coherent and well armed military. In other words, China's relevance to the U.S. was its real military power. In the case of Vietnam, however, Hanoi's only real power was its "relevance" as an active member of ASEAN, and an ARF participant, and a growing economic player in the region. PAVN was an army struggling to define a post–Cold War mission, contending with decrepit and outdated hardware and mediocre leadership, and diverted by a profound economic role in the country's reform plans. It was difficult to tease out a strategic motivation for a defense relationship with Hanoi in the face of these realities.

The Defense Department itself had not determined what it wanted from this relationship. There was broad but unenthusiastic consensus that moving forward in the realm of defense relations was the right thing to do, but there were multiple and not easily reconciled motivations for taking this step. Some U.S. officials argued that cementing a relationship with Vietnam was the most effective way to offset China's influence in the area. Others argued that a policy decision to develop ties with the Vietnamese military would launch the U.S. in the direction of solving future access issues. Still others thought that it made sense to cement a relationship with PAVN given the U.S. government's continuing interests in regional stability, alliances with some ASEAN members, and Vietnam's new membership in ASEAN. The first argument overstated the extent to which the U.S. could exert influence or telegraph a meaningful message to the Chinese by drawing close to the Vietnamese. It also ignored the extent to which Hanoi had steeled itself against the possibility of being drawn into a situation in which it might become the lever used by third countries to offset the influence of China, by designing a foreign policy that was based on maintaining a wide array of relationships and avoiding entangling alliances. The second argument ignored the U.S. government's commitment to the "places not bases" approach, an adjustment to the growing allergy in Asia to affording the U.S. the basis for a long-term military presence. The third argument neglected the extent to which the region was not at all disturbed by, and in some instances quite positively predisposed toward the slow-moving, cautious approach to efforts to build defense relations between the U.S. and Vietnam. It made sense to avoid overstating the leverage that would accrue to the U.S. by cultivating a link with Vietnam. Pressing this "Vietnam card" ran the risk of having the opposite of the intended effect, especially since the Vietnamese remained committed to preserving stability in their relationship with China.

Additionally, there were sound domestic political reasons for not moving too quickly to establish a U.S.–Vietnamese defense relationship. A speedier pace would have put the administration crosswise with the coalition of domestic forces that had managed to complicate the process of confirming the U.S. ambassadorial appointee, and had actively sought to disaggregate DPMO through legislative tactics. There was no reason to push the defense relationship in a manner that would end up putting DoD out in front of the pace and scope of normalization in other areas of the relationship, particularly in the economic and political realm. Finally, there was good reason to avoid placing a policy priority on the relationship with Vietnam in a manner that suggested the Administration viewed it exclusively as a lever against China. Moving in deliberate, cautious steps avoided the problem of suggesting that the U.S. government had real strategic equities wrapped up in the effort to cultivate military relations with Vietnam.

During January and February, some DoD officials looked for a means to divide the defense relationship into a series of phases. That was probably, at least in part, a result of the earliest efforts to configure a model for the relationship that consisted of stages, but even in these earliest configurations, the relationship was not described as something that would unfold in a series of diachronic steps. ISA was seriously concerned that the U.S. side might end up expending considerable quantities of bureaucratic energy defining stages and phases that placed a premium on accomplishing particular steps before moving on the next level in the relationship, only to have the Vietnamese lean forward in a manner that would prod the U.S. side to take steps out of sequence as a response to some positive development in the relationship. That would scuttle the phased approach, and in the end leave the U.S. without a means of controlling the interaction once the decision was made to depart from an elaborately structured game plan to telegraph appreciation for some conceivably minor Vietnamese gesture. The entire "Roadmap" experience had made some in the Defense Department, and others in the interagency group, wary of an approach that established benchmarks intended to determine when both sides should move to the next phase of the relationship. The benchmark moment was always open to interpretation and challenge that could propel either side to a political decision on "next steps" simply to keep the other side wedded to the plan.[1] ISA deliberately avoided defining benchmark moments, and left ambiguous the sense of exactly when the U.S. side would be satisfied that a basic framework for a relationship, the "scaffolding," had come together in a manner that would allow the players to progress to the next highest level of contacts between defense establishments.

Early in the year some senior U.S. State Department officials favored inviting a Vice Minister of Defense to the U.S. in the late spring or early summer, once the Senior Colonels delegation, the CINCPAC visit, and the NDU and Air War College delegations had completed their trips to Vietnam. ISA dissented from this and other initiatives aimed at pushing the pace ahead, because it seemed that a ministerial level visit should not be scheduled until DoD had achieved something that could be described as a decent record of regular, routine contacts between military specialists. To ISA, the military relationship had to remain a step or two behind efforts to develop the political and economic relationship. Some State Department officials argued that the U.S. should confine itself to minor initiatives, as agreed to by both sides in late 1996, but that as soon as a trade agreement had been concluded, Washington should plan a ship visit to Vietnam.

Throughout early 1997, some U.S. government interests persisted in looking at a ship visit to Vietnam as a benchmark moment that would have immense bilateral significance, and would serve mutual security needs. It appeared, though, that the Vietnamese would not be nearly as enamored of the idea of a U.S. naval vessel calling at a Vietnamese port, even if the event were configured in the most benign shape, revolving around a small vessel landing an extremely small number of visitors with a humanitarian mission. The Vietnamese were looking for a symbolic achievement in the form of a meeting at the highest levels of the two defense establishments. There was sufficient reason to believe the Vietnamese would see a ship visit as a one sided event which would leave the U.S. with the bulk of the dividends and put Vietnam in the position of having to explain why U.S. warships were steaming into Vietnamese territorial waters.

To ISA, it made more sense to agree to a sequence of events that preserved the spirit of the earliest plan that placed a primacy on keeping events low keyed, quiet and non-controversial, in a manner that was unlikely to attract headlines, and in a way that would allow DoD to draw the Vietnamese military out at the working level, and get the MND into the habit of routine dialogue and technical level interaction.

Finally, ISA believed it was critical that the U.S. side refrain from depicting the military relationship as a hedge against the advantages that China might derive from a closer relationship with Vietnam. The U.S. had stuck to a vocabulary that communicated Washington's interest in building a connection to Vietnam for the sake of that relationship itself, not as an insurance policy against third countries or a means of telegraphing strategic messages to Beijing. The Pentagon understood that the China dimension would always be a variable in policy calculations regarding

Vietnam, but felt that the U.S.–Vietnamese defense relationship should be pursued in a manner that explicitly ruled out efforts to develop military contacts with PAVN as a means of coping with Chinese behavior in the region.

Vietnam's Viewpoint

The process of planning for the senior colonels delegation offered a good indication of the manner in which the ERD would manage routine discussions with the U.S. side on the implementation of the six activities to which the U.S. and Vietnam had agreed in October 1996, and a sense of the specific concerns the ERD harbored regarding interaction with the U.S. military.

The visit to the U.S. by a Vietnamese Defense Ministry delegation of senior PAVN colonels, for discussions ranging from efforts to sustain POW/MIA cooperation to regional security issues and the next steps in building a bilateral defense relationship, was envisioned by the U.S. side as an "orientation visit" for department-level MND officials. Following the October discussions in Hanoi, the invitation was tailored to fit the ERD's central role in managing the start-up relationship with the U.S. military. The original U.S. plan called for one or two stops between Hawaii and Washington, at military facilities such as Fort Bragg and Fort Lewis, to provide the visiting delegation with a view of operational U.S. military units, and to set an example for the treatment and access to be accorded delegations that would be exchanged between DoD and the MND. That plan, however, did not fit with the ERD's sense of what was appropriate in the relationship at this start-up stage. Early in the planning work, the International Affairs Office of the ERD made it clear that the visit should not involve stops apart from Washington and PACOM, and that the trip should not take more than a week, suggesting that the Vietnamese were not necessarily looking for a full itinerary in the U.S., and were certainly not inclined to see this as a chance to become familiar with the American military in the field. Moreover, it was an indication that Hanoi had a very different view of the kinds of things visiting U.S. military delegations would be able to see in future visits to Vietnam.

The first effort at working jointly to define an itinerary for the senior colonels was awkward, slow moving, and at times simply failed to produce any results. For example, beginning in late November 1996 ISA envisioned a three day visit to Washington, D.C. for Senior Colonel Vu Tan and his ERD colleagues that would involve courtesy calls at ISA, the Joint

Staff, and the offices of the chiefs of the armed services, plus some opportunities to familiarize the visitors with various Pentagon agencies such as the Defense Intelligence Agency and DPMO, meetings with working level Pentagon Asian specialists, office calls at the State Department, and an opportunity to meet local academics focused on Indochina. ISA also supported a meeting with the U.S.–SRV Defense Working Group; a luncheon with representatives of the U.S. Army Center for Military History, the U.S. Air Force and the U.S. Navy historian, and the USMC historical unit; briefings and discussions at the National Defense University; and a side trip to Quantico and other local military facilities such as Fort McNair and Fort Belvoir. ISA tried to work out a schedule that would get the visiting delegation to West Point, Gettysburg, the Air Combat Command, the Air University at Maxwell Air Force Base in Alabama, and Fort Hood, Texas. Through late 1996, the ERD had not settled on a date, and had not yet spoken about their preferences for the length of the visit.

In early January 1997 the ERD took the position that it was "not the right time" to go ahead with three activities proposed by the U.S. side: (1) a delegation of U.S. military justice experts and lawyers, which was to have continued discussions begun in Washington in late 1996 on the principles of freedom of navigation, law of the sea issues, and other regional matters; (2) a delegation of DoD and PACOM humanitarian affairs specialists, which planned to meet with non governmental organization (NGO) and private voluntary organization (PVO) representatives and Foreign Ministry personnel[2]; and (3) a U.S. Coast Guard survey team. In response, ISA told Ambassador Le Van Bang in Washington that the Pentagon wanted to work with the ERD to determine the right timing for these events, and was prepared to provide clarifications regarding the military lawyers delegation that might satisfy lingering questions on the intentions behind this proposed visit. If the planned visit was to be shelved by the ERD, ISA wanted agreement that the cancellation of the visit would be discussed at the working level meeting with the ERD scheduled to take place in the summer. Ambassador Bang was receptive, but clearly not in a position to comment on, or exert influence over, the ERD's decision.

Not until mid–January did the Vietnamese comment on the Defense Department's proposed itinerary for the Senior Colonel's delegation. At that point, they made it plain that there was little interest in visiting U.S. military installations in Hawaii and no real desire to meet with DIA representatives for briefings. Additionally, the ERD gave voice to their concern that the visit to Washington would trigger anti–Vietnamese demonstrations. The ERD was not very willing to provide concrete indications of Defense Ministry interests and to contribute ideas in U.S. efforts to plan for the visit. They were late to offer a proposal for specific time frames for the trip. They were indifferent to the necessity to postpone the CINCPAC trip planned for January, and did not offer explanations of the extent to which their own calendar in January would prohibit additional travel by senior MND policy advisors.

Interestingly, by late January–early February there appeared to be some unsettled questions regarding the role of various Defense Ministry subordinates in the upcoming senior colonels visit that played out in a manner suggesting distinct differences of approach between the ERD and other department-level MND offices. In early February, ISA told the Vietnamese Embassy that Senior Colonel Vo Dinh Quang, who had just been granted *agrement* as the Vietnamese Defense Attaché to Washington, should be included in the activities of the senior colonels delegation. ISA reserved a place for him at all the events on the delegation's itinerary. At the time it was presumed that Senior Colonel Quang would arrive in the U.S. no later than 4 March. The ERD appears to have expressed the preference that Quang not join the delegation. In conveying this decision, the Vietnamese embassy noted the "inconvenience" of pairing the new Attaché with the PAVN delegation, in a manner that suggested a command decision to exclude Quang from the delegation's activities had been made by the Director of the ERD. In the event, Quang lingered in Paris before proceeding to New York and Washington, eliminating the need to address this question as a practical matter. From all appearances, though, the ERD and the Attaché handlers in the General Political Department had different reporting chains, and worked hard to keep their missions separate and distinct. Moreover, there was limited contact on this aspect of the visit between the ERD and appropriate Foreign Ministry offices, and no communication with the SRV Embassy in Washington on the matter.

The Vietnamese side, then, was troubled by plans for a lengthy itinerary intended to familiarize the Senior Colonels delegation with the Defense Department, and with the armed services, through trips to carefully selected sites and facilities, presumably because of the extent to which the visit would be viewed as a public embrace of the idea of extensive U.S.–Vietnamese military relations, and the risks that the visit would be seen in the region, and by China, as a repudiation of Hanoi's policy of non-alignment. The ERD was concerned with the risk that a jam-packed schedule would eventually bring the delegation into contact with the U.S. media. This first official visit should not, in the thinking of the ERD, be an occasion for public posturing, especially when so many fundamental questions about the defense relationship remained unanswered.

Moreover, the ERD feared that the delegation would be forced to confront the POW/MIA issue, and garner unfortunate headlines in the course of the visit. For that reason, the Vietnamese Embassy, and the ERD, carefully described the visit as an event that needed to be kept firmly in military channels. ISA looked at the planned visit as an opportunity to begin working level dialogue on a broad range of security and defense issues. The relationship with the Defense Ministry that would emerge from this process would, in ISA's view, pay positive dividends in other realms of the broader relationship, including the effort to account for missing U.S. personnel. The ERD shared that concept, but looked at the prospect of meetings with non-governmental organizations involved in the POW/MIA issue as an awkward situation that would press the delegation into areas it was not chartered to discuss. Both the Embassy and the ERD were prepared to agree to official briefings, and in the event were equipped with appropriate talking points underscoring the Defense Ministry's continued commitment to this issue. However, for the ERD, exposure on the POW/MIA represented a detour that could compromise the positive optics of this working-level visit, and sour the atmosphere as seriously as would an untoward moment with the anti–SRV ethnic Vietnamese organizations in the United States. In early February, Senior Colonel Tran Bien, head of the MND's MIA Office, told a U.S. official that the delegation of Senior Colonels preparing to visit the U.S. did not want to meet with any interests, organizations, or individuals apart from those on the notional DoD schedule, which had been proposed to the ERD by that time via the SRV Embassy in Washington and the U.S. Defense Attaché in Hanoi. Senior Colonel Bien, who was to be the only one of the six members of the delegation with any POW/MIA-relevant experience, stated that he would be prepared to agree to such meetings with non-governmental organizations involved in the POW/MIA issue in April, when he was scheduled to return to the U.S. as a guest of the Defense POW/MIA Office.

The ERD was also sensitive to the manner in which the delegation might be peppered with questions concerning U.S. interests in former bases in South Vietnam, and USN ship visits to Vietnamese ports. Though ISA had taken great pains to disabuse the press in Washington, and political analysts and commentators, that the U.S. military was jealously eyeing Cam Ranh Bay, or hoping for an opportunity to berth U.S. ships while elements of the 6th Fleet enjoyed shore leave in Saigon, the ERD was concerned that the matter would be raised in their meetings with policy makers and service representatives anyway. Notwithstanding the DoD position on this issue, in the weeks before the ERD delegation departed Vietnam bound for the U.S., the western press, sometimes citing Administration sources, breathed life once again into the notion that the U.S. was anxious to steam into Cam Ranh, pay a ship visit to Hue or some other site, and begin discussions with the Socialist Republic that would result in regular port calls.[3] These views, and statements attributed to U.S. sources, did not escape the attention of the Vietnamese. The Vietnamese Embassy in Washington accepted assurances that this matter would not be part of the agenda during the visit at any point, though the delegation would be briefed on the U.S. Navy's global port call practices and policies, to clarify misgivings about ship visits, to set the issue in context, and to provide basic data aimed at dispelling fundamental Vietnamese misunderstandings of U.S. Naval diplomacy. However, the Embassy was bemused that the press would argue that ship visits and access issues would be central to discussions between the Pentagon and the visiting delegation despite DoD statements to the contrary.

These concerns underscored the cautious position the ERD had taken on the prospects for a normal defense relationship, the tentativeness with which the ERD agreed to press forward with the proposed six point plan put forward by the U.S. side in late 1996, and the number of significant and sensitive issues that would influence the shape of working level dialogue between ISA and the ERD over the course of the next three years. Interestingly, on the U.S. side of the equation, the only contentious part of the planning for this visit was the ISA proposal that the Senior Colonels receive a briefing from the Defense Security Assistance Agency on foreign military sales policies and laws governing the sale of military equipment and training to foreign countries. State Department's Bureau of Political Military Affairs opposed including this briefing as part of the delegation's itinerary in Washington because it might suggest a willingness to begin arms sales. It seemed, though, that a factual presentation of the thicket of legislation governing this process would elucidate for the Vietnamese the extent to which such sales would not be part of the landscape of a normal defense relationship for many years. Armed service representatives in the working group felt that a DSAA briefing would take the heat off the services on the weapons sales issue. In the end, since this was the only sticking point in the proposed visit schedule, ISA removed the proposed briefing from the draft itinerary.

The Senior Colonels Visit

In late February, the delegation of Senior Colonels representing the People's Army of Vietnam traveled to Washington and Hawaii for the first exchange in the calendar of events discussed during the October 1996 meeting in Hanoi. Of the seven senior colonels who traveled to PACOM and Washington in late February 1997, only one had combat experience. So much of PAVN from the top levels of the Defense Ministry to the department-level executive offices of the various general departments on down was composed of "specialists" and staff officers who made their rank doing bureaucratic things for the military. Rifle platoon commanders who, first, survived the war and, second, worked their way up the ladder of ranks, were relatively rare by the early–1990s.

The delegation was headed by Vu Tan, a native of Vinh Phu Province, who joined the People's Army in 1960, spent four years in officers' training, and ascended the ranks from platoon leader as a second lieutenant in 1965–67 to company commander as a first lieutenant in 1970–71. Following three years as a battalion commander, with the rank of captain, in 1976 Tan was assigned to the school of diplomacy, and between 1978 and 1980 served as the Defense Ministry's expert on the Soviet Union in the External Relations Department. From 1980 to 1984 he was the deputy military attaché in Poland, with the rank of major. Tan spent two years in the Political Military Academy, as a lieutenant colonel, and emerged in 1985 to head the International Division of the ERD, a position he held until 1990 with the rank of colonel. He returned to the National Defense Academy between 1993 and 1995, and in 1995, with the rank of senior colonel, became the Director of the ERD. He was promoted to the rank of major general in 2000.

The visit presented an opportunity to reiterate the central messages delivered by the DASD/AP during his October trip: that the defense relationship should unfold in measured, careful ways, at a pace comfortable for both countries, and in a manner that was not aimed at targeting any third country. Further, the visit by the senior colonels would enable the U.S. side to restate the view that military-to-military relations should sustain the priority placed on POW/MIA cooperation by the U.S. government, and should keep pace with the development of other dimensions of the relationship.[4]

During the Washington component of the visit, the delegation, hosted by the Office of the Assistant Secretary of Defense for International Security Affairs, received a briefing from the Defense POW/MIA Office, called on representatives of the armed services, visited the Coast Guard headquarters, met with Assistant Secretary of Defense for International Security Affairs Franklin Kramer, DASD/AP Campbell, Deputy Assistant Secretary of State Jeffrey Bader, and conducted discussions with Defense Department specialists on regional security issues at the National Defense University, an event hosted by the Commandant of the National War College.

Throughout the visit, the delegation leader, Senior Colonel Vu Tan, emphasized that the most important message he would take back to Vietnam was that high-ranking U.S. government officials shared the view that promoting friendship and establishing military-to-military contacts was important and appropriate at this time. The PAVN delegation offered an upbeat assessment of Vietnam's domestic stability, and the effectiveness of the economic reforms, and reiterated the commitment to hew to a foreign policy approach that stressed building friendly relations with many countries. Vu Tan repeatedly stated his view that the U.S.–Vietnamese military-to-military relationship was moving forward, beginning with the exchange of several delegations. The Defense Ministry would dispatch a Defense Attaché to Washington, and CINCPAC was scheduled to visit Vietnam in March, Tan noted. Vietnam was prepared to receive a U.S. National Defense University delegation in mid-year. This part of the relationship, Tan observed, should continue to develop, especially in the face of current "favorable conditions," including a good understanding of the potential for bilateral military relations, and a willingness to "overcome difficulties" by "exchanging perspectives."

Tan reiterated Vietnam's commitment to continued POW/MIA cooperation. Foreshadowing a theme that would figure prominently in subsequent ISA-ERD meetings, Tan pointed out that Vietnam still counted more than 300,000 service personnel as missing soldiers. This meant that "hundreds of thousands" of Vietnamese mothers endured anguish similar to what the families of American MIAs experienced. However, Tan concluded, whereas the U.S. and Vietnam had jointly resolved more than one-third of America's MIA cases, Vietnam had managed to recover the remains of only 7,000 of the 300,000 missing PAVN troops. Tan characterized the POW/MIA matter as a sensitive issue, and stressed that even after normalization had been achieved, Vietnam's level of cooperation had not slacked off as many U.S. officials had speculated would happen, demonstrating the real strength of Hanoi's promises and commitments. On bilateral issues, Tan repeated his Ministry's desire to move in a quiet, phased and cautious manner to build the defense relationship. That contrasted with off-line probes from members of Tan's delegation concerning the potential for a visit to the U.S. by Defense Minister Doan Khue.

The visit by the Senior Colonel's delegation was the first ice-breaking step of the process, intended to begin the business of becoming acquainted. The proposal was concocted in advance of the October 1996 meeting in Hanoi as a means of attracting the Defense Ministry to take some step that could be understood as a signal of their interest in exploring the possibilities of a military relationship. The Vietnamese demonstrated a reluctance to get drawn into practical, program-oriented cooperation with the U.S. military; they were reluctant to agree to host military training teams even on such generic topics as airport safety. When it appeared that most everything the U.S. brought to the table would be greeted with skepticism, the idea for an "orientation visit" was hatched as a means of getting agreement to something substantial in the way of an inaugural event.

The visit brought the two working level offices that would manage the start-up stage of the relationship, ISA and the ERD, into close proximity for the first time, highlighting the information gaps between the two systems, differences in leadership, and the distinct styles of operation and extent of authority that each office brought to the table.

For the ERD, the trip was a prolonged, often tiring, civics lesson about the organization and structure of the U.S. defense establishment. The six PAVN officers came with little real comprehension of the size and shape of the armed forces, and much less of an understanding of defense policy making, the constitutional concept of civilian control of the military, the practical relationship between the uniformed services and the civilian defense leadership, the laws that governed defense and security assistance, and aspects of professional military life including educational requirements, career paths, and promotion standards.[5] For its part, ISA had understood, but not comprehended, the extent to which the Defense Ministry functioned in essential isolation from the Foreign Ministry, with little daily oversight, interaction and coordination on policy issues. For the ERD, the trip revealed the profound cultural differences that would require special attention to the effort to sustain a dialogue between U.S. civilian policy advisors and political appointees, and uniformed Vietnamese defense officials. For ISA, the visit underscored the extent to which the ERD functioned as a transmission belt, and operated with little flexibility in narrowly draw confines, requiring the intervention of a senior defense official at many decision points that simply did not require the same level of decision within the Pentagon. For the ERD, official America must have seemed awash in facts, data sheets, slides and handouts. From the perspective of a system accustomed to controlled information, and a bureaucratic culture that essentially eschewed sharing data, the Pentagon clearly struck the ERD as an example of information anarchy. From the vantage point of a system with clear cut, simple, direct lines of authority, the Washington decision making environment which the ERD met for the first time during this visit must have seemed incomprehensible. For ISA's part, the first introduction to ERD showed a stiff, unyielding and decision-adverse structure, a conveyor belt for information rather than a factory for original policy initiatives. Senior Colonel Vu Tan functioned as the spokesman through the visit, eclipsing the other members of the delegation. He was the sole voice at meetings, though on the margins of all formal events various members of the delegation were prepared to speak to issues or volunteer their own views. In general, Tan's remarks were rehearsed reiterations of conventional policy positions. He carefully relied on the script, and would not be drawn out on most issues beyond a circumscribed perimeter. He was especially reticent about discussing what he described as "Chinese internal affairs." When it was quietly made clear that the second day of the National Defense University round table would be judged as something other than a success if no discussion took place, Tan took the cue but only provided a slightly expanded version of his mission statement as his contribution to the dialogue.

"Next Steps" Issues

In January, and again during the Senior Colonels visit in February, ISA proposed that a "working level" meeting with the ERD be convened to discuss the next steps in the defense relationship. The original proposal called for a June or July session which would put the DoD Working Group together with ERD staffers, shifting the process to a notch below the DASD level to enable both sides to dispense with the protocol associated with higher level meetings. In ISA's view, the session would facilitate a frank dialogue regarding the problems associated with developing an agenda for the defense relationship, and allow the two sides to clarify issues, such as the ERD's discomfort with the proposed visit of DoD humanitarian affairs program specialists, and a military law experts delegation, both of which had been vetoed by the ERD.

However, the Vietnamese side was not quite enamored with the idea of tamping things down to a lesser level. During March, and through early April, the Vietnamese urged that the Defense Minister be invited to visit Washington in late spring or early summer. In his written response to the end-of-tour letter from Secretary of Defense William Perry, sent to defense ministers worldwide, Defense Minister Doan Khue noted his own desire to visit Washington to discuss security issues. Though the Vietnamese were serious about this, and had been hinting at it since September 1996, ISA believed that the timing was not right for such a step. A visit before the two sides had articulated a relationship would consist entirely of optics, which might have been sufficient for Khue but which would have hurt the DoD commitment to fashioning a relationship aimed at encouraging practical bilateral cooperation.[6] However, the ERD continued to drive hard to secure agreement to such a meeting. The Vietnamese Defense Ministry appeared less concerned with the optics of defense relations with the U.S. than with securing an agreement to a visit by Khue, and had grown weary of countering the argument that a precipitous pace in the U.S.–Vietnamese defense relationship would unnerve China, with negative consequences for all the players in this equation. The Vietnamese were stressing the protocol, and ISA was urging practical, lower-level opportunities for dialogue and cooperation. When ISA declared that rushing into an embrace signaled by a meeting between the Secretary of Defense and the Minister would guarantee that the region, and others attentive to this relationship, would see the mutual goal as being aimed at keeping China off balance, the ERD response showed that the Vietnamese felt that they had insulated themselves against negative consequences by continuing to accord the relationship with Beijing top priority.

In ISA's view, there were ample domestic policy and political reasons for proceeding cautiously. But there was also sufficient reason to attempt to consolidate achievements, and push forward to implement the basic agreements struck in October 1996. To accomplish these goals, ISA supported proposed activities that were not part of the six point plan discussed and agreed to in October 1996, approaching such events on a case by case basis, and setting them firmly and explicitly in the context of the concept of the relationship articulated at the October 1996 meeting and in subsequent working level interactions with the ERD.[7] For example, in February 1997 ISA took the position that Vietnam should be invited to the 14th International Seapower Symposium scheduled to be held in Newport, Rhode Island, in November 1997. Though this conference was not discussed at the October 1996 meeting, it fell well within the parameters of blessed multilateral activities to which the Vietnamese could be invited. Moreover, it fit with ISA's interest in gradually expanding the parameters of bilateral defense interaction, and drawing the Vietnamese into such multilateral environments encouraging dialogue on defense issues. Additionally, in mid–March ISA supported the proposal for meetings with the Foreign Ministry and Defense Ministry for a delegation representing the Chief of Naval Operations Executive Panel's Task Force on Pacific Security.[8] Though this activity was not part of the six point plan laid out for the Vietnamese Defense Ministry in October 1996, it represented an opportunity to bring senior American academic and think tank specialists focused on Asia into contact with Vietnamese foreign policy and defense officials and experts. ISA sought to convince the ERD that the visit by the six well-known American experts could contribute to the first stages of dialogue on defense and security issues, a goal that fit with the aim articulated at the October 1996 of coaxing the Vietnamese Defense Ministry to bring military specialists into contact, expand dialogue on national security issues, organize visits between military schools and institutions, and gradually elevate the level of official interaction between U.S. and SRV defense officials, while maintaining the priority focus on accounting for missing U.S. service personnel.

The Vietnamese were not at all comfortable with these attempts to include activities in the calendar of events that had not been explicitly discussed during the October 1996 meeting, even when they could be accurately depicted as falling within the broad contours of the original plan. The ERD bridled at what they saw as DoD efforts to push the envelop in a way that did not necessarily advance the primary Vietnamese goal of arranging a meeting between the Defense Minister and the Secretary of Defense. The highest levels of the Defense Ministry were inclined to strictly interpret the opening agreements, and to deflect requests to add activities to the agreed-upon calendar. ISA sought some flexibility so that activities that fell within the trajectory of the first steps to develop a defense relationship could be included in the plan. The ERD was not inclined to consider "add-on" events, and essentially blunted attempts to press proposals forward on a case-by-case basis.

It was hard to square ERD concerns over efforts to push this envelop on low-level activities with the Defense Ministry's desire to press ahead toward a ministerial-level visit. On one hand, the MND leadership was not prepared to go beyond the six original initiatives until both sides had defined what the system would bear during the scheduled summer meeting between the ERD and ISA. On the other hand, the Vietnamese defense leadership believed that the Vietnamese defense relationship with the U.S. should resemble the U.S.–Chinese defense relationship. Anything less than the treatment accorded China's Defense Minister during Chi Haotian's visit to the United States in December 1996 would shortchange the strategic importance of Vietnam. Hanoi eagerly looked forward to meetings between U.S. and Vietnamese defense officials that matched the high level of interaction characterizing the Sino-American defense relationship.[9]

The Vietnamese looked at a Defense Minister visit as a means of gaining a seal of approval for the idea of a bilateral defense relationship. Once the highest levels of the defense establishment had sat down together, it would become easier for the Ministry to agree to all manner of military-to-military interaction. The U.S. side was more concerned with shaping the contours of a relationship, and taking the first few steps in a manner that demonstrated a real, practical interest in military relations. The Vietnamese believed the multilateral meetings and efforts to put military specialists together would be easier in a context in which the two defense chiefs had met. ISA took the view that a ministerial level meeting would be an empty gesture unless there was some record of the most basic sorts of interaction and dialogue between the U.S. and the Vietnamese defense ministries that could serve as an example of what the future might hold.

Though there were few practical breakthroughs in the first quarter of 1997, the Vietnamese remained positively predisposed to normal relations in general and the military-to-military relationship in particular. In mid–April broadcasts and articles in the Vietnamese news media suggested that the success of the visit to Vietnam by U.S. Treasury Secretary Rubin, Vietnam's signing of the agreement to assume responsibility for settling loans belonging to the former Government of South Vietnam, and the general agreement to "resolve outstanding differences" paved the way for the confirmation of Ambassador Peterson, and would help nudge the issue of Most Favored Nations trading status to the front of the queue. Media essays rejected the argument that "wounds of war" still dictated the shape of Washington's approach to Hanoi, though all commentaries carefully avoided direct reference to the POW/MIA issue.

That is not to suggest the Vietnamese had begun to downplay the importance of the POW/MIA issue. In fact, they were acutely aware of the continued sensitivities of this priority matter. They could not have missed the fact that Ambassador Peterson was confirmed by the Senate only after National Security Advisor Sandy Berger signed a letter to the Senate Intelligence Committee restating the Administration's pledge to sustain priority attention to the POW/MIA issue, undertake an intelligence estimate evaluating Vietnamese cooperation in the process of accounting for missing U.S. service personnel, and complete a report on the two "Soviet documents" which were found in Russian archives and contained assertions regarding the number of live U.S. prisoners in Vietnamese custody during the early 1970s.

The Vietnamese government remained scrupulously attentive to cooperation with the JTFFA. Operationally there was no diminishment of the attention paid to the issue of missing U.S. personnel, though politically it was increasingly difficult for the Vietnamese to portray the relationship with the U.S. as being in their sovereign interest as long as there was a single issue orientation that determined the pace and scope of all matters. Cooperation will continue, Vietnamese news articles suggested, and senior Foreign Ministry officials echoed that message, but there would be real sensitivities to the message that progress in areas such as the trade agreement and Most Favored Nations trading status were contingent upon POW/MIA progress. Vietnamese officials took pains to point out that all these dimensions of the relationship must proceed simultaneously; one aspect of the relationship should not determine the pace of progress in other areas.[10] Vietnamese officials stressed that the development of the U.S.–Vietnamese military relationship must be seen in the context of the continuing normalization of the overall relationship. There had been gradual and deliberate advances in economics, in scientific and technological exchanges, and in trade and economic relations. Progress in the defense and security realm fit into this process in a meaningful way.

However, Vietnamese officials noted the need for caution and perspective in moving into discussions of "next steps," especially as follow-on activities became larger, more visible and consequential public events that required considerable planning and strategic evaluation. According to a senior party official, Vietnam engaged in relationships with other militaries that included, among other things, ship visits and other exchanges "of a friendly nature." There were various forms such relationships could take, and the U.S. and Vietnam must probe for the one that was sensible for both sides at the moment. The two countries should pursue ways to follow up these initial steps taken through the end of the first quarter of 1997. The party official noted that Vietnam did welcome ship visits, and had agreed to port calls by Thai, Indonesian and French naval vessels. However, that form of military cooperation required very specific and technical cooperation between defense ministries and sustained, detailed discussions of modalities. It was important to Vietnam, the party official observed, that no country misunderstand the meaning of the U.S.–Vietnamese military relationship, and this was especially true as both countries explored the feasibility of a ship visit.

Suspending the Program

In late April, the ERD notified the U.S. Defense Attaché of their intention to postpone the three events scheduled for May and June, explaining that the Defense Ministry would be occupied during those months with preparations for the upcoming National Assembly elections, and could not go forward with the National Defense University visit, one of the six initiatives agreed to in October 1996; the West Point historians visit, agreed to under the rubric of contact between military specialists, the last of the six initiatives; and the visit by the Chief of Naval Operations' Executive Panel Pacific Task Force visit scheduled for May or June. Though not part of the package of six initiatives discussed in October 1996, the proposal for the visit by the Pacific Task Force did not elicit an objection from the ERD when the trip was first proposed. The U.S. Defense Attaché's interlocutor from the External Relations Department, Colonel Phan The Minh, indicated that other visits and events involving third countries would also be cancelled for the same reason. He added, enigmatically, that some foreign relations had more complex histories than others, suggesting some additional motivations behind the ERD decision to alter the plan for the remaining 1997 activities. Importantly, a full 72 hours after the ERD explained the cancellations to the U.S. Defense Attaché, the Foreign Ministry had still not been informed of the Defense Ministry's decision.[10] The Defense Ministry may have been preoccupied with activities related to preparations for the 20 July National Assembly elections. There were military issues at stake in that process. For example, in mid–April the ninth National Assembly adopted revisions of the 1992 law on the elections of deputies to the legislature, including a provision that raised the maximum number of deputies to 450 from 400. As of late April there was no indication of whether candidates not approved by the party would be allowed to stand for election, but there was precedent that suggested such a step was not entirely out of the realm of possibility. That itself would have been reason enough for the Vietnamese Communist Party to mobilize all forces, including the defense establishment, to protect the balance of power and preserve the party's edge through the election of delegations with the right political complexion. The Defense Ministry's representative to the party, the Military Committee, would have had a real role in strategizing responses to an election that seated delegates representing interests not entirely in sync with the party. However, the Defense Ministry was well aware that there would be an election when they agreed to the six initiatives intended to stand as the first steps in the U.S.–Vietnamese defense relationship in October 1996, and the MND could have anticipated their obligations at that point. The VNCP may have viewed this as a fundamentally important election, but they did not suddenly proclaim it a critical event at the end of April 1997. Later, a senior Vietnamese Foreign Ministry official confessed surprise that the Defense Ministry would have any obligations that would compel changes in scheduled events as the result of impending National Assembly elections.

The decision to cancel the three events in advance of the July National Assembly election may have been part of a "circling of the wagons" before a major political event. The cancellation might have been part of an effort to emphasize national security equities and caution about foreign threats at a juncture at which Vietnam was signing up to many regional and international initiatives. A flare-up of concerns regarding Voice of America criticisms of alleged Vietnamese "forced labor" policies, and the approach of the anniversary of the liberation of South Vietnam in late April may have combined to give the government reason to stand down temporarily, regroup and undertake a reassessment of the trajectory of specific foreign relationships, including the U.S.–Vietnamese defense relationship.

Importantly, after the cancellation of the three events, senior Vietnamese defense and Foreign Ministry officials took great pains to convey the message that there was no political meaning behind the decision to "postpone" the activities. The Defense Ministry recognized that it would be extremely busy with meetings in advance of the election that would not be limited to hand picked candidates approved by the party, according to such officials. Since anyone could stand for election, the military found it necessary to "meet with the people," to travel to constituencies to explain policies, answer questions, and support the candidacy of delegates. These SRV officials emphasized that the unfortunate inability to go forward with the planned trips did not represent anything that should be construed as an anti–American statement, and reiterated the need for patience and understanding in this early stage of the U.S.–Vietnamese defense relationship.

The decision could have reflected Hanoi's concerns regarding Beijing's view of the growing relationship between the U.S. and the SRV. Desaix Anderson has speculated that the quid pro quo for China's agreement in March 1997 to discuss the issues of the Spratleys and other South China Sea islands in a multilateral forum "may have involved a slowing of Vietnam's development of military ties with the United States."[11] However, subsequent Chinese expressions of encouragement for bilateral defense relations between Washington and Hanoi; strong Vietnamese reluctance to alter foreign and defense policy decisions in response to Chinese influence when those policies represented consensus determinations about the national good; Vietnam's own calculation that its security future required more than just a solid and stable relationship with Beijing; and Hanoi's commitment to securing a sound alignment with ASEAN and other foreign players combine to suggest that the decision to cancel the remainder of the planned events for 1997 was probably not the result of Hanoi's perception that presumed Chinese concerns over the development of U.S.–Vietnamese military ties required a quick and public ratcheting down of the fledgling defense relationship.

Additionally, there was circumstantial evidence suggesting that the consensus regarding foreign and defense policies was unraveling as more orthodox party and government officials asked whether the effort to expand relations needed to be more selective, and questioned whether the investments in developing the normal relationship with Washington had been disproportionate to the gains for Vietnam so far. That may have explained some of the Vietnamese military's nervous response to already agreed upon events, as PAVN prepared to defend its policies and actions in front of increasingly active, educated and critical National Assembly committees. Those committees required full reports about national policy issues that were prepared through laborious exercises coordinated by the VNCP's External Relations Department in conjunction with the Foreign Ministry's party organization, provincial external services, and appropriate Foreign Ministry regional bureaus.

That, however, did not quite explain why this decision to postpone the three events was undertaken in such an uncoordinated manner, with the Foreign Ministry and the Embassy in Washington left out of the loop. It is clear that the Vietnamese were not satisfied with the pace and scope of economic normalization, and may have been seeking ways to telegraph that view in a manner that was not costly to the overall relationship. The Defense Ministry, taking the view of the government, wanted to move quickly toward a trade agreement, and was not happy with having to deal with immigration issues as required by the Jackson-Vanik amendment. Later, when it became clear that a bilateral trade agreement would negatively impact on the military's investments in state owned enterprises, the MND's ardor for the BTA cooled, and the Defense Ministry was somewhat less of a forceful proponent for a quick, early agreement to the terms of the BTA. During 1996–1998, the MND's strong support for granting Vietnam MFN status had less to do with defining a short route toward a BTA than the military's sense that by withholding this status, the United States was acting highhandedly and insultingly to the Socialist Republic.

If the Vietnamese intended to express dissatisfaction with the pace at which the relationship was unfolding, they could have selected a more meaningful way of demonstrating their position, sought wider agreement to the postponement within the government, coordinated the approach, and managed the announcement of it in a more consequential manner, selecting a route with more visibility than a letter from the ERD to the U.S. Defense Attaché. That is, the MND would probably have taken steps to remove the ambiguity from the message, and perhaps announced it at a higher level. The events in question were of such modest consequence that it was difficult to see under what circumstances the ministry might have understood the cancellation of these visits to be a good means of communicating its concerns to the U.S.

In retrospect, it appears that the ERD made a decision to abort the last three activities scheduled for 1997, presumably with at least the knowledge of senior Defense Ministry officials, with the intention of showing the DoD that planned military contacts offered Vietnam some clear though minor dividends, and that Vietnam was prepared to take advantage of those — the first three steps in the "six pack" were Vietnam-centered events. However, Vietnam was not enamored enough with the U.S. plan for the first stages of defense relations, and could walk away from that part of the agreement that was composed of U.S.-centered events, signaling the MND's desire for a greater degree of Vietnamese control over the pace and scope of the start-up process. The message, and the uncoordinated nature of the decision, suggest that the MND was prepared to allow the ERD to act on its instincts, in order to demonstrate the hesitancy, suspicion and lingering second thoughts of the military officials managing the initial talks with the U.S. side. One senior Vietnamese official stated that the ERD was not necessarily effective or experienced enough in discerning the importance of events such as the three postponed visits. While the ERD could appreciate the importance of the CINCPAC visit, they had no real understanding, according to this official, of what a delegation such as the proposed NDU visit represented in the context of the U.S. system. Other Vietnamese defense officials made much of the fact that this was a "postponement," not a cancellation, in order to drive home the point that the decision to pull the plug on the three activities did not portend bad news for the entire concept of defense relations with the U.S. DoD made it plain that no matter what it was called, the deci-sion ended activities for the year, walked back on the ideas discussed and agreed to in October 1996, and thereby undermined DoD confidence that Vietnam was genuinely interested in a military relationship with the U.S.

The official ISA response was a muted statement of disappointment. The Vietnamese response sought to minimize the consequences of the cancellations, and restate confidence in the normalization process. In a 29 April meeting at the Pentagon, Vice Minister of Foreign Affairs Nguyen Dinh Bin told ASD/ISA Kramer that the "postponements" reflected the practical realities of the Defense Ministry's work schedule in advance of the mid–July National Assembly elections. Bin pointed approvingly at the events that had taken place — the exchange of defense attachés, the DASD/AP visit to Hanoi, and the senior colonels delegation. He urged continued progress in the military relationship in the context of improvements to the entire bilateral relationship, in which economic normalization represented the most important part of the process. Kramer replied that the Pentagon hoped to be able to go forward with plans to convene a working level meeting in Hanoi in August to agree to concepts and plans for the next steps in the defense relationship.

In subsequent exchanges with Vietnamese defense officials, embassy representatives, and in communications with the ERD, ISA sought to show that the decision to postpone the three events had changed the rules of engagement, and resulted in a decision to confine further discussions and decisions to the working level until there was sufficient reason to believe, confidently, that the Vietnamese side was serious about the relationship, and would adhere to agreements. ISA was not inclined to risk another rebuff at the deputy assistant secretary level, and made it clear that until the U.S. side felt that solid and sustainable agreements were in place, the nuts and bolts of the start-up phase of defense relations would be managed at a level below the deputy assistant secretary of defense. ISA emphasized the importance of making certain that both sides understood the need to come to the August working level meeting prepared to scrutinize a laundry list of alternatives for the next 12 to 18 months. Both the U.S. and the SRV needed to emerge from that meeting with a high degree of certainty that a calendar of events for the military-to-military relationship acceptable to both sides had been hammered out at the working level.

The Vietnamese did not appear to hesitate at this juncture, or react negatively to ISA's description of how the work of developing future plans would proceed. There was some concern about the optics of conducting the working level meetings with the senior colonel who headed the ERD. The Vietnamese initially questioned, in quiet ways, the equivalence of ISA and ERD, and may have been ill at ease about matching a senior military officer with a civilian bureaucrat for such talks. Ambassador Bang and the MFA America's Department may have taken steps to much to convey the view that ISA was the right office with which ERD should be doing business.

As a result of the cancellation of the last three events in the 1997 plan, both sides drifted toward more clearly circumscribed, less ambitious recommendations for future events. In the aftermath of the cancellations, the Vietnamese shifted their position on the timing, if not importance, of a visit to Vietnam by the Secretary of Defense. The ERD came to take the view that a senior U.S. defense official should visit Vietnam before a senior Vietnamese MND official visited the U.S. In late April, Vietnam's Defense Attaché, Vo Dinh Quang, suggested that there should be a senior level visit by an MND representative in early or mid–1998. He did not specify the level of such a visit, but he did say that his own Ministry had made it clear that 1998 would be more convenient for such a visit to the U.S. He also observed that since the U.S. had already dispatched a DASD to Vietnam, followed by the CINCPAC visit, it would make sense that the next high-level delegation should be from the Vietnamese side so that the program did not look to be entirely focused on American travel to Vietnam. Quang later explained that if the Vietnamese visited Washington first, this would trigger all manner of speculation about Vietnam's purpose, about Vietnam's alliance with the U.S., and generate considerable concern in Beijing, whereas a visit by the Secretary of Defense could be more easily explained, would not raise as many eyebrows, prompt diplomatic gossip about Vietnam's unholy plans to buy its security from Washington, or stimulate potentially harmful speculation that such an event was configured to isolate China.

Though the Vietnamese did not respond to the proposal for a working level meeting until mid–June, by May it appeared that the MND had no objections to such a session. However, the Ministry would not make the formal decision until after the National Assembly election. In the interim, ISA and the ERD conducted discussions on the modalities of the working level meeting. At ISA's urging, the ERD agreed that a working level meeting could avoid excessive protocol, enable direct, straightforward talk, and make it easier to figure out what was acceptable to each side without having to be overly concerned with courtesies.[12] The presumption, on the U.S. side, was that would be easier for one side to say "no" to a working level counterpart than to reject a proposal placed on the table by a Deputy Assistant Secretary of Defense or a Vice Minister. The planning session would facilitate a "joint" approach to the construction of a calendar of events, with each side contributing to the process and working to nail down mutually acceptable programs that would then be presented to senior-level officials for their blessing. The Vietnamese MND appeared to agree to this course, but offered no specific thoughts on how to insure that the meeting would be productive and involve a two-way sharing of proposals for military-to-military events.

What emerged was a set of operating procedures for working level meetings that placed a primacy on openness, transparency, and real two-sided efforts, and a group of rules governing interaction that aimed at eliminating surprise issues, and guaranteeing that sensitive or complex proposals from either side received some prior airing. In theory, the working level meeting, from the U.S. side's perspective, was to be a wrestling match out of which would emerge a set of proposals for a calendar year of events that would then be presented to the Pentagon decision-makers, and the MND leadership, for their formal agreement. From the ERD's perspective, the meeting was to be a chance for an unceremonious presentation of proposals that would require vetting at levels considerably above the pay grade of the ERD.

During May and June, PACOM pressed for a quicker pace in the relationship, endorsing the idea of moving rapidly to the level of a visit to Vietnam by the Secretary of Defense, and urging a robust and "balanced" calendar, with an equal number of Vietnamese and American events in the final U.S. proposals to be put before the ERD. Some PACOM officials urged that the U.S. attempt to get agreement to a port call in Vietnam soon after the Hong Kong reversion. ISA thought this was the wrong course, especially since the U.S. had been saying that there was no strategic imperative driving an interest in ship visits to Vietnam. To suddenly declare an abiding interest in pressing forward with a port call would change the ground rules that had emerged in discussions between the two sides.

By mid-June, the Joint Staff, PACOM, and ISA agreed to four sets of activities: senior level visits by DoD officials and service representatives; working level delegations from the U.S. side (including the three visits that had been cancelled in April 1997); joint activities in the areas of medical research, humanitarian action, and military-to-military exchanges of information; and invitations to Vietnamese MND representatives to attend multilateral events hosted by U.S. regional commands or service commands. The calendar formulated by ISA and the Joint Staff went beyond the original notion of planning for 1998 activities, and instead devised a plan for events through the year 2000.

However, in the end, Walt Slocombe, the Under Secretary of Defense for Policy, decided that the Department could not describe a proposal that envisioned activities through to the turn of the century as a modest, incremental approach. Slocombe felt that the U.S. proposals were too robust and needed to be slimmed down so the U.S. could keep to the idea of presenting a bare bones, incremental program. Part of that viewpoint may have been the result of continued sensitivity regarding the domestic political impact of the POW/MIA issue, but it is important to note that by this juncture the POW/MIA issue had a diminished influence on military-to-military contacts, and on other aspects of the bilateral relationship. Washington continued to accord the issue priority attention, worked to focus the Vietnamese leadership on the positive impact that their cooperation could have on normalization, and made clear the negative consequences of any lessening of Vietnamese assistance to the operational efforts to account for missing Americans. However, the issue had been fenced off from the broader aspects of the relationship. The Administration had backed away from language that tied the pace and scope of normalization to proportionate POW/MIA cooperation from Vietnam or accounting results. The Administration had begun to stress the need to continue cooperation without the exacting description of how, in the event that Vietnam decided to ratchet down its POW/MIA cooperation, progress in all other areas of the relationship would be frozen. Moving away from the customary expression of the consequences for the relationship of a Vietnamese failure to comply with U.S. POW/MIA requirements was a politically difficult decision, but it was one that had a positive impact on the tone of the overall relationship. The Vietnamese grew less concerned with the political outbursts from POW/MIA interests, including activist U.S. legislators who now tended to command fewer headlines and enjoyed diminished support from colleagues on the Hill. Hanoi became more confident that their credible record of productive cooperation had helped turn this issue from a troublesome political problem to a manageable foreign policy issue.

Two pieces of POW/MIA-related draft legislation, both introduced Senator Bob Smith, remained problematic through May. The first piece (introduced in cooperation with Senator Sam Johnson) provided statutory authority and procedures aimed at enhancing the activities of the U.S.–Russia Joint Committee on POW/MIAs. The second was a section in the Intelligence Authorization Bill that sought to place the budget for the Defense POW/MIA Office back in the hands of the intelligence community. The price of Ambassador Peterson's confirmation was a letter signed by National Security Advisor Sandy Berger committing the Administration to commissioning an intelligence community assessment of the two Soviet Documents uncovered in GRU archives that concluded there were more POWs in Hanoi's control in 1972–73 than were repatriated at Operation Homecoming. That was the opening gambit in a concerted effort by Smith to replace DPMO with a more malleable mechanism.

At the mid-year point, overall bilateral relations were proceeding in a positive way. Hanoi understood that the U.S. was obligated by law to seek assurances on remaining emigration issues in order to proceed with a Jackson-Vanik waiver and the opening of EXIM bank financing that would provide a major boost to U.S. businesses in Vietnam. State Department felt action on the waiver would help convince Vietnam that Washington was serious about full normalization as both sides worked through the remaining steps in preparing a trade agreement.

The U.S. had provided Vietnam with a draft text of the trade agreement. Working level talks were to resume to write the annexes to the agreement explaining how the Vietnamese would implement its provisions. The conclusion of a bilateral copyright agreement and a debt settlement agreement in May, Treasury Secretary Rubin's April visit to Vietnam, and Secretary of State Madeline Albright's June visit were critical steps. State Department favored moving ahead on OPIC and Trade Development Assistance, and was set on opening a consulate general in Ho Chi Minh City as soon as possible. American consular services issues and problems were concentrated in the south, and American businesses were clamoring for the support that a consulate could provide. Growing relations required the adjudication of tourist or B-2 visas, which could most effectively be accomplished through a consulate. State Department was pressing for a suitable downtown property for the new Embassy in Hanoi. The Vietnamese opened a consulate general in San Diego in July, headed by a talented Foreign Ministry official who had long been chief of the Americas Department, Nguyen Xuan Phong. On 30 May, the Foreign Ministry passed to the U.S. Embassy a partial list of individuals who had received exit permits under the Resettlement Opportunities for Vietnamese Returnees (ROVR), demonstrating that the highest levels of the Vietnamese government wanted to work cooperatively to reach closure on the refugee issue.

The Question of Pace

At mid-year, PAVN was preoccupied with modernizing its arms inventories, rationalizing all aspects of military education, developing an indigenous arms repair and production capability — still at an extremely rudimentary level — and altering strategic thinking to reflect post–Cold War defense requirements. To most PAVN officers, the sources for inspiration in these areas, and the most likely sources for material assistance, were like-minded ASEAN allies, and China. At the same time, PAVN was focused on the maritime border issue and the dispute with China over claims to various islands. The military had attempted to integrate into its thinking a new way of looking at neighbors and the region. PAVN senior officers visited their Royal Thai Armed Forces counterparts, retained a close relationship with the Indonesian military, remained concerned about the border shared with Cambodia, and committed to maintaining a positive relationship with China's military through consultations and senior-level visits. To most PAVN officers, the promise of a defense relationship with the U.S. could not offer any assurances that Vietnam's defense equities would be served in the context of the thicket of regional diplomacy over disputed territories and land border disagreements.

According to Vietnamese military officers, in his 12 June meeting with Ambassador Peterson, Defense Minister Doan Khue had stressed that the development of military relations was important and should be approached in a manner that was attuned to progress in the overall relationship. Khue stated that Vietnam accepted the U.S. assessment that the military relationship had an important position in the overall bilateral relationship. He agreed with Peterson to continue to exchange delegations including possible high level visits during the Ambassador's tenure. Such exchanges, Khue noted, should be aimed at increasing friendship in accordance with mutual respect and understanding. Both sides should move forward to eliminate any remaining suspicions rooted in the past. Finally, Khue told Peterson that the Defense Ministry agreed in principle to "officers at the working level" meeting in August to "discuss and plan" the next steps in the bilateral defense relationship.[13]

This was the highest level at which the concept of a working group approach had been acknowledged by the Vietnamese side. In a late June meeting with ISA, the Vietnamese Defense Attaché, speaking on instructions, relayed suggestions to ISA for future activities, informed by his round of consultations with military colleagues in Hanoi conducted before he departed Vietnam to take up his post in Washington.

The military relationship, Quang stated, should be based on mutual respect, and should be mutually beneficial. The defense link must be grounded in Vietnam's policy of being friends to all nations, and conducted in accordance with Vietnam's independent and sovereign foreign policy. It should not represent "cooperation against" any nation. The military relationship should be developed step by step, the Defense Attaché noted, because there were people from both the American and the Vietnamese side who did not understand the intent behind this part of the relationship. The MIA issue was and should still be the number one priority in the relationship, not only for the humanitarian benefit of the U.S. but also for Vietnam's interest in accounting for its own missing soldiers. Beyond this, other humanitarian matters must be taken into consideration while shaping a bilateral defense relationship. For example, Quang offered, if the Vietnamese side conducted research on the impact of the wartime use of Agent Orange, the results could be beneficial to both the U.S. and Vietnam and should be shared accordingly, with this humanitarian motivation in mind. Finally, this process must be implemented in conformity with Vietnamese law.

Quang then offered several recommendations, which he clearly labeled as his own initiatives. Those recommendations seemed to push slightly beyond the kinds of activities that the MND had pronounced acceptable.

Quang urged cooperation in training on advanced technologies, discussions of information warfare and intelligence, radar system modernization, night vision technology (which he explicitly noted was required by troops stationed on the Spratly Islands), ammunition storage methods, as well as English language training and forensic medical training. Quang's recommendations may have reflected his own optimistic commitment to articulating a relationship that moved quickly to deal with practical military issues, and may have had the support of some elements in the Defense Ministry. However, his suggestions reached quite far beyond the anodyne kinds of activities the ERD was prepared to consider.

By early August, the redrafted U.S. proposal concerning the "next steps" in the defense relationship was divided into four categories of activities: (1) the restoration of the three cancelled visits, (2) a schedule of increasingly senior visits by DoD officials, (3) invitations to multilateral events sponsored by PACOM, and (4) bilateral activities between the U.S. and Vietnamese militaries. Under Secretary Slocombe supported the proposal for rescheduling the cancelled events, and the proposal for bilateral activities, but felt the proposed senior U.S. DoD visits were out of balance with expected Vietnamese visits to the U.S. He approved the concept of presenting these next steps at a working level meeting, and ISA resolved the imbalance between U.S. visits and visits the Vietnamese side might propose by reducing the number of U.S. DoD visits contained in the original package. At the working level meeting, which had by mid–August been scheduled for early September, ISA planned to propose five senior-level DoD visits to Vietnam: a trip by the Director of DIA in November 1997, a U.S. "Senior Colonels" visit in January or February 1998, a CINC-PACFLT trip in April or May 1998, a visit by the Chief of Staff of the Army in July 1998, and a September or October 1998 visit by the ASD/ISA and DASD/AP.

In August, ISA told the SRV Defense Attaché that the key expectation for the working meeting with ERD was that the meeting would involve two-way communication. ISA wanted to know the types of interaction between the two militaries that the Vietnamese side believed possible, and made it plain that if the working meeting consisted of the U.S. side pushing its recommendations across the table, and soliciting Vietnamese comments on those thoughts, then only half of the task would have been accomplished. The Vietnamese had to be prepared to present their own list of future events to the U.S. side, so both sides could compare notes, advise the Pentagon's senior leadership, and in the end agree upon a calendar that had something for everyone. Finally, ISA told the Attaché, the U.S. side wanted to share its thinking in a manner that would eliminate the possibility of surprises at the September meeting, a desire strongly shared by the ERD.

Through late August, after having agreed to meet with ISA in early September, the ERD appeared to remain somewhat ill at east with the idea of a working meeting, uncomfortable with the extent to which the entire meeting had not been laboriously pre-scripted, and not entirely prepared to agree to a "two way street" approach to the relationship.

The September Meeting

The ISA-led Working Group met with the Director and Deputy Director of the ERD from 2 to 4 September, and conducted a separate session with Vice Minister of Defense Tran Hanh. The ERD made it clear that their intention was to ratchet down the military aspect of the relationship to a level that corresponded to the rest of the bilateral relationship. The relationship, in the ERD view, had to progress in a more coordinated fashion, until more serious progress was made toward granting Most Favored Nations trading status to Vietnam, and more effective steps were taken toward a trade agreement.

The ERD agreed to recommend that the Defense Ministry's leadership approve participation in a respectable number of PACOM-sponsored multilateral conferences. They were inclined to participate in events that they had already attended, such as the Pacific Armies Management Seminar (PAMS) and the Pacific Area Senior Officer Logistics Seminar (PASOLS), but were not inclined to accept proposals that they send a delegation to the Pacific Areas Special Operations Conference (PASOC), which the ERD explained by alluding to "historic sensitivities" as well as the serious differences between the Vietnamese and the American special forces missions. In the category of bilateral cooperation, the Vietnamese expressed interests in activities that resonated with themes taken up by the ASEAN Regional Forum such as Search and Rescue activities (SAREX, and the Disaster Preparedness Planning Seminar). The ERD stated in-principal support for a U.S. Air Force workshop on aeromedical evacuation and search and rescue methods. They had serious reservations about mapping cooperation, and were inclined to believe that the military should follow the lead of the National Flood Committee on relations with the U.S. Army Corps of Engineers.

The Vietnamese turned aside joint activities including JCET Medical Civic Action Projects, and Engineering and Civic Action Projects (ENCAPs) that could be conducted in conjunction with the activities of the JTFFA. They expressed an interest in DoD's humanitarian assistance program excess property "shopping lists," and emphasized the need for financial assistance and technical equipment in a variety of areas, including demining and HIV disease detection. The Vietnamese side agreed to continue medical research cooperation with the Armed Forces Research Institute of Medical Sciences (AFRIMS), the Naval Medical Research Unit (NAMRU), and the Naval Environmental and Preventative Medicine Unit (NEPMU). The ERD was not enthusiastic about the demining training program, arguing that they had many years of experience with mine removal, and proposing financial or equipment assistance in the area of unexploded ordnance control and demining. The Vietnamese side noted that the U.S. Coast Guard initiatives had to be coordinated with the many other ministries involved in maritime security and law enforcement, and emphasized that the military played less of a role in border patrols than the Border Committee and the Ministry of Interior.

The ERD agreed to three visits for 1998, fewer than requested by ISA, in large part as an indication that the military relationship should continue to be confined to a modest level of activity. They stated their support, pending senior leadership review, for a U.S. Senior Colonels delegation visit in the first quarter of 1998, and a mid-year National Defense University visit, as well as a visit to Vietnam by the Assistant Secretary of Defense for International Security Affairs in September or October 1998. The ERD explicitly asked that visits by U.S. regional commanders and service chiefs be deferred until after 1998. The ERD preemptively stated that in the MND's view the relationship had not yet reached a level at which ship visits would be "appropriate." The U.S. side did not raise the question of ship visits. The ERD requested that the U.S. consider looking for a way to accomplish the West Point historians visit without utilizing the good offices of the Defense Ministry, because of what the ERD described as the lack of a good counterpart for this delegation, and asked that the Air War College visit be put off until 1999.

Finally, the Vietnamese made the point that the U.S. needed to acknowledge humanitarian responsibility for the costs of the wartime use of Agent Orange and other chemical defoliation agents. The ERD also complained about the activities of anti-regime organizations that operated in the U.S. with the goal of destabilizing the government of Vietnam. The ERD reiterated standard concerns regarding Vietnam's MIAs, and restated firm commitments to continued humanitarian cooperation with the U.S. in this area. These were themes to which the ERD would return in subsequent meetings with ISA.

Though the level of activity to which the Vietnamese agreed was below the threshold the Defense Department had hoped to establish as the jumping off point for 1998, and though the ERD had refrained from actively promoting its own ideas, choosing to respond to the menu of proposed activities put forward by the ISA-led working group, the ERD did conduct frank discussions of each initiative, and was direct in evaluating each element of the Defense Department's 1998 calendar. Moreover, they expressed willingness to consider additional information on proposals that had elicited only lukewarm or indifferent responses, which at the time suggested the possibility of convincing the ERD to add some activities to the dance card following clarifications that ISA and PACOM would provide. The result was a fairly successful process, and a calendar that represented the preferences of both the U.S. and the Vietnamese sides for a modest starting program of military interaction. However, The ERD continued to function in a vacuum of its own making. They did not bother to inform their Defense Attaché in Washington of the results of the September meeting. Their decisions appeared to have been made with no coordination outside of the Defense Ministry. Senior Vietnamese officials from other ministries evinced surprise that some of the initiatives had not been accepted by the Defense Ministry, and were puzzled as to why the ERD decided to turn aside proposed training opportunities.

In a late September meeting in Washington with Assistant Secretary of Defense Franklin Kramer, Deputy Foreign Minister Vu Khoan stressed that the September working group discussions were a real signal that a new stage had been reached in the bilateral relationship. The Vietnamese side, Khoan noted, was pleased because in addition to progress in the overall bilateral relationship, a link had been established between "military agencies." Khoan told Kramer that very successful discussions had taken place between ISA and the ERD, representing a good beginning, and suggested that this be understood as part of a step-by-step approach. Vietnam, Khoan said, needed time to prepare for such contacts. The military suffered a shortage of English language speakers. However, through a step-by-step approach the relationship could be expanded, and the Foreign Ministry was ready to cooperate with the Defense Department in order to develop the military dimension of the bilateral relationship. The Foreign Ministry welcomed that development because, as Khoan explained, a military relationship with the U.S. could contribute to developing confidence in the overall relationship, and also make a contribution to stability and security in the region. Khoan proposed a "relationship" between the Department of Defense and the Ministry of Foreign Affairs, in the form of an agreement to routine consultations that would also involve the Defense Ministry, explaining that Vietnam conducted such consultations with Australia, as well as less formal consultations with other countries such as Japan. Khoan concluded by noting that the U.S. and the SRV could use the ASEAN Regional Forum as another means of sustaining such "contacts." In response, Kramer observed that such meetings between the Defense Department and senior Vietnamese officials were remarkable reminders of how far the U.S. and Vietnam had come in the relationship, and represented good reasons to pause and contemplate the possibilities for the future. Kramer acknowledged that the military aspect of the bilateral relationship only represented one small dimension of U.S.–Vietnamese ties, and that there were many other parts to this link, including trade and economic relations. The U.S. and Vietnam needed to find ways to work together to mutually beneficial ends in all aspects of the relationship.

Kramer told Khoan that DoD felt the schedule of events for 1998 that had emerged from the September meetings represented the appropriate level of activity for this stage of the U.S.–Vietnamese defense relationship. The U.S. was prepared to be patient, he told Khoan, and prepared to proceed in a step-by-step fashion to develop military ties. The U.S. had a long-term commitment to the region. Kramer emphasized that he was well aware that both sides had issues that were legacies of the war, and that the U.S. and Vietnam could work on those issues together. The Assistant Secretary concluded by noting that the step-by-step approach to the bilateral defense relationship was sensible, and could create an environment in which the U.S. and Vietnam might find that they could do more. However, for the time being, he observed, both sides should go forward with plans for 1998 events defined during the early September talks in Hanoi.

ISA's goal, in the aftermath of the September planning meeting with ERD, was to resist the impulse to press the Vietnamese to walk back from their opposition to activities specifically rejected during the talks in Hanoi. At this point, there was still a high level of interest within the Pacific Command, and the U.S. Army, as well as the Coast Guard, to nudge things forward beyond the limits the Vietnamese side had set in the working level discussions. The Vietnamese, however, had been clear about the kinds of engagement they found unacceptable at this stage of the relationship. There seemed to be no percentage in attempting to convince the ERD to change their considered positions so soon after the formal discussions.

Social Issues

On 9 December, Colonel Edward O'Dowd, the U.S. Defense Attaché in Hanoi, met with Senior Colonel Nguyen Manh Dau, the Director of the

MND's Social Policy Department, to follow up on points made by the Vietnamese side during an August meeting with a delegation of U.S. veterans representing the Veterans of Foreign Wars regarding the consequences of the wartime use of Agent Orange.

Dau made two points at the December meeting. First, he relayed a "request" from the Vietnamese government that the U.S. government provide "more effective assistance" to Vietnam in its efforts to account for Vietnam's MIAs. Dau asked for access to information and documents in U.S. archives that could shed light on Vietnamese troops killed in combat, or PAVN soldiers who may have died in captivity. Second, he requested, on behalf of the Vietnamese side, that the U.S. government help the SRV with funding and financial assistance to Vietnamese soldiers and civilians who were suffering from the effects of dioxins; that the U.S. provide information to the Vietnamese government on the wartime use of Agent Orange, such as spraying target areas, quantities and types of dioxins used, and details regarding aerial spraying operations; and that the U.S. government provide assistance to Vietnam's efforts to research the environmental and health impact of Agent Orange. Dau emphasized that both the MIA and the Agent Orange issue should be handled as part of the bilateral defense relationship.

Secretary of State Albright had told General Secretary Do Muoi that the U.S. was prepared to be helpful to Hanoi's efforts to account for missing and unaccounted for PAVN troops. However, placing such sensitive and potentially controversial issues at the core of the fledgling military-to-military relationship raised the prospect that U.S. "obligations" connected with these issues could become conditions for future progress. The Defense Ministry's position was that the U.S. government must "acknowledge" its humanitarian responsibilities, particularly concerning efforts to account for missing PAVN troops and the wartime use of defoliants. The Director of the ERD had stated this in the strongest terms at the September working level discussions with ISA.

The Administration was prepared to be helpful on the MIA issue, as long as the resources budgeted for the U.S. POW/MIA effort were not diverted to these other missions. The White House supported past steps to provide the Vietnamese with historical documents pertaining to their losses, and encouraged initiatives taken by American veterans organizations in these areas. By late October 1997, the National Security Council had endorsed the idea of inviting Vietnamese officials to the U.S. to discuss how to use resources in the U.S. National Archives. The NSC also supported continued U.S. efforts to search for data in U.S. government archival holdings that might assist the Vietnamese in accounting for their missing.

On Agent Orange, the Administration was prepared to conclude a bilateral scientific and technological agreement that would enable the U.S. to engage the SRV on important environmental issues, initiate cooperation with Vietnamese science and health officials, and promote government-to-government and private sector cooperation on efforts to improve Vietnam's public health service.

However, the issues were complex enough that fashioning a practical response to the Vietnamese request for assistance in these two areas would consume time and resources, and could easily become a show stopper for bilateral defense relations. For example, the Vietnamese conventional wisdom was that there were between 300,000 and 400,000 unaccounted for personnel. There were no systematic and reliable PAVN personnel histories, unit documents, or wartime records of recruitment and conscription that could form the basis of an effort to identify the missing, and no appreciable forensic capability that could be brought to bear in attempts to analyze and identify remains that might be uncovered. The Vietnamese wartime practice was to bury remains in mass graves, and post-war accounting efforts simply attempted to correlate the location of gravesites with combat operations in the vicinity as the means of identifying units involved in firefights. Individual identifications of casualties were not possible beyond the circumstantial association of identification media and personal effects with physical remains found in the area of wartime combat operations and incidents. Regarding Agent Orange, there was no basis for the assumption that joint scientific research would pay dividends. Soil samples and other data that could be collected would not necessarily reveal useful data, and could probably not distinguish the environmental impact of wartime defoliation from that of naturally occurring dioxin contamination and industrial pollution. It seemed that it would be more fruitful to focus on the systematic collection of data on birth defects, and the establishment of registries, but that was not quite the response the Vietnamese were seeking.

On 17 December, ISA told the Vietnamese Embassy's Deputy Chief of Mission, Ha Huy Thong, and his successor, Pham Van Que, that there was a distinction between making judgments regarding the pace and scope of normalization on the basis of progress in resolving specific humanitarian issues, and making progress in resolving humanitarian issues the condition for forward movement in the bilateral relationship. The Vietnamese MIA issue, and the Agent Orange issue, could become obstacles to normal defense relations, especially if progress in these areas was determined by the Vietnamese side to be a prerequisite to proceeding with activities aimed at enhancing and developing military relations. Thong responded that the Vietnamese government had not asked for financial assistance from the U.S., but rather had created a "fund" for the relief of the suffering of victims of Agent Orange to which any country or organization was free to contribute. He agreed that there was a need for caution in the language used to talk about the Agent Orange issue, and in the steps taken to move from generalities to the practical actions required to manage the issue. Finally, he agreed that the proposed mid–January 1998 meeting between ISA and ERD would be a good opportunity to review these two issues.

Conclusion

Throughout 1997, Vietnam spoke cautiously about the strategic relevance of the U.S., and clearly enumerated policy priorities and security concerns in a manner meant to show that the Socialist Republic believed its policy investments should continue to go to other relationships. Relations with the U.S. were typically last or next to last in most inventories of accomplishment, such as the foreign policy reports to the National Assembly's sessions, prefaced by references to improving ties with the European Union, and followed by passing mention of Canadian assistance programs. Foreign policy officials hailed high-level visits in both directions by increasingly senior officials, progress toward a trade agreement, steps toward normalized economic relations, and the rising levels of investments in the Vietnamese economy by U.S. companies doing business in Vietnam. Clearly, Vietnam's priority was accomplishing full economic normalization with the U.S. That was reflected in the manner in which senior defense ministry officials linked the possibility of increasing the pace and scope of defense relations to the acceleration of efforts to sign a trade agreement and complete the normalization of economic relations.

Part of this may have been the result of leadership changes that brought to the fore an even more cautious group of senior decision makers. General Le Kha Phieu, Director of the Defense Ministry's General Political Department, was named General Secretary of the Vietnamese Communist Party at the 4th plenary session of the Central Committee that closed on 29 December 1997. Incumbent General Secretary Do Muoi; President Le Duc Anh, all but incapacitated by a stroke in 1997; and former Prime Minister Vo Van Kiet, replaced at the November 1997 National Assembly session, retired from their Politburo positions and accepted appointments as Advisors to the Central Committee. Former General Secretary Nguyen Van Linh, former Prime Minister Pham Van Dong, and former

Chairman of the Council of State Vo Chi Cong stepped down from their advisory positions, to which they had been appointed in 1991 and reappointed at the 8th National Party Congress in mid–1995. Kiet, long a strong supporter of cutting edge economic reforms, was replaced by his deputy, Phan Van Khai, in late 1997, leaving the reforms without a powerhouse with the longevity and revolutionary lineage that gave Kiet the leverage necessary to build support for reformist policies. Shedding the first team of Central Committee advisors, including Linh, who jump-started Vietnam's reforms in 1987 during his first year as General Secretary, represented a significant shakeup.[14]

6

MAKING DEFENSE RELATIONS WORK, 1998

Introduction

The U.S. Colonels Delegation (March 1998) and the National Defense University trip to Vietnam (May 1998) enabled military academics to discuss issues frankly and directly. The October 1998 visit to the United States by Vice Minister of Defense Lieutenant General Tran Hanh was the first opportunity to bring a senior Vietnamese military policy maker in contact with the highest levels of the Defense Department's leadership. ISA and ERD continued to conduct planning discussions and to exchange views on regional security issues in a positive and increasingly constructive manner.

In the Pentagon's thinking, the establishment of military relations with Vietnam was consonant with, but not essential to, efforts to reinforce the region's steady progress toward prosperity, stability and cooperation.[1] Vietnam had been a serious participant in ASEAN processes, including the Regional Forum. The U.S. and Vietnam were similarly preoccupied with the consequences for the region of conventional arms proliferation, the threat posed to the fabric of societies by illicit narcotics; the need to formulate humanitarian responses to trans-national issues such as AIDs; and the importance of stability and economic progress. Hanoi and Washington recognized that all these issues impacted on national and regional security. The Defense Department looked to the possibility of developing a formal dialogue on regional security issues that could contribute to mutual understanding, and promote shared goals for a peaceful and prosperous Asia. To serve those purposes, DoD sought to increase the number of official visits, expand the visits to include service counterpart and component commander visits, and increase the range of bilateral "confidence building" activities aimed at enhancing practical bilateral cooperation. However, DoD did not seek to expand the relationship by offering training opportunities, military sales, or by putting access issues on the table, though the question of a future ship visit continued to figure in the bilateral planning dialogue. The relationship had not matured to a point at which any of those aspects of military cooperation would be politically acceptable to either the U.S. or Vietnam.

For their part, the Vietnamese continued to view the military-to-military relationship with skepticism and concern. From the perspective of a variety of senior Vietnamese government officials and diplomats, the overall relationship with the United States had developed at quite a fast pace in 1998. Such officials pointed to the fact that the U.S. was Vietnam's fifth ranking investor, that Vietnam had signed a copyright agreement, and had, in a bilateral agreement with Washington, accepted responsibility for the debts of the Republic of South Vietnam. Some officials saw slow but respectable progress on the trade agreement, and were privately confident that the U.S. would decide to go forward with a decision to grant a Jackson-Vanik waiver to Vietnam.

By the end of the year, Hanoi's assessment was that the primary aid contributors in the region, beset with their own economic problems, would probably begin to ratchet down assistance that had been crucial to Vietnam's economy. In that context, Vietnam's leadership was not inclined to embrace new aspects of the relationship with the U.S. that would not bring relief from the economic problems that the regional ripple effect brought to Hanoi's doorstep.

Reviewing the Bidding: Discussing Next Steps

The mid–January ISA meetings in Hanoi revolved around ERD's concerns about the Asia Pacific Security Studies Center in Hawaii, the upcoming U.S. Colonel's visit, MND views regarding Vietnam's MIAs and the Agent Orange issue, the U.S. Commando Compensation Law, and the issue both sides had referred to as the "reciprocity" problem, denoting the question of opportunities and access for the U.S. and the SRV defense attachés. This was not a planning session. Rather, it was one of several post-planning meeting efforts on the part of ISA to "consolidate" agreements reached at the planning meeting, or to put in place mid-course corrections.[2]

DoD wanted to see Vietnamese participation in the classes taught by the Asia Pacific Center for Security Studies (APCSS), at Pacific Command, which were aimed at fostering regional understanding and cooperation. In September 1997, the U.S. invited two Vietnamese participants for Class 98–1 (January–April 1998), and Class 98–2 (May–July 1998). At that time the ERD stated that it would not make a decision regarding this invitation until the MND's student enrolled in a 1997 session returned to Vietnam and reported on his experience. By December, the MND had decided that it would not avail itself of the opportunity to place students in the 1998 APCSS classes, based on several complaints the 1997 PAVN student reported to the Defense Ministry. One concern arose from an APCSS error involving the display of the old Government of Vietnam flag at a school event. The second concern involved the PAVN student's perception that his term paper was not distributed at the APCSS in a manner that replicated the treatment accorded to the writings of other students representing Asian and Pacific militaries. Finally, it appeared that the PAVN student felt he was called upon to defend his country's policies, and subjected to close questioning on certain issues, such as human rights, by the APCSS staff. ISA apologized for the error regarding the flag, noted that the issue of the distribution given to the student's writings had been rectified, and emphasized that the PAVN students should not shrink from frank, direct and collegial dialogue which was the central purpose of the Center. After a clarifying discussion, appropriate acknowledgement of the issues, and a description of steps taken to address the ERD's concerns, Vu Tan closed the matter. ISA told the ERD that the Asia Pacific Center was intended to promote discussion, dialogue, amicable and scholarly interchanges among and between students and staff of the Center. The MND should understand that the questions were intended in that spirit, as a means of generating interest in frank and open dialogue among friends. It appears that the flag incident did not become a problem area because of the U.S. side's preemptive apology. That eliminated the awkwardness for the Vietnamese side of having to raise the issue, and enabled the ERD to take the high road, essentially minimizing the importance of the issue, and agreeing to reconsider the offer to attend future APCSS sessions. For his part, Senior Colonel Tan noted that his Ministry had received a report that evaluated the performance of the PAVN colonel who attended the APCSS session as satisfactory, though his own MND department recognized the colonel's English language deficiencies prevented him from participating in an effective manner in class discussions. Tan stated that his Ministry would select candidates to attend the next session of the strategic studies course, implying that the ERD would be more exacting in their evaluation of the English language capabilities of candidates for the APCSS course.

ISA raised the subject of a U.S. colonels visit to Vietnam, which was to be the first event in the 1998 calendar of bilateral events. The Vietnamese agreed to this proposal because it represented an act of reciprocation for the hospitality accorded the PAVN Senior Colonels visit. The concept, as ISA saw it, was for a group of ten U.S. colonels and support staffers to travel to Vietnam during 2–13 March. The group, ISA told the ERD, would consist of a "senior" 0–6 from the Joint Staff, and four "senior" 0–6's representing the services, selected in consultation with the Joint Staff. Four additional 0–6's from PACOM, U.S. Army Pacific (USARPAC), Pacific Fleet (PACFLT) and Pacific Air Force (PACAF) would be part of the delegation, headed by the Joint Staff representative.

The visit, ISA noted, should mirror the itinerary that was followed during the trip by the PAVN Senior Colonels. The U.S. delegation should travel to Hanoi for appropriate courtesy calls and meetings, and should call on senior service representatives in the same way that the PAVN Senior Colonels met with representatives of the U.S. Air Force, the U.S. Marine Corps, and the U.S. Navy in February 1997 for briefings on organization and missions. The U.S. colonels, ISA told ERD, should also visit one training facility, in the same way that the Vietnamese visitors toured Quantico, and met with senior officers for discussions about training and doctrine. The U.S. delegation should also visit Vietnam's National Defense Academy and one military region, again parallel to the program set up for the PAVN Senior Colonels by the Pacific Command. Finally, the U.S. colonels should meet with Vietnamese military thinkers, scholars, and strategists for discussions of substance that replicated the opportunity PAVN senior colonels had to talk with U.S. think tank specialists and National Defense University faculty.

Senior Colonel Tan replied that though he understood the U.S. request, and agreed in the broadest of terms with the concept, the structures of the two defense establishments were dissimilar enough to raise questions regarding the identification of appropriate counterparts and interlocutors necessary to duplicate the kinds of site visits, meetings and courtesy calls arranged for the Vietnamese senior colonels visit to Washington and Hawaii in February 1997.

This was not the first time the ERD sought to blunt an ISA initiative by making the case that the differences between the U.S. and the Vietnamese militaries would make it difficult to carve out effective common grounds for military-to-military contacts and cooperation. It was a specious argument, one that frequently represented the most polite way of saying that what the U.S. side had asked was simply too politically sensitive, or might involve elements of PAVN over which the ERD had little or no control.

ISA raised the subject of the 9 December meeting between the U.S. Defense Attaché, the Director of the MND's Social Policy Department, and the ERD Director in which the Vietnamese requested that the U.S. render more effective assistance to the SRV's efforts to account for PAVN's MIAs, and that the U.S. help Vietnam with financial assistance for Vietnamese soldiers and civilians suffering from the effects of the wartime defoliation. ISA took the position that neither of the sides should allow these two issues to become obstacles to the development of a defense relationship. These matters, ISA stressed, should be handled in a "humanitarian channel" in much the same way the U.S. POW/MIA issue had been fenced off with the intention of preventing the "politicization" of the issue. The distinction between these two Vietnamese issues and the U.S. POW/MIA issue, to ISA, was that when Washington was pressing the Vietnamese side to help the U.S. conduct investigations and excavations that would shed light on the fate of missing Americans, a normal relationship did not yet exist. None of the advantages of a normal relationship, in terms of the formal and proper channels for communication and experience in managing bilateral issues were available to those involved in shaping the U.S. POW/MIA issue. With the establishment of a normal bilateral relationship and the diplomatic machinery powering that relationship, multiple means of communicating between systems (through Defense Attachés, Political Sections, and Ambassadorial representation) could be called upon in managing issues in ways that took advantage of the resources of the entire U.S. Government. That is, the Agent Orange issues was a matter that exceeded the expertise and mandate of the Defense Department, and involved the interests of the Health and Human Services Department, the State Department, national level U.S. veterans organizations, and the National Institute of Health, among others. Both sides, ISA concluded, should think twice before attempting to set this issue in exclusively military-to-military channels.

ISA recounted the modest steps taken by the U.S. to be helpful to the Vietnamese side in these two areas. Regarding the MIA issue, in addition to providing archival documents and encouraging the initiatives of American veterans groups aimed at locating war memorabilia and identification media taken off battlefields by American soldiers as keepsakes, the U.S. government was prepared to provide assistance to Vietnamese officials in utilizing U.S. archives. On the issue of Agent Orange, the U.S. government was committed to concluding a bilateral scientific and technological cooperation agreement that would enable the two governments to begin cooperation between science and health officials on a wide range of research. The key point, in ISA's view, was that the U.S. side recognized these were legitimate and important issues that should be approached sensibly and appropriately, in a manner that would not detract from the pace and scope of normalization.

This was not quite enough for the Vietnamese side, which had labored to get the Vietnamese MIA issue on the agenda of POW/MIA technical and policy level discussions, and had argued strongly that Vietnam's humanitarian requirements must become a part of the bilateral dialogue. The ERD made the case that the U.S. effort was minor in proportion to Vietnamese expenditures of man-hours and political capital in addressing the U.S. POW/MIA issue, especially in the face of increasing local disgruntlement over intrusive U.S. excavations and site surveys. The ERD argued that the modesty U.S. efforts created the spectacle of a wealthy country responding to real human needs and issues in a miserly, selfish manner. It was not possible for the Vietnamese people to understand, Tan said, how a resource rich country like the U.S. could begrudge Vietnam this modest assistance. It was also hard to understand, Tan continued, in view of the existing Commando Compensation legislation, why the U.S. would spend money to compensate "criminals," but refuse to spend money to provide aid to victims of the war.[3] Interestingly, Tan did not repeat his earlier argument that Washington's legal obligation to the commandos represented an indication of U.S. support for anti-regime groups. Instead, he acknowledged that this was a national law with a specific goal, but that it was a wrong law that obligated the U.S. Government to an incorrect intent, and should therefore be changed.

Washington's efforts to address the Vietnamese MIA issue were, to Vu Tan, also insufficient. He acknowledged U.S. attempts to locate and provide information to Vietnam that might help account for PAVN troops in a missing status, but noted that such information was partial in nature, of limited use, and could not lead to the location of gravesites. Tan requested greater efforts by the U.S. government to locate and turn over information that would have a practical value to Vietnam's accounting effort. In a follow-up to this line of discussion, the Deputy Director of the MND's Social Policy Department, Senior Colonel Nguyen Manh Dau, told ISA that his office was concerned because the veterans-to-veterans initiative was an entirely non-governmental effort, and the Defense Ministry wanted to see more direct involvement of the U.S. Government.

On the issue of reciprocity, ISA noted that during an 8 October meeting in the Pentagon, the Vietnamese Defense Attaché had asked whether DoD would be able to provide Vietnam with any assistance in the area of defense industry development. It was not clear whether Vo Dinh Quang was operating on the basis of instructions, pushing the envelop to see whether there was any flexibility, or exercising his own discretion in seeking to broaden the dialogue on defense relations. Later discussions suggested that there was an interest at the senior levels of the Defense Ministry in determining what the limits were regarding U.S. thinking about military sales; that subject may have come up in the instructions Quang reportedly received in a meeting with the Defense Minister before Quang's departure for the U.S. It is hard to see how any Vietnamese defense official could have misunderstood the manner in which existing legislation, and political decisions, militated against exploring foreign military sales to the Socialist Republic.

At that time, ISA offered to brief Vietnam's Defense Attaché on the subject, in return for an agreement to schedule a meeting between the U.S. Defense Attaché in Hanoi and representatives of the MND's Science and Technology Institute. The key point in all this was that the Vietnamese Defense Attaché should not be allowed to become smarter about the U.S. system and policies than the U.S. Defense Attaché might become about any facet of the Vietnamese system.

In view of the fact that the maneuverings over the science and technology briefing were awkward and at least initially unproductive, ISA offered that perhaps what both the U.S. and the Vietnamese were talking about was not reciprocity, in the form of a "tit for tat" replication of the courtesies and access afforded to each defense attaché by the host country. Although that was a good goal, perhaps it was not quite possible to expect each side to establish the same procedures governing such opportunities for sharing information. Instead, what made sense, especially at this stage in the relationship, was the expectation that reasonable efforts would be taken to extend courtesies and access beyond the level that existed at the outset of the relationship. If the Department of Defense allowed the Vietnamese Defense Attaché to be briefed by DoD experts on procurement and scientific cooperation agreements, the Vietnamese side should be amenable to a courtesy call by the U.S. Defense Attaché on the MND's Director of the Science and Technology Institute. ISA asked that the ERD agree to set up such a meeting, and to continue to work closely, through the two defense attachés, to establish opportunities for both sides to better understand one another.

Responding, Tan restated the regulations that guided the activities of foreign military attaches in Vietnam, and spoke of the need to refrain from singling out one Attache for special treatment. He did acknowledge that it was realistic to expect that the access of the two attaches would have expanded beyond the level that existed at the outset of the relationship, and appeared to agree with the notion that while perfect reciprocity might not be possible, some reasonable level of enhanced opportunities should spring from the fact that both sides had moved beyond the initial stage of the relationship. Tan noted a misunderstanding involving the request for a briefing on science and technology policies, paralleling the briefing provided for Senior Colonel Quang in Washington, suggesting that his office had not been clear as to whether the U.S. Defense Attaché wanted to be briefed by the Institute responsible for training and procurement or a research body subordinate to the MND that had responsibilities for scientific and technological cooperation policies. Tan signaled the ERD's willingness to arrange the briefing for Colonel O'Dowd with the office responsible for training and procurement. It was not necessarily a good explanation of what happened, but it did show that the ERD could be coaxed beyond lines it had drawn in the sand.

The meetings with the ERD were positive and upbeat, even as they addressed some difficult issues. Tan spoke freely and frankly, concluding his tougher points with a clear reiteration of the importance of bilateral security relations. He couched his strongest rejoinders to the U.S. side's points as personal views. That is, his chagrin over how the U.S. could have a law to compensate "criminals," and his suggestion that DOD work to "overturn" this law, were expressed as his own views.

The ERD was able to prepare itself effectively for this January meeting, in large part as the result of deliberate efforts to clarify intentions for this session early, and to cover the basic messages in repeated advanced communications through the Vietnamese Defense Attaché to the ERD, and the U.S. Defense Attaché to the ERD's Director for International Relations. The ERD was also slightly more familiar with the process of communication with ISA hammered out through trial and error, and not unaccustomed to the formalities and structure that had begun to emerge for working level interactions between the MND and DoD. The Vietnamese side knew there were some set piece dimensions to the dialogue, and some extemporaneous efforts to resolve issues and clarify positions, and had come to understand the importance of both these kinds of interaction. The Vietnamese side knew that ISA would review accomplishments, discuss upcoming events, and explore the extent to which recent successes could be used as the basis for incremental forward movement. The meeting was more orderly, and the process began to have a more comfortable feeling for both sides. The ERD leadership was still stiff and formal, but was beginning to relax into the formula for meetings, which by and large still had the character of a dialogue with a practically silent partner. The positions the ERD took on issues ISA brought up for debate — Agent Orange, "reciprocity," the itinerary for the U.S. colonels delegation — were inflexible, in large part because the ERD had no leeway to compromise at the discussion table, and no authority to concoct alternative solutions to practical problems.

Bilateral Meetings and Events, March Through May

The U.S. "Senior Colonels" visit to the Socialist Republic was the first event in the 1998 military-to-military calendar. The category of "senior U.S. colonels" was invented in order to stress the way the U.S. side thought of this proposed event as an exact replica of the February 1997 PAVN Senior Colonels visit. While in the Vietnamese system, the rank of Senior Colonel (Dai Ta) was a meaningful grade, a step above colonel (Thuong Ta), the term had no relevance in the U.S. rank system, but rather brought to mind a group of geriatric O-6's approaching mandatory retirement. The U.S. Colonels arrived in Hanoi in early March, and visited the National Defense Academy, the 308th Mechanized Infantry Division in Son Tay, Vietnamese Navy Headquarters in Haiphong, the 921st PAVN Air Force Regiment, the 5th Military Region Headquarters in Da Nang, the 7th Military Region Headquarters in Ho Chi Minh City, and Infantry Officer School Number Two in Dong Nai Province. The delegation met with Lieutenant General Tran Hanh, a Vice Minister of Defense, as well as Nguyen Manh Hung, the head of the Foreign Ministry's Americas Department.[4]

During the course of the visit, the Vietnamese side broached the issue of ship visits, if only to politely reiterate their sense that the relationship had not yet matured to the point at which a port call by a U.S. Navy vessel was appropriate. The Vietnamese military hosts emphasized that economic development was the single most important priority for the military. Regional military commanders focused on commercial options for developing sources of hardware and modernizing indigenous arms production capabilities, and the possibility for joint ventures and foreign investment, at the expense of more conventional security issues. The military hosts did not conceal their concern over what China represented to the region, and to Vietnam in particular, and were especially interested in discussing People's Liberation Army modernization and Beijing's South China Sea policies.

During January–March, the MND stated its willingness to "expand" the defense relationship in decidedly modest but symbolically important ways, in recognition of positive developments, such as the Administration's decision to press forward on the Jackson-Vanik waiver. For example, the MND invited Ambassador Peterson to tour the 92nd PAVN Air Force

Flying Dragon Division and the 308th Division Headquarters; informed the U.S. Defense Attaché that the Ministry had arranged a visit to the Institute of Military Science and Technology, something the U.S. side had sought to organize since October 1997; and completed arrangements for a courtesy call by the Deputy U.S. Defense Attaché, a USMC officer, on the Commander of the Vietnamese Navy.

In March, perhaps buoyed by the success of the U.S. Colonels visit and the MND's nods toward positive steps forward in the relationship, Ambassador Peterson sought Washington's agreement to pursue a "flyout" for 15 senior Vietnamese military officers who would be ferried by helicopter from Hanoi to the 7th Fleet flagship in the area in mid–March for a tour and a briefing aboard the vessel. The date, according to the ERD, was not convenient for the Vietnamese, and a later time for the event was explored, but in the end the Vietnamese demurred.

It is worth looking at the reasons why this proposal failed. It was an article of faith with the Vietnamese side that once DoD and the MND shook hands on the calendar, there would be no "add ons." This represented the MND's way of complying with the foreign policy leadership's instruction to make certain that the military relationship remained coordinated with the rest of the relationship, and did not surge beyond an invisible line that represented what the Politburo believed should be the pace and scope of normalization. The "flyout" was probably viewed as an "add on." Moreover, the newly appointed Defense Minister, Pham Van Tra, was inclined to interpret the bilateral relationship in strict terms, leaving little room for question on what was possible in the U.S.–Vietnamese military relationship. According to a senior military officer, from the start of his tenure Tra was not inclined to deviate even slightly from the dance card defined at the planning meetings. Senior Vietnamese military officers who sought to get the Defense Ministry to move beyond the single visit they were prepared to make to the U.S. in 1998 were roundly criticized for breaking ranks. In the end, the ERD conveyed that the "flyout" event would not fit with the schedules of the Defense Ministry's leadership, though it was entirely possible that the second thoughts entertained by the MND had more to do with the level of discomfort the PAVN senior officers anticipated they would feel when confronted with a guided tour of the technological superiority of the U.S. military.[5]

By the end of the first quarter of 1998, the government in Hanoi provided Washington with the assurances that exit permit regulations would not be used to bar certain types of people from legally departing Vietnam. That was sufficient basis for the State Department to argue that there was enough reason to go forward with a waiver under the Jackson-Vanik amendment. By late March the Secretary of State had signed the two remaining waivers that were the last obstacles to the legal provision of assistance to Vietnam: the provision prohibiting assistance to communist countries, and the prohibition against providing assistance to countries that assisted terrorist states.[6] Both provisions could be waived on the basis of national interests. The State Department also planned to waive the provisions prohibiting EXIM for "Marxist Leninist states."

This, however, did not translate into a burst of activities in the bilateral defense relationship. By the end of the first quarter, it became clear that the Vietnamese military would not necessarily allow the good news in other parts of the U.S.–Vietnamese relationship to lead to even the most modest ratcheting up of activities in the defense relationship. The ERD restated the decision to defer visits by Pacific Command component commanders and the Chief of Staff of the Army until after 1998, took the position that substantive discussions of ship visits would not be possible until 1999, and rejected humanitarian activities such as demining that would have involved U.S. service members operating on Vietnamese soil as trainers. The Vietnamese also rejected CINCPAC-sponsored Title Ten activities involving U.S. Special Forces, such as the Pacific Area Special Operations Conference and Medical Civic Action Projects conducted as Joint Combined Exercise Training events by Special Operations Command, Pacific (SOCPAC).

For the U.S., concern about the prospects of congressional battles over the Administration's desire to renew the Jackson-Vanik waiver, and the likelihood that such a tussle would include Hill objections to a renewal of the waiver for China, prompted the NSC and the State Department to agree that the bilateral relationship with Vietnam was not yet ready for an expansion of military-to-military activities. During April–May, the defense relationship was confined to Vietnamese participation in a search and rescue conference in which the National Committee for Search and Rescue was the central player. The Vietnamese sent PAVN representatives to PACOM-hosted conferences on law, operational readiness and military medicine. In May, Vietnamese military officials received a delegation of U.S. military and civilian students from the National Defense University, and met with U.S. military officers representing the Joint Interagency Task Force-West (JIATF-West), responsible for providing DoD support to law enforcement agencies and U.S. diplomatic missions in Southeast and Southwest Asia focused on disrupting international drug trafficking.[7]

The activities of the first quarter were all conducted in a positive, cordial way and all resulted in real dividends for the bilateral relationship.

The U.S. Colonels delegation was accorded unprecedented access to military facilities during tours in northern and central Vietnam. The Search and Rescue (SAR) Conference generated request from the SRV government for U.S. support to Vietnamese SAR training. The NDU visit was well organized and thoughtfully executed, and resulted in profitable contacts and exchanges between U.S. regional specialists and Vietnamese military counterparts. The JIATF-West interaction with Vietnamese government representatives led to the possibility of cooperation between law enforcement support agencies on problems related to the trafficking in illicit narcotics. However, these activities suggested that it was easier for the Vietnamese military to participate in multilateral activities sponsored by the U.S., and to play a role in meetings and visits involving the Department of Defense, when the MND was not the SRV government's lead agency with primary responsibilities for the activity.

Midyear Developments

In late May, a Russian built aircraft piloted by Lao nationals crashed in Xieng Khouang Province, killing over 25 passengers and crew, including Vietnam's Deputy Minister of Defense and Chief of the General Staff Department Dao Trong Lich who was leading a delegation on a "working visit" to Laos.[8] The Vietnamese government did not release the list of those who lost their lives in the accident until mid–June. The list included two senior military region officials, seven senior General Staff Department officers, the Vietnamese Defense Attaché in Vientiane, and three PAVN officers assigned to the ERD.

The Vietnamese military was stunned by the crash, and devasted by the loss of these senior officers. The accident led to a raft of rumors about replacements, and left the Ministry dazed and unprepared to get back to business in a focused way. Through late June, the MND remained inattentive to ISA's suggestions to begin planning the vice ministerial visit. The MND never responded to efforts by the U.S. Defense Attaché to initiate discussions of the "terms of reference" for the October visit. At the time, it appeared that the Defense Ministry was seeking to delay planning actions for the October visit, without having to explain themselves. Indeed, during a 23 June meeting, Senior Colonel Quang stated that there had been "no official acceptance" of the invitation to undertake a vice ministerial level visit to the United States. Quang added that nothing negative was intended by this, that the Vietnamese side had agreed to the proposal but had merely not indicated the delegation's plans to travel. Quang's words may have been intended as the first bit of backpeddling in the process, which in a roundabout way seemed connected to the substance of the rumors regarding MND leadership changes.

Around June, a senior Vietnamese Foreign Ministry official stated that though bilateral military-to-military relations were still "premature," it was important to sustain the security dialogue between defense establishments alongside of efforts to develop other areas of the relationship. The Foreign Ministry, according to this official, was pleased with the progress made through mid–1998, and remarked that both countries had achieved substantial advances in humanitarian accounting for wartime missing. The U.S., the official stressed, must realize that assistance to Vietnam's efforts to account for missing PAVN troops, and the U.S. response to Vietnam's appeals for help on the Agent Orange issue, could have a very important impact on the tone of the relationship.

The Vietnamese government, according to the Foreign Ministry official, was looking forward to the visit to the U.S. by Vice Minister Tran Hanh, scheduled for October 1998, which would be the first visit at such a senior level. Defense relations should progress in a modest manner, the official continued, complimented by developments in the ASEAN Regional Forum organized to address regional security issues. ASEAN Regional Forum activities fit well with U.S.–Vietnamese aims in the bilateral defense relationship, according to the Foreign Ministry official.

The official made it plain that Hanoi was concerned that President Clinton's visit to China, and the momentum that this trip would engender in the Washington-Beijing relationship, could overshadow regional security issues, and displace ASEAN's importance to the U.S. at a critical moment when the organization was looking forward to its end of year summit, which Hanoi was to host. The concern in Hanoi was that there had never been both a strong China and a strong Japan at the same time. To cope with this situation, ASEAN must have an equivalent importance. The Vietnamese, according to the Foreign Ministry official, feared that an improvement in U.S.–China relations would enable Beijing to pressure Vietnam into resolving bilateral issues in a manner that was detrimental to Hanoi's interests. The Sino-Vietnamese meeting on border issues reminded Hanoi that they were dealing with an imperious China. This confluence of variables—Japanese and Chinese strength, Beijing's indifference to Hanoi's equities, and improvements in the Sino-American relationship—prompted senior Vietnamese military officials and diplomats to look to the possibility of a significant visit to Vietnam by a senior American official, and to explore Washington's views on America's presence in Asia, U.S. government plans and intentions regarding military basing requirements in Southeast Asia, and recent strides in relations with other ASEAN countries such as the visiting forces agreement with the Philippines.

For the U.S. side, in the aftermath of the NDU visit in May, the several multilateral conferences during April and May, plus a brief visit to Hanoi by the Director of the Defense Intelligence Agency in July, there were no further activities in the defense relationship until the fall. All of ISA and ERD's interaction became focused on planning for Tran Hanh visit to the U.S.

In early June, in connection with a recommendation to extend his general authority to grant Jackson-Vanik waivers, the President transmitted a determination to Congress stating that continuation of the waiver for Vietnam would substantially promote the freedom of emigration objectives of the amendment.[9]

Also in June, U.S. lawmakers involved in prior attempts to reinvigorate attention to the POW/MIA issue fashioned Senate Bill 2260, modifying section 405 of the State Department's Appropriations Act so as to require that the President annually certify to Congress that Vietnam had met a list of requirements related to U.S. efforts to account for Americans lost during the Vietnam War. The Bill expanded the provisions of Senate Bill 1022 of July 1997, which required the Administration to demonstrate that Vietnam was "being fully forthcoming and fully cooperating in good faith with the United States...." Section 405 required certification of Vietnam's good faith efforts to facilitate live sighting investigations, to investigate and resolve wartime reporting and postwar live sighting reports, recover and repatriate American remains, accelerate unilateral efforts to provide documents that would assist the U.S. government in obtaining the fullest possible accounting, provide "full access to relevant information contained in Communist Party and other government archives," and address concerns relating to the two "Soviet documents" that referred to a higher number of American POWs being held in captivity during the Vietnam War than those repatriated by the Vietnamese Communists in 1973. The Administration responded with vigorous criticisms of the intentions underlying this Bill, and confronted the assumption of non-cooperation on the part of Vietnam that informed this modification of Section 405, pointing to a record of accomplishments in accounting for missing Americans on the basis of Hanoi's helpful actions in conjunction with the work of the JTFFA. In the end, though, the Jackson-Vanik waiver issue was addressed directly, on its own merits, and the POW/MIA issue did not become much of a factor in debates over this aspect of the bilateral economic relationship. Indeed, testimony offered by POW/MIA activists had little resonance on the Hill, was seriously out of date, and did not stand up well to the testimony by Administration witnesses who spoke to the issue of joint U.S.–Vietnamese cooperation on archival research, field investigations, and live sighting investigations. On 30 July the House of Representatives voted down House Joint Resolution 120, a resolution to disapprove the waiver. Boeing, Caterpiller, Citibank/Citicorp, Craft Corporation and General Electric testified on the Hill in favor of preserving the waiver. Individual letters supporting the waiver were sent to House members from Bechtel, GE, IBM, Motorola, Coudert Brothers, Raytheon, Nike, Mobil and many others. The National Association of Manufacturers, the Pacific Basin Economic Council, several American Chambers of Commerce (including Hong Kong's ACC), the American Farm Bureau and many other trade associations signed letters to House members against Resolution 120.

Between late May and early July, in anticipation of a possible October 1998 planning meeting with the ERD on the margins of a visit to the U.S. by Vice Minister Tran Hanh, ISA drafted some first thoughts on goals for the bilateral relationship in 1999. ISA wanted to increase the number of official visits in the defense calendar of events from three to a total of four U.S. visits. ISA wanted to expand the range of visits to include service counterpart and component commander visits; in 1997 the MND stated that the relationship had not yet reached the point where it would make sense to have a visit by, for example, the Chief of Staff of the Army or CINCPACFLT. ISA factored in a USD(P) visit to Vietnam for 1999. DoD wanted to work toward an agreement to begin a humanitarian demining program, and focused on what seemed to be the easiest, least intrusive form of assistance: equipment transfer and training in assistance to demining victims. DoD hoped to gradually move Vietnam to accept the "train the trainer" part of the program, which would place U.S. military engineers and demining experts in country providing the necessary instruction to develop a cadre of Vietnamese trainers. DoD also wanted to begin discussions regarding a port call that would involve a humanitarian building project such as the construction of a clinic or schoolhouse because such an activity could be a useful precursor to a ship visit in the year 2000. DoD wanted to see the Vietnamese increase the number of visits they were prepare to commit to, beginning with a late 1999 visit to the U.S. by the Defense Minister. Finally, DoD wanted to rely less and less on working level meetings to plan calendars for the relationship. Both sides, in ISA's argument, should begin to move the relationship into normal channels, where military planners, regional command representatives, and defense attachés brokered proposals, managed the flow of visitors, and oversaw events in the relationship. Policy makers would continue to set the pace and determine the scope of the relationship, and impart content and purpose, deferring to "normal channels" to manage bilateral defense contacts.

All this became moot in late July when Secretary of Defense Cohen communicated his desire to visit Vietnam in January 1999.

Decisions, Revisions, Reversals: The SecDef Visit, Take One

Cohen's interest in traveling to Vietnam in January or February 1999 was first voiced to his policy team during a mid-summer trip to Indonesia to attend the ASEAN Ministerial meeting, and may have been motivated by a desire to convince Hanoi to participate in the Asia Pacific Dialogue organized by the Asia Pacific Policy Center, a nongovernmental organization that developed briefing and orientation programs for U.S. lawmakers and businessmen focused on Asian affairs. Between July and mid–September, the presumption made by senior Pentagon policymakers was that the Secretary intended to travel to Vietnam in January or February. Consequently, all other initiatives in the U.S.–Vietnamese defense relationship became relatively unimportant, and the proposals for the early October 1998 ISA-ERD meeting to plan the 1999–2000 calendar of military activities remained unapproved through mid–September.

From ISA's perspective, bilateral military activities beginning with the events of 1997 had not yet yielded a consistent record of military interaction. Vietnam had not demonstrated a seriousness about some of the proposals for bilateral activities put before them, including involvement in demining training initiatives as well as agreement to meetings between service and component commander leadership, and the initiation of regional security consultations. ISA believed that there should be more to the relationship before things could be nudged to a level where a visit by the Secretary of Defense would have an impact. It was entirely possible that once the Vietnamese got their trophy in the form of a visit by the Defense Secretary, there would be little incentive to move forward with the working-level efforts to develop bilateral cooperation, multilateral engagement through Title Ten conferences, and senior DoD visits.

Moreover, both the U.S. and the Vietnamese had agreed that the relationship must be carefully paced so as to not press ahead of any other part of the effort to build normal relations. A Secretary of Defense visit in early

1999 would have represented a quantum leap, not a carefully phased step in the gradual expansion of bilateral military relations. DoD was on record with a commitment to Congress to keep the defense relationship with Vietnam carefully calibrated to fit with overall normalization plans, and deliberately low keyed. The Vietnamese had agreed to consider the visit by the ASD/ISA, scheduled for December 1998, as the next appropriate step in the context of "visit diplomacy." Pushing the process to the cabinet level would press beyond the level of activity that had so far been acceptable to both sides.

Additionally, significant human right issues complicated the overall bilateral relationship. The Vietnamese government had indicated that Doan Viet Hoat, whose imprisonment following convictions for seditious activities was an important issue for the White House, would be released in the January 1999 amnesty. However in mid–1998 there were reasons to believe that the Ministry of Interior, responsible for managing the prison system and the amnesty process, was not prepared to go forward with the release because Hoat's "attitude" had not changed. A visit to Hanoi by the Secretary of Defense at a moment when the Vietnamese were reneging on the commitment to release Hoat would not have been right. In the end, Hoat was released in the September amnesty, along with several other high profile Vietnamese who had been under SRV lock and key for political transgressions involving the exercise of free speech and other basic human rights.

Finally, there were sound domestic political reasons for not moving too quickly to elevate this relationship to the cabinet level. A speedier pace in pressing relations forward would put the Pentagon crosswise with the coalition of domestic forces that rematerialized as a force in the context of the appropriations process for the Departments of Commerce, Justice, State and related agencies with a bill that expanded the provisions of 16 July 1997 and added new requirements for Presidential certification of Vietnam's POW/MIA cooperation. Although these interest groups had spent much of their force, commanded little attention, and suffered from diminished credibility in their opposition to the granting of the Jackson-Vanik waiver, it was apparent that they had sufficient juice remaining to generate potentially uncomfortable press attention during a visit that would certainly command headline attention. The Administration was committed to improving relations with Vietnam in a variety of areas, while pursuing the fullest possible accounting. In defending this policy the U.S. government had found itself in disagreement with some of the veterans groups, congressional interests, and POW/MIA organizations. The goal had been to remain in sync on key principles with these groups. An early visit by the Secretary of Defense promised to galvanize strong criticism from these vocal interests.

On the Vietnamese side of the equation, the issue of an early visit by the Defense Secretary was troublesome to Hanoi from the moment it was broached by Cohen in a 1 October meeting in the Pentagon with Deputy Prime Minister Nguyen Manh Cam. The Vietnamese side was politely receptive but noncommittal from the beginning. Cam took note of Cohen's interest in promoting U.S.–Vietnamese relations and in developing contacts between Vietnam's provinces and various U.S. states. Cam referenced several Vietnamese provincial delegations, including one from Nghe An, Cam's province of birth, that visited the U.S. in 1998 and stopped in Maine, Cohen's home state. Cam appreciated the effort to boost local economies.[10]

Cohen told Cam that the various parts of the bilateral relationship, including diplomacy, trade, economic relations and defense relations, must develop simultaneously. The relationship must be transparent to reduce the chance for misunderstandings. The POW/MIA issue must continue to be the most important issue in the bilateral relationship. Referencing the U.S. involvement in demining training initiatives in Thailand, Cambodia and Laos, the Secretary encouraged Cam to agree to participate in this program in 1999. Cohen noted his desire to visit Vietnam early in 1999.

Cam stated that Vietnam's approach to relations with the United States was based on the notion that what happened in the past should be left in the past, and that the U.S. and Vietnam should try to establish "a new framework for a new relationship." Cam observed that he would not be sincere if he argued that Vietnam was ready to forget the past. Forgetting was not easy, but it was Vietnam's strong tradition to put the past behind in order to build a future. Cohen, gesturing to the Chairman of the Joint Chiefs of Staff and others on the U.S. side of the table, interjected that some of the DoD officials at the meeting would themselves find it difficult to forget, but their presence at the session was indication that the U.S. was ready to move forward to establish a new relationship. The tradition of helping to rebuild relations between countries once at war was also a strong tradition in the U.S., the Secretary concluded. The Deputy Prime Minister observed that the relationship had thus far focused on economic and trade ties, but Vietnam had not ignored defense relations. A number of military delegations had traveled between the U.S. and Vietnam, and that itself was an important part of building closer, cooperative relations. Vietnam, Cam stated, appreciated the role the U.S. played in maintaining peace and stability in Southeast Asia. The bilateral relationship should indeed move ahead, and all agencies in both governments should seek closer links at the same time.

The U.S. and Vietnam, Cam continued, had been able to cooperate fully on issues of mutual concern. President Clinton's statement of appreciation for Vietnam's cooperation with the U.S. on the matter of missing U.S. personnel was significant to Vietnam. The MIA issue itself was a good reason why forgetting the past was so difficult for Vietnamese, but the people were still prepared to cooperate with American efforts to account for MIAs. Vietnam was grateful for information provided by U.S. veterans groups that enabled the SRV government to resolve questions regarding unaccounted for PAVN troops. This cooperative spirit enabled progress in other areas, such as the Resettlement of Vietnamese Returnees. Cam emphasized the importance of assisting victims of the war, an effort he described as a potentially significant confidence building measure that would improve relations. He recalled his recommendation to the Secretary of State on 30 September, during their meeting in New York, regarding joint scientific research on the effects of Agent Orange, and described Vietnam's establishment of a fund intended to provide financial assistance to victims of Agent Orange. Though this was primarily a domestic effort for Vietnam, Cam said that Vietnam welcomed international contributions to this effort. Cam concluded by telling Cohen that a recent delegation of U.S. Congressmen who had served in Vietnam during the war asked Vietnamese villagers why the Americans had been received positively and treated warmly during their visit. The Congressmen were told that though they had come as war fighters before, now they came as friends and therefore the Vietnamese were obliged to receive them in that spirit. Cam expressed his appreciation for what the Secretary had contributed to normalization, told Cohen that Vietnam would welcome a visit by the Secretary of Defense, and said that Hanoi would consider such a visit an important step in bilateral relations.

It is difficult to characterize the importance of such meetings. Though mostly confined to courtesies, and largely devoid of substance and profundity, sessions of this sort tended to be important moments that represented gateways to future possibilities. They offered the opportunity for each participant to take the measure of the leader across the table. These high level courtesy calls provided a sense of how each side operated, and offered important clues concerning pecking orders, issue priorities, and the seriousness with which each side intended to pursue agenda items. For working level staffs, such meetings became a means of determining the trajectory of the relationship, and the intensity with which individual issues should be addressed.

The meeting between Cohen and Cam was important to the Vietnamese because it represented the Deputy Prime Minister's first foray into defense relations in a public way. Cam had been involved in POW/MIA interactions beginning with his appointment as Foreign Minister. He played a role in the policy process that yielded agreement to the late 1996 visit to Hanoi by the DASD/AP that rolled out the first proposals for military relations. Cam retained an interest in defense issues, as reflected in the active voice department-level Foreign Ministry officials and diplomats employed when commenting on the positive aspects of the relationship between Vietnam and the U.S. His visit to the Pentagon was a personally important moment, and a significant meeting that appeared to bolster his confidence (at least momentarily) at a time when the relationship was not yielding the dividends Hanoi hoped for, especially in terms of a trade agreement and Most Favored Nations trading status.

The visit was important for the handful of Pentagon policy and operations personnel involved in managing this relationship, including ISA and the Joint Staff, because it attracted a significant level of attention to the defense relationship. The Secretary's agreement to schedule the meeting, his willingness to convene a session with the Vice Defense Minister shortly after Cam's visit, and his interest in traveling to Vietnam galvanized levels of attention to the relationship throughout the building, a positive development in a bureaucratic environment so focused on Middle Eastern crises, U.S.–China relations, North Korea, and the economic crisis in Asia. Attention translated into the possibility of real resources being dedicated to the relationship, systematic focus to the public affairs aspect of the issue, the development of coherent thinking about the way to address lingering Congressional concerns, and a renewed cooperation between officials with disparate interests in aspects of the relationship— POW/MIA (DPMO), demining (OASD/SOLIC), ship visits (the Office of the Chief of Naval Operations), and Defense Attaché Affairs (the Office of the Director of the Defense Intelligence Agency), for example.

The meeting with Cam also demonstrated the Secretary's personal willingness to expand dialogue between the U.S. and Vietnamese defense establishments on select humanitarian matters. Cohen underscored that Hanoi's agreement to join the U.S. in tailoring a demining training program for Vietnam would be a major step forward, a real signal that Vietnam was prepared to cooperate in practical "confidence building" steps in the defense relationship. He acknowledged Vietnamese cooperation on the POW/MIA issue, and referred to U.S. actions that showed the Department's willingness to be helpful to Vietnam's efforts to search for the remains of PAVN personnel. Cohen's statements would become rosetta stone-like indications that the full weight of the Pentagon should be placed behind interagency efforts to design an approach to demining training that would meet with the approval of the Vietnamese government, and to provide additional assistance to the Vietnamese effort to account for their wartime battlefield casualties. The latter issue elicited varying degrees of concern over the potential for veterans group backlash, opposition from the Hill, and criticism from POW/MIA organizations. Prior to the Secretary's meeting with Cam, those concerns had insured that DoD decision makers would be hesitant about even the most low-keyed steps such as inviting Vietnamese archivists to explore wartime records in the U.S. National Archives for the purposes of addressing Vietnam's own MIA issues. The Defense Secretary's willingness to acknowledge the legitimacy of Vietnam's concerns on these sensitive issues was important and allowed a slight but positive momentum to develop on this and other issues.

However, the one area where the Cohen-Cam meeting made little difference was the question of a visit to Vietnam by the Secretary. In private discussions, senior Vietnamese diplomats suggested that a later visit by the Secretary of Defense would be "more convenient." The Vietnamese were not prepared to work this issue hard from the start; Hanoi had to be prodded toward a policy decision. Their preference seemed to be to let the clock tick until time for preparations had run out. They were politely encouraging and privately positive about the prospects for a trip, but there was no sense of urgency in accomplishing the myriad of administrative tasks required to insure the success of such a visit. By late October, senior SRV military officers and diplomats were almost obsessively concerned with discerning the Secretary's concept for his trip, and learning the particulars about the traveling party. However, there was no reason to believe that this showed the Vietnamese government would agree to go ahead with the visit.

Tran Hanh's Visit

For both sides, the October 1998 visit to the U.S. by Vice Minister of Defense Lieutenant General Tran Hanh was a key event in the start-up relationship between the two militaries. The Vietnamese saw the trip as an important "symbolic" visit to the U.S. by a ministerial level defense official, a significant opportunity to expose senior officials to American culture, and a potentially important opportunity for discussions on military and strategic issues with senior American defense officials.[11] For the U.S., Hanh's visit was a chance to demonstrate the Pentagon's commitment to developing a frank and serious dialogue with Vietnam about regional security issues of mutual concern. Finally, the visit represented another opportunity to drive home the continuing importance of the POW/MIA issue.

Vice Minister Hanh arrived in Washington on 3 October.[12] During the course of meetings with Defense Secretary Cohen, ASD/ISA, DASD/AP and other senior Pentagon officials from 5 to 6 October, Hanh stated that at some point in the future of the U.S.–Vietnamese defense relationship, there would indeed be a visit to Vietnam by a U.S. Navy vessel, but for now it should not be part of the program. Hanh said that the ship visit issue was something the Defense Minister and Secretary of Defense Cohen should take up at their first meeting. The Vice Minister reaffirmed Vietnam's unconditional commitment to cooperation with the U.S. government in efforts to account for missing Americans, emphasizing the humanitarian nature of this issue. He raised Vietnam's own MIA problem in most of his meetings with DoD, State Department, and White House officials.

The ISA and ERD planning meeting took place on 6 October. The ERD rejected the recommendation from the U.S. side that future visits to Vietnam by the National Defense University and the Air War College classes be considered as routine study group visits, and that they not be counted as part of the quota imposed on senior DoD visits. The Vietnamese side argued that they afforded a delegation's welcome to these groups, and therefore they should be counted in the overall number of visits. The ERD rejected the proposal that the DoD and the MND begin to move the relationship into normal channels, where planners, regional command representatives, and defense attachés would manage the flow of visitors, and oversee events in the relationship. The planning process, Deputy ERD Director Bui Trong Nhu argued on behalf of the ERD, should continue to be handled in the manner that it had been since October 1996 to insure that the pace and scope of proposed activities remained modest. The Vietnamese side agreed to expand the range of visits to include service counterpart and component commander visits. However, they only consented to an incremental increase in high-level visits, moving from 2 or 3 delegations in 1998 to 3 or 4 in 1999. Regarding the demining training initiative, the ERD stated that the U.S. could dispatch an assessment team to visit Vietnam to "discuss plans for the future" in the beginning of 1999.

As ritual, and in terms of protocol, the 3–7 October visit to Washington by the Vice Minister of Defense was a success. The Vietnamese were pleased with the access granted the delegation; agreed that the meetings with the senior officials of the Department of Defense were positive and "constructive;" and were relaxed and content with their treatment, accommodations, the security afforded the delegation, and the opportunity to see parts of Washington.

It was clearly important to Hanoi to minimize the extent to which strategic issues and policy matters were discussed during the Vice Minister's visit. Tran Hanh's delegation, and the Vietnamese Embassy, sculpted a press statement that hailed the visit as having strengthened relations between the two defense ministries and armed forces, strengthened mutual understanding, and at the same time contributed to regional peace and stability. The draft press statement, which became the authoritative basis for press coverage of the trip in the VNCP and the army newspapers in mid–October, highlighted the American side's positive statements about Vietnam's cooperation in U.S. efforts to locate the remains of American service personnel lost during the war in Vietnam. Both sides, the statement stressed, agreed to cooperate to resolve Vietnamese humanitarian problems (cac van de nhan dao), such as locating the remains of Vietnamese service personnel, removing mines, and conducting research to overcome the consequences of Agent Orange. Clearly, the subtleties of the American positions were not as important to the Vietnamese as the public affairs spin that the U.S. had committed to addressing its obligations to resolving problems that were caused by the war.[13]

It is instructive to look at the manner in which the Vietnamese chose to describe the visit to friends in the region. Concerned with how the visit would resonate in Southeast Asia, the SRV Defense Attaché told his Chinese and Singaporean counterparts that the visit was a positive event which contributed to the development of the relationship, and provided an important opportunity to discuss five humanitarian issues at the core of the relationship: U.S. and Vietnamese MIAs, demining, search and rescue, counter narcotics issues, and Agent Orange. The SRV Defense Attaché told his counterparts that the visit resulted in steps to promote cooperation in resolving these five humanitarian issues.[14]

The visit did not secure agreement to some important aspects of the plans for the next steps in the military-to-military relationship that ISA had hoped the Vietnamese would accept. The delegation was proper in its response to Cohen's statement of his interest in visiting Vietnam, but in private conversations on the margins of the visit to Washington, they wavered on the issue of timing, the appropriateness of an early visit, and the likelihood of getting a quick answer from the top leadership of Vietnam. Hanh told Cohen that it was necessary to discuss the proposed visit to Vietnam in the framework of world events, providing the first hint that the Defense Ministry had not yet made a ruling on the visit, and that the timing of the visit would take into account U.S. actions in other parts of the world, and thus be judged on the basis of criteria that were global, and well beyond the control of the DoD. The Vice Minister, and representatives of the ERD, made it clear that developing defense relations would continue to be an incremental process, but they envisioned a scheme that was even slower moving that the blueprint the Defense Department had coordinated during preparations for Hanh's visit.

The Saga of the SecDef Trip

During his talks in Washington, Vice Minister Hanh made it clear that he was not able to go beyond the position that a visit to Vietnam by Secretary Cohen would have many advantages. In meetings with the ASD/ISA and DASD/AP, he delivered the message that his delegation must report the proposal for a visit by the Secretary back to the Defense Minister, who would make the decision and issue the invitation. Privately, the Vice Minister said that the Minister would have to seek the views of the government, and a Politburo decision would have to be made before the proposal for an early 1999 visit was accepted. Hanh would not comment on the possibility of a visit prior to the Vietnamese New Year, although two other senior SRV Embassy officials separately suggested that March or April might be more realistic.

The Vietnamese side wanted to make certain that the visit by the Secretary of Defense took place in a manner that would reflect positively on Vietnam's status and standing in the region, and within ASEAN. Hanoi wanted to be in control of the event from the beginning, and was acutely sensitive to optics that might suggest the SRV was passively prepared to accept the preferences of the U.S. side. The MND also wanted to sculpt an appropriate explanation for the visit, one that did not necessarily rely on the framework conveyed to the Vietnamese during Hanh's meetings with Defense Department officials.[15] Finally, the Defense and Foreign Ministries wanted to have time to evaluate the scheduled November 1998 visit by the DASD/POW-MIA and to assess how the "ten year review" of POW/MIA cooperation and progress would impact on the overall U.S.–Vietnamese relationship.

The crux of the matter, though, was that the Secretary of Defense had personally communicated his travel proposal to both the Deputy Prime Minister and the Vice Minister of Defense. The Vietnamese side had grown comfortable with the low keyed, working level approach to planning senior level delegations that placed a primacy on vetting these initiatives thoroughly, carefully and deliberately, before they became scheduled events.

The ERD could manage the process when it involved organizing and explaining proposals that derived from the working level meetings with ISA. The ERD could devise the concept for running an event, and define the parameters of the proposed activity, essentially shaping the activity before it had to be defended within their own Ministry, and explained to the Foreign Ministry and the External Relations Department of the Central Committee, which took an interest in the defense relationship beginning in early 1997. However, Cohen's direct request to Cam and Hanh altered the process.

This also put ISA in the position of having to actively pursue the goal of an early 1999 visit to Vietnam through a concerted effort to persuade the ERD, the Foreign Ministry, and the Central Committee's External Relations Department that the trip should be allowed to go forward. By late October, to explain their obvious efforts to back away from an enthusiastic embrace of the idea of such a trip, the Defense Ministry and the Foreign Ministry began to quietly point to a series of scheduled meetings and events that would limit their flexibility to agree to a visit by Secretary Cohen, including the last quarter National Assembly sessions and follow-on requirements that would derive from those meetings, which would keep ministries busy through the first quarter of 1999; the likelihood that a first quarter interim party conference would be scheduled, an event that would take the remaining months of 1998 and the pre-lunar new year period to prepare; and the extent to which Vietnam's hosting of the 6th ASEAN summit in December 1998, and the Francophone Conference, would exhaust the resources of the government, and leave it ill-prepared to welcome the Defense Secretary in January or February of 1999.

On 21 October, Ambassador Peterson told Vice Minister Hanh that the U.S. would like to begin serious preparations for a January visit by Cohen, and requested support for this endeavor. A visit by the Defense Secretary, Peterson told Hanh, would be a serious step in the overall bilateral relationship, as well as a major event in the fledgling defense relationship. The same coordinated message was delivered by the U.S. Defense Attaché to the ERD's Director for International Affairs, and repeated in Washington during an ISA meeting with Vietnam's Defense Attaché. Not long after that meeting, at a regularly scheduled session of the Military Attachés in Hanoi, Senior Colonel Tan announced that the Secretary of Defense would visit Vietnam in early 1999. However, the Defense Ministry was still saying that the Minister and the government leadership must make a final decision on the visit, compounding the complexity of the mixed messages being spoken in a variety of Vietnamese channels.

The Defense Ministry promised a decision by 28 November. By 3

December there was still no indication that Vietnam was prepared to follow through with a formal invitation. Between 22 November and the first week of December, the ERD drafted an invitation to the Secretary, for signature by Minister Pham Van Tra, who had not yet returned from a trip to Japan. Ambassador Bang and Senior Colonel Quang felt the invitation would be signed shortly. In late December, the Defense Department released a major policy statement, The United States Security Strategy for the East Asian-Pacific Region, which included a section that described the U.S. long-term commitment to defense and security relations in Asia. In early December, Bang and Quang separately offered positive comments on that report, focusing especially on the paragraph about Vietnam, indicating that the public statement of U.S. intentions would probably be a useful means of underscoring Washington's reasonable view about the defense relationship with the SRV. Ambassador Bang thought the report's special mention of Vietnam would be an important part of the equation in convincing senior Defense Ministry officials to move ahead on proposals for bilateral military activities, including the plan for the January visit by the Defense Secretary.

On 9 December, ERD informed the U.S. Defense Attaché that the proposed trip should not take place, and that the Defense Ministry would issue a formal note to that effect in due course. The Vietnamese were not enamored with the idea of a January 1999 visit from the moment it was first suggested, if only because of the proximity to the lunar new year. But the visit also threatened to crowd an already busy December–January time frame. The Vietnamese system's bureaucracies were taxed by meetings, burdened by reporting requirements, poorly staffed, and a large event such as a visit by the U.S. Defense Secretary would have required diverting already committed and exhausted Defense Ministry personnel.

Beyond complicating an already busy schedule, the Secretary's visit raised more questions than it answered for the Vietnamese. While DoD sought to present the proposal as recognition of the positive developments in the relationship, the Defense Ministry was not satisfied with that explanation. ERD officials, Embassy representatives, and the SRV Defense Attaché were tasked by their home offices with the job of discerning the precise intent of the Secretary's visit. Interlocutors with whom ISA spoke on the subject were clearly not satisfied with a "visit for visit's sake" explanation, and continued to press with some urgency for explanations and details throughout the period leading up to the early December decision. In one sense, that was the first indication that the system was unprepared to say "yes" to this proposed visit, reluctant to say "no," and distinctly uncomfortable with the whole idea. At the point when the Vietnamese bureaucracies began searching for more information, seeking to collect ever increasing increments of nuanced data and particulars, it should have become clear that they had arrived at a decision to say "no" and were merely marking time until they were prepared to declare their position. This was, after all, a system that was not fueled by information, and reached decisions based on political instinct, ideological confidence, and personal preference.

The most important motivations for the Vietnamese decision to defer the visit by the Defense Secretary came on the policy side of the equation. Senior Vietnamese diplomats and MND officials privately stated that the Defense Ministry was not unified on the subject of moving the U.S.-Vietnamese relationship forward, and that some senior officials were concerned with the impact that a visit by Secretary of Defense might exert on the trajectory of Sino-Vietnamese relations. The U.S. government had not budged on the requirements for a trade agreement since mid-summer, and were not likely to alter the standing position. The Vietnamese had spent a lot of energy attempting to chip away at what it considered to be unrealistic expectations of the Vietnamese economy. The Defense Ministry, reflecting the government's position, had made it clear since September 1997 that the economic dimension of the relationship with the U.S. was the most important thing to Vietnam, and other aspects of the relationship, including defense ties, would wait until a trade agreement had been secured before proceeding in a more sure footed manner. Additionally, the Vietnamese had declared themselves to be enthusiastic supporters of Cambodia's entry into ASEAN. That put them at loggerheads with Singapore, the ASEAN chair for the annual rotation. Singapore, Thailand and others were reluctant to support early entry for Phnom Penh, and the U.S. government had staked out the position that this was an ASEAN decision to make. Hanoi had isolated itself and caused other ASEAN members, including Thailand, to begin to contemplate the possibility that Vietnam was angling to position itself as the leader of an "Indochinese caucus" within ASEAN. This seemed to have fed into Vietnamese concerns that the U.S. was working with other friends and allies in Southeast Asia to isolate Hanoi.

Moreover, Vietnam's Defense Minister had traveled to Japan in early December, and reportedly went home with some unpublicized training agreements. The visit was hailed in the Vietnamese media as a milestone. A senior Vietnamese military officer privately said that Vietnam would not need to request training from the U.S., that PAVN needs could be satisfied through training arrangements with countries such as Japan, and that the MND was perfectly satisfied with the model for military relations that the link with Japan offered. Vietnam had a political desire to proceed cautiously in approaching military-to-military relations with Washington, but it also had a set of practical needs that suggested reasons to move toward at least a tepid, partial embrace of Washington's overtures in the area of defense relations. Now, with renewed confidence that the MND could reap dividends through relations with other counties, some senior MND leaders appeared to have concluded that Vietnam had both a practical ability to move slowly and in the most modest increments in its relationship with the U.S. The Secretary's visit could be postponed, with no potential for blowback.

ISA recommended that the basic response to the MND's decision should begin with a statement of disappointment by Ambassador Peterson to Vice Minister Hanh. There should be no further expressions of concern. CINCPAC should not react. JCS should not react. State Department should not react. There should be no commentary by DoD officials at any level to media inquiries, beyond the statement that this was a scheduling issue only. ISA argued that DoD should express interest in proceeding with the calendar discussed at the 6 October 1998 working level meeting with ERD. The seven initiatives formulated as "deliverables" for the Secretary of Defense visit should, as appropriate, be acted upon in a manner that afforded the U.S. the best advantage. For example, the DPMO initiative to invite SRV archivists to the U.S. should be implemented on its own merits. Pending a decision by the Demining Interagency Working Group, the demining assessment team should still go forward as discussed in early October, with a March 1998 deployment date as the target. Ship visits as a subject for discussion should be dropped from any consideration of future possibilities in statements, forward looking projections, or idle speculation by DoD officials. Uncoordinated statements that suggested the highest levels of service leadership had ship visits in mind as part of the relationship, even for the future, would compromise any negotiating space that remained available to the U.S., and would also continue to spook the Vietnamese. Hanoi had demonstrated that it was closely attentive to public reflections to the effect that the U.S. was intent on steaming into familiar ports, and wanted a lot more control over the process leading up to a ship visit. Hanoi was as cognizant as the U.S. side that "no" answers had an impact on the tone of the relationship, and sought to avoid them. But Hanoi was also aware that "no" answers gave Vietnam an optical victory that offered some leverage in the context of planning the next steps in the relationship. Finally, ISA thought that the U.S. should begin to acknowledge that the 1999 calendar for bilateral events would include only a visit to Vietnam by the National Defense University and the Air War College, and any of the multilateral CINCPAC-sponsored conferences the Vietnamese elected to attend.

7

NUDGING THINGS ALONG, MUDDLING TOWARD DÉNOUEMENT, 1999–2000

Throughout 1999, the Vietnamese military continued to maintain that the defense relationship could begin to blossom at a snappier pace when the U.S. granted Most Favored Nations trading status to Vietnam, and signed a bilateral trade agreement. Vietnam understood that from the U.S. perspective, Hanoi needed to make significant progress in economic reforms, particularly in liberalizing access for foreign companies, before the SRV could carry out the provisions of the U.S.–proposed bilateral trade agreement and be ready to accede World Trade Organization. However, Hanoi felt that Vietnam's relatively low level of development should elicit a more realistic U.S. approach. Washington expected Vietnam to take positive steps toward a more transparent set of economic practices in line with world standards in four areas: trade practices, intellectual property rights, trade and services market access, and investment policy. By mid-January, there was little reason to believe that this would happen, and considerable evidence suggesting that the matter would remain frozen, especially given Vietnam's early January decision to accord "non Most Favored Nations Status" to the United States, a decision that threatened to impose higher tax burdens on U.S. businesses.

For the U.S., progress in the relationship between militaries was premised on continued POW/MIA cooperation. Progress in the military relationship was also contingent upon (1) consistent Vietnamese cooperation in facilitating activities and visits agreed to in annual working level planning sessions; and (2) progress toward some bilateral cooperation on practical activities, such as the demining training program. The U.S. side offered a range of suggestions intended to engender Vietnamese interest in proceeding with low-keyed visits, meetings, and discussions between defense officials, including the March 1999 plan for a U.S. Demining Assessment Team visit; the Defense POW/MIA Office's plan to invite SRV archivists to Washington to review National Archive holdings on Vietnam's wartime losses; and a DoD-funded project to compile data on herbicide missions, an effort which looked ahead to joint scientific research on the impact of Agent Orange and health risks in the context of the Scientific and Technological Cooperation Agreement that was under negotiation with Vietnam.

To a certain extent, these were symbolic markers intended to sustain efforts to modestly develop the relationship. The risk, of course, was that symbolism would beget symbolism, and little else. For example, an attempt to respond to Vietnam's long standing position on the Agent Orange problem, by fashioning a response focused on sharing information that might contribute in a small way to telegraphing the Pentagon's sincerity about the issue, several times came close to eliciting a Vietnamese response that dismissed the gesture rather than embracing the spirit in which it was offered. An invitation to Vietnam to send several archival researchers to Washington to look at U.S. wartime records in the National Archives was seen by some Vietnamese as an inconsequential step intended to place the ball back in Hanoi's court, a tactical act rather than a meaningful decision.

Essentially, by early 1999 the effort to develop initial relations between the two militaries had ground to a halt.

Bottom Line ERD Positions

Through early 1999 the ERD remained unprepared to take advantage of unscripted opportunities. The ERD was scrupulously literal about each and every agreement with the U.S. side, unwilling to evince flexibility in anything other than the most minor ways, and focused on blunting the potential for the U.S. to take uncharted initiatives, even minor ones.

In mid–January 1999, for example, Vietnam's Defense Attaché in Washington informed ISA/AP that the Deputy Director of the Defense Ministry's Training Department was scheduled to participate in the Cross Country Championship of the International Council for Military Sports in Florida in late February. A representative of the DoD Armed Forces Sports Council was the primary organizer for this event. ISA proposed that the Deputy Director, Senior Colonel Pham Huu Kham, and his assistant visit the Pentagon for talks with U.S. military training specialists following the sports event. This would have been in keeping with the November 1996 and the September 1997 agreements to bring Vietnamese and U.S. military specialists together for ground-floor level dialogue on specialized military topics where discussion could contribute to the relationship. The Vietnamese side, however, was reluctant to look at this as an opportunity to encourage dialogue between specialists. The ERD questioned the appropriateness of the proposal, saw this as an uncharted event that was not explicitly part of the working level agreements of January 1997 and October 1998, a step which risked giving the U.S. side a home court advantage. The ERD saw this as an event that might place Vietnamese military officers unfamiliar with ERD's management of the relationship out of the reach of MND officials.

For the Vietnamese Defense Ministry, it was important to stick to the plan, because the temptation of a flexible response would mean that the rules of engagement had changed, and the nature of the relationship had changed with it. By mid–January, the MND had shown no interest in reprogramming the calendar to include visits of significance before the proposed late 1999 Defense Secretary visit. Some senior Vietnamese officials were privately prepared to look at the logic of the argument that both sides needed to have more to show for all the efforts in order to invest this relationship with some semblance of substance. However, the ERD did not embrace the idea of adding events to the plan for 1999, and suggested that it would be hard to get a positive answer back to the U.S. in sufficient time to proceed with additional activities. Further, by the first week of February there was reason to believe that the Defense Ministry was inclined to walk back from some of the October 1998 agreements.

For example, the ERD complained about the planning for the first steps in organizing the Air War College visit set for March. In late January, the ERD informed its Defense Attaché in Washington that the proposed Air War College visit did not coincide with the dates requested during the October 1998 working level meeting, but that the ERD would go forward with planning for the mid–March visit anyway. In fact, in October 1998 ISA had told ERD that the visit would take place during the first quarter of 1999, and that ISA would inform the ERD of the proposed travel dates at a later time. Later, the ERD formally complained about the size of the delegation. The ERD clearly confused the main body of the Air War College student group with the list of the U.S. military air crew. There was no reason why the normally careful SRV Embassy passport processing office would have made an error of that sort. It seemed more likely that the ERD was being mischievous, cranky, or both.

Additionally, by the end of the first week of February, it appeared that the ERD had turned against the idea of a demining experts group visiting Vietnam in late February or early March, a trip that had been fashioned on the basis of discussions with a receptive Vice Minister Tran Hanh during his October 1998 visit to Washington.

The Vietnamese looked at efforts to add "beef" to the relationship and concluded that the U.S. was fiddling with existing frameworks and concepts, and attempting to move ahead without a plan. The ERD saw itself as the stable force, the stickler for the letter of an agreement, and the steady and reliable player that would take the long view and refrain from minor mid-course corrections for a process that was essentially on track. That the DoD could offer changes after planning meetings had concluded suggested to the Vietnamese that Washington was interested in achieving tactical goals, but had few long-term and well thought out strategic interests at stake in the defense relationship with Vietnam.

To DoD, the Defense Ministry was stubbornly reluctant to venture beyond platitudes about the positive advantages of the defense relationship, and preoccupied with the consequences of offending China by developing a potentially close relationship with the U.S. Consequently, the Ministry was perceived incapable of identifying the real advantages of a military to military connection with the U.S. Defense Department officials felt that MND's continued unwillingness to demonstrate flexibility on the number of visits, on devolving the process of planning the calendar for the relationship to program managers, and on the distinction between working level study visits and high level delegations indicated Vietnam's reluctance to press forward with the defense relationship. The MND's determination that the issue of port calls could only be decided after a meeting of the Defense Minister and the Secretary of Defense was taken by senior Pentagon policy officials to mean that Hanoi was decidedly unprepared to move the relationship forward in a meaningful way.

Interestingly, quite apart from these interpretations, Pentagon decision makers were surprisingly undaunted by the negative vibes and temporizing responses from the Vietnamese side. To a certain extent, the novelty of the interaction with Vietnamese defense officials, and the generally positive meetings with the talented representatives of the Defense Ministry since early 1997, engendered an interest in playing out these hands, and a willingness to defer gratification. Some Pentagon policy makers saw themselves on the cusp of a new historic moment, however fleeting and strategically inconsequential it might be, and were willing to sustain attention to the issue of defense relations with the SRV for the minor reward of contributing to ice-breaking opportunities, especially since the equities involved were not overwhelming and the "heavy lifting" entailed in taking these decisions would not break any backs.

By early 1999, some U.S. policy makers had concluded that the Pentagon had done the "easy" things in terms of setting the stage for a military relationship. The question of what would come next still had to be addressed. First, in practical terms, DoD had to determine whether to press forward with initiatives such as inviting Vietnamese students to the military academies, nominating military medical interns to study at Walter Reed, and lifting the restrictions on technology transfers that prohibited the sale of select military items to Vietnam. Second, in strategic terms, DoD had to answer the question, where would this relationship go in the next decade, and what did the Pentagon envision in terms of resources for investment and likely dividends from developing these defense ties? Would the relationship involve access to facilities, strategic coordination on regional issues of mutual importance, joint and combined training exercises, and meaningful information exchanges bearing on security matters? Many felt that the relationship was stymied by the inability to move the trade agreement forward, as well as a conservative swing in overall Vietnamese economic and foreign policy. This had begun to show up in the defense relationship in the form of the MND's decision to sustain the cautious approach to future military-to-military activities in the October 1998 meetings, as well as the way the MND handled the proposed January 1999 visit by the Secretary of Defense.

Defense Ministry Program Decisions

In early February, through the Defense Attaché in Washington, the MND informed DoD of its readiness to welcome the Secretary of Defense either after September or in mid–2000. The ERD rejected the possibility of a separate ASD/ISA visit in March or April, and "postponed" the proposed early March visit by a team of U.S. demining experts, selected three multilateral conferences to attend, and politely declined an invitation to the CINCPAC change of command ceremony, while stating that they might rule positively on a proposed June 1999 CINCPAC visit.[1] At the same time, the ERD stated that the Vietnamese side would send a two-person delegation—one senior colonel and one lieutenant colonel—to the January–April session of the Asia Pacific Center for Security Studies. The

Defense Ministry also indicated its readiness to welcome the U.S. Air War College, and the National Defense University delegation scheduled for May, but explicitly noted that these two visiting groups would be received as "high level delegations," demonstrating that the MND had still not accepted the DoD argument that such working level visits should be a "routine" part of defense diplomacy.

These early February decisions to reject initiatives aimed at nudging the relationship forward, and to unceremoniously curtail high level delegations such as a visit by ASD/ISA, suggested that the Vietnamese were nervous about taking any steps forward in any foreign defense relationship before General Secretary Le Kha Phieu had paid his long awaited visit to China.

Phieu's China Trip

Party General Secretary Le Kha Phieu paid an official visit to China from 25 February to 2 March. He conducted wide ranging talks with senior Chinese party and government officials aimed at reiterating the importance of the relationship; establishing goals for the resolution of the proverbial "outstanding issues," including land border delineation and Tonkin Gulf demarcations; and restating commitments to dialogue on issues of mutual importance such as economic and trade development, technological cooperation, and relations between party organizations, governments and mass organizations. Vietnam reiterated its One China policy in the joint declaration issued on 2 March. Interestingly, while the Chinese media referred to this as a "working visit," the Vietnamese press termed it an "official visit."[2] The Chinese press also appeared to draw an equivalence between the Phieu trip and the visits to Beijing paid by the Cambodian and the Lao Prime Ministers, suggesting that the three Indochinese countries were equally important to Beijing. Vietnam was not accorded the primacy it might have expected, though Hanoi had sought to underscore the singular importance of the visit by scheduling it as the first major diplomatic foray following the lunar New Year.[3]

In recounting the visit, Deputy Prime Minister Nguyen Manh Cam underscored the importance of the in-principal agreement to focus on the long term bilateral development of economic and trade cooperation, accelerate investment in one another's economies and cross border trade, as well as efforts to crack down on smuggling. Cam highlighted the agreement to accelerate efforts to address the smuggling issue, efforts to create mechanisms that would speed up sea and land border negotiations, and the attempt to establish a schedule of annual high level meetings to facilitate the process.[4]

Le Kha Phieu took a longer view in describing the trip, characterizing it less as a breakthrough in practical economic and trade aspects of the relationship, and more as a continuation of the positive trend toward increased proximity between the two communist parties, the governments and the people that dated from the 1991 Chengdu Conference, at which the Vietnamese and the Chinese agreed to mend party and state ties and put aside their differences for the sake of restoring the relationship. Phieu dwelled on the importance of the joint declaration, which Cam avoided characterizing in his 2 March press conference.[5]

The actual visit may have had little appreciable affect on the long-term potential for Sino-Vietnamese relations, and may have only served to set a positive tone for Phieu's future dealings with Beijing. However, this relatively successful maiden voyage to China by the General Secretary made a lot of other diplomatic acts much easier to undertake. Senior Vietnamese officials seemed relieved, and privately noted the extent to which having accomplished this important trip would free up the resources to commit to activities that had been deferred pending the successful execution of this critical first visit to the PRC.

Indeed, there was a burst of activities in the U.S.–Vietnamese defense relationship following Phieu's trip to China, not so much as the result of what was said or done in Beijing, but because the trip itself had taken place, enabling the foreign and defense policy making apparatus to focus on other goals and requirements.

The Air War College completed its trip to Vietnam in mid–March. The ERD produced about five officers from the Military Strategy Institute for discussions with the U.S. visitors, including Major General Nguyen Ngoc Van, the Institute's Deputy Director, who accompanied Vice Minister of Defense Tran Hanh to the U.S. in October 1998. That represented an elevation of the access afforded such U.S. groups, which in the past had been confined to 0-6 level interlocutors. The Air War College visited the flight line at the Nha Trang Pilot's School, a first for any visiting foreign delegation, according to the Vietnamese escorts. Since it appeared likely that the French military delegation scheduled to visit Vietnam in April would get a similar flight line visit, this stood as less of a symbolic breakthrough for the U.S.–Vietnamese military relationship, and more of an indication that the MND was beginning to understand that it needed to produce more substantial itineraries to hold the attention of foreign militaries. In March, the MND sent a representative to the Asia-Pacific Military Medicine Conference in Bangkok. In April, a U.S. demining experts team traveled to Hanoi to explore potential bilateral cooperation on demining training. Two Foreign Ministry officials attended the course taught at CINCPAC's Asia Pacific Center for Strategic Studies from May to July.

Another Lurch Away from Engagement

Between late April and mid–May, editorials carried in the Vietnamese military newspaper condemned what the SRV felt was the manner in which principles of the North Atlantic Alliance had been pushed aside, and the United Nations ignored in the efforts of the West to resolve the crisis in Kosovo.

The government in Hanoi appeared to have left it to the media, and "the broad masses of the Vietnamese people," to reflect Vietnam's severe moral and political objections to NATO's tactics and approach to the pursuit of a diplomatic resolution. Several groups that operated under the umbrella of the Vietnamese Fatherland Front made major shows of publicly protesting NATO bombings. PAVN veterans' rallies against the West's actions in Kosovo were highlighted in the Vietnamese media. The accidental bombing of the Chinese Embassy in Belgrade changed the rules. On 10 May the Foreign Ministry spokesperson in Hanoi issued strongly worded condemnations of the bombing of China's embassy and, by extension, the entire NATO enterprise.

By May it was apparent that Hanoi was poised to take some steps to signal displeasure over NATO and U.S. policies toward Kosovo in a manner that would impact on the military part of the relationship. Senior SRV Embassy officials had privately communicated the extremes to which Vietnamese public statements had gone as a result of the strong feelings in Vietnam about the optics of a sustained air war against a small, helpless country. It was unlikely that Vietnam would choose to pursue business as usual in the midst of these events, especially after the deaths of the Chinese diplomats. In May, the SRV Defense Attaché and ISA agreed to begin talking about the nuts and bolts of a visit to Vietnam by the Secretary of Defense in September or October. Those discussions were deferred, as were plans for a search and rescue workshop scheduled for August, and a CINCPAC visit set to take place in July. The Defense Ministry had begun to employ the diplomatic weapon most frequently relied upon by the Vietnamese military to signal displeasure: inaction on pending activities.

In the end, the SRV response was not as consequential as it could have been. In mid–July, the ERD informed the U.S. Defense Attaché in

Hanoi that the MND would not send representatives to the PAMS or the PACC. By August, activities had resumed. In early August, a senior lecturer from the Military Technical University attended the Spectrum Management Conference in Hawaii. In mid-month, a U.S. Coast Guard team sponsored by the Coast Guard's International Training Division visited Hanoi to discuss training opportunities for the Vietnam Customs and Maritime Police. A Vietnamese POW/MIA archival research delegation, headed by the MND's Director of the Social Policy Department, traveled to Washington in late August to review archival materials in the National Archives pertaining to wartime activities in an effort to shed light on unaccounted for PAVN troops. The Deputy Director of the MND's Research Department attended the Biannual Conference of the Asia Pacific Center for Strategic Studies during late August–early September.

In mid–September, Vietnam dispatched a researcher from the Institute of Military Technology to attend the PACOM-sponsored Pacific Senior Communicator Meeting (PSCM) in Hawaii, and in mid–September two PAVN officers joined the Asia Pacific Center's course. In October, the U.S. Naval Medical Research Unit Number Two (NAMRU-2) visited Vietnam in support of its long term research on endemic tropical diseases conducted in conjunction with the Ministry of Health and the National Institute of Hygiene and Epidemiology, as well as the Louis Pasteur Institute in Ho Chi Minh City. In November, in response to unprecedented levels of flooding in Thua Thien-Hue Province, two U.S. Air Force C-130's from the 353rd Special Operations Group delivered nearly 20 tons of relief supplies to the affected areas. A seven-person U.S. Military Medical and Engineering Assessment Team traveled to Vietnam in early December to assist the International Red Cross in identifying long term preventative measures necessary to stem the potential for flood-related diseases, and to mitigate future flood damage to public health clinics in the province.

If ever there was a point in the relationship when the tempo of activities was itself sufficient to suggest that the Vietnamese had overcome their reluctance to participate in bilateral defense activities, this was it. The Defense Ministry had sent students to the Asia Pacific Center, and dispatched a fair share of experts and ranking officers to various multilateral symposia. They received a variety of U.S. military experts for discussions on issues ranging from demining training to flood relief projects. And they received several U.S. delegations in a manner that telegraphed a real interest in conducting effective military diplomacy and fruitful exchanges of views on enduring security issues.

Nevertheless, with the exception of emergency flood control requirements that worked to dramatically expand the U.S. military role in humanitarian activities in the SRV, the Vietnamese side remained disinclined to expand the area of interaction into activities the Defense Department regarded as confidence building events. The Ministry's allergy to programs that involved placing U.S. military personnel on temporary duty in Vietnam persisted. In terms of dialogue on regional security issues, though the MND was from the start prepared to engage in discussions at the vice ministerial level on regional and bilateral defense and security issues, what emerged by the last quarter of 1999 was a somewhat lopsided exchange, with the American side providing detailed rundowns on current issues and policies, and the Vietnamese side articulating predictable boilerplate, leaving little room for discussion.

Some in the Administration argued that Vietnam would come around and accept the positive contribution a defense relationship with Washington could make to their own security, especially in light of consistent Chinese actions in the South China Sea, and undiminished Chinese efforts to expand its leverage in the region. Proponents of this thinking urged that the U.S. look for ways of providing entry-level military training opportunities, IMET-funded English language training, and defense technological cooperation in areas that would equip Vietnam to undertake modernization in safe ways, and with an eye toward the possibility of future interoperability.

To ISA, though, it did not seem that the Defense Ministry would be prepared to sign up to an expanded defense relationship with the enthusiasm that some proposed would be generated by the signing of the bilateral trade agreement. The Defense Ministry had repeatedly stated that a trade agreement would improve the atmosphere in which discussions of military-to-military relations took place. However, there was little basis on which to conclude that success in the economic part of the relationship would offer an incentive to Hanoi to ramp up its defense and security cooperation with the U.S.[6] The motivations behind the MND's reluctance to press ahead with on-the-ground practical engagement in training, humanitarian cooperation, and high level visits were profound, in some instances emotional, and would probably not be easily assuaged by a success in the area of bilateral trade relations. The Defense Ministry still believed that moving ahead with the U.S. in defense relations would be met with a negative reaction in Beijing. The MND saw more advantage to sustaining links with ASEAN, adhering to non-aligned principles, and investing in multilateral regional efforts to improve security through confidence building methods. The MND had assessed the resources that the U.S. could bring to the table as minimal, not worth the trouble, and in the end probably too legislatively difficult for Washington to actually deliver. Indonesia's position on IMET, and Thailand's views of the U.S. laws restricting economic and security assistance, had not been lost on Hanoi.

As if to drive home the message that, notwithstanding the record of fourth quarter 1999 activities, the Vietnamese military was still of two minds on the defense relationship, in mid-August the MND informed the Pentagon that the visit by the Secretary of Defense would be postponed again.

The Saga of the SecDef Trip, Redux

In late December 1998, the Defense Minister invited Defense Secretary Cohen to visit Vietnam after the month of March. May 1999 proved inconvenient for the Vietnamese side, leaving April and anytime between June and December. ISA aimed for the September–October timeframe, one of the two preplanned timeframes set aside for the Secretary to travel to Asia.[7] In February 1999, apparently acting on instructions, the Defense Attaché in Washington communicated the message that the MND preferred to see the Secretary of Defense travel to Hanoi in April in order to ensure that the Defense Minister could pay a reciprocal visit before the end of 1999. The Vietnamese were decidedly unfriendly to the suggestion that the Cohen trip to Asia would occur during the last quarter of 1999, and that the visit to Vietnam should be factored into that scheduling reality.

ISA did not broach the subject of the proposed trip with the Vietnamese until late May, as Cohen's travel plans began to clarify, at which time a senior Vietnamese military official indicated at least formal receptivity to the visit, showed that the Ministry continued to regard Tra's December letter as the authoritative source on the timing of such an event, and hoped that "world affairs" would not detract from the Secretary's travel plans. In the most blunt terms summoned to define the situation, the Vietnamese military was prepared to say that if the "problem in Belgrade" was not resolved, it "might" be inconvenient to proceed with a visit to the SRV by the Secretary. Scheduled visits to the SRV by British and French military officials had been cancelled by late May, and the Defense Ministry had signaled that it was not prepared to go forward with high level events while Belgrade was being bombed, and in the face of continued conflict in Kosovo.

By late June, the ERD had become comfortable enough with the manner in which the "world situation" had stabilized to offer the U.S. Defense Attaché an in-principal statement of support for a late September–early

October date for the Cohen visit. By that time, for the Vietnamese side, the issue had become one of Defense Minister Pham Van Tra's availability; the ERD hoped to have this resolved by the second week of July. At a late June briefing for the defense and military attaché community in Hanoi, Vu Tan stated that Hanoi hoped the delegations that had been postponed because of the events in Kosovo could now be rescheduled, suggesting that the U.S. role in the actions by the North Atlantic Treaty Organization in Kosovo were no longer an obstacle to active planning efforts for senior level delegations.

However, in early July senior Defense Ministry officials anticipated that by late August there would be a positive response to the proposed timing of a Defense Secretary visit to Hanoi in late September–early October 1999, but that it would not be easy getting to that point, and obtaining the answer desired. The Kosovo issue had been resolved, but not in a manner that solved the problem. The situation was still so unsettled and complicated that the same qualms that led Vietnam to communicate its unwillingness to go forward with senior level visits in the context of the North Atlantic Treaty Organization's (NATO) use of force against Yugoslavia still had validity, and still prompted hesitancy on the part of the Vietnamese leadership.[8] Moreover, at least one senior defense official averred that Vietnam would see efforts to plan for visits by high level delegations as inappropriate in a context in which the U.S. relationship with China was still so troubled by the NATO bombings.

In mid–August, the Defense Ministry informed the Pentagon that the visit by the Secretary of Defense, postponed once in January 1999, would be postponed again.

The Vietnamese may have calculated that a visit by the Secretary could have overloaded the system at a time during which significant advances in the relationship were being contemplated. Hanoi had agreed in principle to a draft bilateral trade agreement in mid-summer, and moved closer to signing other bilateral cooperation agreements (science and technology, counter narcotics, commercial aviation), though in the end they demurred and signed nothing. Hanoi may have also been concerned with projecting the image of a growing defense relationship with Washington that would not quite represent the message Hanoi wanted telegraphed to the region; such a visit represented a ratcheting up of defense relations for which Vietnam was simply not yet ready.

It is fair to say that the Vietnamese had not made up their minds concerning what they wanted from a defense relationship. The Defense Ministry was of the view that the relationship was a good thing, but managing the interaction was potentially complex for them, especially in light of

Sino-Vietnamese relations. Various departments in the Defense Ministry continued to hold differing views.

The General Political Department was content to confine the opportunities for interaction to small-scale events. The Social Policy Department remained focused on Agent Orange and Vietnam's MIAs. The External Relations Department regarded the relationship with the Pentagon as important, but was inclined toward an extremely incremental process of furthering the relationship. The Foreign Ministry was more inclined to endorse programs, including the demining cooperation offered to, but initially rejected by, the Defense Ministry. The result was an only partial inclination to "engage."

The Defense Ministry remained concerned with the manner in which Beijing would react to the prospect of a defense relationship between Washington and Hanoi, especially one sanctified by a meeting between the two highest defense officials. The Defense Ministry's ERD sought to assuage concerns in Beijing by offering regular briefings and reassurances of the low level character of this interaction. Hanoi's own unstated rule was that the China relationship was the most important foreign and defense policy issue. Indeed, the proposed January 1999 visit was cancelled precisely because the General Secretary of the Vietnamese Communist Party did not want to meet with the Secretary of Defense before he had paid his introductory calls in Beijing. So, the proposed September–October time frame became untenable because both the Vietnamese and the U.S. relationship with China had not stabilized to a sufficient degree after a round of sensitive, publicly waged conflicts between Hanoi and Beijing, and between Washington and Beijing.

Planning for 2000

ISA met with the ERD in early October 1999 in Hanoi to review 1999 defense relations, and plan for military-to-military activities in the year 2000. Reviving the pitch made in October 1998, ISA argued that it was time to nudge the relationship forward, end limits on the number of annual activities, and move the relationship into normal channels where operational level officers managed the bilateral dance card. The ERD responded in a decidedly less combative fashion than when these points were first raised in October 1998.

Essentially, ISA took the position that the Pentagon did not intend to function within the confines of the Vietnamese-imposed ceiling on the number of U.S. defense delegations that could visit the Socialist Republic in one year. The intention was to put each proposal before the ERD, via the U.S. Defense Attaché, and ask the ERD to agree to each activity, even those that transcended the ceiling on bilateral activities, in the hope that the ERD would recognize the utility that would derive from proceeding with these initiatives. It was clear that the MND was not prepared to devolve management of the planning process to levels below the defense policy makers. It was also clear that the ERD had the effective veto; they could reject proposed visits and other activities at the point at which they were put before the MND. However, doing otherwise would have guaranteed that the Vietnamese would have continued to blunt ISA efforts to get ERD agreement to turning the process work over to PACOM, which would have run an annual bilateral military consultation meeting to handle the administrative aspects of the relationship. The only way to tuck the issue aside for the moment without unceremoniously dropping it from the U.S. side's talking points was, in effect, to note that DoD intended to define its side of the notional calendar of bilateral military events without regard for the Vietnamese ceiling on annual visits. It was a tactic that allowed each side to represent its posture as the one that prevailed in these discussions.

ISA recommended that the Vietnamese side agree to a tailored bilateral program that focused on exchanging information regarding the military's role in the management of environmental issues, beginning with meetings in Hanoi between DoD experts, led by the Principal Assistant to the Deputy Under Secretary for Environmental Security, and Vietnamese counterparts. The program would structure opportunities for U.S. and Vietnamese military specialists to discuss hazardous materials management, pollution prevention, environmental maintenance of training areas, deforestation, ground water contamination, and environmental planning. ISA also detailed the interest on the part of the Naval Oceanographic Office (NAVOCEANO) to visit Vietnam for discussions regarding cooperative survey efforts, information exchanges, and training opportunities offered by the U.S. Navy.

Additionally, ISA asked the Vietnamese side to agree to the first of what DoD hoped might become regular visits to Vietnam by the CAPSTONE Program of the National Defense University as part of the education of newly selected flag and general officers who participated in a six week long course geared to prepare them for future command responsibilities at the joint task force level and above. PACOM's interest in having a group of lawyers from the Judge Advocates Office visit Vietnam for a "military law exchange" was also placed before the ERD. ISA restated the U.S. side's interest in pursuing bilateral search and rescue initiatives. PACOM and the U.S. Defense Attaché had cooperated to design a proposal to bring a group of Vietnamese search and rescue specialists to Hawaii for a seminar, in conjunction with the regional command components and the U.S. Coast Guard. The U.S. and Vietnam had prior successes in cooperating on SAR issues, including the rescue of a U.S. pilot whose aircraft failed him in the vicinity of a Vietnamese naval vessel in coastal waters in the early 1990s. RADM J.J. McClelland, Commander, 14th Coast Guard District, was scheduled to host the event. The U.S. side planned to review SAR program developments since April 1998, and discuss the new U.S. National SAR plan as well as a host of technical areas including Automated Mutual Assistance Vessel Rescue (AMVER) and Short Range SAR Communications Improvements. The U.S. side intended to review training opportunities, give the Vietnamese side an opportunity to review major SAR developments and challenges, and discuss scenarios for SAR activities. Finally, ISA reiterated the U.S. Navy's interest in ship visits.

The ERD agreed that the relationship was progressing at a satisfactory pace. They committed to working toward a visit by the Secretary of Defense in 2000, and acknowledged the U.S. side's invitations to multilateral conferences. The ERD agreed to review programs offered to enhance the bilateral part of the military relationship, including defense environmental security cooperation, and oceanographic and hydrological cooperation. The Vietnamese did not reject, nor did they enthusiastically embrace, the proposals for demining training, expanded search and rescue cooperation, and bilateral exchanged on medical and dental care, veterinarian work and military law. The MND was still not prepared to discuss port calls until there was an opportunity for the Defense Minister and the Secretary of Defense to discuss this matter directly. In predictable tones, the ERD raised their three "humanitarian" issues: Agent Orange, Vietnamese MIAs, and U.S. Government support for anti-Hanoi organizations. ISA replied, also in predictable tones, that the U.S. hoped to promote private sector cooperation on basic scientific research, and that a bilateral scientific and technological cooperation agreement was necessary to facilitate work with Vietnamese science and health officials on dioxin issues; that the late August visit by Vietnamese archival experts was a positive accomplishment in the area of providing information to the SRV that could help shed light on Vietnam's missing troops; and that the U.S. law mandating that compensation be paid to former Vietnamese commandos did not represent U.S. support for anti–SRV organizations. Those replies were no more satisfactory to the ERD than earlier efforts to explain Washington's positions on these persistent issues.

In the end, the ERD and ISA agreed, subject to higher level concurrence, that the "next steps" in the military relationship for the year 2000 would include a SAR bilateral seminar in Hawaii, set for late 1999 or early 2000; the annual class trips to Vietnam by the National Defense University and the Air War College; a Vietnamese military medical delegation visit to the US; a DoD environmental security working level group visit to Hanoi, as well as a U.S. demining training working level group visit to Hanoi. The two high profile activities were to be a visit to Vietnam by the Secretary of Defense, possibly in mid–2000, and a reciprocal visit by the Minister of Defense to Washington, possibly in late 2000.

2000 Begins

Most of the first three months of the year 2000 were taken up with preparations for the Defense Secretary's visit to Vietnam, which by mid–February had been set to occur in the middle of March. In late February, PACOM sponsored a bilateral search and rescue seminar in Hawaii. In February, the NDU's CAPSTONE class of newly minted general officers visited Vietnam as part of its global familiarization travel, an event that had been discussed for the first time at the October 1999 planning session. ISA and ERD agreed to postpone the visit by an Air War College group scheduled for March in view of the anticipated press of business associated with planning the Cohen trip. By late January, the visit by the Secretary of Defense had become the exclusive preoccupation of both sides, and all DoD-MND dialogue focused on agreeing to a date for the visit, shaping the broad parameters of the event, and defining an itinerary.

In mid–January, Vietnamese military officials told the U.S. Defense Attaché that Hanoi's primary focus for bilateral relations in 2000 would be trade and economics, and the military relationship would have to stay within the framework of overall relations, reinforcing the message that defense relations would not be allowed to move so fast as to get ahead of the trade and economic relationship. The ERD gave no indication of whether an agreement had been reached regarding the proposed July date for the Cohen trip, and reiterated the MND's "two part policy" regarding foreign military delegations: (1) no country should send more than one delegation to Vietnam in any single month, and (2) no single country would be allowed to send more delegations than any other country. The curious thing about this message was the timing and the tone, which seemed intended to telegraph the point that a visit to Vietnam by the Defense Secretary was not the most important piece of business on the MND's mind.

On 31 January the ERD announced to the U.S. Defense Attaché that Defense Minister Pham Van Tra had extended an invitation to Secretary Cohen to visit Vietnam "at the end of March."[9] Senior Vietnamese military officers and diplomats suggested that the MND's leadership had concluded that a visit earlier than the proposed July date would enable both sides to act on initiatives that might spring from the meetings between the two defense chiefs.

ERD officers suggested that the MND's leadership was hesitant to agree to a visit by a lame duck Defense Secretary, which could in part explain the ERD's non-responsiveness to entreaties between November 1999 and late January 2000 to initiate serious trip planning efforts. In January, Ambassador Bang threw his share of cold water into the mix, noting that a foreign policy crisis of the sort represented by the events in Kosovo, or the eruption of another Taiwan-related crisis, could cause a "setback in planning for the visit," notwithstanding his recognition that Washington would have little control over the kind of event that might stop the show. Bang observed that the impending U.S. election was the primary reason a visit should not take place in the last quarter of 2000. The VNCP's own preparations for the national party congress that would begin in earnest in the last quarter of 2000 was another reason for looking to an earlier date. Bang also said that Hanoi must take into consideration the potential costs of a visit by the Secretary. For example, the influence of Overseas Vietnamese in the U.S. "is not insignificant." That community could organize against a trip, and appeal to Senators Helms, Gilman or Rohrbacher as one of several possible public steps that would galvanize opposition to such a trip.

Between 24 January and 2 February, the Office of the Secretary of Defense committed to a 9–20 March trip to Asia, with stops in Hong Kong, Vietnam, Korea and Japan. The Hanoi-Ho Chi Minh City portion of the trip was to take place between 13 and 15 March. Between 3 and 9 February the Defense Ministry replied, through ERD, that a 25–30 March time frame would be preferable.[10] This was perceived in the Pentagon as a potentially serious setback for the trip.

The importance of this blip in the process of nailing down agreement to plans for the visit was that the MND was apparently back to freelancing military diplomacy, without coordinating their positions or discussing the consequences of these actions with the Foreign Ministry. This suggested that the MND was operating without the benefit of Foreign Ministry coordination in much the same way as when the MND precipitously and unilaterally cancelled a half years worth of bilateral activities in April 1997.

In April 1997, ISA pressed the issue of the cancellations with Foreign Ministry officials, and though DoD was not able to get any of the events restored, the end result of the full court response to the cancellations was a chastened ERD that effectively promised to act more reasonably in subsequent efforts to plan annual events. In February 2000, it was not clear how influential the Foreign Ministry channels could be. The new Foreign Minister, Nguyen Duy Nien, did not have the experience of his predecessor in terms of the relationship with the U.S. He did not have the rank and credibility necessary to be a player at the Politburo level. His predecessor, Nguyen Manh Cam, was a Politburo member. At the time, Nien was not. In short, the equation of influence had shifted in ways that appeared to have blunted the Foreign Ministry's ability to manage foreign policy through a rudimentary interagency approach.

Between 9 and 13 February, the U.S. side pressed the importance of agreeing to the original timeframe for the Secretary's visit. Peterson took up the issue in meetings with senior SRV officials in Hanoi, and senior Pentagon officials lobbied Ambassador Bang. On 13 February, the ERD provided a one-page letter on MND stationary to the U.S. Defense Attaché inviting the Secretary to visit Vietnam between 13 and 15 March.[11]

In late January, when the ERD first indicated Minister Tra's decision to invite Cohen to make the trip in late March, ERD Chief Vu Tan said that MND envisioned a welcoming ceremony, "official talks" with the Defense Ministry's leadership, courtesy calls on senior government officials, an official banquet hosted by the Defense Minister, and a visit to Ho Chi Minh's Mausoleum. This was a bare bones schedule which reflected the ERD's interest in insuring that the first visit by a U.S. Defense Secretary established no unmanageable precedents, and invited no comparisons to visits by other foreign defense establishment chiefs.

With the final decision made about the timing of the trip, the ERD grew flexible about the itinerary. For example, Tan understood that the invitation to pay respects at the mausoleum of President Ho might press beyond the Pentagon's comfort level, and the matter was unceremoniously dropped from discussions. When the MND issued its invitation to Cohen, ISA resurrected the notional schedule discussed in anticipation of a September or October 1999 visit as a point of departure. That proposed schedule revolved around a first day spent with JTFFA, and a speech to the National Defense Academy, followed by a second day of calls on the General Secretary, the President, the Foreign Minister, the Defense Minister, and the Chair of the National Assembly, plus a pre-departure visit to the 921st Squadron of the People's Air Force, and a brief trip to Ho Chi Minh City.

The ERD's notional schedule, formulated around 24 February, called for a welcoming ceremony, a "conference" between the two sides, an MND-hosted reception, a visit to the National Defense Academy, courtesy calls on the President, the Chair of the National Assembly, and the Foreign Minister, a visit to the 921 Squadron prior to departing for Ho Chi Minh City, where the delegation would meet with the Chair of the People's Committee and the Commander of the 7th Military Region, and tour the Tan Thuan Production and Export Zone. That plan did not include a call on the party chief, and envisioned a more pro-forma traipse through the National Defense Academy rather than a speech. OSD saw a formal speech with a question and answer period as the Secretary's opportunity to talk with PAVN officers directly, and to deliver the Department's strategic message in a setting distinct from the customary set-piece courtesy calls. So, the job became one of bridging the differences between the Vietnamese side's minimalist interpretation of what it would take to make a successful visit, and the U.S. side's formula for a more public, high level schedule that combined ceremony and substance. By late February, the U.S. side began to look unfavorably on the idea of a site visit to the Tan Thuan Export Zone, arguing that planning for a visit to the JTFFA recovery and excavation site outside of Hanoi, where CILHI and the Task Force were conducting wet screening operations in the area of an F-4B aircraft crash site, was a critically important part of the trip, against which the allocation of time to other events would have to be balanced.

The Vietnamese had some initial concerns that featuring POW/MIA-related activities during the Secretary's visit would lead to a flood of critical comments that questioned the SRV's record of cooperation on this issue. By the end of February, Hanoi had moved on to the larger issue of dealing with the domestic and international response to a visit aimed at broadening the relationship with the U.S. The Vietnamese side was also concerned that an outspoken Secretary might make comments akin to those of U.S. lawmakers on sensitive issues that could impact negatively on the bilateral relationship; Cohen's legislative record on issues such as Burma's human rights practices had not escaped Hanoi's attention. Finally, through the end of February, the Defense and the Foreign Ministry were looking for the practical dividends that would flow their way from the visit, including humanitarian gestures and practical offers of assistance in areas such as flood relief. OASD/ISA officials sought to convince Vietnam that the DoD was looking at the visit as an opportunity to show gratitude for Vietnam's commitment to resolving the POW/MIA issue, and to remind the MND and the MFA that since there were strict legislative limits on the kinds of assistance and development commitments that could be offered by the Secretary of Defense, Vietnam would be wise to avoid establishing impossible measures the success. Additionally, in order to lower the temperature of the Vietnamese leaders who feared that comments the U.S. side might make during the visit would reflect badly on the Socialist Republic, Washington reiterated that the aim of the trip was to stress shared goals and interests including a mutual commitment to maintaining regional stability, finding common ground on how to engage with China in a positive manner, and identifying ways to carefully nudge the bilateral relationship along on a positive path. Such reassurances probably had marginal impact on the level of trepidation in Hanoi.

Early in the planning for this trip, U.S. and Vietnamese working level officials discussed the way in which the sensitive issues in the relationship might be handled during the visit. In a 28 February meeting ISA told Ambassador Bang that the commando compensation issue should not be raised at all, if only because it had been addressed with the Vietnamese at several levels, and the two sides had staked out positions that were amply clear; reiterating those positions would add nothing to the Secretary's interaction with the MND's leadership. Interestingly, Bang replied that the decision would be made by the Minister himself, suggesting that the questions concerning the Pentagon's implementation of this law were important enough to the MND to require a policy determination on this matter at the highest level of leadership. Additionally, the Vietnamese may have been concerned that Cohen would want to meet with "dissidents and religious figures" who would want to use the Secretary's visit to draw attention to their causes.

In early March, Senior Colonel Quang told ISA that in the scheduled 13 March meeting with the Secretary, Minister Tra planned to begin by laying out Vietnam's views of the regional and global security situation.[12] Tra, Quang continued, would also confirm the government's commitment to continued "renovation" in the economic realm. The Defense Attaché stated that the Minister would also review Vietnam's fundamental defense and security policies, stressing the military's role in "safeguarding" the country. Tra would enunciate Vietnam's foreign policy priorities and principles, situate the relationship with the U.S. in this context, and reiterate Vietnam's commitment to continued cooperation on the MIA issue. Finally, the Minister planned to offer some suggestions for future steps, and to discuss Vietnam's humanitarian requirements. Though the ERD did not spell out for their Defense Attaché what those suggestions might be, Quang opined that they might focus on areas where U.S. assistance could have an impact on the relationship, such as demining, Vietnam's MIAs, and Agent Orange. Quang told ISA that the MND would not ask questions regarding the "commandos."

By 9 March, the MND had clarified its position regarding the visit, and the speech to the National Defense Academy, and had come to embrace the event, at least in part as the result of a review of Cohen's trip to Beijing and his address to the Chinese Defense Academy.

The Visit

Secretary of Defense William Cohen arrived in Hanoi on 13 March. There were several arcane debates staged in the Western press over whether Cohen was the first Defense Secretary to visit Vietnam, in view of wartime visits by secretaries to South Vietnam. The media eventually settled on a phrase framing the event as the first visit by a U.S. defense chief to communist Vietnam. However, the visit felt, looked and smelled like a first time event. Every customary act of protocol resembling the courtesies extended by the Socialist Republic to hundreds of other prior visiting foreign delegations was, in this event, extended for the first time to the defense secretary from the United States, from the hoisting of the American flag alongside the flag of the SRV in the Defense Ministry's welcoming ceremony to the Secretary's visit to the headquarters of the 921st Squadron, and his visit to Ho Chi Minh City. And though the visit broke no new ground of fundamental strategic importance, the fact that it occurred at all represented an achievement, one that had the potential to make all subsequent bilateral military-to-military interaction that much easier.

Cohen met with Tra in a 13 March plenary session, and on several other occasions during a 13–15 March visit that was described as positive and constructive in the Vietnamese media. The Secretary also met with Prime Minister Phan Van Khai, President Tran Duc Luong, Foreign Minister Nguyen Duy Nien, as well as the Chair of the Ho Chi Minh People's Committee and the Commander of Military Region 7. Cohen paid a highly publicized visit to a JTFFA/CILHI excavation site outside of Hanoi.

Both Cohen and Tra agreed on the importance of recognizing trends toward global integration, settling regional differences through peaceful means, relying on the regional association as the fulcrum for efforts to insure regional stability, and managing relations with China in positive, effective ways. The Defense Minister and the Secretary exchanged views on regional security, developments on the Korean peninsula, and China's regional and global role.

The Secretary made the case that the Bilateral Trade Agreement would be a useful step toward helping Vietnam take advantage of its significant economic potential, and a means of seizing the opportunity to begin early integration into the regional and global economy. In all his meetings, Cohen stressed the importance of the POW/MIA issue, and the need to move the bilateral defense relationship ahead slowly and in measured stages calibrated to stay in pace with the overall process of bilateral normalization. The Secretary highlighted the U.S. commitment to transparency in the relationship, the importance of dispelling bilateral suspicions, and avoiding regional misunderstandings of U.S.–Vietnamese intentions. He emphasized the need to find common ground on which to develop the basis for practical cooperation, offering as starting points demining, environmental security cooperation, and forensic training for Vietnamese officials responsible for accounting for Vietnamese MIAs.

It is instructive to look at what Tra said about the bilateral relationship, and how he said it. At the plenary session, Tra stated that the biggest question was how will the defense relationship with the U.S. be conducted. At the moment, he observed, most of the relationship was taking place in the form of U.S. visits to Vietnam. On the MIA issue, Tra stated that the MND had established its own office responsible for this problem, and that this office had demonstrated productive cooperation for many years. Vietnam was committed to continuing that cooperation on the basis of a "humanitarian position" taken in the relationship with the U.S. Regarding the question of transparency, Tra referenced the Secretary's remark about the importance of making certain the U.S.–Vietnamese relationship was entirely understood and accessible to foreign countries, and stressed the need for acts that would make the decision to enter into this relationship understandable to the Vietnamese people. In fact, he averred, the Vietnamese had shown special attention to the U.S. MIA issue. Vietnam, Tra noted, sought the same for its soldiers and officers listed as MIA, amounting to about 300,000 personnel. Many soldiers and relatives, he continued, suffered from the effects of chemicals sprayed during the war. Those families received help from the Vietnamese government, which had recently taken the step of providing financial assistance and health care to these people so they could lead normal lives. Vietnam, Tra concluded, hoped the Secretary and the U.S. Congress could "pay attention" to Vietnam's MIAs and victims of chemical spraying. By evoking the need for Congressional and cabinet level attention, Tra seemed to suggest that the Vietnamese were interested in having some legislative acknowledgement of those issues, and assistance blessed by the Hill. Tra stated that Vietnam was prepared to put aside the past and look to the future, but the Vietnamese government had to do something for its own people so the past could be set aside and the people could look toward a better future.

Tra asserted that Vietnam's own policy toward the U.S. was very transparent. He noted that Vietnam understood that some people in the U.S., supported by some "circles" including people who left Vietnam as refugees, did not want to see better relations with the U.S. The Secretary, Tra stated, should do something to keep those people from preventing the development of better relations with the U.S. Cohen's reply started with this issue, and noted that the U.S. had shared intelligence information with the Foreign Ministry and the Ministry of Public Security on possible illegal activities by those who sought to undermine relations. The Secretary suggested that in both the U.S. and Vietnam, some people had opposed normalization, both citizens and officials. The best way to overcome critics was to maximize official contacts, and to demonstrate that the relationship could proceed in a positive way. The goal should be to reduce suspicions and misunderstanding so as to overcome the objections of critics. That argument seemed persuasive enough to eliminate this issue from the agenda of subsequent sessions with the Defense Minister, as well as from the agendas at meetings with other high ranking government officials, including the Prime Minister and the Foreign Minister.

On demining, Minister Tra pointed out that Vietnam had, since the end of the war, been involved in reclaiming land contaminated by mines and unexploded ordnance. He stated Vietnam's need for equipment, particularly mine detectors that could locate mines and unexploded ordnance deeply buried, thus taking the first step toward responding to the U.S. request that Vietnam help determine how to spend the $750,000 in appropriated demining funds earmarked for use by Vietnam. Tra also asked that the U.S. help overcome dioxin contamination around airbases such as Bien Hoa and Da Nang.

Tra noted that, in the step-by-step process of building defense relations, the U.S. and Vietnam would cooperate on search and rescue matters. The U.S. was far more experienced in this area, Tra observed, and reiterated that search and rescue cooperation would figure in the course of developing this phased, incremental, step-by-step process of cementing military relations. That statement in effect authorized continued efforts in this area.

On environmental issues, Tra said that Vietnam was much concerned about the sea, since on a daily basis 100 ships traveled along the coast of Vietnam within 200 kilometers, including oil tankers. He noted U.S. Navy and Coast Guard experience with oil leaks. Both those references to U.S. experience, on search and rescue practices and environmental issues, reinforced that information exchanges aimed at making Vietnam smart on these challenges remained the best way to start incorporating practical cooperation on such matters into the military relationship.

On ship visits, Minister Tra said this issue could be left to the U.S. Defense Attaché, the ERD and the U.S. Embassy. So, after years of the ERD arguing that no headway would be made on the issue of ship visits until the Defense Minister and the Secretary of Defense discussed the issue, Tra turned the issue back to the working levels. Later, Major General Tan noted that this was a key point in that the ERD now had the authority to proceed to cooperation with U.S. DoD counterparts on this issue.

In response to Cohen's reference to global interdependence, regional and global integration, the two sides got involved in spinning out a soccer metaphor over the issue of whether or not a new team's competition in certain leagues could be accelerated regardless of whether that team had developed its strength and capability through minor league experience before moving forward to play with established teams. Though the metaphor addressed questions concerning Vietnam's regional and global fit, the merciless beating to which this metaphor was subjected suggested that the MND was contemplating the parameters within which Vietnam would approach the development of bilateral military relations.

It seemed that Tra was prepared to place the priority on "improving experience," playing effectively with "local teams." This would develop team experience and allow matches across classes of experience. Tra also seemed to make the case that step-by-step improvements in Vietnam's "team" were required before it could play in a global class league. Physical strength and capabilities would have to be developed before Vietnam could enter into effective relations with powers. Doing this at too rapid a pace would hurt Vietnam's chances of developing equal relations in the military realm.

From the Vietnamese perspective, the Cohen visit went well. Senior departmental level MND officials came away with a positive picture of the bilateral defense relationship. The candid talks put a dent in Vietnamese suspicious about Washington's plans and intentions, and generated senior level support for practical steps on some proposals for bilateral cooperation. The positive tone translated into some practical accomplishments at the 17 March ISA–ERD planning meeting.

Planning from a New Vantage Point

Following the Cohen visit, the ISA — ERD planning session in Hanoi reviewed the process of preparing for the Secretary's visit with the goal of deriving planning lessons for future high levels events. ISA and ERD looked at practical programs that would require action from both sides, such as the demining proposal and the environmental security cooperation proposal. Finally, the planning meeting reviewed the ground rules for a visit to the U.S. by Vietnam's Defense Minister.

ISA took the view that the Secretary's endorsement of a modest expansion of areas of cooperation, and Minister Tra's essentially positive response to this line of thinking, was sufficient reason to take a closer look at demining training and expanded search and rescue training and information sharing, environmental security cooperation, as well as exchanges on military medicine, law, airport safety and regionally relevant multilateral activities concerning anti-piracy measures, disaster relief, and peacekeeping.

ISA and ERD discussed Vietnamese equipment and training requirements, MND agreement to the U.S. side's invitation to send a team of PAVN demining experts to the U.S., and Defense Ministry recognition of the DoD offer to provide Vietnam with an enhanced international deminers guide to unexploded ordnance identification, recovery and disposal. ISA reiterated the Secretary's support for efforts to identify ways in which the Army Corps of Engineers could provide assistance to the SRV in areas requiring assistance with flood control measures. ISA also noted the invitation to the November 2000 Chiefs of Defense Conference, and pointed to the success of the bilateral search and rescue symposium in February as an achievement in the military relationship on which both sides should build. On the question of ship visits, ISA suggested that the ERD agree to discuss ship visit diplomacy and port call procedures on a navy-to-navy basis. Finally, ISA restated the Secretary's invitation to the Defense Minister to visit the U.S., and recommended that the ERD study DoD regulations governing the shape of such events as a first step toward defining a workable date.

The ERD was decidedly positive in its responses, acknowledging the importance of the Secretary's visit, and characterizing the bilateral defense relationship in generally upbeat terms. ISA urged that the ERD come to a decision on a date for the Minister's visit to the U.S. ERD suggested an interest in conducting the visit before the U.S. presidential elections, meaning that the trip would have to take place sometime between April and September. That was to be the closest thing to a practical response from the ERD to the request for a good date for a visit by the Minister of Defense.

The ERD essentially fell silent on this issue between April 2000 and August 2001. Major General Vu Tan stated that he would advise the Minister to instruct the PAVN Engineering Command to work out a list of equipment necessary to detect deeply buried unexploded ordnance, and that he would recommend that the Minister issue instructions to PAVN units involved in environmental work to prepare for "engagement" with the U.S. Tan himself noted that while in the past it had been difficult to work on programs such as demining, it would now become easier because the Defense Minister would issue instructions, which would be the key to getting appropriate PAVN units and officials involved in the practical dimensions of bilateral military cooperation. The ERD also agreed to receive delegations representing the NDU, the Air War College, and the U.S. Marine Corps University Group, and to attend CINCPAC-sponsored multilateral activities when resources allowed, appropriately capable personnel were available, and the subject matter coincided with PAVN interests. On the margins of the meetings Vu Tan chided ISA over the fact that the U.S. was still represented by a defense attaché with the rank of lieutenant colonel. This disparity in rank between the U.S. military representative and the SRV Defense Attaché, a senior colonel, yielded awkward moments of protocol, Tan argued, and suggested that the U.S. was not really according the relationship appropriate attention.

Tan toned down the familiar "wounds of war" points, and spoke to these issues in vocabulary that was friendly, philosophical, and oriented to accomplishing practical things in these sensitive areas. The problem with initiatives focused on demining training and environmental security, Tan explained, was that these issues were "consequences of war." He made the case that it was beneficial to the relationship to see U.S. activities aimed at dealing with flooding, and it would be similarly positive if Washington could focus on the two other humanitarian issues that had become part of the landscape of the military relationship, namely Vietnam's MIA issue and the Agent Orange problem. Interestingly, Tan contoured his recommendation so that the emphasis was on "exchanging information" on demining, environmental protection, and dioxin related issues, rather than the more complex Vietnamese effort to prod the U.S. to "addressing the consequences of war" that had characterized earlier efforts to place the ball in the U.S. government's court. Tan said that the Vietnamese side understood that the U.S. was "realistic and practical," but that it was important to understand what was "in the minds of the Vietnamese people." In the end, he argued, the issue boiled down to a question of attitudes. Americans urged Vietnam to "close the past, and look to the future," and to "put aside" the past or "erase" (xoa) the past, which would be impossible for the Vietnamese people. Actually, Tan's reference was to the choice of terms used to translate Cohen's statement emphasizing the need to get beyond the past and work to improve relations in the future. Tan made it clear that he saw a difference between "letting bygones be bygones," itself a difficult enough proposition for Vietnamese, and "erasing" memory of historical events, indisputably more difficult.

2000 Ends

The Secretary's visit contributed to making some things in the defense relationship easier, if only by dispelling some Vietnamese-held suspicions and clarifying Washington's intentions. For example, in early April, the Vietnamese welcomed the USMC University group, and in late April received a U.S. Army Pacific Command surgical survey team. In June, the ERD hosted a U.S. Demining Experts Group. Also in June, the State Department announced that Vietnam would be included in the U.S. humanitarian demining program, and would received assistance including equipment designed to detect and safely remove landmines and unexploded ordnance. In mid–July, the MND welcomed the Principal Assistant to the Deputy Under Secretary of Defense for Environmental Security, and in late July a U.S. Health Clinic Engineering Assessment Team arrived.

The signing of the Bilateral Trade Agreement in August was a politically important moment that led to a high point in the overall relationship, and translated into additional possibilities for defense relations. PAVN's daily newspaper sent reporters to an early August CINCPAC-sponsored international public affairs seminar. Vietnamese military officers participated in the Pacific Armies Management Seminar in early September, and sent representatives to a PACAF international search and rescue conference in late September and the CINCPAC-sponsored Symposium on East Asian Security. However, though the symbolism of the Secretary's trip was important, though it did change the tone and vocabulary in which the practical matters of the defense relationship were discussed, and though the signing of the trade agreement exerted a positive multiplier effect on relations, these events did not alter the basic chemistry of the military relationship, and did not change either side's fundamental starting points.

It was still awkward and difficult to prod the Vietnamese side to widen practical bilateral defense cooperation. It took three years to get the MND to agree to the most modest of steps toward cooperation on demining training.

The humanitarian issues that had become a fixture in the dialogue between the defense establishments were still sensitive matters. In some ways the Vietnamese side was emboldened by the talks that took place between Minister Tra and Secretary Cohen in March, arguing that just as the Pentagon had long spoken of the need for a "track record" of accomplishments that would set the stage for a visit by the Defense Secretary, so the Vietnamese side was prepared to argue that there should be a "record of responsiveness" to Vietnamese humanitarian requirements" that would be a sufficient basis for going forward with plans for a visit to the U.S. by Vietnam's Defense Minister.

Additionally, it was still necessary to factor in the "China veto," to calculate into the equation the way in which U.S. initiatives might play in Beijing, and thereby influence the Vietnamese perspective on U.S.–SRV defense relations. The Vietnamese Defense Ministry probably had more of a comfort level by the time of Secretary Cohen's trip. In part, this may have been because of an intensive period of government-to-government activities in 1999 and 2000 aimed at improving relations with China, including the December 2000 signing of a "Joint Statement on All Around Cooperation in the New Century Between the PRC and the SRV." Successfully completing those milestones enabled Hanoi to focus, between March and June 2000, on defense relations with many other countries. Nevertheless, the China angle remained a critical variable in sizing up Vietnam's readiness to engage. Vietnam remained reluctant to take any steps, such as exploring bilateral military cooperation or committing to high level travel, that might suggest a thriving, close defense relationship with the U.S. Between April, when the Secretary Cohen issued a written invitation to Minister Tra to visit the U.S., and September 2000, the date of the last ISA-ERD planning meeting, the MND was essentially unresponsive to continuous ISA requests to take steps toward planning for a reciprocal visit to the U.S., in effect indicating that the MND might have questioned whether the relationship had reached the point at which such a visit made sense.

Interestingly, in mid–March 2000, the Vietnamese side was, perhaps for the first time in a while, somewhat relaxed about the implications of the Defense Secretary's visit, to the point that a Foreign Ministry spokesperson was prepared to suggest that newspapers had perhaps "gone a bit too far" in their comments suggesting that the Cohen visit had some meaning or message relevant to Sino-Vietnamese relations. The remark that stirred most press attention was Cohen's response to a question raised during his session at the National Defense University. During a meeting with faculty, Cohen stated that "one of the very important and beneficial aspects of ASEAN is that you have collective interests, and those collective interests can in fact, if you act in concert, give considerable leverage in dealing with China in the future on a peaceful and cooperative basis." At least one commentator suggested privately that this remark could have been taken to mean that Cohen had offered a recipe to the Vietnamese for responding to troublesome Chinese actions in the region. In actuality, the point was little more than a statement acknowledging the relevance and utility of ASEAN in coping with security issues that impacted on the interests of member countries. In a side conversation during the Secretary's visit, Vu Tan said that the candid talks put a dent in the suspicions harbored by senior Vietnamese military leaders. He also observed that since U.S.–China relations had transcended the pace and scope of U.S.–Vietnamese relations, it was unlikely that China would view the U.S.–Vietnamese military talks as a problem. This meant that senior Vietnamese military officials did not regard the Cohen visit as having telegraphed any anti–China themes, that they were confident or at least more assured that they were not being drawn into the U.S. embrace as part of some strategic effort to challenge China's interests in the region, and that PAVN leaders were confident that Beijing did not see efforts to develop military relations between Vietnam and the U.S. as threatening to its interests.

In 2000, the Department of Defense maintained the stress on the importance of continued POW/MIA cooperation, and recognized the extent to which Vietnam's MIA issue represented an important policy challenge for the MND. Acting on the offer made by Cohen, DoD sought to organize a visit to the U.S. for three Vietnamese scientists to attend a course on mitochondrial DNA and remains identification. The Pentagon continued to support the Veteran's Initiative of the Vietnam Veterans of America and the Veterans of Foreign Wars, and worked with Ambassador Peterson to provide the SRV with wartime information and artifacts that might help shed light on Vietnam's unaccounted for service personnel. By late 2000, the ERD had begun to talk about the SRV's MIA issue in less strident terms, recognizing that this would be a problem that would take many years to resolve, and that it was an issue Vietnam must resolve itself.

In 2000, ISA conducted two planning meetings with the ERD, in March and in September. In the period following the first planning meeting in 1997, the two sides had developed an effective means of defining annual calendars of military events through sharing views of what was possible in the relationship. ISA and the ERD had arrived at a formula for insuring timely action on proposals, through the use of official channels of communication between the two ministries. That itself demonstrated the extent to which an effective system of managing these yearly programs had been put in place. ISA had nudged beyond the limits of bilateral visits and activities, while preserving the overall modest character of this defense calendar of annual events. By late 2000, there appeared to be agreement that important steps had been taken toward developing a defense relationship through bilateral activities, multilateral seminars and symposia, high level visits, and working level contacts between the two militaries.

The visit by the Air War College had been cancelled, by mutual agreement, in view of the planning required for the March 2000 visit by the Defense Secretary. The ERD met with a group of USMC students from the Corps' Command and Staff College in April. Also in April, Vietnam received a USARPAC Medical Delegation and an Engineering Team, which met with the Vietnam Red Cross Society and the International Federation of the Red Cross to discuss flood damage. The ERD welcomed the National Defense University in May. Vietnam also agreed to a visit by a small group of U.S. Naval Academy students led by a faculty member in June. The ERD also agreed to meet with a second delegation of U.S. experts on demining, and from that June meeting emerged a series of mutually acceptable proposals for a demining program. The U.S. Environmental Security Experts Group conducted useful meetings in Hanoi during late July–early August, demonstrating a willingness from both the U.S. and the Vietnamese side to cooperate on problems that were not traditionally part of conventional defense relations, and validating the proposition that the most effective way of developing the U.S.–Vietnamese military relationship was to begin with "informational exchange" between "defense experts."

The Secretary of Defense and the Minister of Defense had agreed in March that both sides should look for ways to enhance the relationship. Vietnam had agreed to expand working level familiarization visits to include the Marine Corps University and CAPSTONE. However, through the end of 2000 the ERD failed to press forward with plans to get PAVN delegations of military medical officials, science and technology experts, and faculty and staff members from the National Defense Academy to visit the U.S. The Defense Ministry evinced little interest in steps that would make the relationship more of a "two way street." Nor did the ERD believe that the business of managing the relationship should be moved into the hands of planners, regional command representatives, service representatives and the defense attachés who would relieve policy-level officials of the tasks of brokering proposals, managing the flow of visitors, and overseeing the planning and execution of events in the relationship.

The March 2000 visit by the Secretary led both sides to take another look at the issue of senior visits. The Vietnamese had taken the view, before March, that it was premature to discuss visits to Vietnam by senior U.S. military officers. The U.S. side pressed for agreement to visits by several senior military and defense officials in 2001, including the Commanding General of the U.S. Army Region Pacific; a U.S. Navy Battle Group Commander; the Commander of the USMC Forces Pacific; and the Commandant of the Marine Corps. The ERD was politely receptive but noncommittal about the possibility of conducting such visits in 2001. The attractiveness of enhanced bilateral cooperation on demining and flood control, the possibilities for select training opportunities, and the prospect for increased dialogue on regional security issues that could develop as a result of such visits were clearly not decisive selling points for the ERD.

Finally, by late 2000, the ERD and ISA agreed that the discussion between the Secretary and the Minister on U.S. ship visits to Vietnam should lead to working-level talks on the subject. It remained difficult to press beyond that shared understanding, and to define the next step that would result in efforts to explore the practical matters involved in conducting port calls. ISA offered ERD a briefing on ship visits by the Office of the Chief of Naval Operations and the Pacific Fleet Command as a means of jump starting this process. The ERD was receptive to this starting point, but showed no interest in following through on this initiative through late 2000, notwithstanding the notably more positive views spoken by ERD officials on the prospects for a ship visit. In late 2000, the Vietnamese view was that Cohen and Tra had agreed in principle that port calls should be part of the relationship. It was up to both sides to determine the right time to press forward with a ship visit. Vietnamese officials at the ministerial level remained concerned over the larger meaning of ship visits to Vietnamese ports by American vessels, and the risks implicit in seeking to schedule an early port call. Vietnamese veterans, Vu Tan noted, continued to be concerned about the optics of U.S.–Vietnamese military relations. Senior advisors to the Central Committee of the VNCP were also focused on the sensitivities of this matter. The ERD showed that the Vietnamese side must be attentive to public opinion and "diplomatic views" expressed about defense relations with the U.S.

By September, the Vietnamese government had turned its attention to preparing for President Clinton's arrival. The Foreign Ministry, according to one senior Defense Ministry official, was "studying" the experiences of the Defense Ministry gained in managing Secretary Cohen's visit. The President's November 2000 trip, widely judged to have represented a moment of symbolic importance with no real policy punch line, had little impact on bilateral military normalization. The White House was reluctant to add a senior U.S. military representative to the trip, in part because of what the U.S. Embassy sensed was Vietnamese hesitancy about having a defense component for this event, and in part because the White House wanted to carefully maintain control of the spotlight, and make certain that little detracted from the POW/MIA issue. However, the MND appeared to be prepared to receive a senior U.S. military representative as part of the Presidential delegation as early as April or May, and on multiple occasions mentioned the possibility of side meetings with a senior DoD representative that could contribute to "military to military relations."

In the event, the President's visit underscored that there was still much to be done to make certain that the bilateral trade agreement made a difference in the economic relationship. There was still some heavy lifting necessary to make certain the scientific and technological cooperation agreement, signed during Clinton's trip, contributed to a systematic approach to the Agent Orange issue, a matter raised repeatedly during the President's meetings in Hanoi. The President's speech to university students in Hanoi, broadcast nationwide, in which he articulated his message on freedom, market access, private economic initiative, and opportunity were positively received in Vietnam. And though the General Secretary did allow his hackles to show in a meeting that featured predictable VNCP boilerplate, in the end the President's visit symbolized successful normalization, acknowledged Vietnam's significance, and crystallized the issues that would become center stage fixtures in future bilateral discussions.

The President's trip featured the MIA issue, demining, and Agent Orange cooperation. None of the ongoing issues in the defense relationship cropped up, suggesting that bilateral military interaction would continue to be cautious in pace and scope, modest in its goals, and calibrated to keep pace with developments in the overall process of normalization. Incremental steps toward more developed cooperation on practical matters such as demining, environmental security, and search and rescue would take time. A careful ratcheting up of the level of dialogue and diplomacy would follow the Defense Secretary's March visit and the September planning meeting. Both sides were prepared to begin working level discussions on the potential for a ship visit, but that would also take a long time to work out. In the meantime the Pentagon would continue to push the envelope, albeit gently, by seeking more senior level visits, increased practical cooperation and more regular, routine channels for dialogue.

8
CONCLUSIONS, OBSERVATIONS, MUSINGS

Dissecting Motivations

The first discussions between Vietnam and the U.S. on military normalization took place in 1995, well below the ministerial level, on an informal and exploratory basis, in a manner intended to provoke thinking about bilateral defense relations, without necessitating a policy decision at this early juncture. These were "terms of reference" discussions aimed at piquing interest. For the U.S. side, the goal was to be able to stimulate some palpable Vietnamese interest in a dialogue on the subject of military-to-military relations. Attention to the subject by senior Vietnamese embassy officials in Washington, and a reasonable indication that the issue was communicated back to the Foreign Ministry for further study, was sufficient basis for the case that Hanoi would not foreclose on the possibility of discussing this dimension of the normalization process with U.S. officials. That was what ISA required in order to make the case that this was a fertile area for exploration, and to stimulate the interest of the Pentagon's policy makers.

It appears that the SRV Embassy officials who first listened to the argument at least informally communicated the substance of these meetings to the departmental-level within the Foreign Ministry, and that information may have been relayed laterally to relevant Defense Ministry departments, possibly the External Relations Department. That much seems likely, especially in view of the effective manner in which the SRV Embassy under Le Van Bang kept the Foreign Ministry informed of issues in Washington. What is not clear is whether the Vietnamese Embassy's communications stimulated discussions, and prompted the

Defense Ministry, the Foreign Ministry, or the Prime Minister's Office to stake out any policy positions on the matter of U.S.–Vietnamese defense relations.

That is, it is not clear when the question of defense relations between Washington and Hanoi became a policy issue for the Vietnamese. The MND may have thought about dispatching a Defense Attaché as early as January 1996, shortly after the U.S. assigned an Army Colonel to Hanoi as the first military representative. For the Vietnamese, that decision would have been made at the level of the Minister, but it was probably not framed as part of a decision to engage in defense relations with the U.S., given the manner in which the Defense Ministry appeared to look at various parts of the process as disconnected, discreet steps to be judged on their own merit. The Vietnamese may have thought about the possibility of a visit to Hanoi by the Secretary of Defense as early as late 1996, though there is no indication that such an event was calculated as a part of the normalization process, or even that the musings about such a visit within the MND's Research Department and the ERD were couched in discussions about the long term possibilities for U.S.–Vietnamese military cooperation.

The Vietnamese Defense Ministry was not sure what the U.S. intended to accomplish during the talks conducted between the Deputy Assistant Secretary Campbell and Vice Minister Nguyen Thoi Bung in November 1996. Up to the eve of these discussions, senior military officials thought that the U.S. side intended to focus on the POW/MIA issue. At least one senior member of the MND's delegation to those talks was genuinely surprised that the agenda was not primarily POW/MIA-oriented, suggesting that the Vietnamese came to the table with no clarity about U.S. intentions, in spite of efforts to by ISA to put the MND's mind at ease.

Part of that may have been the result of the Defense Ministry's generally cloistered approach to foreign and defense policy issues. The habit of refraining from, or avoiding, interagency discussions with the Foreign Ministry, for example, probably contributed to the MND's disjointed approach to U.S. proposals in the November 1996–April 1997 period.

Another part may have been the MND's preference to stay out of the business of military diplomacy, and to shy away from making new policy, except in instances where there were clear national defense interests at stake, and where guidance and leadership from the government was clear. So, the MND was on safe ground in working to articulate defense relations with China, but on much less settled soil in thinking about new military relations with the U.S.

This means that had the U.S. side not raised the issue of the potential for military-to-military relations, the Vietnamese would probably not have shown any interest in the topic. Vietnam's military was quite content to keep its distance from the increasingly complex question of normalization, and to view the process as critical only insofar as economic relations and trade status were concerned. Indeed, beginning in late 1997, the Vietnamese side was unequivocal on the subject of fine-tuning progress in all areas of the relationship so that the matter of Most Favored Nations status and the Bilateral Trade Agreement were center stage issues in the relationship. To that end, the MND made it clear that military relations could not, and would not, progress in any appreciable way until real forward movement had taken place in the normalization of economic and trade relations. It seemed that the Defense Ministry, and the ERD in particular, were more than happy to cede center stage to the Office of the Prime Minister, and the "economic" ministers, if only to avoid the potentially difficult process of having to devise a policy, and render strategic judgments, about defense relations with the U.S.

The real question, though, is did the Vietnamese military ever look at the bilateral defense relationship with the U.S. as something with potential strategic meaning and value? While the process of formulating a policy position on the question bilateral defense relations with the U.S. was bureaucratically and politically complex for the Defense Ministry, was there any point at which Vietnamese military thinkers looked at the strategic "pros and cons" of such a course?

From the start of the normalization process, the Defense Ministry's thinking about relations with Washington remained focused on the POW/MIA issue. The MND's involvement in this issue was, by 1994, profound, and its memory of politically consequential aspects of the issue was acute. Senior military officers, while recognizing their government's commitment to be helpful to the U.S., were quite prepared to look at this issue as a one-sided, uncomfortable obligation that grated on their nerves, insulted their country, and neglected their own "humanitarian" problems stemming from the war. Additionally, the MND embraced the argument that Washington was intent on destabilizing Hanoi, and that the U.S. supported all manner of insidious schemes hatched by expatriate organizations to accomplish that goal. Given the negative view of U.S. intentions that emerged from this thinking, it is fair to say that the Vietnamese military was not prepared to look at Washington as a potentially reliable friend or partner. Defense Ministry officials were keenly aware of U.S. policy toward Burma, which stressed human rights issues and supported democratization, and studiously attentive to U.S.–Thai conflicts that in-fluenced the tone of that treaty relationship. Many senior Vietnamese defense officials looked at U.S. behavior toward friends in the region and concluded that Washington was incapable of grasping local strategic realities, identifying policy opportunities, and thinking realistically about Southeast Asia. On that basis, senior Defense Ministry officials were not at all confident in Washington's capacity to size up, and satisfy, Vietnam's strategic requirements. Between 1996 and 1997, Vietnam's military leadership concluded that contacts between the U.S. and the Vietnamese military would be a harmless adjunct to the overall normalization process, and a strategically inconsequential commitment. Hanoi would not gain security assurances from this link, and should not suggest that the Socialist Republic was at all invested in the possibility of security cooperation with the U.S. Recognition of basic similarities in regional security views, and shared defense concerns, could not be parleyed into a meaningful relationship. From the perspective of the senior MND leadership, such a relationship could not prosper as long as Washington wielded the cudgels that were America's major foreign policy tools—including human rights, labor standards, market access, intellectual property rights practices, and counterproliferation policies.

More to the point, the Vietnamese military leadership firmly believed that the most strategically consequential relationship for Vietnam was its link with China, and that the Sino-Vietnamese relationship should not be jeopardized by any suggestion that Hanoi was receptive to anything beyond symbolic steps toward normal military relations with the U.S. The Defense Ministry, especially the ERD, went to great lengths to insure that Beijing understood Hanoi's views regarding the relationship with the U.S., and that China was fully informed about all interactions between Vietnam's Defense Ministry and the Department of Defense.

At the same time, Vietnamese defense officials were not at all shy about voicing their qualms regarding the Sino-Vietnamese relationship. Senior SRV officials complained of Chinese highhandedness, Beijing's consistent failure to conduct its relationship with Vietnam in a way that recognized Vietnam's importance and accorded Hanoi appropriate and deserved respect, China's continued efforts to dominate the bilateral dialogue on border issues, and to complicate Vietnam's economy by dumping cheap Chinese goods onto the weak Vietnamese market. In the 1996–97 period, PAVN military officers voiced their concerns over China's force buildups in the South China Sea, and probed for the likely U.S. response to potential conflicts in the Spratly Islands. Through late 2001, Party and Foreign Ministry officials also privately spoke their minds, regarding China's reliability as an ally, and suggested steps the U.S. might take to put some meaning behind the familiar rhetoric describing Washington as Asia's benign benefactor and reliable security guarantor.

The Vietnamese who spoke these views, privately, on the margins of official meetings, or in direct terms on the record in official encounters, did not harbor the view that Washington would alter its thinking about how to best address China, and did not suggest that a closer U.S.–Vietnamese relationship, with a more focused, purposeful defense component, would be the best course for Vietnam. In fact, when such SRV officials did prescribe policies and actions, their recommendations focused on how the U.S. could improve alliance behavior with existing treaty allies, and how Washington could commit to practical plans for regional cooperation, rather than how the U.S. could improve to the tone and content of U.S.–Vietnamese relations.

In short, it is fair to say that though the Vietnamese were slow to make up their minds concerning what they wanted from a bilateral defense relationship, they were quicker to acknowledge what they did not want. They did not want a full-blown partnership, and they did not want much in the way of direct practical cooperation. They wanted the minimum necessary to keep the U.S. interested in interaction, without allowing the relationship to approach the point of strategic relevance.

Old Thinking in Washington

By mid–1996, the military-to-military relationship was accepted and supported by the Department of State and the National Security Council as an integral part of the overall relationship, and a piece of the normalization process. However, at first, the defense relationship was not embraced by the Clinton Administration as a legitimate part of that process. In fact, the defense dimension of the normalization process was fenced off from the mainstream bilateral relationship, portrayed as being a subsidiary of the POW/MIA effort, and characterized as relevant and valuable only insofar as it contributed to broad regional goals, remained inoffensive to China, and had positive impact on larger U.S. security interests such as ASEAN stability and security, resolution of South China Sea disputes, and cooperation regarding transnational threats. The first tentative steps toward defense relations were not accorded much importance in U.S. government statements characterizing the normalization process between 1996 and 1998.[1]

The Clinton Administration sought to walk a fine, delicate line between the business community's interest in developing markets and ending the embargo, and the POW/MIA lobby's concerns with the fullest possible accounting. The Administration wanted to do this without pitting one interest against the other. It wanted to avoid setting up a situation where trade and economic relations would be seen as incompatible with the interests of the veterans, Congress and the families of missing Americans. In the context of efforts to enlist business support for a normalization game plan marked by a gradual pace and controlled scope, the Administration was not prepared to alienate the more conservative business interests, scratch the wrong nerve in the national veterans organizations, or mobilize POW/MIA dissent against plans for U.S.–Vietnamese relations. The Administration had managed to maintain positive, cordial relations with some of the veterans groups over the POW/MIA issue. The differences between the Alliance of Families and the League Families over POW/MIA esoteria, and the differences between the American Legion and the Vietnam Veterans of America, for example, over the pace and scope of normalization and the future of accounting efforts, made it unlikely that such groups would be galvanized into united opposition to the Administration's plans as long as the vision of normalization recognized the importance of long-term POW/MIA accounting goals, and remained restrained in symbolism and pomp, and as long a projections regarding the future of the Washington-Hanoi relationship were cautious. Highlighting efforts to fashion a defense relationship would unite the constellation of interests against normalization.

Introducing the idea of defense normalization, especially since it had become connected in public discourse with the question of a U.S. strategic presence in the region, and the U.S. access to and use of Cam Ranh and Da Nang, struck senior U.S. policy makers as a step that would compromise this uneasy status quo. Though the idea that normalization with Vietnam would have an immediate and positive strategic impact on American interests had been discussed, at least at the level of the Under Secretary of Defense, during the Administration of George Bush, in the earliest days of the Clinton Administration, and in the context of preparations for the exchange of Ambassadors between Washington and Hanoi, this dimension of the relationship was downplayed in favor of a much more constrained sense of what might be accomplished as the Administration continued to press Hanoi for more POW/MIA cooperation.

There were other interests that struck the Administration as requiring a delicate balance in their approach to Vietnam. Several key State Department officials who played a role in the interagency discussion of normalization in 1993–95 had been involved in the efforts during the late 1970s to get Hanoi into a serious dialogue about unconditional normalization. They recalled the difficult discussions over reparations, and claims and counter-claims related to the nationalization of U.S. property in the south, the issue of frozen assets, the wartime use of defoliants, and the question of compensation for collateral damage of civilian property by U.S. bombs. Keeping those issues from spoiling sensitive, precarious dialogue aimed at getting the Vietnamese to agree to normalization weighed heavily on the minds of working level participants in the earlier round of talks. In their roles in the mid–1990s, as members of the interagency groups that managed the process of normalization, they sought to remind the players from Defense and the National Security Council exactly how troublesome such claims issues and other sensitive matters had been to the overall goal of achieving normalization. To those participants in this process, the value added by a defense component to the plan for establishing bilateral relations was minimal. It was hard enough to get the Vietnamese to think of the positive dividends that would derive from overall normal relations without introducing the politically complex topic of military relations, and the attendant issues of Agent Orange, claims to abandoned military equipment ("war booty"), and potential claims against the government in Hanoi by former U.S. Prisoners of War.

U.S. government interagency working group participants looked at the military part of the process as a potentially troublesome way of guaranteeing that the POW/MIA issue would be given an extra shrill emphasis by critics of the process of normalization who would, in this thinking, zero in on the implications of establishing defense relations with a former enemy before the accounting process had been completed to the satisfaction of the U.S. These U.S. officials reasoned that it was difficult enough to satisfy the requirements of domestic constituencies focused on accounting for missing U.S. service personnel. To include a position arguing in favor of military-to-military normalization alongside of economic, trade, cultural, consular and diplomatic normalization ran the risk of disrupting the delicate balance that recognized the POW/MIA issue as the "highest national priority." Additionally, such officials believed that anything suggesting an interest in a military component to normalization would strike the Vietnamese as another way of front loading POW/MIA requirements, and come to be viewed in Hanoi as an unacceptable condition for normalization, and thus become a deal breaker.

Finally, the long standing association between normalization and military access issues, established by the public statements of retired senior flag officers during the late 1980s and early 1990s, suggested to senior State Department officials that injecting a defense component into the mix at this juncture in bilateral discussions of normalization would guarantee that Vietnam would shrink from clearly unacceptable strategic implications that would become associated with the normalization process were it to include an integral defense relationship as part of the start-up process.

Strange Bedfellows

ISA and ERD made a slightly odd couple. The level of authority with which each organization was invested was unequal. ERD reported to one of several vice ministers of defense. ISA reported to an Assistant Secretary, subordinate to the Under Secretary of Defense for Policy, the third ranking defense official in the Pentagon. ERD was headed by a major general.[2] ISA was generally headed by a political appointee or a senior civil servant, nominally accorded the authority of a field grade officer, though this equivalency was more often than not irrelevant in the U.S. system, and unfathomable in the Vietnamese context. ERD had department-level status within the Defense Ministry. ISA was a subordinate entity within the Office of the Assistant Secretary of Defense for International Security Affairs. It did not have the heft of a separate department-level entity.

ERD had a global mandate, bearing responsibilities for managing the diplomatic and foreign policy dimensions of Vietnam's defense relationships; the American relationship was one small portion of the ERD's overall mission. The DoD entity that ran the relationship with Vietnam was part of the office responsible for Asia and the Pacific. ERD was a one-stop shopping organization in that it was entrusted with the management of communications with the system of defense and military attachés as well as with managing defense relationships.[3] ISA did not have such a reach. ISA depended on the Defense Intelligence Agency's human intelligence resource managers and the Defense Intelligence Officers to facilitate communication from the field. Though personal contact between ISA desk officers and U.S. defense attachés was common, customary and routine, ISA did not have any responsibility for the day-to-day care and feeding of U.S. defense attaché personnel.

ERD was, at least in some contexts, the first among equals, meaning that for the most part the ERD "outranked" other departments, such as the MND's Social Policy Department. The ERD had none of the operational level authority invested in the General Staff Department, and lacked the General Political Department's infrastructure in units, where there was a tradition of political officers minding the rectitude of foot soldiers and line and staff officers. However, it did have more of a voice over issues that impacted on defense relations and foreign policy matters than some MND departments that also had global mandates. And it did function in this regard as a "military" organization; it was staffed and led by uniforms, with no civilian personnel attached.

In contrast, the focus of the ISA office that interacted with the ERD was limited to Asian affairs. It's influence and functional scope was diminished somewhat in the early 1990s when the Pentagon established several "stovepipe" organizations with global missions in the areas of counternarcotics policy, peacekeeping, and humanitarian assistance; prior to 1993–94, each regional affairs section in the Office of the Assistant Secretary of Defense for International Security Affairs held collateral responsibilities for the regional manifestations of these global issues.

Further, though ISA and the other regional offices subordinate to the ASD/ISA included a field grade officer as a Director subordinate to the Deputy Assistant Secretary, none of the regional offices in OASD/ISA had any role in military planning and operational matters. ISA worked with the Joint Staff and the regional command when it came to the political dimension of military policy and behavior. ISA's contribution to any strategic dialogue was necessarily focused on the political and policy development, and regional consequences, of defense and security decisions. In interagency policy meetings, U.S. military representatives speaking for the regional commands or the joint staff might be asked what it would take, in terms of personnel, equipment, organization and budget, to accomplish a mission. ISA would be asked whether and how the mission would impact on countries in Asia, regional organizations such as ASEAN, how the mission might be received, and what it would take to extract specific support from friends and allies in the region for a particular military action. ERD appeared to be more directly integrated into MND discussions of strategic military choices.

Negotiating Table Behavior

At least at the outset, through 1997–98, some of these distinctions made for an awkward match between ISA and ERD as negotiating partners. ERD believed that its appropriate interlocutor was at least the Deputy Assistant Secretary of Defense, and initially saw more of a parallel between the ERD and the ASD/ISA. ERD may have been ill at ease with talking across the table to a civilian representative of the Defense Department, flanked by lower ranking officers from the Joint Staff and Pacific Command. ERD was also uncomfortable with ISA's notion that the planning dialogue between ISA and ERD should eventually involve PAVN service representatives. Part of that, at first, may have been a product of the view that direct service-to-service talks should come at a much later point in the relationship, but another part of ERD's discomfiture with this ISA proposal may have been their desire to continue to ride herd on the U.S.–Vietnamese military-to-military dialogue without sharing that responsibility with uniformed elements that would bring to the table their own resources and authority. When in 1998 ISA began proposing that the annual planning meeting be replaced by a meeting of operational experts and planners from the U.S. and the Vietnamese side who could more easily work together to chart events, plan calendars, and strategize about the realities of transportation, accommodations and itineraries, ERD balked at the thought of Vietnamese service level officers and specialists conferring directly with PACOM plans and programs managers. Whereas ISA was perfectly comfortable with the prospect of having its role confined to lofty strategic discussions, fundamental defense policy dialogues, and talks about regional security, the ERD was not prepared to confine its role to the more "ethereal" level of dialogue intended to sustain the broad contours of the relationship.

The conventional wisdom has long been that Vietnamese bureaucrats remain on a very short leash, with little wiggle room in their instructions that left them unprepared to take advantage of negotiating table opportunities. Vietnamese diplomats were not generally capable of responding to a compromise offer that split a difference, or of speaking for their home ministries on an uncharted point; they had to go back to the government for instructions. In contrast, the heads of U.S. delegations generally had a mandate that was flexible enough to accommodate the possibility that unforeseen opportunities might arise.[4]

That conventional wisdom is weakened somewhat by the negotiating table behavior of the ERD. While it may have been on a short leash, the ERD clearly had the authority to make judgments regarding the acceptability of proposals put forth by DoD interlocutors without further instructions from a higher level. That is, the ERD seemed to be able to reject ISA initiatives that were not, in its estimation, compatible with existing rules and agreed upon parameters for the U.S.–Vietnamese defense relationship, without having to consult with the vice defense minister responsible for American issues. Moreover, the ERD was fortified in its position by an extreme reluctance on the part of the vice ministerial level charged with supervising the U.S.–Vietnamese defense relationship to entertain proposals that did not meet with ERD approval, especially in instances where ISA sought to elevate issues to a level above the ERD.

Did the Vietnamese military behave differently than the Socialist Republic's diplomatic service around a negotiating table?

Judging from post–1975 examples of bilateral negotiations on the POW/MIA issue, on refugee related matters, and on trade and economic issues, for the Vietnamese, negotiations had a certain dimension of choreography and ritual to them, and were treated as a politicized theatrical production. The drama maximized the impact of Hanoi's political message. As part of the drama, the Vietnamese diplomatic negotiator probed for the opposite side's bottom line and areas of flexibility, and sought to identify exploitable differences within the opposite side's negotiating team.

Vietnamese diplomatic negotiators often pursued extremes of reciprocity, and could seem less inclined to worry about the meaning of the point at the heart of a particular bargain than about the idea of achieving maximum benefit for concessions. While insisting on extremes of reciprocity appeared to be intrinsically important to Vietnamese negotiators, at the same time it afforded a means of achieving tactical advantages, playing for time, or delaying proceedings. During 1988–1993, in discussions with the U.S. Presidential Emissary for POW/MIA Affairs, Hanoi delayed proceedings, presumably for tactical advantages, by simply stating that it could not proceed until Washington met Hanoi's concerns for equivalent consideration with respect to Hanoi's humanitarian needs. Often, the concessions in question were irrelevant to Hanoi, but being able to exert a chokehold on proceedings earned the Vietnamese side sufficient advantage, especially when Washington became preoccupied with concocting inventive means of meeting Vietnamese demands and anticipating Vietnamese requests for reciprocity.

Vietnamese diplomats established themselves as tenacious, skilled negotiators with infinite patience, a sense of theatre, a flair for the dramatic, and an unrelenting way about them.

While Vietnamese diplomats have shown an attenuated sense of the importance of reciprocity, responding accordingly to Vietnamese hints that a tit-for-tat was required in order to move discussions forward did not necessarily result in appreciable progress toward a negotiating goal. With Vietnamese diplomats, sometimes a negotiated agreement was not the primary end result or expected payoff of a negotiating process. Sometimes the product of discussion and bargaining was more discussion, and more bargaining, and sometimes the end result was an altered playing field that came from actions taken on other fronts during negotiations. Sometimes the end result was a change in the balance of forces, springing in part from the act of demonstrating endurance at the negotiating table, and the legitimacy earned in a bilateral contests of wills.

Finally, Vietnamese negotiators had short tethers. Their wiggle room, and their authority to make on-the-ground decisions in actual bargaining situations was not always as significant as their rank and office suggested. They frequently did not come to the table with the authority to make a decision or deliver an agreement.

There were a number of similarities between the behavior of Vietnamese diplomatic negotiators and the comportment of Vietnamese military negotiators engaged in discussions about the bilateral defense relationship between 1996 and 2000. The Vietnamese military officials who represented the Defense Ministry in discussions with DoD officials during this period — including 0-5 and 0-6 level PAVN officers staffing the ERD, the 0-7 who headed the ERD, and the several vice defense ministers who met with Pentagon representatives during these years, plus the defense attachés assigned to Washington during 1997-2000 — saw the aggressive defense of Vietnam's image and standing as one of their primary obligations in the dialogue with the U.S. They had a lot at stake in terms of status, and demonstrated this in their preoccupation with such things as insuring that Vietnam was received the same treatment as other countries with which the U.S. conducted normal diplomatic discourse, an obsessive concern for the formalities of invitations, and exaggerated attentiveness to the way Vietnam's place in the itineraries of multi-country trips by senior DoD officials would reflect on the SRV's standing. They were especially concerned with seeing their relationship handled with the same care and attention as the Chinese received, and demonstrated this in their preoccupation with insuring that plans for a visit by the SRV Defense Minister would exactly duplicate the minutia of protocol employed in welcoming the Chinese Defense Minister in his December 1996 visit to the United States. At the same time, they were committed to making certain that the United States was not treated any differently than other countries with which the MND conducted normal military relations, and went to great lengths to level the playing field by treating the U.S. Defense Attaché as something significantly less than the first among equals in the defense attaché community in Hanoi. The Defense Ministry's desire in early 1997 to quickly set the stage for a meeting between the Defense Minister and the Defense Secretary did not reflect the strategic importance accorded the bilateral defense relationship as much as it showed the extent to which Vietnam strongly wanted to be on an equal footing with the U.S. in defining the trajectory of the relationship, shaping the manner in which military ties would unfold, and controlling the process of discussions that would define military ties.

The Vietnamese military interlocutors were dogged in their perseverance, and unwavering at the negotiating table, in much the same way as their Foreign Ministry counterparts, though they had little need to seek tactical advantages in discussions aimed at shaping the defense relationship since, for the most part, it was the U.S. that was seeking Vietnamese agreement to various proposals.

However, there were also some compelling differences between military and diplomatic negotiators, which had a great deal to do with the distinction between what the military had to discuss with Washington, and what the Foreign Ministry ended up having to negotiate, but which were also a function of the "operational code" of PAVN officers.

Negotiating was not in the PAVN job description. Vietnamese military officers tended to stake out a position and stick to it, signaling that there was rarely any room for discussion aimed at changing a policy decision. Foreign Ministry officials negotiated. Defense Ministry officials, in contrast, stated their bottom line and struck a pose that was meant to indicate that they would not be moved. Indeed, efforts by ISA to nudge the ERD into a more receptive, reasonable mood on things like demining training required that Pentagon officials dangle the dividends before other potentially interested ministries that would then have to exert their influence to press the Defense Ministry to a less reluctant posture.

Military men carried out policy. Negotiating, in the sense of sitting at a table and hammering out agreements that would shape military-to-military interaction, was too much like making policy for the comfort of the working levels of the Defense Ministry. And the very core of negotiating—the ability to cleverly convince and to build consensus through the manipulation of resources and the use of compromise—ran against the instincts of the ERD, which wanted no surprises in the working level discussions, and pressed ISA to tip its hand before every planning meeting. While ISA looked to these meetings as a means of developing ground-floor level agreement to incrementally push forward with a program of bilateral military activities, the ERD viewed these meetings as a clumsy way of working out a schedule of activities that would have to be blessed by the senior leadership before any movement could take place.

In the context of the working level sessions that were established as the means of communicating between defense establishments after April 1997, the Vietnamese military looked to accomplish their goals in a variety of ways, from informal discussions on the margins of meetings, to strongly stated views laid down as markers in representational events following plenary meetings, to privately stated views masquerading as unofficial positions that were clearly meant to be feelers. Some of that behavior drew on the instruments that SRV government negotiators speaking for the Foreign Ministry, the Office of the Prime Minister, or other government agencies relied on in managing the process of negotiations with the U.S. over POW/MIA problems, refugee-related issues, and other prenormalization matters. But some of that arsenal of negotiating behavior was strictly military, especially statements spoken privately, and in extreme terms, outside of official settings, meant to define the real parameters in which both sides could hope to work. While Foreign Ministry representatives would rely on opportunities apart from the negotiating table to leverage agreements, to discern unity within the ranks of the U.S. delegation, and to define the far ends of the spectrum that might be represented more subtly at formal sessions, diplomats were generally more reserved in their tone, guarded in their vocabulary, and more cautious about using these channels than military figures.

Trade Agreement Realities

The Defense Ministry's position that the bilateral military relationship with the U.S. should not be allowed to develop more quickly than progress toward a trade agreement was both an excuse for moving at the glacial pace the MND found comfortable, and an indication that the MND was prepared to live with the results of an interagency process that placed the military relationship in a larger context, and ultimately called for slow and deliberately small steps in defense ties.

There was no real reason to believe that the MND attached any overriding importance to the signing of a trade agreement with Washington. There would be no real payoff for the Defense Ministry from a trade agreement in terms of things important to PAVN, such as access to technology. In fact, a trade agreement with the U.S. had the potential to undermine PAVN's economic interests by requiring Hanoi to dismantle state owned enterprises in which PAVN had significant investments. However, the MND had come to view the trade agreement in the same way they looked at the early 1990s negotiations over the esoteria of the POW/MIA issue — including access to wartime documents, agreements to conduct investigations at grave and crash sites, and the rules governing site excavations. To the MND, these were tests of the Vietnamese government's resolve and ability to take strong negotiating stands in defense of security and sovereignty, even when these principles were only impacted in the most minor ways by the manner in which the issue unfolded between Hanoi and Washington. The specifics of the trade agreement, or the essential importance of the Jackson-Vanik Amendment in this connection, were probably not fully grasped by the MND. What they saw was a process where the U.S. stood toe to toe with Vietnam; for their part, the entire trade agreement issue was about who would blink first.

The military's insistence, beginning in September 1997, that bilateral military relations with the U.S. should not develop more quickly than progress toward a trade agreement was important because it provided some indication that a legitimate interagency process had begun to evolve, and that it had enough starch to impact on military equities. Between April and August 1997, the Foreign Ministry, the Ministry of the Interior, and the External Relations Department of the Central Committee began to wire the MND's ERD into a fledgling process of coordination that involved more regular consultations. The emergence of the MND position on the bilateral trade agreement that took into account broader foreign policy interests was one circumstantial indication of how this newborn interagency process had impacted on the operational code of the Defense Ministry.

Selling Military Hardware

The issue of bilateral arms and technology transfers and commercial foreign military sales began to surface in 1997 and 1998, at least as an intellectual question of how and when such interaction might be appropriate between Hanoi and Washington. It is instructive to look at the manner in which this issue unfolded in the U.S.–China relationship, in contrast to the dynamics of this issue in the context of the first steps toward U.S.–Vietnamese military relations. From the beginning of the normalization of defense ties between the U.S. and China, U.S. military sales to China were an essential component of the relationship, designed to support a policy of enhancing the defensive capabilities of the People's Liberation Army, while avoiding changes in the military balance in the region. In early 1999, in the thinking in the Pentagon and the State Department, it was unlikely that the U.S. defense relationship with Vietnam would come to the point in the near future, or even within five to ten years, at which the U.S. might consider assisting Vietnam in meeting its legitimate defense requirements within existing weapons and technology transfer policies, consistent with U.S. political and military objectives in the region. First, national laws eliminated the possibility of foreign military sales credits for countries that were still communist. Second, there were very explicit prohibitions against the sale of end use items and technologies controlled by the International Munitions List (IML), licensed by the Department of State, and there was no indication, as of early 1999, that U.S. foreign policy makers were inclined to think about becoming flexible regarding weapons, equipment and technologies associated with the IML. Nor was there any indication of flexibility on issuing licenses to U.S. companies to sell dual use equipment and technology whose transfer to foreign countries was licensed by the Department of Commerce. Third, the structure of threats that motivated the U.S. to look at military technological cooperation in the areas of anti-tank, artillery, air defense and anti-submarine warfare technology in many defense relations did not exist in the region in a way that would make such cooperation relevant to the U.S.–Vietnam relationship. There was no common or shared threat and no security interests that would lead the U.S. to a decision to transfer production technologies and systems to Vietnam that would enable the Socialist Republic to upgrade its own defense industries and begin manufacturing weapons systems and military equipment to meet their own defense requirements. At most, the U.S. defense establishment could begin thinking of assisting Vietnam in airport and maritime safety, and in a manner that would not involve the transfer of IML items, but these were opportunities for cooperation that had been spelled out to the MND as early as 1996, and were greeted with disinterest by the Vietnamese side.

Though some senior Vietnamese officials were prepared to privately explore the possibility of limited military sales with a variety of U.S. government contacts, it is reasonable to conclude that through early 1999 the Vietnamese Defense Ministry did not fool itself at all on the likelihood that Washington would move down this path toward a relationship characterized by even the most modest of defense production cooperation.[5]

Vietnamese Generational Divides

There were subtle shadings of differences within the Ministry of Defense on aspects of the defense relationship with the U.S. Some officers responsible for managing working level affairs with the U.S., with considerable experience in the POW/MIA issue, felt that the long years of negotiations over joint excavations and crash site investigations had taught the two countries useful lessons on getting along, handling tough and intractable issues, and had bred an important familiarity that would make the establishment of the most basic level military relations that much easier. Those officers believed that the course of dealing with each other across a negotiating table at POW/MIA technical meetings, and working together in the field, the U.S. and Vietnamese militaries had learned to solve problems, handle touchy matters, and work through difficult moments to achieve an agreed upon goal. This was, however, a minority view.

Actually, the number of military officers involved in the POW/MIA issue from the late 1980s to the early 1990s was limited. Between December 1990 and January 1991, the VNOSMP expanded the number of military officers participating in POW/MIA work, and enlarged the MND's responsibilities. By 1992, a select handful of officers drawn from the General Staff Department, the Institute for Military History, and the General Political Department composed the newly created MND MIA Office. That office had a growing role in the early 1990s, but the involvement of the MND in this issue was still relatively new, and with few exceptions PAVN officers did not have the exposure to DoD officials representing the Secretary of Defense on the POW/MIA issue that the Foreign Ministry had experienced as a result of its continuous involvement in the POW/MIA issue from the mid–1970s.[6]

The majority of officers who came into contact with U.S. Defense Department officials in the context of efforts to develop military-to-military contacts were skeptical of the stated U.S. intention to develop a modest relationship, suspicious of the agenda for working level meetings, and decidedly unfriendly in contacts with DoD officials. Their demeanor, when explained in private opportunities for discussion, suggested that middle aged PAVN officers who participated in the defense of Hanoi during the 1969–73 period and officers with Soviet or Soviet Bloc training were less likely to believe that the shared wartime history would equip the two countries to cope with tensions and enable the two sides to agree on a practical approach to establishing normal defense relations. Officers with this basic background were bitter, mistrustful, uncooperative and generally unhelpful. Some were intensely interested in extracting some indication of U.S. regret for wartime "wrongdoings," and fixed their attention on manipulating humanitarian issues, such as the Vietnamese MIA problem or the consequences of the use of Agent Orange during the war, to position the U.S. for humiliation. While Foreign Ministry officials looked at the Agent Orange issue as a domestic concern for Vietnam that required a practical effort by the government to address health issues, and generate international interest in providing assistance to Vietnam to cope with these problems, few diplomats saw it as an issue that afforded the Foreign Ministry leverage sufficient to make demands of the U.S. for reparations, for a public confession of the alleged violation of the rules of war, or for acknowledgement, as some PAVN officers saw it, of a fundamental moral wrongdoing that harmed innocent Vietnamese civilians caught in the war. Some Vietnamese military officers saw a real need, as a matter of policy, for Vietnam to wrestle the U.S. into the posture of a supplicant, and to wring such a confession from Washington, before a real normal relationship between militaries could be fashioned.

Older officers who joined the revolutionary cause in the 1920s and 1930s as young men, and had a long history in uniform in multiple wars, including Dien Bien Phu veterans, were more acutely concerned with the strategic variables springing from the decision to move cautiously forward with efforts to normalize defense relations with the U.S. Senior officers with long careers in the Defense Ministry focused on the China angle in assessing the impact of a relationship with the U.S. Some hoped that a U.S.-Vietnamese security link would work to Vietnam's advantage by making modern military equipment and technological know-how available to Vietnam through U.S. commercial sources or, from the perspective of a few officers, U.S. foreign military sales. These officers saw defense and military relations with the U.S. as a positive step toward equipping Vietnam with the hardware and technical capabilities necessary to attend to its own security requirements in the South China Sea. The military relationship with the U.S. would not, in their view, be Vietnam's hedge against China, nor would it serve as a security guarantee. However, by getting PAVN the technology and the training necessary to operate modern military equipment, Vietnam would be able to defend its own interests without relying on the strategic charity and good will of another country.

Some senior department level officers in the MND with responsibilities that brought them into working-level contact with DoD officials did indeed see the possibility of an active U.S.-Vietnamese condominium directed against China. Those officers appeared to be driven less by a conviction that such an alliance was possible on the basis of mutual interest, or momentary convenience, and more swayed by concern for Vietnam's security.

Normalization Strategies

The U.S. looked at military relations as an adjunct to overall normalization. In the U.S. view, there was no reason why defense normalization should not take place. However, there was at the same time no compelling reason why it had to take place. That made military relations a stepchild to normalization on the U.S. side. It was the odd, disconnected part of the process of normalization.

By contrast, in Vietnam's view, there was no reason why defense normalization should take place. There was no reason for it to crop up as a separate dialectic. In the MND's thinking, in general, defense relations emerged on their own, in their own time, with an independence pace and scope. The extent to which the bilateral military relationship with Beijing,

8 — Conclusions, Observations, Musings 239

years after rapproachment, essentially was without substance, and lagged way behind the diplomatic and trade relationship with China, underscores this point. To the MND, as a general rule, bilateral defense relations came about in the aftermath of a sound, reasoned, mutually satisfying diplomatic relationships.

In some ways, these two systems were not ready for one another. Vietnam's defense leadership had no experience in relating to U.S. civilian defense interlocutors. The U.S. defense leadership had only the POW/MIA negotiating experience as a model.

ISA placed a premium on moving forward and minimizing "no" answers, and believed it was important to have something to show for the effort at the end of each year. The real goal was to define areas in which bilateral "practical cooperation" could be achieved. To the ERD, no forward movement meant no failures. The ERD did not have any need to produce policy results. It did not have a stake in military relations. The meeting was not the message.

ISA was content to confine efforts to achieve this to the "technical level." For the ERD, agreements yielded by "technical level" discussions were never considered critical achievements by the ERD.

ISA presumed the Vietnamese didn't have their heart in military relations, but felt that military relations should not be left out of the equation of normalization. The ERD was suspicious of ISA's enthusiasm regarding "military contacts." To the ERD, military relations would follow naturally, and eventually, in the aftermath of "normalization."

ISA set modest goals and celebrated incremental progress as sufficient indication of SRV interest. The U.S.–proposed areas of cooperation (demining, SAR, environment) were not national security interests. While Vietnam's military leadership might speak positively about engagement, it was not mission essential to PAVN.

To what extent did either side have a well thought out approach to military relations in the 1994–96 period, as things were beginning to move forward in the opening phase of normalization? And, to what extent did the views of either side regarding military relations mature and evolve during 1998–2001, after four or five years worth of normalization?

For the Vietnamese, military relations with the U.S. may have been an afterthought. At best, it was a sideshow, another point at which the two countries would intersect. At worst, defense relations were irrelevant to a process essentially controlled by the Foreign Ministry, the Office of the Prime Minister, and the Party's General Secretary, and thus received only the most perfunctory working level attention during the 1995–96 period. Somewhere in between these extremes is a picture of Defense Ministry officials at the 0–5, 0–6, and 0–7 levels spending some time in early 1995 defining an approach to defense relations that emphasized the "humanitarian" dimension of the relationship. It seems that in the earliest part of the process of building military contacts, the working level officials in the ERD believed that defense relations with the U.S. would continue to revolve around the MIA issue, and that normalization represented Vietnam's opportunity to restate "humanitarian needs" issues. In part, this might have been the result of the Defense Ministry's tentativeness about exploring military-to-military relations so early in normalization, and the desire of those officials to set low expectations and define simple goals so as not to experience disappointment and failure so early in the normalization process. However, it seems more likely that the Vietnamese Defense Ministry simply assigned minimal strategic content to a relationship they saw as having little potential to begin with.

In the U.S., on the other hand, senior and middle level Defense Department officials saw a high level of strategic value to such a relationship, and considerable potential for quick, positive developments. During 1993–95, defense policy makers, area specialists and analysts were prepared to argue that Vietnam would see the value of a defense relationship with the U.S. in terms of the potential security insurance such a link could offer the SRV in its relationship with China. A chorus of former senior service officials, commentators, and experts spoke about returning to bases in Vietnam with which the United States armed forces were intimately familiar. Others spoke of the "Asian Decade," the blossoming vitality of the Southeast Asian economies and the growing political importance of the region to U.S. interests.

However, much of this was strategic thinking without strategic content. Amidst other world issues and transnational threats, Vietnam paled to insignificance. It became too difficult to attract the attention of senior defense policy managers to the matter of shaping entry-level military relations with Vietnam. Senior U.S. service representatives were intrigued by the prospect of being able to satisfy long-term training needs through a relationship with Vietnam, but were unwilling to take the short term, nonstrategic steps necessary to make new friends. The newness of the idea of U.S.–Vietnamese military relations raised the possibility of achieving long-standing policy aims in the region by flirting with one more country in the area, but the novelty did not have the propulsive power necessary to convert the idea into a strategic reality. By 1997, everyone was echoing the phrase "Vietnam is a Country, Not a War," as a symbolic means of saying that the new relationship was a way of transcending the difficult past, and that Vietnam's national interests needed to be factored into any equation aimed at creating a sound relationship between the U.S. and Vietnam.

However, U.S. strategic thinking about Vietnam was essentially confined to discussions of the China card (or Vietnam's "America card"), some nods toward the importance of facility access, some eccentric notions that joint training would be a distinct possibility, and the ever present notion that a ship visit would be a good start on the road toward strategic partnership.

Some Final Observations

Beginning in late 1996, when the possibility of a military-to-military relationship was first broached with the Vietnamese, the Defense Department's goal was to keep the first stages of this bilateral interaction modest in pace and scope, and focused on enhancing mutual understanding. The Pentagon postulated three key principles for this start-up phase: (1) the defense relationship must be deliberately and carefully phased, kept to modest goals at the outset, and calibrated to develop in tandem with the overall relationship, (2) the defense relationship must be transparent, leaving no possibility that U.S. intentions might be misunderstood by any country, and (3) the POW/MIA issue must continue to be the most important issue in the bilateral relationship.

The Vietnamese adduced a similar set of first principles, revolving around the critical importance of non-interference and respect for sovereignty, but ultimately reflecting the shared sense that the effort to establish defense relations must proceed with care, consist initially of measured goals, and move forward at a modest and cautious pace. These first principles were a way of focusing both sides on the mission, and insuring that both sides proceeded with appropriate perspective in the first exploratory efforts. The first principles reminded both sides of the parameters in which each side was prepared to conduct defense relations.

DoD believed that a range of critical regional security interests that could be addressed through normal, routine contacts with the Vietnamese military. The Vietnamese had embraced the "confidence building" activities of the ASEAN Regional Forum. Many of the bilateral initiatives intended to develop security relations with Vietnam resonated positively with regional concerns over transnational security threats and multilateral regional cooperation. U.S. regional interests and Vietnamese security concerns ran parallel to a certain, limited extent that was a sufficient basis for introducing a military component into the process of bilateral normalization.

Vietnam's Defense Ministry thought in terms of a relationship that would unfold in slow and deliberate ways, and in a manner that did not compromise their interests in a stable and healthy relationship with China and the region. Hanoi had a clear allergy to certain kinds of bilateral military interaction, such as ship visits and training, and this militated against a broadening of interaction between the two defense establishments. The U.S. Government's own need to be cautious about what would be acceptable to the various constituencies relevant to the process—POW/MIA interests, Congress, human rights lobbies, and the veterans, whose objections to normal relations continued to find expression in letters to the Secretary of Defense through late 2000—underscored the appropriateness of an incremental approach to defense relations.

The annual meetings between the External Relations Department and International Security Affairs that started in 1997 established the basic tools for conducting bilateral business. The interactions yielded an effective means of defining annual calendars of military-to-military interaction through sharing views of what was possible in practical and political terms. The meetings defined a formula for insuring timely action on proposals through the use of working level channels of communication, and helped nudge things beyond the limits that emerged as the starting point in the earliest phases of military-to-military relations. Both offices demonstrated the ability to identify ways of enhancing bilateral relations while sustaining the commitment to pursuing this course in a careful and cautious manner. The ERD was willing to accommodate requests from the U.S. side to press forward with visits by military educational and academic delegations, showing an increasing seriousness about efforts to bring military officers and military specialists together. Both sides moved forward on practical bilateral cooperation by grasping that the most effective way of developing this aspect of the relationship was to begin with informational exchanges between defense experts. That formula helped engender an interest on the part of the Vietnamese military establishment in U.S. demining training assistance, overcoming initial reluctance, and it provided the means of pressing forward with proposals for exchanging information on search and rescue practices. There was every reason to believe that it would help overcome Vietnamese concerns regarding the proposal for PAVN's involvement in U.S. International Military Education Training (IMET) programs. (On 17 June 2005 Vietnam concluded an agreement with the U.S. that would facilitate PAVN's participation in IMET programs.)

The relationship developed and evolved in a positive manner, and at a respectable pace, from the first formal meetings in late 1996. Vice Minister of Defense Tran Hanh visited the U.S. in October 1998. The U.S. National War College visit in 1998 was conducted effectively, and an Air

War College trip in 1999 was successful, with an unprecedented flight line visit at a key air defense unit as the highlight. The visit to Vietnam by the Secretary of Defense in March 2000 set a positive tone for defense relations. Following the second meeting in Hanoi of the U.S. Demining Experts Group and their Vietnamese interlocutors, Vietnam agreed to cooperate with the U.S. on a humanitarian demining program. The first delivery of demining equipment was made in October 2000, and a landmine/unexploded ordnance survey was being planned in late 2000. Additionally, the U.S. and the Vietnamese were taking steps toward search and rescue cooperation, and information sharing on environmental issues. After years of quiet and patient discussion, in March 2000, during former Defense Secretary William Cohen's visit to Hanoi, Defense Minister Pham Van Tra agreed that the proposal for a U.S. naval ship visit should be discussed in earnest, a decision that kicked off more than two years of working level technical discussions. In November 2003, following Minister Tra's visit to Washington, a U.S. naval warship steamed into Ho Chi Minh City. In July 2004 a second port visit took place in Da Nang. A third ship visit was conducted in March 2005. In November 2004, a delegation of Vietnamese military training and education professionals spent a week studying the American military education model, visiting Annapolis, the National Defense University, the National War College, the Joint Forces Staff College, and the Marine Corps University.

In 2000, after four years of annual working level planning sessions, the U.S. felt that the time was right to nudge the relationship forward, develop routine activities such as orientation visits that would take place annually, and move the relationship into operational channels for the purposes of planning and executing events in the annual calendar. However, the Vietnamese were decidedly more inclined to proceed in a low-keyed, slow-paced fashion, limiting the number of annual visits by U.S. military delegations, participating selectively in a small but respectable number of multilateral meetings sponsored by the Pacific Command, and confining bilateral cooperation on practical projects to several essentially humanitarian areas where the emphasis remained on information sharing rather than joint military field cooperation.

By late 2003 the Vietnamese side had agreed, with some temporizing, to conduct bilateral defense discussions with U.S. Pacific Command on an annual basis, with the first one scheduled for September 2004, as a means of planning future events and defining future possibilities in the defense relationship. To the U.S., this was a means of expanding the nature of the planning dialogue, and at the same time crystallizing a separate channel for developing a policy dialogue between defense officials at the assistant secretary level. To the Defense Department, this was a way to routinely communicate about regional and global security and defense issues, to bring military thinkers and strategists together to promote discussion of shared interests. To the Vietnamese, these were the kinds of proposals that would require consultation with friends in the region, internal scrutiny of Washington's plans and intentions, evaluation of the pace and scope of the bilateral relationship with the U.S., and debate over the trajectory of Vietnam's engagement with the U.S.

There was still a lot of heavy lifting to be done by both sides in this relationship to turn promise and potential into reality. There was also sufficient promise and potential to make the exertion worthwhile.

NOTES

Chapter 1

1. Nayan Chanda, *Brother Enemy: The War After the War — A History of Indochina Since the Fall of Saigon*, (New York: Harcourt, Brace, Jovanovich, 1986), p. 269.
2. Luu Van Loi, *1945–1995: 50 Years of Vietnamese Diplomacy*, (Hanoi: The Gioi, 2000), p. 287.
3. Chanda, *Brother Enemy*, pp. 269–70.
4. "The Presidential Commission on Americans Missing and Unaccounted for in Southeast Asia: Report on Trip to Vietnam and Laos, 16–20 March 1977," pp. 6–9.
5. As National Security Advisor Zbigniew Brzezinski pointed out in a July 1978 memorandum, "moving ahead on relations with Vietnam would only be an irritant to expanding our understanding with China." Quoted in Chanda, *Brother Enemy*, p. 272.
6. *POW-MIA Factbook*, Department of Defense, June 1984, pp. 4–5; Testimony of Richard Childress, former staff member, National Security Council, before the Senate Select Committee on POW/MIA Affairs, 12 August 1992, pp. 2–3.
7. Stern, *Imprisoned or Missing in Vietnam: Policies of the Vietnamese Government Concerning Captured and Unaccounted for United State Soldiers, 1969–1994*, (Jefferson, N.C.: McFarland, 1995), pp. 48–49.
8. "POW/MIA Agreements," National League of Families, p. 2; Paul Mather, *The MIA Story in Southeast Asia*, 1990. 3:32; Chanda, *Brother Enemy*, p. 403.
9. Hanoi Voice of Vietnam Network in Vietnamese, 2300 GMT, 19 May 1991, *FBIS-EAS* 91-100, pp. 56–57.

10. Quan Doi Nhan Dan Viet Nam, Tong Cuc Chinh Tri, *Quan Triet Va Thuc Hien Nghi Quyet Hoi Nghi Trung Uong Lan Thu 3 Ve Doi Moi Va Chinh Don Dang Trong Dang Bo Quan Doi*, (Luu Hanh Noi Bo), (General Political Department, People's Army of Vietnam, *Understanding and Implementing the Resolution of the 3rd Plenum of the Central Committee on Renovation and Reorganization in Military Party Chapters*, Hanoi, 1992) [Internal Distribution], Hanoi, 1992, pp, 5–10. (Hereafter, *Quan Triet Va Thuc Hien Nghi Quyet*.)
11. *Quan Triet Va Thuc Hien Nghi Quyet*, pp. 23–41.
12. *Quan Triet Va Thuc Hien Nghi Quyet*, pp. 28–29. One observer stated that the Central Committee heard debate over the nature of Chinese plans and intentions in the region. Some party elders argued that China continued to hew to the socialist road, and therefore bilateral spats should be minimized. Younger party officials made the case that China's goal was to use socialism as a rope to tie Vietnam's hands. See Murray Hiebert, "Unhealed Wounds: Party Plenum Dominated by Concerns Over China," *Far Eastern Economic Review*, 16 July 1992, pp. 20–21.
13. *Quan Triet Va Thuc Hien Nghi Quyet*, pp. 32–34.
14. On the subject of protecting and promoting defense and security, the Defense Ministry's synopsis urged strengthening the quality of party leadership in national defense, modernizing military technology and equipment, focusing on quality of life issues affecting cadres and soldiers, and insuring a steady level of financing to sustain force levels. Finally, the synopsis pointed out the importance

of preserving internal security through sustained attention to political education, cadre management, and the reform of party membership recruitment. See *Quan Triet Va Thuc Hien Nghi Quyet*, pp. 32–41.

15. Hanoi Voice of Vietnam Network in Vietnamese, 1430 GMT, 2 May 1992, BK 0405114792, 4 May 1992.

16. *The Nation* (Bangkok, Thailand), 20 July 1992, p. 8, in *FBIS-EAS*, 92–144, 27 July 1992, p. 50; Hanoi Vietnamese News Agency in English, 0742 GMT, 14 July 1992, *FBIS-EAS* 92–135, 14 July 1992, p. 55; Hanoi Vietnamese News Agency in English, 1420 GMT, 20 August 1992, *FBIS-EAS 92–163*, 21 August 1992, pp. 41–42.

17. Hanoi Voice of Vietnam in English, 1000 GMT, 20 August 1992, *FBIS-EAS* 92–163, 14 July 1992, p. 41.

18. Hanoi Vietnamese News Agency in English, 0652 GMT, 14 July 1992, *FBIS-EAS* 92–135, 14 July 1992, p. 53.

19. Quan Doi Nhan Dan, Tong Cuc Chinh Tri, "Tin Luc Luong Vu Trang: Mot So Net Ve Hoat Dong Cua Dich Co Lien Quan Den Quan Doi," in *Tinh Hinh The Gioi Trong Nuoc Va Luc Luong Vu Trang (9–1992)*, pp. 11–13 Quan Doi Nhan Dan Viet Nam, Tong Cuc Chinh Tri, *Tinh Hinh The Gioi Trong Nuoc Va Luc Luong Vu Trang (9–1992)*(General Political Department, People's Army of Vietnam, *International and Domestic Situation and the Armed Forces*); Hanoi Vietnamese News Agency in English, 1510 GMT, 13 August 1992, *FBIS-EAS* 92–158, 14 August 1992, p. 29.

20. See "POW/MIA: Going Through a Phase (Two)," ISA/AP Memorandum for PDASD/ISA, 13 November 1992 (unclassified).

21. "What Is to Be Done?: Moving to Phase Two," ISA/AP notes, 17 November 1992. The Office of the Deputy Assistant Secretary of Defense for Asia and the Pacific (DASD/AP) addressed a memo summarizing these points to the Under Secretary of Defense for Policy. Assistant Secretary James Lilley was reluctant to send up two contradictory recommendations, one from the office of the DASD/AP and the other from the Office of the Deputy Assistant Secretary of Defense for POW/MIA Affairs (ODASD/POWMIA). In the end, the ODASD/POWMIA paper urging no change in policy was sent forward. The differences of view between the POWMIA Office and AP could not be ironed out at the level of the Deputy Assistant Secretary. My view was that OASD/POWMIA had lost sight of the fact that the real test would come as early as January 1993, and would be independent of whether or not the Vietnamese continued to comply with U.S. POW/MIA requirements. The IMF was scheduled to convene in January, and in late 1992 there was little reason to believe that the Japanese and the French would agree to refrain from urging the lifting of the embargo. The Japanese had agreed to postpone new loans from May to November 1992. There was no reason to believe that Tokyo could be convinced to once more postpone moving forward with new assistance for Vietnam.

22. On 3 December, Vessey called Cheney and National Security Advisor Brent Scowcroft to press the point that taking the remaining steps in Phase Two of the Roadmap was a relatively inexpensive way of sustaining the momentum. Vessey's goal was to argue that moving to Phase Two would show that the U.S. was not dragging its feet to the chagrin of friends such as Japan that were gently arguing in favor of a quicker pace toward U.S.–Vietnamese normalization. Vessey saw an opportunity to put the ball back into Hanoi's court. His view was that the Vietnamese had decided to cooperate, and the U.S. ought to be primed to support and sustain that decision with a confidence-building act. Moving squarely into Phase Two would serve that purpose, without lessening U.S. leverage should the Vietnamese slack off or fail to repatriate remains. Vessey, "POW/MIA Next Steps," 4 November 1992.

23. Author's discussions with a non-governmental organization official with good access to Vietnamese government officials, early December 1992. According to the same source, at roughly the same time Vietnam designated Le Van Bang, then the Director of the Foreign Ministry's Americas Department, as the individual who would become the first SRV Ambassador to the U.S. The plan was to have Bang assume duties at the United Nations until such time as the U.S. moved into Phase Four. Trinh Xuan Lang, the SRV's Permanent Representative to the United Nations, was scheduled to return to Hanoi in May 1993, and retire from the foreign service. Bang, who would be promoted to ambassadorial rank in January 1993, was an intelligent, articulate diplomat who rose to an important departmental-level position following the 7th Congress, along with a group of others including Nguyen Xuan Phong, who would take Bang's place as head of the Americas Department (and eventually become the first Consul-General in San Diego). Lang,

on the other hand, was an old guard conservative who owed his position to Nguyen Co Thach. He regarded U.S. efforts to promote POW/MIA field work and archival research as a means of actively collecting intelligence on the internal situation in Vietnam, and was disinclined to step up joint efforts. His retirement represented the first step in a quiet purge of the holdovers from Nguyen Co Thach's long tenure as Foreign Minister.

24. Quan Doi Nhan Dan Viet Nam, Tong Cuc Chinh Tri, Cuc Tu Tuong Van Hoa, (Thong Bao Noi Bo), "Tinh Hinh The Gioi, Trong Nuoc Va Luc Luong Vu Trang, Thang 1-1993," pp. 1-2. (Ideological and Cultural Department, General Political Department, People's Army of Vietnam, [Internal Bulletin], "International and Domestic Situation and the Armed Forces," January 1993).

25. Quan Doi Nhan Dan Viet Nam, Tong Cuc Chinh Tri, Cuc Tu Tuong Van Hoa, (Thong Bao Noi Bo), "Tinh Hinh The Gioi, Trong Nuoc Va Luc Luong Vu Trang," February 1993. (Ideological and Cultural Department, General Political Department, People's Army of Vietnam, [Internal Bulletin], "International and Domestic Situation and the Armed Forces," February 1993).

26. "Tong Bi Thu Do Muoi Tiep Thuong Si Et Mon Mot-xki," ("General Secretary Do Muoi Receives Senator Edmond Muskie"), *Nhan Dan*, 6 April 1993, pp. 1, 4; "Ve Quan He My-Viet Nam," ("Vietnamese-U.S. Relations"), *Nhan Dan*, 3 April 1993, p. 4; Hong Kong AFP in English, 1232 GMT, 3 April 1993, *FBIS-EAS* 93-063, 5 April 1993, pp. 32-33; Le Van Bang, SRV Permanent Representative to the United Nations, Presentation to the Center for Strategic and International Studies, Washington, D.C., 6 April 1993.

27. Stephen J. Morris, "The '1205' Document: A Story of American Prisoners, Vietnamese Agents, Soviet Archives, Washington Bureaucrats and the Media," *The National Interest*, Fall 1993, pp. 28-42. The Vessey visit is covered in detail in Stern, *Imprisoned or Missing in Vietnam: Policies of the Vietnamese Government Concerning Captured and Unaccounted for United State Soldiers, 1969-1994*, (Jefferson, N.C.: McFarland, 1995), pp. 100-104.

28. Hanoi Vietnamese News Agency in English, 1508 GMT, 8 May 1993, *FBIS-EAS*, 93-088, 10 May 1993, p. 55; Hanoi Voice of Vietnam in English, 1000 GMT, 4 May 1993, *FBIS-EAS* 93-187, 10 May 1993, p. 41.

29. Kerry urged the Vietnamese to allow U.S. specialists greater access to wartime documents, and to improve the program of interviewing witnesses regarding the details of loss incidents. He suggested that the Vietnamese establish a repository in Hanoi that would contain all documents related to the POW/MIA issue. Kerry asked that Vietnam undertake further efforts to shed light on the issues raised by the Soviet document, and stressed the importance of improving the rate at which remains were repatriated. See Hanoi Voice of Vietnam Network in Vietnamese, 1000 GMT, 20 May 1993, *FBIS-EAS*, 93-096, 21 May 1993, p. 49; Hanoi Voice of Vietnam in English, 1000 GMT, 19 May 19934, *FBIS-EAS*, 93-096, 20 May 1993, p. 55; "Chu Tich Le Duc Anh Tiep Thung Nghi Si Giom Ke-ry," ("Chairman Le Duc Any Meets with Senator John Kerry"), *Nhan Dan*, 17 May 1993, pp. 1, 4.

30. During Senator Kerry's 31 May visit to Hanoi, the Vietnamese opened the document repository Kerry had asked them to establish during his mid-May visit. The Vietnamese were unable to respond to some of the specific JTFFA requests for documents, but they did provide a dozen or so documents to the Kerry delegation. "Tong Bi Thu Do Muoi Tiep Doan Nghi Si Va Cuu Binh My," ("General Secretary Do Muoi Receives a Delegation of U.S. Senators and War Veterans"), *Nhan Dan*, 2 June 1993, pp. 1, 4; Hanoi Vietnamese News Agency in English, 1429 GMT, 1 June 1993, FBIS-EAS, 93-103, 1 June 1993, p. 51; Hanoi Voice of Vietnam Network in Vietnamese 1430 GMT, *FBIS-EAS* 93-104, 2 June 1993, p. 51; Hanoi Voice of Vietnam in English, 1000 GMT, 8 June 1993, *FBIS-EAS*, 93-108, 8 June 1993, p. 54.

31. In July, the Defense POW/MIA Office was established as a Pentagon field activity. The Deputy Assistant Secretary of Defense for POW/MIA Affairs headed this office, which became known by the acronym DPMO.

32. The July 1993 issue of the General Political Department's monthly assessment of key events highlighted the 2 July decision by President Clinton to cease blocking efforts to settle Vietnam's arrears with the IMF. The decision, according to the assessment, was a result of Vietnam's "correct foreign policy, our approach and spirited struggle of making a stand for out people, with the support of many countries and broad international opinion." The report noted that many forces in the U.S. vehemently opposed lifting the embargo and normalizing relations with Vietnam. The report further stated that Vietnam's "struggle

respecting America to lift the embargo and normalize relations is still difficult and complex."

33. Hanoi Voice of Vietnam Network in Vietnamese, 0800 GMT 1 July 1993, FBIS-EAS 93–131, 2 July 1993, p. 70.

34. Hanoi Vietnamese News Agency in English, 1510 GMT, 16 July 1993, FBIS-EAS, 93–136, 19 July 1993, pp. 51–52; Hanoi Vietnamese News Agency in English, 1521 GMT, 17 July 1993, FBIS-EAS, 93–133, pp. 52–53; Hanoi Voice of Vietnam Network in Vietnamese, 1430 GMT, 17 July 1993, FBIS-EAS, 93–136, 19 July 1993, pp. 53–55; Hanoi Voice of Vietnam Network in Vietnamese, 1430 GMT, 17 July 1993, FBIS-EAS 93–136, 19 July 1993, pp. 53–54.

35. General Secretary Muoi met with Representative Sam Gibbons on 14 August. On 20 August, Senator Charles Robb was received by Prime Minister Vo Van Kiet, Interior Minister Ngo, and Foreign Minister Cam, all of whom emphasized changes in the security and economic situation in the region, the importance of economic cooperation, and especially the importance of quickly resolving the POW/MIA issue. On 27 August President Le Duc Anh received Representative David McCurdy and affirmed Vietnam's deep sympathy with the concerns of the U.S. Congress and the American people regarding the MIA issue. On 30 August, Senator Shelby, Chairman of the Armed Forces Subcommittee, met with Vice President Nguyen Thi Binh, who pledged continued cooperation with the U.S. Hanoi Voice of Vietnam in English, 1000 GMT, 6 August 1993, FBIS-EAS 93–150, 6 August 1993, p. 39; Hanoi Voice of Vietnam Network in Vietnamese, 0015 GMT, 4 August 1993, FBIS-EAS 93–150, 6 August 1993, pp. 39–40; "Hoat Dong Doi Ngoai," ("Diplomatic Activities") *Quan He Quoc Te*, (International Affairs), August 1993, p. 3; "Hoat Dong Doi Ngoai," ("Diplomatic Activities"), *Quan He Quoc Te*, (International Affairs), September 1993, p. 2; Hanoi Voice of Vietnam in English, 1000 GMT, 10 August 1993, FBIS-EAS 93–153, 11 August 1993, p. 54; Hanoi Voice of Vietnam in English, 1000 GMT, 12 August 1993, FBIS-EAS 93–155, 13 August 1993, p. 53; Hanoi Vietnamese News Agency in English, 1507 GMT, 14 August 1993, FBIS-EAS 93–156, 16 August 1993, p. 39; Hanoi Vietnamese News Agency in English, 1431 GMT, 27 August 1993, FBIS-EAS 93–165, 27 August 1993, p. 28; Hanoi Vietnamese Television Network in Vietnamese, 1100 GMT, 9 August 1993, FBIS-EAS 93–152, 10 August 1993, p. 55; Hanoi Vietnamese News Agency in English, 1442 GMT, 9 August 1993, FBIS-EAS 93–152, 10 August 1993, pp. 55–56.

36. Quan Doi Nhan Dan Viet Nam, Tong Cuc Chinh Tri, Cuc Tu Tuong Van Hoa, (Thong Bao Noi Bo), "Tinh Hinh The Gioi, Trong Nuoc Va Luc Luong Vu Trang," August 1993. (Ideological and Cultural Department, General Political Department, People's Army of Vietnam, (Internal Bulletin), "International and Domestic Situation and the Armed Forces," August 1993).

37. The Vietnamese Foreign Ministry spokesperson responded cautiously by noting that the ministry had not seen the text of Lord's remarks, and did not want to comment, though the spokesperson did say, in words that revealed Hanoi's serious concern, that "if the statement of Mr. Winston Lord includes anything that could compromise the process of normalization between the United States and Vietnam, we will ask for an explanation from the United States." See Hong Kong AFP in English, 0806 GMT, 26 August 1993, FBIS-EAS, 93–169, 26 August 1993, p. 38.

38. However, the 20th plenary session of the Vietnamese Workers' Party Central Committee took place in February 1972, not 1970-early 1971.

39. Hanoi Voice of Vietnam Network in Vietnamese, 1100 GMT 9 September 1993, FBIS-EAS 93–174, 10 September 1993, p. 52; Hong Kong AFP in English, 0636 GMT, 9 September 1993, FBIS-EAS 93–174, 10 September 1993, p. 52; Hanoi Voice of Vietnam in Vietnamese, 0015 GMT, 11 September 1993, FBIS-EAS 93–175, 13 September 1993, pp. 54–55; Hanoi Voice of Vietnam in English, 1000 GMT, 10 September 1993, FBIS-EAS 93–175, 10 September 1993, p. 54; Quang Loi, "Mot Kien Kinh Doanh Tren Noi Dau Nguoi Khac," ("A Commercial Proposal Built on the Misery of Others"), *Quan Doi Nhan Dan*, 12 September 1993, p. 4; Hanoi Voice of Vietnam Network in Vietnamese, 1100 GMT, 9 September 1993, FBIS-EAS 93–174, 10 September 1993, p. 52; Hanoi Voice of Vietnam Network in Vietnamese, 1100 GMT, 22 September 1993, FBIS-EAS 93–182, 22 September 1993, p. 41; Hanoi Voice of Vietnam Network in Vietnamese, 1400 GMT, 20 September 1993, FBIS-EAS 93–182, 22 September 1993, pp. 42–43.

40. *Izvestiya*, 30 October 1993, p. 3.

41. Office of the White House Press Secretary, "Renewal of the Trading with the Enemy Act and U.S. Policy Toward the Embargo Against Vietnam," 13 September 1993.

42. Hanoi Voice of Vietnam in English, 1000 GMT, October 1993, *FBIS-EAS* 93–195, 12 October 1993, p. 59; Hanoi Vietnamese News Agency in English, 1423 GMT, 9 October 1993, *FBIS-EAS* 93–195, 12 October 1993, p. 59. Statement of H.E. Mr. Phan Van Khai at the 48th Session of the United Nations General Assembly, 6 October 1993. Khai reiterated Vietnam's commitment to continued cooperation regarding the POW/MIA issue.

43. Hanoi Vietnamese News Agency in English, 1504 GMT, 14 December 1993, *FBIS-EAS*, 93–239, 15 December 1993, p. 66; Hanoi Voice of Vietnam Network in Vietnamese 1430 GMT, 15 December 1993, *FBIS-EAS* 930239, 15 December 1993, pp. 66–67. For details on the Lord meetings in Vietnam see Stern, *Imprisoned or Missing*, p. 122.

44. Hanoi Voice of Vietnam Network in Vietnamese 1430 GMT, 14 December 1993, *FBIS-EAS* 93–238, 14 December 1993, p. 68.

44. "Phi Ly Va Loi Thoi," ("Irrational and Outdated"), *Nhan Dan*, 17 September 1993, p. 4; Hanoi Voice of Vietnam Network in Vietnamese, 0015 GMT, 18 September 1993, *FBIS-EAS* 93–180, 20 September 1993.

Chapter 2

1. Reuters Transcript Report, Clinton/Vietnam Announcement, 3 February 1994, (17:57 02–03), p. 5. The President described four areas where the U.S. believed additional progress could be made: (1) continuing cooperation in joint field investigations of grave and crash sites, including witness interviews, provincial preparation (including reviews of locally-held archival information and documents bearing on loss incidents), as well as continued live sighting investigations; (2) efforts to organize trilateral cooperation on the Lao-Vietnam border cases involving U.S. service personnel on Lao territory in the area in which the Vietnamese People's Army operated throughout the war; (3) the repatriation of remains of Americans whose fate had been established, and whose remains were at one point through at least 1973 in the custody of Vietnamese authorities. These included the "photograph" cases, the Died in Captivity cases, cases listed on Vietnamese grave registers for which there had been no accounting, and cases where field investigations revealed witnesses who indicated that Vietnamese officials recovered remains from wartime burial sites that had not been repatriated, and (4) archival research in Vietnam's wartime document repositories for information pertaining to loss incidents, wartime burials, and the captivity of American service personnel. See Stern, *Imprisoned or Missing*, pp. 31–37, 83–88.

2. Murray Hiebert and Susuma Awanohara, "Lukewarm Welcome," *Far Eastern Economic Review*, 17 February 1994, pp. 14–17.

3. Quan Doi Nhan Dan Viet Nam, Tong Cuc Chinh Tri, Cuc Tu Tuong Van Hoa, (Thong Bao Noi Bo), "Tinh Hinh The Gioi, Trong Nuoc va Luc Luong Vu Trang," February 1994, pp. 1–2, (Ideological and Cultural Department, General Political Department, People's Army of Vietnam, (Internal Bulletin), "International and Domestic Situation and the Armed Forces," February 1994).

4. "Hoc Bao Quoc Te," ("International Press Conference"), *Nhan Dan*, 5 February 1994, pp. 1, 4; Hanoi Voice of Vietnam Network in Vietnamese, 1100 GMT, 4 February 1994, *FBIS-EAS* 94–024, 4 February 1994, pp. 40–41; Philip Shenon, "Vietnam Welcomes U.S. Decision on Embargo," *New York Times*, 5 February 1994, pp. 1, 5; From the beginning of the year, U.S. legislators, including John Kerry, had called for the lifting of the embargo, and supported the President's approach to the POW/MIA issue. The Vietnamese were aware of the importance of congressional support for the White House strategy on normalization. See "Tuong Nghi Si My Gio Ke-ri: Bay Gio La Luc My Can Bai Bo Lenh Cam Van Buon Ban Doi Voi Viet Nam," ("Senator John Kerry: It Is the Time American Must Lift the Trade Embargo with Vietnam"), *Nhan Dan*, 27 January 1994, p. 4; "Thu Thuong Vo Van Kiet Va Chu Tich Quoc Hoi Nong Duc Manh Tiep Thuong Nghi Si J. Ke-ri," ("Prime Minister Vo Van Kiet and Chairman of the National Assembly Nong Duc Manh Meet with Senator John Kerry"), *Nhan Dan*, 17 January 1994, pp. 1, 3.

5. The Office of the Deputy Assistant Secretary of Defense for Asia and the Pacific, subordinate to the Office of the Assistant Secretary of Defense for International Security Affairs, was generally referred to as Asia and the Pacific, or "AP," and in acronyms as ISA/AP, within the U.S. government. In meetings with the Vietnamese Defense Ministry's External Relations Department, the working level Pentagon delegation referred to itself as being headed by "ISA." Hereafter, the acronym "ISA" will be used as a shorthand for the Office of the Deputy Assistant Secretary of Defense for Asia and the Pacific.

6. During the early August 1987 meetings in Hanoi, General Vessey obtained agreement to resume and expand cooperation on POW/MIA and other humanitarian issues of mutual concern. Vessey told the Vietnamese that the U.S. could not consider direct assistance to Vietnam without a Cambodian settlement, but that the Administration would encourage American non governmental organizations to provide prosthetics assistance to Vietnam's disabled. These suggestions were referred to as the "Vessey Initiative." See "POW/MIA Agreements Between the U.S. and SRV, February 1982–Present," National League of Families, June 1992, pp. 7–8; "POW/MIA Significant Events," Office of the Assistant Secretary of Defense for Public Affairs, 7 August 1991, p. 1; "De Cuong Phat Bieu Tai Cuoc Gap Doan Tro Ly Thuong-Ha Vien My Sang Tim Hieu Tinh Hinh Giai Quyet Van De Nguoi My Mat Tich O Viet Nam," 21 July 1991, pp. 3–4 ("Outline of Statements at Meeting with Staff Aides to the U.S. Senate and U.S. House of Representatives Regarding the Effort to Resolve the Issue of Americans Missing in Action in Vietnam"); Hanoi International Service in English, 1000 GMT, 3 August 1987, *FBIS*, 3 August 1987, p. N.3. Assistant Secretary of State Richard Solomon traveled to Hanoi in March 1992 for the first contact at that level since then Assistant Secretary of State Paul Wolfowitz's 1986 visit to Hanoi. Solomon announced that the U.S. would provide about one million dollars in additional prosthetics assistance, 1.5 million dollars in new assistance to displaced children, and 250,000 dollars of excess Veterans Administration equipment. The U.S. also agreed to conduct military-run Medical Care Projects (MEDCAPS) during POW/MIA field operations, and announced Vietnam's eligibility for free transport for NGO-sponsored humanitarian assistance on a space available basis aboard U.S. military aircraft directed to support POW/MIA efforts in Vietnam, in accordance with the provisions of the Denton Amendment.

7. In February 1994, following the decision to lift the embargo, I sought DoD agreement to devolve authority to ISA to grant requests for Vietnamese citizens to visit U.S. military facilities, such as AFRIMS in Bangkok, Thailand. AFRIMS had requested permission to extend an invitation to two Vietnamese medical researchers to pursue shigellosis studies. AFRIMS planned to collaborate with the Institute of Hygiene and Epidemiology in Hanoi. The chief of the shigellosis vaccine testing project at the Institute visited AFRIMS in late 1993 to lecture on the studies undertaken at his facility. The proposed visit, and the planned collaboration, complemented a range of U.S. government initiatives, including the U.S. Navy malarial research team, and prosthetics and child care assistance provided under the umbrella of the "Vessey Initiative," all of which were aimed at responding to Vietnam's humanitarian needs in order to sustain Hanoi's cooperation on the POW/MIA issue. Following the Presidents decision to lift the embargo, it made sense to begin to treat these initiatives as routine, rather than as exceptions to policy. I felt that DoD needed to begin encouraging low-level contacts with the PAVN. At the time, there was a certain amount of skittishness at the White House regarding any further steps in the relationship with Vietnam. I was persuaded to separate the AFRIMS proposal, which would receive working level NSC support, from the pitch to allow DoD personnel to make modest, low profile familiarization visits to Vietnam, which would be considered at a later date.

8. In his report to the interim party conference in January 1994, General Secretary Do Muoi stated that Vietnam "persisted in the renovation undertaking, accelerated socioeconomic development, broadened the process of democratization, firmly maintained political stability, consolidated out national defense and security capabilities, diversified our diplomatic activities, and gradually overcame the impact of the blockade and embargo," terms that suggested that the SRV would look at the continuation of the trade freeze as an extreme and unfriendly act.

9. "Tu Lien Quoc Te: Dien Bien Quan He Viet-My," ("Transforming the Vietnamese-American Relationship"), *Nhan Dan*, 5 February 1994, p. 3.

10. "Bo Cam Van Chong Viet Man Se La Tot Lanh Khong Nhung Cho Hai Nuoc Viet Nam Va My Cho Ca Cong Dong Quoc Te," ("Lifting the Embargo Against Vietnam Will Benefit Not Only Vietnam and the U.S., but the Entire International Community"), *Nhan Dan*, 4 February 1994, p. 4.

11. In March, General Vessey broached the issue of eliminating the position of Presidential Emissary for POW/MIA Affairs with the National Security Advisor. Vessey made the case that the right mechanism had emerged to handle the POW/MIA job, involving the VNOSMP, the MND MIA Office, the MOI office, the Joint Document Center, the south-

ern office of the VNOSMP. These structures had established good working relations and effective communication with the JTFFA. The opening of Liaison Offices in Hanoi and Washington helped facilitate government-to-government dialogue, and added a useful means of bringing human and institutional resources to bear on the POW/MIA issue. The existence of a fairly clear cut policy structure obviated the need for a Presidential Emissary. The Vietnamese were more likely to be confused by multiple authorities, and prone to try and leverage to their advantage a system in which multiple high level U.S. policy players exerted influence in this area. Eliminating the position of Presidential Emissary would put the issue back in the Pentagon where it could be managed by policy bureaucrats and casualty resolution experts in a way that would make it unnecessary for the topmost policy officials to intervene in the daily grind of POW/MIA business.

12. In response to requests for specific documents, including provincial records of U.S. aircraft shot down by local military units, senior Vietnamese officials told the League representatives that they would take "rapid steps" to locate and provide these documents.

13. The League argued that the Joint Task Force was focused on initial surveys and investigations of all cases, and that the Task Force placed little emphasis on "achieving real accountability" and "no focus on pursuing unilateral SRV efforts." The League concluded that "this focus told Vietnamese officials that there was no need or desire on the U.S. part" for unilateral SRV efforts. The League also made the case that the "highly publicized Joint Document Center" had more value as propaganda than as a mechanism that contributed to focusing joint efforts on real research. Further, the League averred that U.S. government statements commending Vietnamese support for the center also eroded the message that Vietnam should be responsible for coming across with archival documents unilaterally. See "Report on National League of Families Trip to Vietnam, Laos, and Cambodia," Washington, D.C., no date.

14. "Tu Lien Quoc Te: Dien Bien Quan He Viet-My," ("Transforming the Vietnamese-American Relationship"), *Nhan Dan*, 5 February 1994, p. 3.

15. Hanoi Vietnamese News Agency in English, 0914 GMT, 2 March 1994, *FBIS-EAS*, 94–041, 2 March 1994, p. 41; "Dam Phan Viet Nam — My Ve Van De Tai San Va Lap Co Quan Lien Lac," ("U.S.–Vietnamese Talks on Property and Establishing Liaison Offices"), *Nhan Dan*, 7 March 1994, p. 4. In April, the Foreign Ministry publicly protested an American oil firm;s decision to conduct a seismological survey in preparation for exploratory drilling to evaluate oil and gas potential of a contract area that Hanoi claimed was located entirely within its exclusive economic zone and continental shelf. The U.S. company had signed an oil exploration contract with the Chinese Offshore Oil Company in 1992. Hanoi Voice of Vietnam Network in Vietnamese, 1100 GMT, 20 April 1994, *FBIS-EAS*, 94–077, 20 April 1994.

16. Hanoi Voice of Vietnam Network in Vietnamese, 1000 GMT, 27 May 1994, *FBIS-EAS*, 94–104, 31 May 1994, pp. 72–73.

17. Quan Doi Nhan Dan Viet Nam, Tong Cuc Chinh Tri, Cuc Tu Tuong Van Hoa, (Thong Bao Noi Bo), "Tinh Hinh The Gioi, Trong Nuoc va Luc Luong Vu Trang," March 1994. (Ideological and Cultural Department, General Political Department, People's Army of Vietnam, (Internal Bulletin), "International and Domestic Situation and the Armed Forces," March 1994).

18. Melbourne Radio Australia in English, 0630 GMT, 2 May 1994, *FBIS-EAS*, 94–084, 2 May 1994, pp. 54–55. During this period the Vietnamese cast around for all manner of ways to encourage the U.S. government to normalize quickly, and grasped at odd straws to communicate the importance of continued forward movement and to demonstrate friendliness and openness. The pinnacle of this was the mid–May reception accorded to the former heavyweight champion Muhammad Ali, who saw a number of sports officials as well as representatives of the State Committee for Cooperation and Investment, and Finance Ministry representatives. See Hanoi Vietnamese News Agency in English, 0620 GMT, 14 May 1994, *FBIS-EAS*, 16 May 1994, p. 54.

19. Hanoi Vietnamese News Agency in English, 1357 GMT, 8 June 1994, *FBIS-EAS* 94–110, 8 June 1994, p. 69.

20. Hanoi Voice of Vietnam in English, 1000 GMT, 24 June 1994, *FBIS-EAS* 94–122, 24 June 1994, p. 57.

21. Hanoi Vietnamese News Agency in English, 1401 GMT, 18 June 1994, *FBIS-EAS* 94–121, 23 June 1994, pp. 52–53. Quang returned for a similar visit in May 1995. See Hanoi Vietnamese News Agency in English, 0614 GMT, 30 May 1995, *FBIS-EAS* 95–103, 30 May 1995, p. 81.

22. "Day Toi Mot Buc Su Nghiep Cong Nghiep Hoa, Hien Dai Hoa Dat Nuoc Vi Muc Tieu Dan Giau, Nuoc Manh, Xa Hoi Cong Bang, Van Minh," Dang Cong San Viet Nam, *Van Kien: Hoi Nghi Lan Thu Bay Ban Chap Hanh Trung Uong, Khoa VII*, Hanoi, August 1994, pp. 3, 30. ("Taking a Step in the Effort to Industrialize and Modernize the Country to Enrich the People, Strengthen the Country, Establish a Just Society and Culture," Communist Party of Vietnam, Documents: Seventh Plenary Session of the Central Committee, Seventh Tenure, Hanoi, August 1994).

23. Mai encouraged an informal give and take, and very effectively presented his own views on a range of key issues, including the U.S. role in the region, the North Korean crisis, and the question of MFN status for Vietnam. Mai was authoritative in his presentation, but he was not totally empowered to reflect Vietnamese foreign policy views. He expressed his own views on some strategic issues, but demurred when asked to comment on Vietnam's official positions on matters involving third countries.

24. "U.S., Vietnam Discuss MIA Issue," *Washington Post*, 3 July 1994, p. A.24.

25. Remarks to the National League of Families of POWs and MIAs from Southeast Asia, Washington, D.C., 15 July 1994, pp. 10–11.

26. Remarks of Samuel R. Berger, Deputy National Security Advisor, to the Annual Meeting of the National League of Families of POWs and MIAs from Southeast Asia, Washington, D.C., 15 July 1994, pp. 3–4.

27. Hanoi Vietnamese News Agency in English, 1430 GMT, 2 July 1994, *FBIS-EAS* 94–128, 5 July 1994, pp. 67–68; Hanoi Voice of Vietnam in English, 1000 GMT, 3 July 1994, *FBIS-EAS* 94–128, 5 July 1994, p. 68; Hanoi Voice of Vietnam in English, 1000 GMT, 4 July 1994, *FBIS-EAS* 94–128, 5 July 1994, pp. 68–69; Hanoi Voice of Vietnam Network in Vietnamese, 1430 FMT, 4 July 1994, *FBIS-EAS* 94–129, 6 July 1994, p. 65; Hanoi Voice of Vietnam in English, 1000 GMT, 5 August 1994, *FBIS-EAS* 94–151, 5 August 1994, pp. 77–78; Hanoi Vietnamese News Agency in English, 1418 GMT, 4 August 1994, *FBIS-EAS* 94–151, 5 August 1994, p. 78; "Tong Bi Thu Do Muoi Tiep Doan Cap Cao My," ("General Secretary Do Muoi Receives a High-Ranking American Delegation"), *Quan Doi Nhan Dan*, 3 July 1994, p. 4; *Report to Congress*, 10 August 1994, p. 3; George Esper, "Vietnam Hands Over More MIA Remains," *Washington Times*, 3 August 1994, p. 10.

28. Department of State, *Technical Steps Required to Implement Economic Measures Concerning Vietnam*, 27 November 1994.

29. Hanoi Voice of Vietnam in English, 1430 GMT, 12 August 1994, *FBIS-EAS* 94–156, 12 August 1994, p. 67.

30. Regarding the U.S. call for trilateral cooperation on the Lao Border cases, in late 1994 a senior Vietnamese diplomat suggested that the persistent difficulties regarding this problem had more to do with the nature and quality of U.S.–Lao relations than with the content and tone of Lao-Vietnamese relations. The Lao wanted to be treated as equals in their relationship with Washington, and strongly desired MFN status. The Vietnamese diplomat made the case that a consistent level of humanitarian assistance for Laos, not tied to POW/MIA activities, would significantly improve the relationship. Laos, the diplomat argued, looked at Cambodia and saw the United States developing programs and sustaining a level of relationship that far exceeded the treatment accorded to Vientiane. The Lao wondered why Washington was unwilling to make a similar investment in Laos.

31. VNOSMP, "Report: Recent Work to Resolve the MIA Issue," 14 September 1994.

32. Hanoi Vietnamese News Agency in English, 1449 GMT, 5 October 1994, *FBIS-EAS* 94–194, 6 October 1994, p. 81.

33. Hanoi Voice of Vietnam Network in Vietnamese, 1000 GMT, 5 October 1994, *FBIS-EAS*, 94–193, 5 October 1994, p. 63.

34. Greg Pierce, "Last POW Symbolically Buried," *Washington Times*, 5 October 1994, p. 3; *Far Eastern Economic Review*, 6 October 1994, p. 13.

35. Hanoi Vietnamese News Agency in English, 1424 GMT, 15 November 1994, *FBIS-EAS* 94–221, 16 November 1994, p. 85; Hanoi Vietnamese News Agency in English, 1501 GMT, 15 November 1994, *FBIS-EAS* 94–221, 16 November 1994, p. 86.

36. Hanoi Vietnamese News Agency in English, 1000 GMT, 16 November 1994, *FBIS-EAS* 94–221, 16 November 1994, p. 85; Hanoi Vietnamese News Agency in English, 1000 GMT, 1 December 1994, *FBIS-EAS* 94–231, 1 December 1994, p. 43.

37. Bruce Stanley, "U.S. Sees a Breakthrough in MIA Search in Laos," Associated Press Story Category, 1 December 1994, APTU-12-01-94 0720 EST; Hanoi Voice of Vietnam in English, 1100 GMT, 2 December 1994, *FBIS-EAS* 94–233, 5 December 1994, p. 77.

38. Hong Kong AFP in English, 1005 GMT,

Notes—Chapter 2

2 December 1994, *FBIS-EAS* 94–232, 2 December 1994, p. 53.

39. National Defense Authorization Act for Fiscal Year 1995, Conference Report to Accompany S.2182, House of Representatives, 103rd Congress, second session, Report 109–701, 12 August 1994, pp. 181–195.

40. In mid-November, Senator Smith supported the efforts of a coalition of family and veterans groups to establish an ad hoc working group aimed at presenting to Congress an "Action Plan" on accounting for the MIAs, and in effect supplanting the Administration's efforts to manage this issue. The effort fizzled but did not dampen Smith's desire to discredit the Administration's policy toward Vietnam. See "Veterans Form POW/MIA Action Group," *The American Legion*, 16 November 1994; VSO and Family POW Organizations, "POW/MIA Ad Hoc Working Group Meeting," 16 November 1994.

41. In a paper prepared for a May 1994 conference sponsored by the U.S.–Vietnam Reconciliation Project, I noted that there were significant strategic "values" to entering into a relationship with Vietnam, including Vietnam's growing market potential for U.S. businesses, Vietnam's increasing significance to ASEAN, the Southeast Asian notion that in the end economic forces will be the integrating force that reintroduces countries such as Cambodia and Vietnam into the region. "There will come a time," I suggested, "when the substance of our relationship with Vietnam will focus on shared concepts of regional tranquility, common strategic interests in preserving regional balances, and agreed-upon concepts of global responsibility in areas such as counter-proliferation." The senior Vietnamese representatives, including Le Van Bang, nodded in agreement but ventured no clarifying positions of their own on the possibility for future bilateral defense relations. See Stern, "U.S. government Strategic Interests in Vietnam," May 1994. Also see "Looking to the Future: Vietnam and Regional Policy Issues," Remarks prepared for the U.S.–Vietnam Policy Forum, sponsored by the U.S.–Vietnam Trade Council and the Georgetown University School of Foreign Service, Georgetown University, Washington, D.C., 21–22 July 1994.

42. Hanoi Vietnamese News Agency in English, 0734 GMT, 28 January 1995, FBIS-EAS 95–019, 30 January 1995, p. 86; Statement by Christine Shelling, Acting State Department Spokesman, on the opening of liaison offices, 27 January 1995, U.S. *Department of State Dispatch*, February 1995, Vol. 6, No. 6, p. 84.

43. In mid-January 1995, the Vietnamese reacted angrily to the publication of a book written with the assistance of a consultant engaged in 1992 by the Department of Defense to develop leads and extract documents from the holdings of the Vietnamese military museum pertaining to missing Americans. See Malcolm McConnell, *Inside Hanoi's Secret Archives: Solving the MIA Mystery*, New York: Simon and Schuster, 1995. In a 19 January Foreign Ministry press conference, spokesperson Ho The Lan strongly denied allegations that U.S. POWs had been tortured, categorically rejected the claim that POWs had been killed during 1966 and 1972 while in Vietnamese custody, and argued that such claims were aimed at obstructing normalization. See Hanoi Vietnamese News Agency in English, 0723 GMT, 20 January 1995, *FBIS-EAS* 95–013, 20 January 1995, p. 72; Hanoi Voice of Vietnam Network in Vietnamese, 1430 GMT, 19 January 1995, *FBIS-EAS* 95–013, 20 January 1995, p. 71; Hong Kong AFP in English, 1142 GMT, 19 January 1995, *FBIS-EAS* 95–012, 19 January 1995, pp. 71–72; *Boston Globe*, 18 January 1995, p. 64.

44. Kevin Fedarki, "Washington: The Last POW," *Time*, 24 April 1995, p. 42; Adam Schwartz, "Unfinished Business: MIA Issue Continues to Bedevil Ties with U.S.," *Far Eastern Economic Review*, 4 May 1995, pp. 24–25; U.S. General Accounting Office, Report to Congressional Committees, "U.S. Vietnam Relations: Issues and Implications," GAO/NSIAD-95-42, April 1995.

45. The Interior Ministry representative cited a 20 September 1994 communique from the Ministry's General Department One to provincial and municipal public security service directors containing these instructions. The directive was included as an appendix to the VFW trip report. See Ministry of Interior, General Department One, Number 1001/TC 1 (MIA), 20 September 1994, signed by Bui Quoc Huy, Chairman, General Department One, contained in VFW Junior Commander James E. Neir's "Southeast Asian POW/MIA Trip Report," 5–17 April 1995.

46. "Southeast Asian POW/MIA Trip Report," 5–17 April 1995, pp. 1–13.

47. Schwartz, "Unfinished Business," *Far Eastern Economic Review*, 4 May 1995, pp. 24–25.

48. The four areas specified by the President in July 1995 as the key areas where the

U.S. expected enhanced Vietnamese cooperation were: the recovery and repatriation of remains, the resolution of the remaining discrepancy cases, the conduct of investigations of Lao Border area cases, and accelerated efforts to provide the U.S. government with POW/MIA-related documents from Vietnamese archives.

49. The Commission sifted through 270 pages of Soviet archival material, including 64 pages of Soviet military intelligence reporting on the air war in Vietnam, and interviewed 60 witnesses to events in Vietnam during the war years. See *Interim Report of the Joint Commission on POW/MIAs*, and *Vietnam Working Group Report*.

50. Hanoi Voice of Vietnam in English, 1000 GMT, 4 May 1995, *FBIS-EAS* 95–087, 5 May 1995, p. 56; Jim Wolf, "No Vietnam-Era U.S. POWs Were Sent to Moscow, Report Says," Reuters, 2 May 1995 (wire service copy); Associated Press, 2 May 1995 (wire service copy); U.S. Government, "Recent Reports on American POWs in Indochina: An Assessment," September 1993.

51. The two Soviet documents were (1) a document from the former Soviet Union's Communist Party Central Committee archives that purported to be an official Vietnamese report on 1,205 American POWs held in northern Vietnam in 1972, which was released to the U.S.–Russia Joint Commission in April 1993, and (2) an intelligence document from the archives of Central Committee of the Communist Party of the Soviet Union that was purportedly a part of a report given to a Vietnamese Communist Party Central Committee plenary session in late December 1970–early January 1971 on 735 American "fliers" incarcerated in Hanoi during those years.

52. The Vietnamese plenary team consisted of 14 officials representing four ministries, under the leadership of Vice Foreign Minister Le Mai.

53. Those cases included the "photograph" cases, the Died in Captivity List cases, cases in which the names of Americans were listed on Vietnamese grave registers but no remains had been repatriated, and cases where field investigations revealed witnesses who indicated that Vietnamese officials recovered remains from wartime burial sites but those remains had never been repatriated.

54. In late 1993 the U.S. government began asking the Vietnamese to provide detailed information regarding how, over the years, they acted independently to investigate leads and track down witnesses and grave/crash sites for the cases involving individuals who died in Vietnamese custody, but whose remains had not been repatriated. Two versions of this list, both signed by Vice Minister Le Mai, were rejected as evasive, skimpy or hastily compiled. In July 1994, the U.S. government told the Vietnamese that they still needed to provide more information, even if the SRV had already provided the U.S. with information on a case-by-case basis because what Washington wanted was a comprehensive report that included all the information Vietnam had on each of the 84 cases. The Vietnamese, especially at the outset, were confused by the request, and wondered why their willingness to engage in special joint activities with reference to these cases was not an entirely satisfactory response to the U.S. government request.

55. Only four items that were included in the list of requests provided to the Vietnamese by the June 1994 Presidential Delegation were not provided: a Department of Military Justice list of U.S. remains that were recovered by 1978, records from provinces similar to the Ha Bac Province daily journal of wartime actions, a list of verified graves in Lang Son Province, and pages two and three of a Military Region Four roster of "bodies killed and torn apart," which was provided to the U.S. in 1993. Regarding the Department of Military Justice list, during the war PAVN's General Political Department was responsible for managing prison facilities, caring for prisoners, exploiting the American POWs for propaganda value, and retaining records regarding the fates of U.S. casualties and the disposition of U.S. prisoners. Subordinate elements of the General Political Department, including the Department of Military Justice, managed the prison system in cooperation with the General Department of Rear Services and the Public Security Service of the Interior Ministry. The "list" was assumed to exist by members of the U.S. Interagency Working Group in the early 1990s. There was no independent confirmation that such a document existed. VNOSMP officials and others told JTFFA that some provinces simply did not keep records and chronologies similar to the Ha Bac daily journal. VNOSMP officials, and collateral source information, indicated that Vietnamese archival holdings, safehavened in Lang Son, were destroyed in 1979 during China's invasion. By mid–1995 the JTFFA concluded that there was no basis for presuming that the two pages of the MR 4 roster existed.

56. John McCain, "U.S.–Hanoi Ties Seen as Strategic," *Washington Times*, 10 July 1995.
57. Robert McNamara, *In Retrospect: The Tragedy and Lessons of Vietnam*, New York: Times Books, 1995.
58. Hanoi Voice of Vietnam in English, 1000 GMT, 4 May 1995, *FBIS-EAS* 95–087, 5 May 1995, p. 56. Hanoi Voice of Vietnam in English, 1000 GMT, 2 June 1995, *FBIS-EAS* 95–106, 2 June 1995, p. 84; "U.S. Vietnam War Crash Wreckage Believed Found," Reuters Wire Service, 30 May 1995. Hanoi Voice of Vietnam in English, 1633 GMT, 31 May 1995, *FBIS-EAS* 95–105, 1 June 1995, p. 70. Hanoi Voice of Vietnam in English, 1000 GMT, 9 June 1995, *FBIS-EAS* 95–112, 12 June 1995, pp. 96–97.
59. Remarks by President Clinton, President of France Jacques Chirac, and President of the European Union Jacques Santer, Office of the Press Secretary, White House, 14 June 1995, p. 1. Hanoi Voice of Vietnam in English, 1000 GMT, 20 June 1995, *FBIS-EAS* 95–119, 21 June 1995, p. 71. Also see George Moffet, "U.S. Faces Last Battle Over Vietnam War," *Christian Science Monitor*, 22 June 1995, p. 4; Todd S. Purdum, "Clinton on Spot on Vietnam Issue," *New York Times*, 26 June 1995, p. 1. In late June, the Vietnamese media noted the commencement of a new round of joint field activities. This media article departed from the usual formula of simply announcing the fact that joint activities were about to or had taken place, and pointed out that the search was launched as the debate over normalization intensified in the U.S. See Hanoi Voice of Vietnam in English, 1000 GMT, 23 June 1995, *FBIS-EAS* 95–121, 23 June 1995, p. 80.
60. According to testimony before Congress by DASD/POW-MIA Wold, "a special investigator conducted a thorough field investigation of Hendon's claims that a prison was hidden in a mountain at a specific location in Vinh Phuc Province, approximately 50 miles northwest of Hanoi. Using the coordinates provided by Hendon and a global positioning system receiver, the investigator went to several sites in question. One site turned out to be a truck depot; the other was in the middle of a rice paddy. There were no mountains near either site and no indications of underground facilities. The investigation concluded with no evidence of American POWs being uncovered." James Wold, "Keeping Faith with MIAs," *Defense '95*, p. 21.
61. The Vietnamese media coverage extensively quoted Defense Department personnel who emphasized Vietnam's cooperation, and who denied that live American prisoners remained in Vietnam. The maximum that was said of Hendon was that his statements were "incorrect" and that no evidence had been uncovered to show that the 200 to 300 POWs Hendon claimed had been detained at the site in question were ever incarcerated there. The Vietnamese press coverage was free from the shrill denunciations of Hendon that might have been expected. See Hanoi Voice of Vietnam in English, 1000 GMT, 8 June 1995, *FBIS-EAS* 95–117, 19 June 1995, p. 99.
62. Hanoi Voice of Vietnam in English, 1000 GMT, 20 June 1995, *FBIS-EAS* 95–119, 21 June 1995, p. 71.
63. DPMO, "Fact Sheet: Vietnam POW/MIA Issue—Progress Since the Lifting of the Embargo, (February 1994–Present), 26 June 1995; "Assessment of the Government of the Socialist Republic of Vietnam Documents Presented to the May 1995 Presidential Delegation," Office of the Assistant Secretary of Defense for International Security Affairs, 28 June 1995; "Fact Sheet: Background Paper on POW/MIA Accounting," Office of the Press Secretary, the White House, 11 July 1995.
64. AmVets National Headquarters National Affairs Newswire Release Number 95–44; Dear Colleague Letter from Senator John McCain, 19 June 1995. Michael Dobbs, "Two POWs, Two Views of Vietnam," *Washington Post*, 9 July 1995, p. 1. At about the same time, General William Westmoreland, the retired commander of U.S. troops in Vietnam, stated that he did not believe that "the incumbent political leadership in Hanoi" merited recognition. See "Westmoreland Against Hanoi Relations," *Washington Times*, 9 July 1995, p. 4.
65. Kiet told the delegation that Vietnam had continued to cooperate after the lifting of the embargo, and could be expected to stay its course on this humanitarian issue in the aftermath of normalization. Le Mai emphasized the shared feelings of the Vietnamese and the American people toward their respective MIAs. Mai observed that several days prior to the arrival of the delegation, a mass grave containing the remains of more than one hundred PAVN troops had been uncovered near Tan Son Nhut airport. Though the Vietnamese government did not have the means of identifying any of the soldiers, the Vietnamese people recognized how important accounting for the missing was to the American people on the basis of Vietnam's own "sacred values." Mai stressed the involvement of a wide range

of organizations in Vietnam's efforts to locate information on missing American service personnel. He cited the efforts of the Veterans Association, the Red Cross, the Ministry of Labor, War Invalids and Social Affairs, all of which worked with the Lao and the U.S. on the Border Cases. Mai reiterated that the remaining cases were the most difficult ones to investigate because of the paucity of information and the extent to which the physical evidence had been destroyed or worn away by time. See "Thu Thong Vo Van Kiet Tiep Doan Thuong Nghi Si My," ("Prime Minister Vo Van Kiet Receives a U.S. Presidential Delegation"), *Nhan Dan*, 4 July 1995, p. 1.

66. In early June the National Security Advisor had stated that he would not recommend any policy until the assessment was completed.

67. George Moffett, "U.S. Faces Last Battle Over Vietnam War," *Christian Science Monitor*, 22 June 1995, p. 4.

68. James Wold, "Keeping Faith with MIAs," Defense '95, Issue 4, 1995, pp. 20–21; Statement by Brigadier General Charles R. Vitale, Command of the JTFFA, before the House Committee on National Security, Military Personnel Subcommittee, 28 June 1995.

69. In late November 1995, that delegation, which was scheduled to visit Vietnam in early December, postponed the trip to enable the Administration to complete the family notifications and congressional consultations prior to revealing the contents of the comprehensive POW/MIA review to the Vietnamese.

70. "Bao Chi Cac Nuoc Noi Ve Quan He Viet-My," ("The International Press on Vietnamese-American Relations"), *Nhan Dan*, 15 July 1995, p. 4; "Du Luan The Gioi Ve Quan He Viet-My," ("World Opinions Regarding Vietnamese-American Relations"), *Nhan Dan*, 16 July 1995, p. 4; "Hoan Nghenh Viec Binh Thuong Hoa Quan He Viet Nam-My," ("Welcoming Normalization of Vietnamese-American Relations"), *Nhan Dan*, 17 July 1995, p. 4.

71. "Noi Dung Hop Bao Cua Thu Truong Le Mai Ve Van De Binh Thuong Hoa Quan He Viet Nam-My," 12 July 1995, p. 2. ("The Contents of the Press Conference of Vice Minister Le Mai on the Problem of Normalization of Vietnamese-American Relations")

72. Vo Thu Phuong, "Buoc Tien Moi Trong Quan He Viet-My," ("A New Step Forward in Vietnamese-American Relations"), *Tap Chi Cong San*, Number 9, August 1995, pp. 47–48. Also see Hoan Lien, "Binh Thuong Hoa Quan He Viet-My — Viec Phai Den Da Den," ("Normalizing Relations Between Vietnam and the United States: The Inevitable Has Finally Come to Pass"), *Nhan Dan*, 23 July 1995, pp. 1, 4; "Du Luan My Va The Gioi: Binh Thuong Hoa Quan He Voi Viet Nam So Co Khong Doi Voi My Ca Trong Kinh Te, Chinh Tri Va Ngoai Giao," ("U.S. and World Opinion: Normalizing Relations with Vietnam Means Nothing to the U.S. Economically, Politically, and Diplomatically"), *Nhan Dan*, 23 July 1995, pp. 1, 4.

Chapter 3

1. I am indebted to Colonel Edward O'Dowd, U.S. Army (retired), for his recollections regarding USMC interest in the bilateral relationship by June-July 1995. By this point, the Marine Corps already had their selectee for the position of deputy defense attaché in training for that position, and may have already designated his successor so as to allow for the necessary lead time in scheduling long term training, thus demonstrating a seriousness about the relationship that put them far out in front of the other armed services.

2. See Draft unclassified Memorandum for the Assistant Secretary of Defense for International Security Affairs, "U.S.–Vietnamese Military Contacts Policy," 18 September 1995. Also see Stern, Memorandum for DASD/AP, "Some Thoughts on Mil-to-Mil U.S. Viet Relations," 13 June 1995; Stern, "Long Term Plans for Mil-to-Mil Relations with SRV," undated unclassified background paper; Stern, "Memorandum for DASD/AP, "Timing for Starting a Mil-to-Mil Relationship with Vietnam," 7 July 1995.

3. Richard Fisher, "Beyond Normalization: A Winning Strategy for U.S. Relations with Vietnam," Heritage Foundation Backgrounder Update, Number 257, 18 July 1995; Letter from Stern to Fisher, 24 July 1995; Stern, "U.S.–Vietnamese Relations: The Security Dimension — An Apriori Stab at the Facts," presented to the Asia Foundation Seminar on Issues for Post-Normalization With Vietnam, Washington, D.C., 19 July 1995.

4. U.S. Department of State, Office of the Spokesman, "American's Strategy for a Peaceful and Prosperous Asia-Pacific," National Press Club Briefing by Secretary of State Warren Christopher, 28 July 1995.

5. Memorandum, "PAG Subject: Normalization," Working Draft Document, 22 June 1995.

6. Hanoi Voice of Vietnam Network in Vietnamese, 1100 GMT, 12 July 1995, *FBIS-EAS* 95-134, 13 July 1995, pp. 68–69; Vo Thu Phuong, "Buoc Tien Moi Trong Quan He Viet-My," ("A New Step Forward in Vietnamese-American Relations"), *Tap Chi Cong San*, Number 9, August 1995, pp. 47–48.
7. Quan Doi Nhan Dan, Tong Cuc Chinh Tri, Thong Bao Noi Bo, "Tin The Gioi Trong Nuoc Va Luc Luong Vu Trang, January 1995," pp. 1, 2 (Ideological and Cultural Department, General Political Department, People's Army of Vietnam, (Internal Bulletin), "International and Domestic Situation and the Armed Forces," January 1995).
8. Nguyen Thoi Bung, "May Van De Can Quan Triet De Nang Cao Hieu Qua Cong Tac Doi Ngoai Quan Su," ("Several Problems Which Must Be Understood in Order to Improve the Effectiveness of the Military's Foreign Relations Activities"), *Tap Chi Cong San*, July 1995, pp. 1–4.
9. Hanoi Voice of Vietnam Network in Vietnamese, 1430 GMT, 13 July 1995, *FBIS-EAS*, 95–135, 14 July 1995, pp. 54–55.
10. *Saigon Giai Phong*, 14 May 1995, pp. 1, 2, FBIS-EAS 95–159, 17 August 1995; Hanoi Voice of Vietnam Network in Vietnamese, 1430 GMT, 25 August 1995, *FBIS-EAS* 95–167, 29 August 1995, pp. 86–87; Vo Thu Phuong, "Buoc Tien Moi Trong Quan He Viet-My," ("A New Step Forward in Vietnamese-American Relations"), *Tap Chi Cong San*, Number 9, August 1995, pp. 47–48. For articles on "peaceful war" and "peaceful evolution schemes" in the November issue of the Army's monthly journal, see *FBIS-EAS* 95–236, 8 December 1995, pp. 73–74; *FBIS-EAS* 95–218, 13 November 1995, pp. 99–102. Also see *FBIS-EAS* 95–218, 13 November 1995, pp. 97–99; Hanoi Voice of Vietnam Network in Vietnamese, 1100 GMT, 24 August 1995, FBIS-EAS 95–166, 28 August 1995, pp. 78–79; Hanoi Voice of Vietnam Network in Vietnamese, 2330 GMT, 16 August 1995, FBIS-EAS 95–164, 24 August 1995, pp. 70–72.
11. Quan Doi Nhan Dan, Tong Cuc Chinh Tri, Thong Bao Noi Bo, "Tin The Gioi Trong Nuoc Va Luc Luong Vu Trang, March 1994: Quan He Viet Nam-My Sau Khi My Bo Cam Van," pp. 1, 2 (Ideological and Cultural Department, General Political Department, People's Army of Vietnam, (Internal Bulletin), "International and Domestic Situation and the Armed Forces," March 1994: "Vietnamese-American Relations After the U.S. Lifts the Embargo").

12. Nguyen Thoi Bung, "May Van De Can Quan Triet De Nang Cao Hieu Qua Cong Tac Doi Ngoai Quan Su," ("Several Problems Which Must Be Understood in Order to Improve the Effectiveness of the Military's Foreign Relations Activities"), *Tap Chi Cong San*, July 1995, pp. 1–4.
13. In a side meeting during the Christopher trip, Vice Minister of Foreign Affairs Le Mai told DASD/POW-MIA James Wold that cooperation on the POW/MIA issue would increase, especially in view of the involvement of veterans from both sides. Mai once again stressed the complexity of the remaining cases of missing Americans. He also stated that the spectacle created by former Congressmen Hendon had placed the Foreign Ministry under considerable pressure to explain the situation to other ministries involved in managing relations with the U.S. Mai responded to Wold's promise to brief the Vietnamese on the "Comprehensive Review" of the remaining 2,198 cases of missing Americans, once the report had been coordinated within the U.S. government and briefed to Congress, by agreeing that experts from both sides should meet to discuss the individual cases in detail. In late September, in a continuation of the Veterans-To-Veterans Initiative, the president of the Vietnam Veteran's of American turned over maps, photographs and other documents collected from U.S. veterans to Vietnam's veterans association. Then Vice President of the Veteran's Association, Nguyen Trong Vinh, accepted the items as an indication of mutual willingness to put the past behind and "look to the future."
14. U.S. Department of State, Office of the Spokesman, Address by Secretary of State Warren Christopher to the Youth of Vietnam: "U.S.–Vietnam Relations: A New Chapter," Institute for International Relations, Hanoi, Vietnam, 6 August 1995; Michael Dobbs and Keith Richburg, "Hanoi Urged to Reject Repression," *Washington Post*, 6 August 1995; Hanoi Voice of Vietnam in English, 1000 GMT, 5 August 1995, *FBIS-EAS* 95–151, 7 August 1995, pp. 65–66 (meeting with Foreign Minister Cam); Hanoi Voice of Vietnam in English, 2300 GMT, 5 August 1995, *FBIS-EAS* 95–151, 7 August 1995, pp. 67–68, (meeting with President Le Duc Anh); Hanoi Voice of Vietnam in English, 1100 GMT, 6 August 1995, *FBIS-EAS* 95–151, 7 August 1995, p. 68, (meeting with General Secretary Do Muoi); Hanoi Voice of Vietnam in English, 1413 GMT, 6 August 1995, *FBIS-EAS* 95–151, 7 August 1995, p. 68, (meeting with Prime Minister Vo Van Kiet).

15. Vo Thu Phuong, "Buoc Tien Moi Trong Quan He Viet-My," ("A New Step Forward in Vietnamese-American Relations"), *Tap Chi Cong San*, Number 9, August 1995, pp. 47–48; *Tap Chi Cong San* editorial, August 1995.

16. Hanoi Voice of Vietnam Network in Vietnamese, 1430 GMT, 17 August 1995, *FBIS-EAS* 95–159, 17 August 1995, p. 60; I am grateful for the recollections of Mr. Mark Sidel, who attended the Christopher speech at the Institution for International Relations in his capacity as Asia Foundation Representative in Hanoi.

17. Section 403 (19 USC 2433).

18. The one thing that Vietnam had achieved in this list was membership in the IMF.

19. Vietnam Interagency Working Group, "Economic Normalization: Pace and Procedures," 21 August 1995; "Technical Steps Required to Implement Economic Measures Concerning Vietnam," 27 October 1994; Robert G. Sutter, "Vietnam Procedural and Jurisdictional Questions Regarding Possible Normalization of U.S. Diplomatic and Economic Relations," CRS Report 94–663, 4 August 1994. DoD did not participate in the July 1995 Interagency Working Group review of an unclassified August 1994 paper on the pace and procedures for economic normalization. I did participate in the 25 August 1994 meeting and the 19 July 1995 meeting at the State Department. The August 1994 meeting was one of the first IWG meetings on Vietnam that was not focused exclusively on the POW/MIA issue, and that widened participation to include representatives from Commerce, Trade and a myriad of State Department offices beyond the regional office responsible for Vietnam, Cambodia and Laos.

20. Hanoi Vietnamese News Agency in English, 1556 GMT, 5 October 1995, *FBIS-EAS* 95–194, 6 October 1995, p. 82.

21. In early September, former President George Bush traveled to Vietnam. During the trip, which was sponsored by CitiCorps, and must have confronted the Vietnamese as yet one more confusing piece to the puzzle of U.S. intentions, Bush proposed the establishment of a humanitarian organization to "function as a bridge between American veterans and family members and Vietnamese veterans and family members most affected by the war." Bush also raised several cases of missing servicemen on behalf of two families, stressed the mutual benefit that should spring from normalization, and supported Clinton's decision to normalize relations. The Vietnamese media mentioned Bush's trip, and his meetings with senior leaders, but did not discuss any of Bush's proposals. "Chu Tich Le Duc Anh, Thu Tuong Vo Van Kiet Tiep Cuu Tong Thong My Bu-So," ("Chairman Le Duc Anh and Prime Minister Vo Van Kiet Receive U.S. President Bush"), *Nhan Dan*, 6 September 1995, pp. 1, 3.

22. Department of Defense, *A Zero-Based Comprehensive Review of Cases Involving Unaccounted for Americans in Southeast Asia*, 13 November 1995; "567 MIAs Lost Forever, Pentagon Says," *Washington Times*, 14 November 1995, p. 3.

23. For example, Organizational Department Director Le Phuoc Tho addressed cadre from Nam Ha, Hai Hung, Ha Tay, Haiphong and Thai Binh Provinces in early July, at the outset of the local party congresses. He analyzed the results of pilot congresses conducted in three districts in Thai Binh Province, emphasized economic development issues and party-people relationships as two key objectives of the grassroots congresses, and implied that security matters and "peacefully transformation" themes would be a central part of the local congressional agendas.

24. Hanoi Vietnamese News Agency in English, 0610 GMT, 28 August 1995, *FBIS-EAS* 95–167, 29 August 1995, p. 84.

25. Ha was accompanied by his Vice Chairman, Mr. Pham Van Chuong, and Bui The Giang, the Director for People-to-People Relations Department of the External Relations Department, as well as Ambassador Le Van Bang in his capacity as charge, SRV Embassy, and his Deputy Chief of Mission Ha Huy Thong.

26. Hanoi Vietnamese News Agency in English, 0610 GMT, 28 August 1995, *FBIS-EAS* 95–167, 29 August 1995, p. 84; Hanoi Voice of Vietnam in English, 1000 GMT, 29 August 1995, *FBIS-EAS* 95–167, 29 August 1995, p. 84.

27. In a meeting on 24 October 1995, Ha Huy Thong, DCM in Vietnam's Embassy in Washington, told me that there were additional bureaucratic steps within the Vietnamese system in the process of approving the exchange of military attaches that had yet to be taken. Since this was a new initiative, Thong told me, the senior-most Vietnamese governmental leadership must review and approve the proposal. The government wanted to assure that the U.S. and the Vietnamese military attaches were assigned at the same time, in a manner that paralleled Vietnamese thinking about the designation of ambassadors. Nevertheless,

when it was clear that the Vietnamese side was not going to name a candidate and move forward with their side of the process of exchanging Defense Attachés, I urged that the U.S. Defense Attaché-designate be allowed to take up his place in the U.S. Embassy, notwithstanding Vietnam's sluggish response to our proddings. In early 1997, senior Vietnamese military officers suggested that one reason for the delay was a debate within the Defense Ministry on who to send to Washington, an older or a younger officer. Vietnam was concerned that sending an older officer would be taken to mean that PAVN could not come up with a well trained young officer.

28. The waiver, however, did not have to be approved by Congress. Eight Senators, including McCain, Harkins, Kerrey, and Kerry, had urged that a waiver be granted and that the U.S. government begin programs to support U.S. businesses operating in Vietnam. The steps that could be taken after granting the waiver were incremental, and were likely to be spread out over time in a manner that would satisfy those who did not want to move too quickly. At the time, specialists estimated that EXIM programs could probably begin before the end of the year. OPIC insurance and reinsurance and investment guarantees would follow, but not before Vietnam implemented laws to extend internationally recognized worker rights to its population. MFN status would have to await the completion of a trade agreement, which would have to be blessed by Congress.

Chapter 4

1. The Jackson Vanik waiver would secure EXIM funding for Vietnam; enable the Overseas Private Investment Corporation (OPIC) to insure, reinsure, guarantee or finance projects of private U.S. companies seeking to break into the Vietnamese market; activate Trade Development Assistance (TDA) which would be used to promote U.S. private sector participation in development projects; and enable the Administration, under the provisions of the Agricultural Trade Development and Assistance Act of 1954 (PL 480), to transfer on a loan or grant basis U.S. surplus agricultural commodities to Vietnam to help cope with foreign exchange shortages, difficulties in purchasing food, food deficits, malnutrition and emergency food requirements. See Vietnam Interagency Working Group, "Economic Normalization: Pace and Procedures," 21 August 1995.

2. Hanoi Voice of Vietnam Network in Vietnamese, 1430 GMT, 19 January 1996, *FBIS-EAS* 96-014, 22 January 1996, p. 88.

3. Hanoi Voice of Vietnam in English, 100 GMT, 14 February 1996, *FBIS-EAS* 96-032, 15 February 1996, pp. 77–78; Hanoi Voice of Vietnam Network in Vietnamese, 1100 GMT, 14 February 1996, *FBIS-EAS* 96-032, 15 February 1996, pp. 76–77.

4. "Accounting for the Missing in Southeast Asia: Text of a 'Zero-Based Comprehensive Review of Cases Involving Unaccounted for Americans in Southeast Asia,'" a DoD Report to Congress and the Nation Prepared by the Office of the Deputy Assistant Secretary of Defense for POW/MIA Affairs, released on 13 November 1995, in *Defense Issues*, Volume 11, Number 1.

5. In April 2001, Senior Colonel Bien died in the crash of a helicopter, along with seven U.S. JTFFA and nine VNOSMP personnel who were returning from a POW/MIA field mission in Quang Binh Province.

6. Stern, "Perspectives: The Other MIAs," *Vietnam*, October 1996, pp. 62–66.

7. The White House hoped for a reasonably quick confirmation, which was by April no longer a possibility given Senator Jesse Helm's posture on this and other nominations. Nevertheless, there was talk of dispatching Peterson to Hanoi during the summer of 1996, suggesting that the White House had a new level of confidence.

8. According to a foreign journalist, by mid–December 1995 the Vietnamese had selected a PAVN officer for this position. Through early 1996, senior Vietnamese military officers were not prepared to acknowledge that an individual had been selected to fill this job. In early January 1996 a senior Vietnamese military officer told the U.S. Defense Attaché in Hanoi that a decision had been made to assign a PAVN officer to the defense attaché position, though a candidate had not yet been named.

9. Desaix Anderson, *An American in Hanoi: America's Reconciliation with Vietnam*, New York, EastBridge, 2002.

10. See SNIE 14.3.87, "Hanoi and the POW/MIA Issue," Approved for release, 29 October 1996; "Vietnamese Storage of Remains of Unaccounted for U.S. Personnel," ICA-96-05, October 1996; Memorandum for USD(P), "POW/MIA: Declassification of 1988 SNIE,"

Information Memorandum, I-96/56696 (unclassified).

11. Katherin McIntire Peters, "The Endless Search," *Government Executive*, April 1996, pp. 27-31; Kristin Huckshorn and Tim Larimer, "Vietnam Cashes in on MIA Hunt," *San Jose Mercury News*, 28 April 1996; Huckshorn, "Hanoi Probe Complete; Pentagon Officials Mum on MIA Funds," *San Jose Mercury News*, 22 December 1995.

12. Hanoi Voice of Vietnam Network in Vietnamese, 1000 GMT, 18 April 1996, pp. 96-97; Julie Zasany, "Vietnam Mystery Exhumed by Mom," *The Journal Gazette*, (Fort Wayne, Indiana), 10 April 1996, pp. 1, 4.

13. "My Cham Dut Lenh Coi Viet Nam La Khu Vuc Chien Su," ("The U.S. Cancels Order Listing Vietnam as a War Zone"), *Nhan Dan*, 16 May 1996, p. 1.

14. The Presidential Determination noted that Section 609 raised "grave constitutional concerns" because it purported to use a condition on appropriations as a means to direct the execution of responsibilities reserved exclusively to the President by the Constitution. However, the Administration decided to provide the certification required by Section 609 "as a matter of comity," and without prejudice to the position that the condition enacted in Section 609 was unconstitutional. See Memorandum for the Secretary of State, from the White House, Subject: Vietnamese Cooperation in Accounting for United States Prisoners of War and Missing in Action (POW/MIA), 29 May 1996.

15. Kent Wiedemann, "Vietnam: U.S. Commitment to the Fullest Possible Accounting of POW/MIAs," U.S. *Department of State Dispatch*, 24 June 1996, pp. 342-343; James Wold, Written Statement Submitted to Congressional Hearing on U.S. POW/MIA Issue, "The Presidential Determination of Full Faith Cooperation by Vietnam, before the House Committee on National Security, Military Personnel Subcommittee, 19 June 1996.

16. *Quan Doi Nhan Dan*, 31 March 1996, p. 2.

17. Kristin Huckshorn and Tim Larimer, "Vietnam Cashes in on MIA Hunt," *San Jose Mercury News*, 28 April 1996.

18. In November or December 1996, Defense Minister Doan Khue signed a memorandum authorizing the dispatch of a PAVN officer to serve as Defense Attaché in Washington. He reiterated that decision in June or July of 1997, by which time Senior Colonel Vo Dinh Quang had taken up his post as the first Vietnamese Defense and Military Attaché in the SRV Embassy in Washington.

19. Dang Xuan Ky, "Vung Buoc Di Con Duong Xa Hoi Chu Nghia," ("Steady Step Forward on the Road to Socialism"), *Tap Chi Cong San*, Number 4, February 1996, pp. 3-6; Bui Ngoc Thanh, "Khong Co Su Lua Chon Nao Khac," ("No Other Choice"), *Tap Chi Cong San*, Number 4, February 1996, pp. 7-11; Nguyen Khac Hien, "Kinh Te Thi Truong Va Dinh Huong Xa Hoi Chu Nghia Co Doi Lai Nhau Khong?" ("Are a Market Economy and a Socialist Orientation Inherently Contradictory?), *Tap Chi Cong San*, Number 4, February 1996, pp. 12-15; Nguyen Van Oanh, "Ve Khai Niem Dinh Huong Xa Hoi Chu Nghia," ("Regarding the Concept of Socialist Orientation"), *Tap Chi Cong San*, Number 4, February 1996, pp. 16-19; Vu Hien, "Cuc Dien Moi Va Dinh Huong Di Len Cua Dat Nuoc," ("The New Face and the Progressive Orientation of the Nation"), *Tap Chi Cong San*, Number 4, February 1996, pp. 20-24; Nguyen Ngoc Khoa, "Buc Tien Moi Cua Dang Bo Huyen Thanh Oai," ("New Step Forward by the Thanh Oai District Party Chapter"), *Tap Chi Cong San*, Number 4, February 1996, pp. 50-54; Nguyen Duy Quy, "Doc Lap Dan Toc Gan Lien Voi Chu Nghia Xa Hoi," ("National Independence is Directly Linked to Socialism"), *Tap Chi Cong San*, Number 5, March 1996, pp. 4-8.

20. Nguyen Phu Trong, "Dinh Huong Xa Hoi Chu Nghia Va Con Duong Di Len Chu Nghia Xa Hoi O Nuoc Ta," ("Socialist Orientation and the Road to Socialism in Our Nation"), *Tap Chi Cong San*, Number 5, March 1996, pp. 9-16. Also see Phong Hai, "Nam Vung Dinh Huong Xa Hoi Chu Nghia-Thuoc Do Pham Chat, Nang Luc Cua Can Bo, Dang Vien Trong Su Nghiep Doi Moi Dat Nuoc," ("Firmly Maintaining Our Socialist Orientation: Measuring the Quality and Capabilities of Cadre and Party Members in Our National Cause of Renovation"), *Quan Doi Nhan Dan*, 27 May 1996, pp. 1, 4.

21. Ha Xuan Truong, "Dinh Huong Xa Hoi Chu Nghia Mot Khai Niem Khoa Hoc," ("Socialist Orientation, a Scientific Concept"), *Tap Chi Cong San*, Number 7, April 1996, p. 18.

22. Khong Doan Hoi, "Dinh Huong Xa Hoi Chu Nghia O Nuoc Ta," ("Socialist Orientation in Our Nation"), *Tap Chi Cong San*, Number 5, March 1996, pp. 15-17; Le Huu Nghia, "Vai Tro Cua Chinh Tri Trong Viec Bao Ve Dinh Huong Xa Hoi Chu Nghia," ("The Role of Politics in Protecting Our Socialist Orientation"), *Tap Chi Cong San*, Num-

ber 5, March 1996, pp. 18–20; To Huy Rua, "Con Duong Va Dieu Kien Bao Dam Dinh Huong Xa Hoi Chu Nghia O Nuoc Ta," ("The Road to and Conditions to Ensure the Socialist Orientation of Our Nation"), *Tap Chi Cong San*, Number 6, March 1996, pp. 19–22; Nhat Tan, "Chu Nghia Mac-Le Nin Va Tu Tuong Ho Chi Minh Voi Dinh Huong Xa Hoi Chu Nghia O Nuoc Ta," ("Marxism-Leninism and Ho Chi Minh Thought in Relation to Socialist Orientation in Our Nation") *Tap Chi Cong San*, Number 6, March 1996, pp. 26–29; Ha Xuan Truong, "Dinh Huong Xa Hoi Chu Nghia Mot Khai Niem Khoa Hoc," ("Socialist Orientation, a Scientific Concept"), *Tap Chi Cong San*, Number 7, April 1996, p. 18.

23. To Huy Rua, "Con Duong Va Dieu Kien Bao Dam Dinh Huong Xa Hoi Chu Nghia O Nuoc Ta," ("The Road to and Conditions to Ensure the Socialist Orientation of Our Nation"), *Tap Chi Cong San*, Number 6, March 1996, pp. 19–22.

24. The Gia, "Dai Hoi Dang Bo Quan Khu 7: Xay Dung The Tran Quoc Phong Toan Dan Gan Voi The Tran An Ninh Nhan Dan," ("Military Region 7 Party Congress: Developing a National Defense Posture Involving the Entire Population Is Linked with Our People's Security Posture"), *Nhan Dan*, 5 April 1996, pp. 1, 4.

25. Duy Phuc, "Dai Hoi Dang Bo Quan Khu 3: Nang Chat Luong Ba Thu Quan, Xay Dung Phong Thu Va The Tran Quoc Phong-An Ninh Vung Chac," ("Congress of the Military Region 3 Party Chapter: Increasing the Size of Our Three Types of Soldiers, Building Defenses and a Solid National Defense and Security Posture"), *Nhan Dan*, 8 April 1996, pp. 1, 4.

26. Xuan Phong, "Dai Hoi Dang Bo Co Quan Tong Cuc Chinh Tri: Tap Trung Nang Luc Tri Tue, Thuc Hien Tot Chuc Nang Tham Muu Tren May Tran Chinh Tri, Tu Tuong, Van Hoa," ("Congress of the General Political Department's Headquarters Party Chapter: Concentrating our Energies and Our Minds to Correctly Perform Our Staff Function on the Political, Ideological, and Cultural Fronts"), *Nhan Dan*, 6 April 1996, pp. 1, 4.

27. Quang Trong, "Dai Hoi Dang Bo Quan Khu 3: Dong Vien Moi No Luc Quan Va Dan Tren Dia Ban, Xay Dung Quan Khu Thanh Phao Dai Phong Thu Vung Chac," ("Military Region 3 Party Chapter Congress: Mobilize All Military and Civilian Efforts in the Region to Build the Military, *Quan Doi Nhan Dan*, 1 April 1996, pp. 1, 4. Also see Tran Nhung, "Tu Day Moi Ve Hoat Dong Doi Ngoai," ("Moving Forward Regarding Foreign Activities"), *Nhan Dan*, 20 April 1996, pp. 1, 4; Nguyen Quoc Pham," Tang Truong Kinh Te Gan Lien Voi Tien Bo Va Cong Bang Xa Hoi," ("Economic Growth Is Directly Linked to Social Progress and Social Justice"), *Quan Doi Nhan Dan*, 17 April 1996, pp. 1, 4; Nguyen Dinh Uoc, "Quoc Phong, An Ninh Voi Su On Dinh Chinh Tri Cua Dat Nuoc," ("National Defense and Security in Relation to the Political Security of the Nation"), *Quan Doi Nhan Dan*, 18 April 1996, pp. 1, 4; Doan Chuong, "Gop Phan Tim Hien Du Thao Bao Cao Chinh Tri Dai Hoi VIII Cua Dang: Giu Vung Dinh Huong Xa Hoi Chu Nghia," ("To Help Understand the Draft Political Report of the 8th Party Congress: Firmly Maintaining Our Socialist Orientation"), *Quan Doi Nhan Dan*, 16 April 1996, pp. 1, 4. These *Quan Doi Nhan Dan* commentaries on the draft political report emphasized the threats posed by external and internal forces that sought to undermine the Vietnamese system through "peaceful evolution."

28. D.T., "Dai Hoi Dang Bo Khoi Cac Co Quan Doi Ngoai Trung Uong; Nang Hoat Dong Doi Ngoai Len Tam Cao Moi," ("Congress of the Party Chapters of the Central Foreign Relations Agencies: Raise Foreign Relations Activities to New Heights"), *Nhan Dan*, 28 March 1996, pp. 1, 4, which describes the 4th congress of the Central Committee's Foreign Relations Bloc, convened from 26 to 27 March with the participation of Foreign Minister Nguyen Manh Cam and Hong Ha, Chief of the Central Committee's External Relations Department.

29. U.S. Department of State, Transcript: Lake 7/13 Press Conference in Vietnam, p. 2. Lake also visited Quang Tri and was briefed at a JTFFA recovery site. See Remarks by Anthony Lake, Assistant to the President for National Security Affairs, to the Japan-America Society, Washington, D.C., October 23, 1996; Kevin Fedarko, "Washington: The Last POW," *Time*, 24 April 1995, vol. 145, no. 17; 30 January 2002 telephonic conversation with Anthony Lake.

30. Lake had no specific memory that the question of defense relations figured prominently in his discussions with senior SRV officials. He believed that his decision to visit Vietnam did not trigger an internal U.S. government debate over the question of the utility of presidential delegations. He also felt that his decision to visit Vietnam was not a function of a personal decision to serve for only one presidential term as National Security Ad-

visor. However, he did note that alongside of the substance of the visit, he did have a serious personal interest in visiting Vietnam, given his wartime assignment in the south, and he did have an invitation to visit dating from a trip to Hanoi in 1983 or 1984. Author's 30 January 2002 telephonic conversation with Anthony Lake.

31. "Southeast Asia–ROK–U.S.: Thai, Vietnamese, South Korean Media Portray Lake Visit in Positive Light," Foreign Media Note, Foreign Broadcast Information Service, FBIS-FMN 96-00543, 15 July 1996. Also see Hanoi Voice of Vietnam Network in Vietnamese, 2300 GMT, 13 July 1997, FBIS-EAS 96–136, 15 July 1996, p. 89; Hanoi Vietnamese News Agency in English, 1530 GMT, 13 July 1996, *FBIS-EAS* 96–137, p. 103.

32. Hanoi Voice of Vietnam in English, 1000 GMT, 11 July 1996, *FBIS-EAS* 96–135, 12 July 1996, p. 93.

33. 18 July 1996 letter to Ha Huy Thong.

34. Hanoi Voice of Vietnam in English, 1000 GMT 2 August 1996, *FBIS-EAS* 96–152, 6 August 1996, p. 94.

35. The U.S. delegation, headed by DASD/AP Campbell, consisted of Deputy Assistant Secretary of State Jeffry Bader, Joint Staff Deputy Director for Political-Military Affairs Major General Robert Fogelson (USAF), National Security Council Director for Asian Affairs Colonel Jack Pritchard (USA), a CINCPAC representative (Major David Corwin, USAF), a Joint Staff desk officer (Lt.Col. Bill Thomas, USAF), Chief of the State Department's Bureau for Indochina, Thailand and Burma (Ms. Marie Huhtala), a DPMO representative (Mr. Joe Harvey), and myself, representing ISA.

36. *Vietnam News*, an English language paper published by the Vietnam News Agency, carried an article in the 9 October issue that noted the visit by an "American Military Delegation" which met with Vietnamese officials from the Defense and Foreign Affairs Ministries for talks on "matters of common interest." The article stated that the delegation called at the Vietnam Veterans Association, the JTFFA and the Vietnamese MIA Office, and was received by Defense Minister Doan Khue. *Hanoi Moi*, the municipal daily paper, noted that the exchanges with the MND and the MFA took place in "an open, relaxed atmosphere" and covered "problems important to both sides." *Hanoi Moi* said that the U.S. delegation had been received by both Doan Khue and General Tran Van Quang of the Veterans' Association. The party's daily paper, *Nhan Dan*, and the military's daily newspaper, *Quan Doi Nhan Dan*, did not cover the visit.

37. Khue seemed to say that an SRV Defense Attaché would be placed in Washington according to his Ministry's own schedule. However, Khue made this statement in a manner that suggested the SRV Defense Attaché might not be assigned until the U.S. upgraded its representation in Hanoi to the ambassadorial level. In his words, the U.S. had a defense attaché, and the Vietnamese had a "working embassy," headed by a diplomat with ambassadorial rank.

38. Indeed, in 1997 the Vietnamese allowed the Atlantic Council's invitation to send an officer for a nine month long orientation visit to go unanswered. At first, the MND identified a candidate, and later withdrew the name of the officer with the explanation that ill health prevented travel by that individual. The MND never responded to entreaties from ISA and the Atlantic Council to nominate another candidate for this orientation trip.

Chapter 5

1. On the Roadmap, see *Imprisoned or Missing*, pp. 61–69, 87–98.

2. In November 1996, the ERD evinced disinterest in meeting with a humanitarian assistance program officer from the Office of the Assistant Secretary of Defense for Strategy and Resources (OASD/S&R/PKO/HAP). The ERD told the U.S. Defense Attaché that the DoD travelers should work with the Foreign Ministry.

3. Jim Mann, "U.S. Steps Up Military Linkage to Vietnam," Los Angeles Times, 15 January 1997, p. 7; Jim Mann, Reuters report, 19 February 1997.

4. Barbara Opall, "Pentagon Forges Military Relations with Vietnamese," *Defense News*, 3–8 March 1997, pp. 1, 28; "Vietnam Military Delegation, In U.S., Expected to Go Beyond MIA Issues," *Boston Globe*, 20 February 1997, p. 10.

5. One senior officer in the delegation privately expressed confusion upon observing uniformed officers in the corridors of the Pentagon, wondering why military personnel would be present in the building that was supposed to be an entirely civilian entity.

6. Khue posted a letter to Secretary of Defense William Cohen dated 29 March which

offered congratulations on his appointment to the cabinet. He briefly described the first three steps in the development of the military relationship, and looked forward to "positive contributions" to developing the relationship during Cohen's tenure. Secretary Cohen's response, which I drafted, noted that no region in the world was of greater significance that the Asia-Pacific region. Vietnam had recently joined ASEAN, and was working with the ASEAN Regional Forum to find creative approaches to resolving regional security issues and fostering productive regional dialogues. Secretary Cohen expressed his hope that Vietnam and the U.S. would be able to build on common security objectives in a manner that contributed to the growing bilateral defense dialogue, which itself would contribute to regional stability. The letter did not reference Khue's interest in visiting the U.S., nor did it refer to the future possibility of a visit to Hanoi by Cohen.

7. There were proposals that were not part of the original "six pack" which I regarded as seriously premature. For example, in mid–April 1997, the Coast Guard requested advice regarding the feasibility of a three day port visit by a USCG cutter to Da Nang, Vietnam, in late May or early June. This step went far beyond anything envisioned by the U.S. and Vietnam. The White House was not at all prepared to entertain this kind of a leap in the relationship. PACOM, PACFLT, and DAO Hanoi agreed with ISA that the proposed port call was not appropriate to the relationship at that juncture. In March, Martin Lancaster, Assistant Secretary of the Army for Civil Works, proposed a visit to Vietnam. He had been invited to address the second Asian and Australian Ports and Harbors Conference in Saigon, scheduled for mid–April. ISA thought that such a visit by a policy representative of the Army Corps of Engineers would get ahead of the six point plan, and would elevate official contacts to the Assistant Secretary level before we were prepared to do so. Also, such a visit proposal was, by March, out of step with the sequence of events envisioned by the ISA-ERD working level meeting as the means of planning for next steps in the defense relationship. Moreover, the Vietnamese Defense Ministry had already demonstrated an allergy to humanitarian assistance proposals.

8. The Executive Panel was created in the 1970s and charged with the responsibility of bringing together knowledgeable U.S. civilians from different walks of life to provide analysis, advice and guidance to the Chief of Naval Operations. In 1997, the Chief of Naval Operations, Admiral Johnson, directed the Task Force to conduct a study of long-range Pacific security issues. The Task Force was directed to pay particular attention to the role of the U.S. Navy over the next ten to fifteen years. As part of their mission, the Task Force was to travel to Thailand, Malaysia, Singapore, the Philippines and Indonesia.

9. Chinese Defense Minister Chi's December 1996 visit to the U.S. was a Secretary of Defense-funded counterpart visit. In addition to the Minister, there were 18 government and military officials in his delegation, of whom 16 were members of the People's Liberation Army. The U.S. military installations on the itinerary included the U.S. Military Academy, Langley Air Force Base, Fort Hood, Sandia National Lab, Camp Smith, and the Pearl Harbor Naval Base. No restricted areas were visited. The U.S. and the Chinese sides agreed to next steps in the bilateral military relationship and to several confidence building measures aimed at reducing the likelihood of dangerous misunderstanding and enhanced regional stability. The visit included meetings with the President, the Secretary of Defense, the Deputy Secretary of State, the National Security Advisor, and members of Congress. The itinerary was designed to show Minister Chi the capabilities of the U.S. armed forces, and to allow him to see first hand the free and open society that serves as the foundation of the strength of the United States. In the end, oddly, the Vietnamese Defense Attaché, after being briefed on this itinerary, asked whether his defense minister would be put up at the same hotel as Chi. This was a theme that would come up often during monthly conversations I conducted with Senior Colonel Quang between his 1997 arrival and the end of his tour in 1999.

10. Cuc Doi Ngoai Bo Quoc Phong Cong Ha Xa Hoi Chu Nghia Viet Nam, ("The External Relations Department of the Ministry of Defense, Socialist Republic of Vietnam"), Letter to U.S. Ambassador, 28 DN, 27 April 1998.

11. See Desaix Anderson, *An American in Hanoi: America's Reconciliation with Hanoi*, (New York: EastBridge, 2002), p. 69. Anderson adds that "Even if this speculation is correct, I would judge that Vietnam's strategic imperative is to align itself with ASEAN and the other friendly powers in the region, including especially the United States, against

the day when China might attempt to use its growing power against its neighbors."

12. This did not always work out as envisioned. It was difficult to pry the Vietnamese away from their commitment to formalities and strict protocol. In advance of the Vietnamese Senior Colonels visit, ISA appealed to the Vietnamese Embassy, and to ERD through the U.S. Defense Attaché, to agree to dispense with the practice of exchanging gifts to mark an official event. I made the case that we could do away with the inconvenience of hauling trinkets across oceans, and eliminate unnecessary protocol requirements and administrative procedures necessary to authorize the use of official monies for acts of generosity and symbolic expressions of appreciation for hospitality. It would be a mark of the extent to which both sides were serious about conducting meetings of substance as opposed to generating newsworthy gestures. That negotiation failed, and the U.S. side was deluged with keepsakes, trinkets and souvenirs of the visit at the airport. The pre-boarding gesture elicited a shocked response from the U.S. side. I noted that a "no gift" policy had been negotiated, to which the ERD responded that the Vietnamese understanding of this arrangement was that it did not preclude the possibility of an exchange of souvenirs. So, in advance of the September 1997 meetings, ERD pressed for the end to the "no gift policy," and the installation of an agreement that would allow "souvenirs," or parting gifts. My solution was to begin providing the ERD with large tomes published by the Office of the OSD Historian, on the history of the Department of Defense, excessively weighty hard covered books that would easily press luggage weight limits to the edge. The Vietnamese side responded by stockpiling larger scrolls, calendars and keepsakes, impossible to pack in commercially available valises.

13. Khue emphasized how important it was that he pay an early visit to Washington, and suggested that some U.S. officers supported a more rapid pace that went beyond the modest steps in defense relations to which the U.S. had agreed. In late June, the U.S. Embassy in Hanoi recommended a meeting with the ERD Chief to conduct an initial reconnaissance of the Defense Minister's intentions regarding a visit to the U.S. I was not confident that this was the best approach. I thought that broaching the subject with the ERD would signal to the Vietnamese that we were prepared to meet their requirements. I preferred leaving it to the ERD to raise the visit in the context of the upcoming planning meeting. Additionally, though ISA had not yet approved the plan, there was fairly broad support in the Pentagon for the notional schedule in the proposal, which kicked a visit to the U.S. by the Minister of Defense down to the last years of the Clinton Administration.

14. Linh passed away in May 1998. The 4th plenum also announced the election of four additional Politburo members to replace the retirees.

Chapter 6

1. Department of Defense, *The United States Security Strategy for the East Asian-Pacific Region*, Washington, D.C., 1998.

2. Besides Vu Tan, I also met with Nguyen Manh Hung, the Director of the MFAs Americas Department; Ha Huy Thong, who had returned to the Americas Department; Hoang Thuy Giang, the Director of the Party Central Committee's External Relations Department; and Pham Dung of the Interior Ministry's External Relations Department.

3. The Vietnam Commando Compensation legislation, Section 657 of the National Defense Authorization Act (PL 104–201), required the Secretary of Defense to pay $40,000 to $50,000 to any Vietnamese operative who participated in OPLAN 34A or OPLAN 35 during the war.

4. John D. Mills, "U.S. Colonels Visit Vietnamese Military," *Asia Pacific Defense Forum*, Summer 1998, pp. 2–11.

5. The flyout proposal would surface again in late 1998 as part of ISA's proposed package of next steps, without attracting appreciably more support from the Vietnamese side. The discomfort associated with such events surfaced periodically in the course of charting next steps in the relationship. Faced with the armed prowess of American military hosts, Vietnamese military officers relied on their sense that their long history of tactical and strategic cleverness in the face of overwhelming odds equipped them to speak for a tradition of military greatness. So, for example, when exposed to concepts and achievements in information warfare during the February 1997 visit to the National Defense University, Senior Colonel Tan suggested that the easiest way to disarm a computer driven war machine was to simply pull the plug out of the wall socket.

6. Vietnam's gift of rice to Cuba and North Korea placed Hanoi on the list of countries providing assistance to terrorist states.

7. The NDU group that traveled to Vietnam in May concluded that the Vietnamese military looked at the relationship with the U.S. in positive terms, and saw the calendar of events for 1998, especially the scheduled visit for the Vice Minister of Defense, as important. Vietnamese officers and government officials accepted the importance of a U.S. military presence in Asia as a guarantee of regional stability and security, believed that Washington should be doing more for Vietnam in terms of postwar reconstruction assistance, and were extremely attentive to the development of U.S.–Chinese relations. There was some sense that the U.S. needed to be more explicit about what lay ahead in terms of defense relations. According to one member of the NDU delegation, one SRV military official suggested that the U.S. present Vietnam with a "roadmap" of future steps in the security relationship, an odd view for an MND official to take, especially in view of the experience with the "Roadmap." I am grateful to Dr. Marvin Ott of the National War College for sharing his impressions of the visit with me.

8. Vice Minister Lich was a Central Committee member, a member of the Party's Military Committee, and Chief of the General Staff. Some have claimed that the aircraft was shot down by the Hmong resistance. See Stephen Young, "Vietnam Policy Workshop: Background Statement," 31 January 2002, p. 10.

9. On 10 March President Clinton granted Vietnam a waiver of the Jackson-Vanik amendment under section 402 of the Trade Act of 1974. According to the amendment, in order to be granted Most Favored Nations status, Vietnam must comply with certain requirements relating to Vietnamese emigration. The requirements of the Jackson-Vanik amendment could be fulfilled by either (1) a presidential determination that Vietnam was in full compliance with the freedom of emigration requirements of the amendment, or (2) a waiver of such compliance by the president on the basis of his determination that such a waiver would "substantially promote" the objectives of the amendment. The president was required to submit a report to Congress on 30 June and 31 December of each year describing the nature of Vietnam's emigration laws and policies.

10. Severin M. Beliveau, the President of the U.S. Chapter of the "Forum Francophone Des Affaires," headquartered in Lewiston, Maine, hosted the Nghe An trade delegation during its visit to Main in early June. Cohen signed a letter to Nghe An Governor Ho Xuan Hung welcoming the delegation and expressing his hope that Hung's visit to Maine would help define opportunities for commercial cooperation that would be to the mutual benefit of Vietnamese and American businesses.

11. In Washington, the delegation met with Secretary of Defense Cohen; ASD/ISA Kramer; DASD/AP Campbell; DASD/POW-MIA Robert Jones; Vice Chairman of the Joint Chiefs of Staff General Joseph W. Ralston; Chief of Staff of the Army General Dennis Reimer; Chief of Staff of the Air Force General Michael Ryan; Vice Chief of Naval Operations Admiral Donald Pilling; Assistant Secretary of State for East Asia Mr. Stanley Roth; and Director for Asian Affairs, National Security Council, Dr. Kenneth Lieberthal. The ISA-ERD meeting took place the morning of 6 October. From 7 to 9 October, the delegation visited Nellis Air Force Base in Nevada for an Air Warrior exercise briefing; the National Training Center at Fort Irwin, California; and the Pacific Command in Hawaii where they were able to meet with the Commander in Chief of the Pacific Command, Admiral Prueher. In Hawaii, the delegation received the Pacific Command Strategy Brief, a briefing by the Joint Task Force-Full Accounting, and a briefing by the Special Operations Command-Pacific (SOCPAC) on demining. The delegation departed Hawaii for Vietnam on 10 October.

12. Hanh's delegation consisted of Major General Nguyen Ngoc Van, Deputy Director, Military Strategy Institute; Senior Colonel Nguyen Ngoc Giao, Director, Research Department; Senior Colonel Bui Trong Nhu, Deputy Director, ERD; Senior Colonel Dinh Van Binh, Secretary to the Vice Minister; and Colonel Nguyen Quang Bieu, the American Expert in the ERD. When the Vietnamese Defense Attaché and I first sat down to discuss the visit, Senior Colonel Quang made the case that the delegation from Vietnam should consist of fourteen officials, not counting himself and "security personnel." His initial list included the directors of the Office of the General Staff, the General Staff's Operations Department and Combat Training Department, the deputy commanders of the Air Force and the Navy, and the commanders of Military Regions 5 and 7, in addition to three officers representing the ERD, the director of the Office of the Defense Minister, and the Director of

the National Defense College. In shaping this first list, Quang appears to have looked to visits to the U.S. by Chinese military delegations, including the December 1997 visit by Defense Minister Chi Haotian. Defense Minister Chi's delegation consisted of 14 officials, including military region officials, general staff officers, and representatives from each of the services at the deputy chief of staff level. He may have also looked at the delegation led by Zhang Wannian, the Vice Chairman of the Central Military Commission, which traveled to the U.S. in March 1998.

13. "Doan Dai Bieu Quan Su Cap Cao Viet Nam Tham Hoa Ky," labeled "tin do Doan Ta cung cap sau khi da duoc Truong doan duyet," [a message sent by our high level delegation after approval from the delegation head], dated 12 October 1998. In a handwritten note, Quang recorded that the item would be published in *Nhan Dan* following the return of the delegation.

14. Senior Colonel Quang told me that he mentioned DoD's interest in more visits by senior level officials to his Chinese and Singaporean counterparts in Washington, D.C.. Embassies, but he did not discuss DoD's views regarding the initiation of a strategic dialogue, nor did he recount discussions with senior U.S. military officials aimed at getting Vietnamese agreement to what Quang described as "quiet cooperation." Quang thought these two things were far too sensitive, and left them out of his briefings to Asian colleagues. The meaning of his reference to "quiet cooperation" was not clear to me, but probably referred to the U.S. sides desire for a measured increase in practical cooperation and interaction in strictly military-to-military channels. Quang did tell the Chinese Defense Attaché that the Secretary of Defense and the Minister of Defense would take up the issue of ship visits when they met.

15. In his discussions with Hanh, DASD/AP Campbell stated that the U.S. and Vietnam must publicly portray the visit by the Secretary as in no way being part of a strategy intended to offset China's influence in the region. This proposed visit should be, Campbell noted, a normal part of a growing bilateral relationship. How the U.S. and Vietnam explained the visit to the region would be very important. Campbell told Hanh that Cohen and Pham Van Tra should publicly support a continuation of the modest pace and scope of the bilateral military relationship. The U.S. side, Campbell noted, will want to discuss the idea of a ship visit, and would be interested in hearing the Defense Ministry's views about the timing of such a future port call, but the U.S. would not press Vietnam to go forward with plans for a ship visit. Hanh quietly absorbed the messages, but did not respond to any of the specific points except in the broadest of platitudes celebrating the positive developments in the bilateral military relationship. He was probably not prepared to speak to these issues, and was uncomfortable with the idea of laying groundwork and discussing concepts for a trip proposal on which his leadership had not yet ruled.

Chapter 7

1. The Vietnamese elected to send delegations to (1) the Pacific Area Special Operations Conference (PASOC) scheduled for February 1999; (2) the PACOM International Operations and Law Conference, also in February; and (3) the Asia-Pacific Military Medicine Conference, which was scheduled to take place in Bangkok in early March. In the instruction cable sent to the SRV Defense Attaché's Office from the ERD, the Vietnamese noted their plans to participate in a February conference on weapons of mass destruction, to be conducted under the auspices of the Arms Control and Disarmament Agency.

2. Beijing Xinhua in English 1126 GMT, 3 March 1999, Serial OW0303114399; Hanoi Voice of Vietnam Network in Vietnamese, 1100 GMT, 26 February 1999, Serial BK102084299.

3. Beijing Xinhua in English, 1126 GMT, 3 March 1999, Serial OW0303114399. Interestingly, in his remarks during a dinner in honor of Phieu, Li Peng noted that China was building socialism with its own "characteristics," and Vietnam was building socialism "in its own national conditions," suggesting that Vietnam's pursuit of this historical end was rooted less in the fundamental character of the country than in the physically limiting circumstances in which Vietnam found itself, economically and developmentally. See Vietnam News Agency WWW in English, 26 February 1999, Serial BK0103091899.

4. Vietnamese News Agency WWW in English 2 March 1999, Serial BK030305099, 2 March 1999.

5. Hanoi Voice of Vietnam Network in Vietnamese, 1100 GMT, 2 February 1999, Serial BK03003081799, 2 March 1999.

6. By early September, there was a mixed

picture regarding the likelihood of getting a signable bilateral trade agreement in time for the mid–September APEC meeting. The Secretary of State planned to travel to Hanoi to coax that process along during 6–7 September. Some minor tariff issues struck SRV trade officials as manageable, though Deputy Prime Minister Nguyen Manh Cam suggested that the highest levels of the Vietnamese government were not inclined to push forward on an agreement, making it unlikely that the document would be able to wind its way through the National Assembly in six or eight months time. Some senior Vietnamese officials felt the bilateral trade agreement had been rushed through in the last few weeks, giving important ministries less than adequate time to "study" the document.

7. Cohen intended to travel to China in April. I sought to decouple a Vietnam trip from his plans for a China visit, and argued against a visit to the SRV during the anniversary month commemorating the 1975 communist victory.

8. *Cuoc Chien Cua My — NATO Chong Nam Tu; NATO Trong Chien Luoc Toan Cau Cua My*, Hanoi: Nha Xuat Ban Quan Doi Nhan Dan, 1999. ("The American-NATO War Against Yugoslavia; NATO in the Global Strategy of America," Hanoi: People's Army Publishing House, 1995).

9. On 24 January, Ambassador Peterson was informally told that the General Secretary intended to issue a formal invitation to Cohen to pay a visit to the Socialist Republic. At that time, the MND had not yet signaled that such an invitation was forthcoming. Perhaps putting the General Secretary's name behind the first inkling that an invitation was being formulated lent more stature to this, and invested it with the sturdiness required to convince the U.S. that this was a date by which Vietnam would stand.

10. During his remarks at the SRV Embassy's New Year's reception on 9 February, in the course of recounting achievements in U.S.–Vietnamese relations, Ambassador Bang announced the proposed March visit. Later, in a private conversation, Bang expressed surprise that the Defense Ministry had stated its preference for late March dates that fell outside of the parameters of Cohen's 9 — 20 March travel plans. He had not been briefed on the problem, and was at a loss for words. He had not been apprised of the fact that the DASD/AP had signed a letter on the subject, addressed to the MND, noting the importance of sticking with the 9–20 March travel schedule. Bang stated his conviction that it was essential to make this visit work this time; a third try must be successful. He committed to working as hard as he could to get the MND to agree to the 13–15 March dates.

11. Bo Quoc Phong (Ministry of Defense), 13 February 2000, Number 13 CH-DN.

12. It had taken ISA four years to get the ERD to a point at which it was comfortable enough to preview major issues that would be on the agenda for senior level meetings. I had made a point of responding to ERD requests for a pre-brief on the content of planning sessions, and had provided detailed advance notice of the content that would be on the agenda for all of Tran Hanh's meetings. ISA was not able to get the ERD, which initiated these requests for pre-meeting sharing of highlights, to tip its hand until the Vietnamese side took the initiative and laid out the MND's approach to the meeting with the Secretary.

Chapter 8

1. See, for example, Testimony of Douglas Peterson, U.S. Ambassador to Vietnam, House Committee on Ways and Means, Subcommittee on Trade, 18 June 1998; "Background and Talking Points on Vietnam," National Security Council, 11 July 1995; White House Office of the Press Secretary, "Press Package: The President's Announcement on Vietnam," 11 July 1995; U.S. Department of State, Office of the Spokesman, "U.S.–Vietnam Relations: A New Chapter," Secretary of State Warren Christopher, Presented to the Institute for International Relations, Hanoi, Vietnam, 6 August 1995; Vietnam Interagency Working Group, "Economic Normalization: Pace and Procedures," 21 August 1995; and White House Office of the Press Secretary, "Press Package: The President's Announcement on Vietnam," 11 July 1995.

2. During the early 1990s, a lieutenant general headed ERD. Between 1995 and 1998, a senior colonel held the top spot in ERD, before being promoted to major general.

3. The Defense Ministry's Research Department was the intelligence collection entity, and held responsibilities for assigning military personnel to embassies abroad, tasking attachés, supporting officers attached to SRV embassies, and sustaining communications with the defense attachés. There were points at which the missions of the ERD and

the Research Department converged and contexts in which the level of communication was deficient.

4. Stern, *Imprisoned or Missing in Vietnam: Policies of the Vietnamese Government Concerning Captured and Unaccounted for United States*, (Jefferson, N.C.: McFarland, 1995), pp. 127–150.

5. The 1998 MND White Paper was obscure on the issue of procurement and supply of weapons from "outside" sources. The paper merely suggested that such needs should be met by expanding "association and cooperation inside and outside the army so as to acquire advanced technologies and, at the same time, to promote and bring the Vietnamese defense industry to a new stage of development. See *Consolidating National Defense, Safeguarding the Homeland*, p. 68. However, though by no means a reliable indication of Vietnam's intentions, by late 1999 the various informal queries about the accessibility of U.S. technologies and military equipment that had figured in earlier meetings with the SRV Defense Attaché had dropped out of our continuous dialogue. Senior Colonel Quang had introduced the importance of acquisition of technology into our regular discussions in early 1999, stressing the need to support troops deployed to the Spratly Islands, and recommending that the U.S. make water purification technology available to Vietnam to serve that purpose. This line of discussion dropped out of Quang's agenda in our subsequent routine monthly meetings, and was replaced by much more reasonable requests intended to probe U.S. thinking on matters such as whether or not the U.S. government would support SRV access to demining innovations.

6. I am grateful to Mr. Robert Destatte for sharing his recollections of the staffing patterns of the VNOSMP and the MND MIA Office.

BIBLIOGRAPHY

Vietnamese Periodicals

Hanoi Moi
Lao Dong Nhan Dan
Quan Doi Nhan Dan
Quan He Quoc Te

Saigon Giai Phong
Tap Chi Cong San
Tap Chi Quoc Phong Toan Dan
Tuoi Tre

Vietnamese-Language Periodicals (published outside of Vietnam)

Hoa Thinh Don Viet Bao
Phu Nu Viet Nam

Thu Do Thoi Bao Tu Do
Xay Dung

Vietnamese Language Books

Duong Thong, *Mot So Van De Ve "Dien Bien Hoa Bien" O Nuoc Ta.*) Hanoi: Nha Xuat Ban, 1994. ("Several Problems Relating to "Peaceful Evolution" in Our Country.")

Bao Ninh, *Than Phan Tinh Yeu,* Hanoi: Nha Xuat Ban Hoi Nha Van, 1991. (Bao Ninh. "Destiny of Love." Writers Association Publishing House, 1991.)

Ban Chi Dao Tong Ket Chien Tranh (Truc Thuoc Bo Chinh Tri). *Tong Ket Cuoc Khanh Chien Chong My, Cuu Nuoc Thang Loi Va Bai Hoc.* Hanoi: Nha Xuat Ban Chinh Tri Quoc Gia. 1995. (Guidance Committee for Reviewing the War) (Directly Subordinate to the Politburo.) "Review of the Resistance War Against the Americans to Save the Nation: Victories and Lessons." National Political Publishing House, 1995.)

Bo Quoc Phong, Vien Lich Su Quan Su Viet Nam. *50 Nam Quan Doi Nhan Dan Viet Nam.* Hanoi: Nha Xuat Ban Quan Doi Nhan Dan, 1995. (Military History Institute, Ministry of Defense. "50 Years of the People's Army of Vietnam." Hanoi: People's Army Publishing House, 1995.)

Tai Lieu Tham Khao: Am Muu Va Hoat Don "Dien Bien Hoa Binh" Cua Cac The Luc

Thu Dich Tren Dat Nuoc Ta. ("Toi Mat"), Hanoi: January 1994. ("Study Document: Plots and Actions by Hostile Forces to Carry Out 'Peaceful Evolution' in Our Nation." Top Secret, Hanoi, 1994.)

Cuoc Chien Cua My — NATO Chong Nam Tu; NATO Trong Chien Luoc Toan Cau Cua My. Hanoi: Nha Xuat Ban Quan Doi Nhan Dan, 1999. ("The American-NATO War Against Yugoslavia; NATO in the Global Strategy of America." Hanoi: People's Army Publishing House, 1995.)

Vietnamese Language Articles (signed)

Nguyen Le Bach. "Co Phai Duong Ta Di Da Het Chong Gai." *Nhan Dan*, 7 August 1995, p. 3. (Nguyen Le Bach. "Is Our Path Now Clear of Thorny Problems?")

Tran Danh Bang. "Tong Ket Cong Tac Huan Luyen Nam 1996." *Quan Doi Nhan Dan*, 14 January 1997, p. 1. ("Review of 1996 Training Operations.")

Nguyen Thoi Bung. "May Van De Can Quan Triet De Nang Cao Hieu Qua Cong Tac Doi Ngoai Quan Su." *Tap Chi Cong San*, July 1995, pp. 1–4. ("Several Problems Which Must Be Understood in Order to Improve the Effectiveness of the Military's Foreign Relations Activities.")

Nguyen Manh Cam. "Tren Duong Trien Khai Chinh Sach Doi Ngoai Theo Dinh Huong Moi." *Quan He Quoc Te*, April 1993, pp. 2–3. ("On the Road Toward Employing Foreign Policy in Accordance with Our New Orientation.")

_____. "Ngoai Giao Viet Nam Gop Phan Xung Dang Vao Su Nghiep Cach Mang Cua Dan Toc." *Tap Chi Cong San*, Number 10, August 1995, pp. 9–24. ("Vietnam's Foreign Policy Makes Worthy Contributions to Our People's Revolutionary Cause.")

Thuy Chi, and Van Yen. "Dai Su My Tai Viet Nam D. Pi-To-Xon Tra Loi Phong Van Bao QDND: To Lac Quan Ve Cac Cau Hoi Cua Cong Dong Kinh Doanh My Tai Viet Nam." *Quan Doi Nhan Dan*, 23 May 1997, p. 4. ("American Ambassador Peterson Responds to an Interview by Quan Doi Nhan Dan: Demonstrating Optimism in Response to Questions Raised by the American Business Community in Vietnam.")

_____, and Van Yen. "Dai Su Viet Nam Tai My Le Van Bang Tra Loi Phong Van Bao QDND: Mot Buoc Quan Trong Trong Qua Trinh Binh Thuong Hoa Quan He Viet-My." *Quan Doi Viet Nam*, 16 April 1997, p. 4. ("Vietnam's Ambassador to the U.S., Le Van Bang, Interviewed by QDND: An Important Step in the Normalization of U.S.–Vietnamese Relations.")

Tran Dinh Chinh. "Quang Tri: Nhieu Viec Lan Tinh Nghia Tri Gia Hang Ty Dong; Kon Tum: Cho Gia Dinh Chinh Sach Vay Von, Tao Viec Lam." *Nhan Dan*, 18 July 1995, p. 1. ("Quang Tri: Many Humanitarian Actions Contributing Billions of Dong; Kontum: Capital Loan Policy for Families to Create Jobs.")

Doan Chuong. "Gop Phan Tim Hien Du Thao Bao Cao Chinh Tri Dai Hoi VIII Cua Dang: Giu Vung Dinh Huong Xa Hoi Chu Nghia." *Quan Doi Nhan Dan*, 16 April 1996, pp. 1, 4. ("To Help Understand the Draft Political Report of the 8th Party Congress: Firmly Maintaining Our Socialist Orientation.")

Tran Quang Co. "50 Nam Ngoai Giao Viet Nam: Hoa Nhap Quoc Te Va Gin Giu Ban Sac." *Thong Tin-Tu Lieu*, September 1995, pp. 8–12, 24. Reprinted in *Tuan Bao Quoc Te*, Number 35, 31 August–6 September, pp. 3, 19.) ("50 Years of Vietnamese Diplomacy: Blending into the International Community While Still Maintaining Our Own National Character.")

Le Cao Dai. "Trach Nhiem Truoc Nhung Con Nguoi, Nhung Cuoc Doi." *Tuoi Tre Chu Nhat*, 27 July 1997, p. 8. ("Responsibilities to People and Lives.")

———. "Hau Qua Cua Chat Doc Mau Da Cam." *Tuoi Tre*, 27 July 1997. ("Consequences of Agent Orange.")
Vu Dat. "Chuyen Cua Nhung Chien Si Xu Ly: Bom Min." *Quan Doi Nhan Dan*, 13 May 1998, p. 2. ("Stories of Soldiers Responsible for Clearing Bombs and Mines.")
Dong Dung. "May Net Lon Ve Chien Luoc Chau A — Thai Binh Duong Cua My Cho The 21." *Tap Chi Quoc Phong Toan Dan*, March 2000, pp. 77–79, 59. ("Several Major Points About American Strategic Policy for Asia and the Pacific in the 21st Century.")
Pham Chi Dung. "Qua Khu Nau Da Cam: Mot Chung Nhan Lich Su." *Saigon Giai Phong*, 17 October 1997, p. 2. ("The History of Making Agent Orange: A Witness to History.")
The Gia. "Dai Hoi Dang Bo Quan Khu 7: Xay Dung The Tran Quoc Phong Toan Dan Gan Voi The Tran An Ninh Nhan Dan." *Nhan Dan*, 5 April 1996, pp. 1, 4. ("Military Region 7 Party Congress: Developing a National Defense Posture Involving the Entire Population Is Linked with Our People's Security Posture.")
Phong Hai. "Nam Vung Dinh Huong Xa Hoi Chu Nghia-Thuoc Do Pham Chat, Nang Luc Cua Can Bo, Dang Vien Trong Su Nghiep Doi Moi Dat Nuoc." *Quan Doi Nhan Dan*, 27 May 1996, pp. 1, 4. ("Firmly Maintaining Our Socialist Orientation: Measuring the Quality and Capabilities of Cadre and Party Members in Our National Cause of Renovation.")
Nguyen Khac Hien. "Kinh Te Thi Truong Va Dinh Huong Xa Hoi Chu Nghia Co Doi Lai Nhau Khong?" *Tap Chi Cong San*, Number 4, February 1996, pp. 12–15. ("Are a Market Economy and a Socialist Orientation Inherently Contradictory?")
Vu Hien. "Cuc Dien Moi Va Dinh Huong Di Len Cua Dat Nuoc." *Tap Chi Cong San*, Number 4, February 1996, pp. 20–24. ("The New Face and the Progressive Orientation of the Nation.")
Dang Vu Hiep. "Quan Doi Nhan Dan Trong Cuoc Dau Tranh Chong 'Dien Bien Hoa Binh.'" Bao Ve Doc Lap Dan Toc Va Chu Nghia Xa Hoi," *Tap Chi Cong San*, Number 14, October 1995, pp. 17–20. ("The People's Army in the Struggle Against Peaceful Evolution: Defending National Independence and Socialism.")
Nguyen Hoa. "Cau Chuyen Quoc Te: Hon Mot Nam Viet Nam Gia Nhap ASEAN." *Nhan Dan*, 1 January 1997, p. 5. ("International Story: More Than One Year After Vietnam's Entrance Into ASEAN.")
Khong Doan Hoi. "Dinh Huong Xa Hoi Chu Nghia O Nuoc Ta." *Tap Chi Cong San*, Number 5, March 1996, pp. 15–17. ("Socialist Orientation in Our Nation.")
Phan Van Khai. "Tinh Hinh Dat Nuoc Tiep Tuc Chuyen Bien Tot, Nhung Chua Vung Chac, Con Nhung May Teu Va Kho Khan Lon Phai Khac Phuc." *Nhan Dan*, 17 June 1993, p. 2. ("Our National Situation Continues to Change for the Better, but Still Unsteadily; There are Still Major Obstacles to Overcome.")
Pham Van Khanh. "Nhan Quyen Va Con Duong Thuc Hien Nhan Quyen." *Nhan Dan*, 24 July 1995, p. 3. ("Human Rights and the Path to Achieving Human Rights.")
Nguyen Ngoc Khoa. "Buc Tien Moi Cua Dang Bo Huyen Thanh Oai." *Tap Chi Cong San*, Number 4, February 1996, pp. 50–54. ("New Step Forward by the Thanh Oai District Party Chapter.")
Vu Kiem. "Lam Cho Tet Viec Muon Nha." *Nhan Dan*, 2 February 1994, p. 1. ("Properly Handling the Renting of Houses.")
Dang Xuan Ky. "Vung Buoc Di Con Duong Xa Hoi Chu Nghia." *Tap Chi Cong San*, Number 4, February 1996, pp. 3–6. ("Steady Step Forward on the Road to Socialism.")
Hoan Lien. "Binh Thuong Hoa Quan He Viet-My — Viec Phai Den Da Den." *Nhan Dan*, 23 July 1995, pp. 1, 4. ("Normalizing Relations Between Vietnam and the United States: The Inevitable Has Finally Come to Pass.")

Quang Loi. "Mot Kien Kinh Doanh Tren Noi Dau Nguoi Khac." *Quan Doi Nhan Dan*, 12 September 1993, p. 4 ("A Commercial Proposal Built on the Misery of Others.")

Le Xuan Luu. "Kinh Nghiem Xay Dung Nhan To Tinh Than Cho Quan Doi." *Tap Chi Cong San*, Number 9, May 2000. ("Experience in Developing Moral Factors for the Army.")

Hoang Gia Minh. "Noi Dau Dai Dang Cua Chien Tranh." *Quan Doi Nhan Dan*, 12 June 2000, p. 2. ("The Protracted Misery of War.")

Le Huu Nghia. "Vai Tro Cua Chinh Tri Trong Viec Bao Ve Dinh Huong Xa Hoi Chu Nghia." *Tap Chi Cong San*, Number 5, March 1996, pp. 18–20. ("The Role of Politics in Protecting Our Socialist Orientation.")

Tran Nhung. "Tu Day Moi Ve Hoat Dong Doi Ngoai." *Nhan Dan*, 20 April 1996, pp. 1, 4. ("Foreign Activities to Date.")

Nguyen Duy Nien. "Quan He Viet Nam Va Cac Nuoc Tay, Bac Au Trong Tinh Hinh Moi," *Tap Chi Cong San*, Number 10, August 1995, pp. 61–63. ("Vietnam's Relations with Western and Northern European Nations in the New Situation.")

Nguyen Van Oanh. "Ve Khai Niem Dinh Huong Xa Hoi Chu Nghia." *Tap Chi Cong San*, Number 4, February 1996, pp. 16–19. ("Regarding the Concept of Socialist Orientation.")

Vu Oanh. "Trach Nhiem Va Tinh Nghia Sau Nang Voi Nhung Nguoi Con Trung Hieu Cua Dat Nuoc." *Nhan Dan*, 31 March 1993, p. 3. ("Responsibility and Profound Affection Toward the Loyal Children [Sons] of the Nation.")

Nguyen Quoc Pham. "Tang Truong Kinh Te Gan Lien Voi Tien Bo Va Cong Bang Xa Hoi." *Quan Doi Nhan Dan*, 17 April 1996, pp. 1, 4. ("Economic Growth Is Directly Linked to Social Progress and Social Justice.")

_____. "Tang Truong Kinh Te Gan Lien Voi Tien Bo Va Cong Nguyen Dinh Bang Xa Hoi." *Quan Doi Nhan Dan*, 17 April 1996, pp. 1, 4. ("Economic Growth is Directly Linked to Progress and the Era of Social Equality.")

Tranh Phong, and Bang Chan. "Cac Dia Phuong, Don Vi Nhan Dan Phung DUong Ba Me Viet Nam Anh Hung." *Nhan Dan*, 25 July 1995, p. 1. ("Localities: The People's Unit to Care for the Heroic Mothers of Vietnam.")

Xuan Phong. "Dai Hoi Dang Bo Co Quan Tong Cuc Chinh Tri: Tap Trung Nang Luc Tri Tue, Thuc Hien Tot Chuc Nang Tham Muu Tren May Tran Chinh Tri, Tu Tuong, Van Hoa." *Nhan Dan*, 6 April 1996, pp. 1, 4. ("Congress of the General Political Department's Headquarters Party Chapter: Concentrating our Energies and Our Minds to Correctly Perform Our Staff Function on the Political, Ideological, and Cultural Fronts.")

Duy Phuc. "Dai Hoi Dang Bo Quan Khu 3: Nang Chat Luong Ba Thu Quan, Xay Dung Phong Thu Va The Tran Quoc Phong-An Ninh Vung Chac." *Nhan Dan*, 8 April 1996, pp. 1, 4. ("Congress of the Military Region 3 Party Chapter: Increasing the Size of Our Three Types of Soldiers, Building Defenses and a Solid National Defense and Security Posture.")

Ngoc Phuong. "Ke Hoach Stephen Young." *Xay Dung* (California), 20 October 1993, # 51, pp. 30–40. ("The Stephen Young Plan.")

Vo Thu Phuong. "Buoc Tien Moi Trong Quan He Viet-My." *Tap Chi Cong San*, Number 9, August 1995, pp. 47–48. ("A New Step Forward in Vietnamese-American Relations")

_____. "Y Kien Nho Ve Thang Loi Lon Cua Ngoai Giao Viet Nam." *Tap Chi Cong San*, Number 13, October 1995, pp. 49–52. ("A Few Thoughts About the Great Victory Won by Vietnamese Diplomacy.")

Vo Dinh Quang. "On the Security Situation in Our Region and the Armed Forces of Vietnam." Informal Forum for Defense Authorities in the Asia-Pacific Region, 29–31 October 1996.

Nguyen Duy Quy. "Doc Lap Dan Toc Gan Lien Voi Chu Nghia Xa Hoi." *Tap Chi Cong San*, Number 5, March 1996, pp. 4–8. ("National Independence is Directly Linked to Socialism.")
To Huy Rua. "Con Duong Va Dieu Kien Bao Dam Dinh Huong Xa Hoi Chu Nghia O Nuoc Ta." *Tap Chi Cong San*, Number 6, March 1996, pp. 19–22. ("The Road to and Conditions to Ensure the Socialist Orientation of Our Nation.")
Phan Van Son. "Cuoc Song Moi Cua Nguoi Linh Cu." *Nhan Dan*, 30 April 1993, p. 3. ("A New Life for Old Soldiers.")
D.T. "Dai Hoi Dang Bo Khoi Cac Co Quan Doi Ngoai Trung Uong; Nang Hoat Dong Doi Ngoai Len Tam Cao Moi." *Nhan Dan*, 28 March 1996, pp. 1, 4 ("Congress of the Party Chapters of the Central Foreign Relations Agencies: Raise Foreign Relations Activities to New Heights.")
Nhat Tan. "Chu Nghia Mac-Le Nin Va Tu Tuong Ho Chi Minh Voi Dinh Huong Xa Hoi Chu Nghia O Nuoc Ta." *Tap Chi Cong San*, Number 6, March 1996, pp. 26–29. ("Marxism-Leninism and Ho Chi Minh Thoughts in Relation to Socialist Orientation in Our Nation.")
Bui Ngoc Thanh. "Khong Co Su Lua Chon Nao Khac." *Tap Chi Cong San*, Number 4, February 1996, pp. 7–11. ("No Other Choice.")
Huy Thiem. "Bon Diem Noi Bat Trong Cong Tac Quoc Phong Nam 1996." *Quan Doi Nhan Dan*, 1 January 1997, p. 2. ("Four Outstanding Points in National Defense Activities During 1996.")
Phan Van Toan. "Chuyen Cua Nguoi Bat Song Phi Cong My." *Quan Doi Nhan Dan*, 7 August 1994, pp. 1, 4. ("The Story of a Person Who Captured an American Pilot.")
Nguyen Phu Trong. "Nhan Quyen-Dao Ly Viet Nam." *Nhan Dan*, 14 May 1993, p. 3. ("Human Rights—Vietnamese Ideals.")
_____. "Dinh Huong Xa Hoi Chu Nghia Va Con Duong Di Len Chu Nghia Xa Hoi O Nuoc Ta." *Tap Chi Cong San*, Number 5, March 1996, pp. 9–16. ("Socialist Orientation and the Road to Socialism in Our Nation.")
Quang Trong. "Dai Hoi Dang Bo Quan Khu 3: Dong Vien Moi No Luc Quan Va Dan Tren Dia Ban, Xay Dung Quan Khu Thanh Phao Dai Phong Thu Vung Chac." *Quan Doi Nhan Dan*, 1 April 1996, pp. 1, 4. ("Military Region 3 Party Chapter Congress: Mobilize All Military and Civilian Efforts in the Region to Build the Military Region into a Solid Fortress for National Defense.")
Ha Xuan Truong. "Dinh Huong Xa Hoi Chu Nghia Mot Khai Niem Khoa Hoc." *Tap Chi Cong San*, Number 7, April 1996, p. 18. (Socialist Orientation: A Scientific Concept.")
Nguyen Dinh Uoc. "Quoc Phong, An Ninh Voi Su On Dinh Chinh Tri Cua Dat Nuoc." *Quan Doi Nhan Dan*, 18 April 1996, pp. 1, 4. ("National Defense and Security in Relation to the Political Security of the Nation.")
P.V. "Hoai Thao Thuong Mai Cap Cao Viet Nam-My," *Nhan Dan*, 8 April 1997, p. 8. ("High Level U.S.-Vietnamese Commercial Conference.")
Tran Huynh Hoang Vu. "Nguoi Linh Quan Gioi Lam Kinh Te." *Quan Doi Nhan Dan*, 3 January 1997, p. 3. ("Ordnance Soldiers Perform Economic Tasks.")
Van Yen. "Ong Pi-To-Xon Duoc Thuong Vien My Phe Chuan Lam Dai Su Tai Viet Nam." *Quan Doi Nhan Dan*, 12 April 1997, p. 4. ("The U.S. Senate Approves Mr. Peterson as Ambassador to Vietnam.")
_____. "Quy Che MFN Va Trien Vong Xuat Khau Cua Viet Nam Tren Thi Truong My." *Quan Doi Nhan Dan*, 26 April 1997, p. 4. "MFN Status and Vietnam's Prospects for Exporting to the American Market.")

Vietnamese Language Articles (Unsigned, in chronological order)

"Ve Quan He My-Viet Nam." *Nhan Dan*, 3 April 1993, p. 4. ("Vietnamese–U.S. Relations.")
"Tong Bi Thu Do Muoi Tiep Thuong Si Et Mon Mot-xki." *Nhan Dan*, 6 April 1993, pp. 1, 4. ("General Secretary Do Muoi Receives Senator Edmond Muskie.")
"Tong Thong My B. Clinton: Chinh Phu Viet Nam Thanh Thuc Hoc Tac Trong Van De POW/MIA." *Nhan Dan*, 26 April 1993, p. 4. ("President B. Clinton: The Vietnamese Government is Sincerely Cooperating on the POW/MIA Issue.")
"Tong Bi Thu Do Muoi Tiep Doan Nghi Si Va Cuu Binh My." *Nhan Dan*, 2 June 1993, p. 4. ("General Secretary Do Muoi Receives a Delegation of U.S. Senators and War Veterans.")
"Hoat Dong Doi Ngoai." *Quan He Quoc Te*, August 1993, p. 3. ("Diplomatic Activities.")
"Hoat Dong Doi Ngoai." *Quan He Quoc Te*, September 1993, p. 2. ("Diplomatic Activities.")
"Phi Ly Va Loi Thoi." *Nhan Dan*, 17 September 1993, p. 4 ("Irrational and Outdated.")
"Thu Tuong Vo Van Kiet Va Chu Tich Quoc Hoi Nong Duc Manh Tiep Thuong Nghi Si J. Ke-ri." *Nhan Dan*, 17 January 1994, pp. 1, 3. ("Prime Minister Vo Van Kiet and Chairman of the National Assembly Nong Duc Manh Meet with Senator John Kerry".)
"Thuong Nghi Si My Gion Ke-ri: Bay Gio La Luc My Can Bai Bo Lenh Cam Van Buon Ban Doi Voi Viet Nam." *Nhan Dan*, 27 January 1994, p. 4. ("Senator John Kerry: It Is the Time American Must Lift the Trade Embargo with Vietnam.")
"Bo Cam Van Chong Viet Nam Se La Tot Lanh Khong Nhung Cho Hai Nuoc Viet Nam Va My Cho Ca Cong Dong Quoc Te." *Nhan Dan*, 4 February 1994, p. 4. ("Lifting the Embargo Against Vietnam Will Benefit Not Only Vietnam and the U.S., but the Entire International Community.")
"Bo Ngoai Giao Ta Ra Tuyen Bo Ve Viec Tong Thong My Quyet Dinh Bo Cam Van Doi Voi Viet Nam." *Nhan Dan*, 5 February 1994, p. 1. ("Our Foreign Ministry Issues an Announcement Regarding the American President's Lifting of the Trade Embargo Against Vietnam.")
"Tu Lien Quoc Te: Dien Bien Quan He Viet-My." *Nhan Dan*, 5 February 1994, p.3. ("Transforming the Vietnamese-American Relationship.")
"Hop Bao Quoc Te." *Nhan Dan*, 5 February 1994, pp. 1, 4. ("International Press Conference.")
"Dam Phan Viet Nam — My Ve Van De Tai San Va Lap Co Quan Lien Lac." *Nhan Dan*, 7 March 1994, p. 4. ("U.S.–Vietnamese Talks on Property and Establishing Liaison Offices.")
"Thu Tuong Vo Van Kiet Tiep Doan Dai Dien Tong Thong My." *Nhan Dan*, 16 May 1995, pp. 1, 4. ("Prime Minister Vo Van Kiet Receives a U.S. Presidentiual Delegation.")
"Tong Bi Thu Do Muoi Tiep Doan Dai Dien Tong Thong My." *Nhan Dan*, 17 May 1995, p. 4. ("General Secretary Do Muoi Receives a U.S. Presidential Delegation.")
"Tong Bi Thu Do Muoi Tiep Doan Cap Cao My." *Quan Doi Nhan Dan*, 3 July 1994, p. 4. ("General Secretary Do Muoi Receives a High-Ranking American Delegation.")
"Thu Thong Vo Van Kiet Tiep Doan Thuong Nghi si My." *Nhan Dan*, 4 July 1995, p. 1. ("Prime Minister Vo Van Kiet Receives a Delegation of American Senators.")
"Mat Tran To Quoc Viet Nam Phat Dong Phong Trao Cham Soc Thuong Binh, Gia

Dinh Liet Si, Phung Duong Ba Me Viet Nam Anh Hung." *Nhan Dan*, 6 July 1995, pp. 1, 3. ("The Vietnam Fatherland Front Initiates a Movement to Care for the Wounded, Families of War Dead, and to Support the Parents of Vietnam's Heros.")
"Toan Dan Cham Soc Thuong Binh, Gia Dinh Liet si Va Nguoi Co Cong Voi Nuoc." *Nhan Dan*, 6 July 1995, p. 1. ("The Entire Population Cares for the Wounded, Families of War Dead and Those Who Made Contributions to Our Nation.")
"Huong Ung Loi Keu Goi Cua MTTQ Viet Nam." *Nhan Dan*, 15 July 1995, pp. 1, 3. ("Responding to the Appeal by the Vietnam Fatherland Front.")
"Bao Chi Cac Nuoc Noi Ve Quan He Viet-My." *Nhan Dan*, 15 July 1995, p. 4. ("The International Press on Vietnamese-American Relations.")
"Du Luan The Gioi Ve Quan He Viet-My." *Nhan Dan*, 16 July 1995, p. 4. ("World Opinion Regarding Vietnamese-American Relations.")
"Ha Tay, Toan Dan Cham Soc Cac Doi Tuong Chinh Sach: Tong Cong Ty Buu Chinh Vien Thong Tang Moi Ba Me VNAH Trong Nganh 2 Trieu Dong." *Nhan Dan*, 16 July 1995, pp. 1, 4. ("Ha Tay: The Entire Population Helps Care for Targets of Our Policy: The General Postal and Telecommunications Corporation Gives Every Vietnamese Hero Mother Throughout the Corporation Two Million Dong.")
"Du Luan The Gioi Ve Quan He Viet-My." *Nhan Dan*, 16 July 1995, p. 4. ("World Opinion on U.S.–Vietnamese Relations.")
"Tong Cong Ty Buu Chinh vien Thong Tang Moi Ba Me Viet Nam Anh Hung Trong Nganh 2 Trieu Dong." *Nhan Dan*, 16 July 1995, p. 4. ("The General Postal and Telecommunications Corporation Gives Every Vietnamese Hero Mother Throughout the Corporation Two Million Dong.")
"Noi Dung Hop Bao Cua Thu Truong Le Mai Ve Van De Binh Thuong Hoa Quan Du Luan The Gioi Ve Quan He Viet-My." *Nhan Dan*, 16 July 1995, p. 4. ("Contents of Deputy Minister Le Mai's Press conference on Normalization and World Opinion on U.S. Vietnamese Relations.")
"Hoan Nghenh viec Binh Thuong Hoa Quan He Viet Nam-My." *Nhan Dan*, 17 July 1995, p.4. ("Welcoming Normalization of Vietnamese-American Relations.")
"Thi Xa Long Xuyen Nang Cao Muc Song Thuong Binh, Gia Dinh Liet Si." *Nhan Dan*, 17 July 1995, pp. 1, 3. ("Long Xuyen City Improves the Lives of Wounded Veterans and of the Families of Martyrs Who Gave Their Lives During the War.")
"Huong Ung Loi Keu Goi Ung Mat Tran To Quoc Viet Nam." *Nhan Dan*, 19 July 1995, p. 1. ("Response to the Appeal by the Vietnam Fatherland Front.")
"Du Luan My Va The Gioi: Binh Thuong Hoa Quan He Voi Viet Nam, Con So Khong Doi Voi My Ca Trong Kinh Te, Chinh Tri Va Ngoai Giao." *Nhan Dan*, 23 July 1995, pp. 1, 4. ("U.S. and World Opinion: Normalizing Relations with Vietnam Means Nothing to the U.S. Economically, Politically, and Diplomatically.")
"Nhieu Dia Phuong Mo Rong Phong Trao Phung Duong Ba Me Viet Nam Anh Hung, Tang Nha, So Tiet Kiem Tinh Nghia." *Nhan Dan*, 24 July 1995, pp. 1, 3. ("Many Localities Expand the Movement to Support Vietnamese Hero Mothers, Providing Them Homes and Savings Accounts.")
"Nhieu Don vi Tang Qua Cac Gia Dinh Chinh Sach." *Nhan Dan*, 26 Jul 1995, p. 1. ("Many Units Provide Gifts to Policy Families.")
"Chu Tich Nuoc Le Duc Anh Gui Thu Cho Thuong Binh, Benh Binh, Gia Dinh Liet si Va Gia Dinh Co Cong Voi Cach Mang." *Nhan Dan*, 27 Jul 1995, p.1. ("State Chairman Le Duc Anh Sends a Letter to Wounded and Sick Veterans, Families of Martyrs, and Families Which Have Made Contributions to the Revolution.")
"Cac Dia Phuong, Nganh, Doan The Mo Rong Phong Tran, Phung Duong Ba Me VNAH, Tang Nha, So Tiet Kiem Tinh Nghia." *Nhan Dan*, 27 July 1995 , pp.1 , 3. ("Localities, Branches, and Groups Expand the Movement to Support Vietnamese Hero Mothers, Providing Them Homes and Savings Accounts.")

"Doan Dai Bieu Dang, Quoc Hoi, Chinh Phu, Mat Tran To Quoc Thanh Pho Hanoi Vieng Nghia Trang Liet Si Hanoi." *Nhan Dan*, 28 July 1995, pp.1 , 4. ("Party, National Assembly, Government, and Hanoi Fatherland Front Delegation Visits the Hanoi Martyrs Cemetery.")

"Chu Tich Le Duc Anh, Thu Tuong Vo Van Kiet Tiep Cuu Tong Thong MY Bu-So." *Nhan Dan*, 6 September 1995, pp. 1, 3. ("Chairman Le Duc Anh and Prime Minister Vo Van Kiet Receive U.S. President Bush.")

"Hoi Cuu Chien Binh Viet Nam Tiep Doan Hoi Cuu Chien Binh My." *Nhan Dan*, 26 September 1995, p. 4. ("Vietnam Veterans Association Receives a Delegation from the American Veterans Association.")

"Bo Chinh Tri Ban Hanh Nghi Quyet Ve Tiep Tuc Doi Moi To Chuc Va Hoat Dong Thuong Nghiep, Phat Trien Thi Truong Theo Dinh Huong Xa Hoi Chu Nghia." *Nhan Dan*, 19 January 1996, pp. 1, 3. ("The Politburo Passes a Resolution on Continuing Renovation of Commercial Organizations and Activities and Developing Markets with a Socialist Orientation.")

"My Cham Dut Lenh Coi Viet Nam La Khu Vuc Chien Su." *Nhan Dan*, 16 May 1996, p. 1. ("The U.S. Cancels Order Listing Vietnam as a War Zone.")

"Bao Cao Chinh Tri Cua Ban Chap Hanh Trung Uong Dang Khoa VII Tai Dai Hoi Dai Bieu Toan Quoc Lan Thu VIII Cua Dang." *Nhan Dan*, 30 June 1996, p. 2. ("Political Report of the Central Committee, 7th Party Congress, to the 8th National Party Congress.")

"Hoi Cuu Chien Binh Viet Nam, Cho Dua Tin Cay Cua Dang Va Chinh Quyen." *Quan Doi Nhan Dan*, 4 December 1996, p. 3. ("The Vietnam Veterans Association, a Trustworthy Source of Support to the Party and the Government.")

"Cac Nghi Si Cong Hoa Se Khong Chong Viec Bo Nhiem Ong D. Pi To Xon Lam Dai Su My Tai Viet Nam?" *Quan Doi Nhan Dan*, 5 January 1997, p. 4. ("Republican Senators Will Not Oppose the Appointment of Mr. D. Peterson as U.S. Ambassador to Vietnam.")

"Ve Viec Bo Nhiem Dai Su My Tai Viet Nam." *Nhan Dan*, 5 January 1997, p. 8. ("Regarding the Appointment of the U.S. Ambassador to Vietnam.")

"Ong Hyn-Xton Lot: Binh Thuong Hoa Quan He My-Viet La Thanh Thu Co Y Nghia Nhat." Nhan Dan, 17 January 1997, p. 8. ("Mr. Winston Lord: Normalization of Relations Between the U.S. and Vietnam Is the Most Significant Achievement.")

"Ong Pi-To-Xton: Hien Dai Ngoai Giao Chinh Thuc Tai Viet Nam Se Giup My Phat Hien Nhung Co Hoi Kinh Doanh Moi." *Nhan Dan*, 17 February 1997, p. 8. ("Mr. Peterson: Official Diplomatic Presence in Vietnam Will Help America Find New Business Opportunities.")

"Tong Tu Lenh Bo Chi Huy Thai Binh Duong Hoa Ky Tham Viet Nam." *Quan Doi Nhan Dan*, 22 March 1997, pp. 1, 4. ("U.S. Commander in Chief Pacific Visits Vietnam.")

"Ong Pi-To-Xon Duoc Thuong Nghi Vien My Phe Chuan Lam Dai Su Tai Viet Nam." *Nhan Dan*, 12 April 1997, p. 8. ("U.S. Senate Approves Peterson as Ambassador to Vietnam.")

"De Ra Chuong Trinh Hanh Dong Ve Giao Duc-Dao Tao Va Khoa Hoc Cong Nghe Sat Thuc Te Nhiem Vu Cua Don Vi." *Quan Doi Nhan Dan*, 1 May 1997, pp. 1, 4. ("Proposing Action Programs for Education and Training and for Science and Industry in Line with the Realities of Unit Missions.")

"Dai Su Hoa Ky: Hy Vong Hai Nuoc Se Som Ky Ket Hiep Dinh Thuong Mai Toan Dien." *Nhan Dan*, 10 May 1997, p. 8. ("U.S. Ambassador: Hopes That Both Nations Will Soon Sign an Overall Commercial Agreement.")

"Du Luan Ve Quan He Giua Viet Nam Va My." *Nhan Dan*, 12 May 1997, p. 8. ("Public Opinion on U.S.–Vietnam Relations.")

"Giai Quyet Ton Tai Cu Ve Tai Chinh Giua Viet Nam Va Hoa Ky." *Nhan Dan*, 12 May 1997, p. 8. ("Resolving Outstanding Financial Problems Between Vietnam and the United States.")

"Bo Truong Ngoia Giao My M. On-Brai Tham Chinh Thuc Viet Nam." *Nhan Dan*, 28 June 1997, pp. 1, 7. ("U.S. Secretary of State M. Albright Makes an Official Visit to Vietnam.")

"Tong Bi Thu Do Muoi Tiep Dai Su Hoa Ky." *Nhan Dan*, 4 June 1997, pp. 1, 3. ("General Secretary Do Muoi Receives the U.S. Ambassador.")

"Hoi Thao Ve Chien Tranh Viet Nam." *Nhan Dan*, 25 June 1997, p. 8. ("Conference on the Vietnam War.")

"Du Luan Ken Goi My Binh Thuong Hoa Day Du Quan He Kinh Te Voi Viet Nam." *Nhan Dan*, 3 July 1997, p. 8. ("Public Opinion Calls for the U.S. to Fully Normalize Economic Relations with Vietnam.")

"Giao Su Bac Si Le Cao Dai: Trach Nhiem Truoc Nhung Con Nguoi, Nhung Cuoc Doi." *Tuoi Tre Chu Nhat*, 27 July 1997, p. 8. ("Professor/Doctor Le Cao Dai: Duty to People and to Lives.")

"Tong Bi Thu Do Muoi Noi Chuyen Voi Can Bo Chu Chot Cong Doan Va Doanh Nghiep Ve Nghi Quyet Dai Hoi VIII." *Quan Doi Nhan Dan*, 1 August 1997, pp. 1, 4. ("General Secretary Do Muoi Speaks with Key Industrial and Trade Cadres About the Resolution of the 8th Party Congress.")

"Doan Ha Nghi Vien Hoa Ky Tham Nuoc Ta." *Nhan Dan*, 14 August 1997, p. 8. ("Delegation of the U.S. House of Representatives Visits Our Country.")

"Chu Tich Quoc Hoi Nong Duc Manh Tiep Doan Uy Ban An Ninh Quoc Gia Ha Nghi Vien My." *Nhan Dan*, 22 August 1997, pp. 1, 8. ("Chairman of the National Assembly Nong Duc Manh Receives a Delegation From the National Security Committee of the U.S. House of Representatives.")

Vietnamese Documents (chronological order)

"Bao Can Thuc Luc Vat Tu," U-6 A, D34, SRV Document, undated. ("Report on Supply Strength")

Bo Quoc Phong Vien Lich Su Quan Su Viet Nam. *May Van De Tong Ket Chien Tranh va Viet Su Quan Su*. Hanoi, 1987. (Military History Institute of Vietnam, Ministry of Defense, *Several Problems Regarding Reviewing the War and Writing Military History*, Hanoi, 1987.)

Dang Cong San Viet Nam. *Van Kien: Hoi Nghi Lan Thu Hai Ban Chap Hanh Trung Uong (Khoa VII)*, Hanoi: November-December 1991. (Communist Party of Vietnam, *Documents. Second Plenum of the Central Committee (7th Party Congress)*, Hanoi, November-December 1991.)

"De Cuong Phat Bieu Tai Cuoc Gap Doan Tro Ly Thuong-Ha Vien My Sang Tim Hieu Tinh Hinh Giai Quyet Van De Nguoi My Mat Tich O Viet Nam." 21 July 1991. ("Outline of Statements at Meeting with Staff Aides to the U.S. Senate and U.S. House of Representatives Regarding the Effort to Resolve the Issue of Americans Missing in Action in Vietnam.")

Ban Tu Tuong-Van Hoa Trung Uong. *Tai Lieu Gioi Thieu Nghi Quyet Hoi Nhi Lan Thu 2 Ban Chap Hanh Trung Uon Dang Cong San Viet Nam, Ve Nhiem Vu Va Giai Pha On Dinh Phat Trien Kinh Te Xa Hoi Trong Nam 1992-95*. Hanoi: Nha Xuat Ban Tu Tuong-Van Hoa, 1992. (Central Ideological and Cultural Committee: Document Introducing Resolution of the 2nd Plenum of the Vietnamese Communist Party Central Committee on Responsibilities and Measures to Stabilize Economic and

Social Development During the Period 1992–1995, Hanoi; Ideological and Cultural Committee Publishing House, 1992.)

Quan Doi Nhan Dan Viet Nam. Tong Cuc Chinh Tri, *Tinh Hinh The Gioi Trong Nuoc Va Luc Luong Vu Trang (9-1992)*. (General Political Department, People's Army of Vietnam, International and Domestic Situation and the Armed Forces (9-1992).)

Quan Doi Nhan Dan Viet Nam, Tong Cuc Chinh Tri. *Quan Triet Va Thuc Hien Nghi Quyet Hoi Nghi Trung Uong Lan Thu 3 Ve Doi Moi Va Chinh Don Bang Trong Dang Bo Quan Doi*. Hanoi: August 1992. (General Political Department, People's Army of Vietnam, Understanding and Implementing the Resolution of the 3rd Plenum of the Central Committee on Renovation and Reorganization in Military Party Chapters, Hanoi: August, 1992.)

Dang Cong San Viet Nam. *Van Kien: Hoi Nghi Lan Thu Tu Ban Chap Hanh Trung Uong, Khoa 7*, Luu Hanh Noi Bo, Hanoi, February 1993. (Communist Party of Vietnam, Documents: Fourth Plenum of the Party Central Committee, 7th Congress, Internal Distribution Only, Hanoi, February 1993.)

Quan Doi Nhan Dan Viet Nam, Tong Cuc Chinh Tri, Cuc Tu Tuong Van Hoa, (Thong Bao Noi Bo). "Tinh Hinh The Gioi, Trong Nuoc Va Luc Luong Vu Trang." January, April, May, June and July 1993. (Ideological and Cultural Department, General Political Department, People's Army of Vietnam, (Internal Bulletin), "International and Domestic Situation and the Armed Forces," January, April, May, June, and July 1993.)

Ban Tu Tuong Van Hoa Trung Uong. *Tiep Tuc Doi Moi va Phat Trien Kinh Te-Xa Hoi Nong Thon: Tai Lieu Hoc Tap Nghi Quyet Hoi Nghi Lan Thu Nam Ban Chap Hanh Trung Uong (Khoa VII) Dung Cho Co So Nong Thong*. Hanoi: Nha Xuat Ban Chinh Tri Quoc Gia, July 1993. (Central Ideological and Cultural Committee, Continuing Renovation and Economic-Social Development of the Rural Countryside: Study Document on the Resolution of the Fifth Plenum of the Party Central Committee, for Use by Rural Organizations, Hanoi: National Political Publishing House, July 1993.)

Statement of H.E. Mr. Phan Van Khai at the 48th Session of the United Nations General Assembly, 6 October 1993.

Dang Cong San Viet Nam. *Tai Lieu Tham Khao: Am Muu Va Hoat Dong "Dien Bien Hoa Binh" Cua Cac The Luc Thu Dich Tren Dat Nuoc Ta*. Hanoi: January 1994. (Communist Party of Vietnam: Study Document: "Peaceful Evolution" Plots and Actions Carried Out by Hostile Forces in Our Nation, Hanoi: January, 1994.)

Quan Doi Nhan Dan Viet Nam, Tong Cuc Chinh Tri, Cuc Tu Tuong Van Hoa, (Thong Bao Noi Bo). "Tinh Hinh The Gioi, Trong Nuoc va Luc Luong Vu Trang." March, February 1994. (Ideological and Cultural Department, General Political Department, People's Army of Vietnam, (Internal Bulletin), "International and Domestic Situation and the Armed Forces, March, February 1994.)

Dang Cong San Viet Nam. *Van Kien: Hoi Nghi Lan Thu Nam Ban Chap Hanh Trung Uong, Khoa VII*. Hanoi: August 1994. (Communist Party of Vietnam, *Documents: Fifth Plenum of the Party Central Committee, 7th Congress*, Hanoi: August, 1994.)

VNOSMP. "Report: Recent Work to Resolve the MIA Issue." 14 September 1994.

Bo Noi Vu, Tong Cuc So Mot, So 1001/TC 1 (MIA), 20 September 1994. Bui Quoc Huy, Chu Tich, Tong Cuc So Mot. (Ministry of Interior, General Department One, No. 1001/TC 1 (MIA), 20 September, 1994, Bui Quoc Huy, Chairman, General Department One.)

Quan Doi Nhan Dan, Tong Cuc Chinh Tri, *Thong Bao Noi Boi, Tinh Hinh The Gioi, Trong Nuoc Va Luc Luong Vu Trang*, Hanoi: June 1990–January 1995. (General Political Department, People's Army, Internal Bulletin, International and Domestic Situation and the Armed Forces, Hanoi: June-January 1995.)

Ban Tu Tuong-Van Hoa Trung Uong. *Tiep Tuc Xay Dung Va Hoan Thien Nha Nuoc Cong Hoa Xa Hoi Chu Nghia Viet Nam Trong Tam La Cai Cach Mot Buoc Nen Hanh Chinh: Tai Lieu Quan Triet Nghi Quyet Hoi Nghi Lan Thu 8 Ban Chap Hanh Trung Uong Dan Khoa VII.* Hanoi: Nha Xuat Ban Chinh Tri Quoc Gia, 1995. (Central Ideological and Cultural Committee: Continue Building and Improving the State Government of the Socialist Republic of Vietnam, with Primary Focus on Taking the First Step in Administrative Reform: Study Document for Understanding the Resolution of the 8th Plenum of the Party Central Committee, 7th Congress, Hanoi: National Political Publishing House, 1995.)
"Noi Dung Hop Bao Cua Thu Tuong Le Mai Ve Van De Binh Thuong Hoa Quan He Viet Nam-My, 12 July 1995." ("The Contents of the Press Conference of Vice Minister Le Mai on the Problem of Normalization of Vietnamese-American Relations")
Statement of the Spokesperson of Vietnam's Ministry of Foreign Affairs on the Decision by the United States President to Grant Vietnam a Waiver of the Jackson-Vanik Amendment, Embassy of Vietnam, Washington, D.C., Press Release Number 2, 11 March 1998.
The External Relations Department of the Ministry of Defense, Socialist Republic of Vietnam. Letter to U.S. Defense Attaché, 24 April 1997, 11/QT-M.
The External Relations Department of the Ministry of Defense, Socialist Republic of Vietnam. Letter to U.S. Ambassador, 28 DN, 27 April 1998.
Letter from Defense Minister Pham Van Tra to Secretary of Defense William S. Cohen, 12 December 1998.
The External Relations Department of the Ministry of Defense, Socialist Republic of Vietnam. Letter to U.S. Ambassador, 13 CH-DN, 13 February 2000.

English-Language Periodicals

Asian Wall Street Journal
Congressional Record
Department of Defense
POW/MIA Newsletter
Far Eastern Economic Review
Foreign Broadcast Information Service-East Asian Service

Indochina Interchange
National League of Families Updates
New York Times
Washington Post
Washington Times

English Language Books

Brown, Frederick Z. *Second Chance: The United States and Indochina in the 1990s.* New York: Council on Foreign Relations Press, 1989.
Chanda, Nayan. *Brother Enemy: The War After the War.* New York: Harcourt Brace Jovanovich. 1986.
Loi, Luu Van. *1945–1995: 50 Years of Vietnamese Diplomacy.* Hanoi: The Gioi, 2000.
Mather, Paul. *M.I.A.: Accounting for the Missing in Southeast Asia.* Washington, D.C.: National Defense University Press, 1994.
McConnell, Malcolm. *Inside Hanoi's Secret Archives.* New York: Simon and Schuster, 1995.
McNamara, Robert. *In Retrospect: The Tragedy and Lessons of Vietnam.* New York: Times Books, 1995.

Stern, Lewis M. *Renovating the Vietnamese Communist Party: Nguyen Van Linh and the Programme of Organizational Change*. Singapore: Institute of Southeast Asian Nations, 1993.

_____. *Imprisoned or Missing in Vietnam: Policies of the Vietnamese Government Concerning Captured and Unaccounted for United States Soldiers, 1969–1994*. Jefferson, N.C.: McFarland, 1995.

English Language Articles and Papers

Alexander, Paul. "Vietnamese General: U.S. Should Help." Associated Press, AP-NY-04-08-00, 9 April 2000.

Anderson, Desaix. "America's Relations with Vietnam: Accomplishments, Challenges, Potential." U.S.–Vietnam Trade Council. Hanoi, Vietnam, 7 April 1998.

Baker, Peter. "U.S. Will Waive Anti-Communism Law to Lessen Trade Restrictions on Vietnam." *Washington Post*, 19 December 1997, p. A.19.

Bang, Le Van. "U.S.–Vietnam Relations: Past and Future." Remarks at the National Press Club, Washington, D.C., 10 February 1998.

_____. Speech to Conference on Vietnam and the U.S. After 25 Years of Peace." Co-sponsored by the Fund for Reconciliation and Development, the Asia Pacific Center for Justice and Peace, the Mennonite Central Committee Washington Office, and the Vietnam Veterans of America Foundation, 12 April 2000.

Brown, Frederick Z. "Vietnam Since the War (1975–1995)." *Wilson Quarterly*, Winter 1995, pp. 65–87.

_____. "The United States and Southeast Asia Enter a New Era." *Current History*, December 1995, pp. 401–405.

_____. "Vietnam's Tentative Transformation." *Journal of Democracy*, Vol. 7, No.4, October 1996, pp. 74–87.

_____. "President Clinton's Visit to Vietnam." Asia Society Update, November 2000.

Buchan, Alex. "House Pastors Jailed in New Crackdown." *Christianity Today Magazine*, 6 January 1997, vol. 41, no. 1, p. 63.

Carroll, James. "Vietnam Buddies." *The New Yorker*, 21 and 28 October 1996, pp. 131–152.

Chanda, Nayan. "Vietnam in Post Cold War Asia: A Cautious Hand at the Wheel." in *China, India, Japan and the Security of Southeast Asia*, edited by Chandran Jeshurun, Singapore: Institute of Southeast Asian Studies, 1993, pp. 234–252.

Childress, Richard, and Stephen Solarz. "Vietnam: Detours on the Road to Normalization." in *Reversing Relations with Former Adversaries: U.S. Foreign Policy After the Cold War*, edited by C. Richard Nelson and Kenneth Weisbrode, University Press of Florida, 1998, pp. 88–194.

"Clinton Promises Full Effort to Account for MIAs." *New York Times*, 30 May 1995.

Crossette, Barbara. "Hanoi Official Sees MIA Searches as Spying." *New York Times*, 9 August 1992, p. 17.

Dai, Le Cao. "Agent Orange and Conscience of American People." *Viet Nam News*. 27 July 1997, p. 3.

Dobbs, Michael. "Two POWs, Two Views of Vietnam." *Washington Post*, 9 July 1995, p. 1.

Dzung, Vu Dan. "Vietnam's Perspectives: Establishing the ASEAN Free Trade Area." The Asia Pacific center for Security Studies Annual Conference, Honolulu, Hawaii, 3–6 November 1997.

Elliott, David W .P . "Vietnam Faces the Future." *Current History*, December 1995, pp. 412–419.

Esper, George. "Vietnam Hands Over More MIA Remains." *Washinqton Times*, 3 August 1994, p. 10.
Fedarko, Kevin. "Washington: The Last POW." *Time*, 24 April 1995, p. 42.
Fisher, Richard. "Beyond Normalization: A Winning Strategy for U.S. Relations with Vietnam." Heritage Foundation Backgrounder Update, Number 257, 18 July 1995.
Goldich, Robert L. "POWs and MIAs: Status and Accounting Issues." Congressional Research Service Issue Brief, IB92101, updated 24 April 1997.
Grant, Jeremy. "Asian Whirlwind Could Soon Prove Vietnam's Problem Too." *Financial Times*, (London), 31 December 1997.
Grinter, Lawrence. "Indochina's Slow Opening to the Future." *The Korean Journal of Defense Analysis*, Vol. IX, No. 2, Winter 1997, pp. 191- 208.
"Hanoi Seeks Settlement." *Vietnam News*, 16 May 1995, p. 1.
Harding, Harry. "The United States and China in the Asian Quadrangle." Vietnam–U.S. Workshop, Institute of Relations, Hanoi, Vietnam, 20–21 March 1998.
Herr, Don. "The Future of U.S.–Vietnam Security Relations." National War College, 6 March 1998.
Hiebert, Murray. "Unhealed Wounds: Party Plenum Dominated by Concerns Over China." *Far Eastern Economic Review*, 16 July 1992, pp. 20–21.
_____, and Susuma Awanohara. "Lukewarm Welcome." *Far Eastern Economic Review*, 17 February 1994, pp. 14–17.
Huckshorn, Kris. "Hanoi Probe Complete; Pentagon Officials Mum on MIA Funds." *San Jose Mercury News*, 22 December 1995.
_____, and Tim Larimer. "Vietnam Cases in on MIA Hunt." *San Jose Mercury News*, 28 April 1996.
Hung, Nguyen Manh. "Vietnam in 1999: The Party's Choice." *Asian Survey*, Vol. 39, No. 1, January/February 1999, pp. 98–111.
_____. "Vietnam–U.S. Relations: Achievements and Prospects." Vietnam–U.S. Workshop, Institute of Relations, Hanoi, Vietnam, 20–21 March 1998.
Hunt, Albert R. "On Vietnam, Clinton Should Follow a Hero's Advice." *Wall Street Journal*, 1 June 1995, p. A.15.
Kenney, Hank Kenney. "Which Way, Vietnam? " *Assembly*, March 1995, vol. 53, no.4, pp. 10–13.
Mann, Jim. "U.S. Steps Up Military Linkage to Vietnam." *Los Angeles Times*, 15 January 1997, p. 7.
Marr, David. "Vietnam Strives to Catch Up." The Asia Society, February 1995.
Mills, John D. "U.S. Colonels Visit Vietnamese Military." *Asia Pacific Defense Forum*, Summer 1998, pp. 2–11.
Moffet, George. "U.S. Faces Last Battle Over Vietnam War." *Christian Science Monitor*, 22 June 1995, p. 4.
Morris, Stephen J. "The '1205' Document: A Story of American Prisoners, Vietnamese Agents, Soviet Archives, Washington Bureaucrats and the Media." *The National Interest*, Fall 1993, pp. 28–42.
"Most of the MIA Issue Has Been Resolve — Do Muoi." Vietnam News, 17 May 1995, p. 1.
Neir, James E., Junior Vice Commander in Chief, VFW, "Southeast Asian POW/MIA Trip Report." 5–17 April 1995.
Ngoc, Dao Huy. "Asia-Pacific and Regional Security Cooperation," in *Multilateral Activities in South East Asia*. edited by Michael W. Everett and Mary A. Sommerville, Washington, D.C.: National Defense University Press, 1995, pp. 195–207.
O'Dowd, Edward. "Vietnamese Military Modernization: A Status Report." unpublished manuscript, 2000.
Opall, Barbara. "Pentagon Forges Military Relations with Vietnamese," *Defense News*, 3–8 March 1997, pp. 1, 28.

Peters, Katherin McIntire. "The Endless Search." *Government Executive*, April 1996, pp. 27–31.
Pierre, Andrew F. "Vietnam's Contradictions." *Foreign Affairs*, vol. 79, no. 6, November/December 2000, pp. 69–86.
Pierre, Greg. "Last POW Symbolically Buried." *Washington Times*, 5 October 1994, p. 3.
Pike, Douglas. *Report from Vietnam: 1991*. Berkeley, California: Indochina Studies Project, 1991.
Purdum, Todd S. "Clinton on Spot on Vietnam Issue." *New York Times*, 26 June 1995, p. 1.
Reuters Transcript Report. Clinton/Vietnam Announcement. 3 February 1994 (17:5702-03), p. 5.
Richmond, Melvin R., Jr. "United States National Interests in the Socialist Republic of Vietnam," U.S. Army War College Research Project. 16 September 1996.
Scalapino, Robert A. "Asia-Pacific on the Eve Century." Vietnam–U.S. Workshop, Institute of II Relations, Hanoi, Vietnam, 20–21 March 1998.
Schwartz, Adam. "Unfinished Business: MIA Issue Continues to Bedevil Ties with U.S.," *Far Eastern Economic Review*, 4 May 1995, pp. 24–25.
"Senior Clinton Aides Urging Full Relations with Vietnam," *New York Times*, 20 May 1995, pp. 1, 4.
Sheehan, Neil. "Report from Vietnam: The Last Battle." *New Yorker*, 24 April 1995, p. 85.
Shenon, Philip. "Vietnam Welcomes U.S. Decision on Embargo." *New York Times*, 5 February 1994, pp. 1, 5.
Sidel, Mark. "Philanthropy, Development of New Forms of Social Organizations, and the New Context for Corporate Philanthropy in Vietnam." Prepared for presentation at the International Symposium on Corporate Citizenship, Council on Foundations, Hong Kong, September 1995.
_____. "The United States and Vietnam: The Road Ahead." Asia Society Asian Update, 1996.
_____. "Vietnam's America Watchers in a New Era." *SAIS Review: A Journal of International Affairs*, Summer-Fall 1996, Vol. 26, No.2, pp. 43–69.
_____. "Vietnam in 1997: A Year of Challenges." *Asian Survey*, Vol. 38, No. 1, January 1998, pp. 80–90.
_____. "Vietnam in 1998: Reform Confronts the Regional Crisis." *Asian Survey*, Vol. 39, No. 1, January/February 1999, pp. 89–98.
_____. "Corporate Philanthropy in Vietnam: Initial Data and Initial Problems." manuscript, nd.
Stanley, Bruce. "U.S. Sees Breakthrough in MIA Search in Laos." Associated Press Story Category, 1 December 1994, APTU-12-01-94 0720 EST.
Stern, Lewis M. "Comments on Vietnamese Historiography and the Second World War." Prepared for the Panel on Teaching Outcomes and Legacy, Conference on the Teaching of the Vietnam War, sponsored by the Indochina Institute at George Mason University, Twin Bridges Marriott Hotel, Arlington, Virginia, 23 April 1988.
_____. "USG Strategic Interests in Vietnam." May 1994.
_____. "Vietnam's New Concept of Integrated National Defense", 17 July 1994.
_____. "Looking to the Future: Vietnam and Regional Policy Issues." Remarks prepared for the U.S.–Vietnam Policy Forum, sponsored by the U.S.–Vietnam Trade Council and the Georgetown University School of Foreign Service, Georgetown University, Washington, D.C., 21–22 July 1994.
_____. "U.S.–Vietnamese Relations: The Security Dimension — An Apriori Stab at the

Facts." presented to the Asia Foundation Seminar on Issues for Post-Normalization with Vietnam, Washington, D.C., 19 July 1995.
_____. "Perspectives: The Other MIAs." *Vietnam*, October 1996, pp. 62–66.
_____. "American Security Interests in Indochina," Prepared for presentation to the Advanced Area Studies Course: Mainland Southeast Asia, National Foreign Affairs Training Center, Department of State, Arlington, Virginia, 6 May 1998.
_____. "When You Wish Upon a Star: U.S.–Vietnamese Defense and Security Relations." Prepared for the Conference on the United States and Vietnam: Three Years After Normalization, Sponsored by the Stanley Foundation, Queenstown, Maryland, 11–13 December 1998.
_____. "Phieu and Far Between: The General Secretary and the 6th Plenary Meeting," unpublished manuscript, 4 February 1999.
_____. "Vietnam Security, Defense and Foreign Policies and Institutions in the 1990's: A Review of Key Developments and a Stab at Future Trends." Prepared for Project Asia, Center for Naval Analysis, Alexandria, Virginia, April 1999.
_____. "Vietnamese Public Statements on Kosovo." Prepared for the Roundtable on the Impact of Kosovo on Asia and the Pacific, Center for Naval Analysis, Alexandria, Virginia, 19 May 1999.
_____. "American Security Interests in Vietnam." Prepared for presentation to the Advanced Area Studies Course: Mainland Southeast Asia, National Foreign Affairs Training Center, Department of State, Arlington, Virginia, 3 June 1999.
_____. "Vietnam." *Asian Security Handbook 2000*. New York: M.E. Sharpe, 2000, pp. 305–318.
Sutter, Robert G. "Vietnam Procedural and Jurisdictional Questions Regarding Possible Normalization of U.S. Diplomatic and Economic Relations." CRS Report 94-663, 4 August 1994.
Thanh, Nguyen Trong. "ASEAN 10: Opportunities and Challenges." Vietnam–U.S. Workshop, Institute of Relations, Hanoi, Vietnam, 20–21 March 1998.
Thayer, Carlyle. "Vietnam in 2000: Toward the Ninth Party Congress," *Asian Survey*, Vol. 39, No. 1, January/February 1999, pp. 98–111.
_____. "Vietnam's Doi Moi: Progress and Prospects." Concurrent Session 6, 15th Asia Pacific Roundtable, Organized by ISIS-Malaysia, Kuala Lumpur, Malaysia, 4–7 June 2001.
Turley, William S. "Vietnamese Security in Domestic and Regional Focus: The Political-Economic Nexus." in *Southeast Asian Security in the New Millennium*, edited by Richard J. Ellings and Sheldon W. Simon, New York: M.E. Sharpe, 1996, pp. 175–220.
"U.S. Congressional Legislation." *The Mekong Digest*, Vol. 9, No. 23, 2 October 1996, p. 1.
"U.S., Vietnam Discuss MIA Issue." *Washington Post*, 3 July 1994, p. A. 24.
"U.S.–Vietnam Trade Talks." *The Mekong Digest*, Vol. 9, No. 23, 2 October 1996, p. 1.
"U.S. Vietnam War Crash Wreckage Believed Found." Reuters Wire Service, 30 May 1995.
Van Ness, Peter. "Alternative U.S. Strategies with Respect to China and the Implications for Vietnam." Vietnam–U.S. Workshop, Institute of International Relations, Hanoi, Vietnam, 20–21 March 1998.
Vessey, John W. Jr. "Vietnam War — POW/MIA and National Priorities." The John M. Olin Lecture Series in National Security and Defense Studies, Final Report for Academic Year 1993-1994, United States Air Force Academy, August 1994.
"Vietnam Military Delegation, in U.S., Expected to Go Beyond MIA Issues." *Boston Globe*, 20 February 1997, p. 10.
"Westmoreland Against Hanoi Relations." *Washington Times*, 9 July 1995, p. 4.

Wiedemann, Kent. "Vietnam: U.S. Commitment to the Fullest Possible Accounting of POW/MIAs." *U.S. Department of State Dispatch*, 24 June 1996, pp. 342–343.
Wold, James. "Keeping Faith with MIAs." *Defense '95*, p. 21.
Wolf, Jim. "No Vietnam-Era U.S. POWs Were Sent to Moscow, Report Says." II Reuters, 2 May 1995 (wire service copy).
Young, Stephen. "Vietnam's Turn." *Washington Post*, 13 June 1993, p. A.15.
_____. Memorandum via facsimile, 23 November 1993.
Zasany, Julie. "Vietnam Mystery Exhumed by Mom." *The Journal Gazette*, (Fort Wayne, Indiana), 10 April 1996, pp. 1, 4.

U.S. Government Documents and Congressional Testimonies (chronological order)

The Presidential Commission on Americans Missing and Unaccounted for in Southeast Asia: Report on Trip to Vietnam and Laos, 16–20 March 1977, pp. 6–9.
"POW/MIA Significant Events." Office of the Assistant Secretary of Defense for Public Affairs, 7 August 1991.
Testimony of Richard Childress, former staff member, National Security Council, before the Senate Select Committee on POW/MIA Affairs, 12 August 1992, pp. 2–3.
Vessey, John W. Jr. "POW/MIA Next Steps." 4 November 1992.
_____. "Vietnamese Cooperation." 18 February 1993.
Office of the White House Press Secretary. "Renewal of the Trading with the Enemy Act and U.S. Policy Toward the Embargo Against Vietnam." 13 September 1993.
Remarks of Samuel R. Berger, Deputy National Security Advisor, to the Annual Meeting of the National League of Families of POWs and MIAs from Southeast Asia, Washington, D.C., 15 July 1994, pp. 3–4.
Congressional Research Service. *Vietnam: Procedural and Jurisdictional Questions Regarding Possible Normalization of U.S. Diplomatic and Economic Relations.* 4 August 1994.
National Defense Authorization Act for Fiscal Year 1995, Conference Report to Accompany S.2182. House of Representatives, 103rd Congress, 2nd Session, Report 109-701, 12 August 1994, pp. 181–185.
President's Report to Congress on Vietnamese POW/MIA Cooperation. 22 August 1994.
"Technical Steps Required to Implement Economic Measures Concerning Vietnam." 27 October 1994.
"Veterans Form POW/MIA Action Group." The American Legion, 16 November 1994.
VSO and Family POW Organizations."POW/MIA Ad Hoc Meeting." 16 November 1994.
Department of State. *Technical Steps Required to Implement Economic Measures Concerning Vietnam.* 27 November 1994.
Statement by Christine Shelling, Acting State Department Spokesman, on the opening of liaison offices, 27 January 1995, *U.S. Department of State Dispatch*, February 1995, Vol. 6, No. 6, p. 84.
General Accounting Office. Report to Congressional Committees. U.S.–Vietnam Relations: Issues and Implications. GAO/NSIAD-95-42, April 1995.
U.S. General Accounting Office, Report to Congressional Committees. "U.S. Vietnam Relations: Issues and Implications." GAO/NSIAD-95-42, April 1995.
U.S.–Russian Joint Commission on POW/MIAs, *Interim Report of the Joint Commission on POW/MIAS*, Washington, D.C., May 1995.

U.S.–Russian Joint Commission on POW/MIAs. *Vietnam Working Group Report.* Washington, D.C., May 1995.
Remarks by President Clinton, President of France, Jacques Chirac, and President of the European Union, Jacques Santer, Office of the Press Secretary, White House, 14 June 1995, p. 1.
White House Office of the Press Secretary. "Press Package: The President's Announcement on Vietnam." 11 July 1995.
"DPMO Response to 7 June 1995 Congressional Questions Regarding the POW/MIA Issue," 19 June 1995.
Defense POW/MIA Office Response to 7 June 1995 Congressional Questions Regarding the POW/MIA Issue, 19 June 1995.
Defense POW/MIA Office. "Fact Sheet: Vietnam POW/MIA Issue — Progress Since the Lifting of the Economic Embargo (February 1994–Present), 26 June 1995.
DPMO. "Fact Sheet: Vietnam POW/MIA Issue — Progress Since the Lifting of the Embargo, (February 1994–Present)." 26 June 1995.
Assistant Secretary Winston Lord. Policy Statement on Accounting for U.S. POW/MIAs Before the House Subcommittee on Military Personnel, 28 June 1995.
Statement by Brigadier General Charles R. Viale, Commander, JTFFA, before the House Committee on National Security, Military Personnel Subcommittee, 28 June 1995.
"Report to the President by the Presidential Delegation on POW/MIA Issues.," 6 July 1995.
Office of the Press Secretary, the White House. "Fact Sheet: Vietnam War POW/MIA Cases: Progress Under the Clinton Administration." 11 July 1995.
Office of the Press Secretary, the White House. "Fact Sheet: Background Paper on POW/MIA Accounting." 11 July 1995.
U.S. Department of State, Office of the Spokesman. "America's Strategy for a Peaceful and Prosperous Asia-Pacific." Secretary of State Warren Christopher, Presented to the National Press Club, 28 July 1995.
U.S. Department of State, Office of the Spokesman, "U.S.–Vietnam Relations: A New Chapter." Secretary of State Warren Christopher, Presented to the Institute for International Relations, Hanoi, Vietnam, 6 August 1995.
Vietnam Interagency Working Group. "Economic Normalization: Pace and Procedures." 21 August 1995.
"Accounting for the Missing in Southeast Asia: Text of a 'Zero-Based Comprehensive Review of Cases Involving Unaccounted for Americans in Southeast Asia.'" DoD Report to Congress and the Nation Prepared by the Office of the Deputy Assistant Secretary of Defense for POW/MIA Affairs, released on 13 November 1995.
Department of Defense. *Zero-Based Comprehensive Review of Cases Involving Unaccounted for Americans in Southeast Asia.* 13 November 1995.
Memorandum for the Secretary of State, from the White House Subject: Vietnamese Cooperation in Accounting for United States Prisoners of War and Missing in Action (POW/MIA). 29 May 1996.
James Wold. "The Presidential Determination of Full Faith Cooperation by Vietnam." Presented to the House Committee on National Security, Military Personnel Subcommittee, 19 June 1996.
"Southeast Asia-ROK-US: Thai, Vietnamese, South Korean Media Portray Lake Visit in Positive Light." Foreign Media Note, Foreign Broadcast Information Service, FBIS-FMN 96-00543, 15 July 1996.
Remarks by Anthony Lake, Assistant to the President for National Security Affairs, to the Japan-America Society, Washington, D.C., October 23, 1996.
Vietnamese Storage of Remains of Unaccounted U.S. Personnel, Intelligence Community Assessment. October 1996.

SNIE 14.3.87, "Hanoi and the POW/MIA Issue," Approved for release, 29 October 1996.
"Vietnamese Storage of Remains of Unaccounted for U.S. Personnel." ICA-96-05, October 1996.
"U.S.–Vietnam Relations." Hearings Before the Subcommittee on Asia and the Pacific of the Committee on International Relations, House of Representatives, 150th Congress, First Session, 18 June 1997.
Department of Defense. *The United States Security Strategy for the East Asian-Pacific Region*. Washington, D.C., 1998.
Roth, Stanley. Statement before the Senate Foreign Relations Committee, 10 March 1998.
———. Assistant Secretary of State for East Asia, "Regional Security Policy in East Asia and the Pacific." Hearing of the House International Relations Committee, Asia and the Pacific Subcommittee, 7 May 1998.
Slocombe, Walter. Under Secretary of Defense for Policy, "U.S. Security Interests in the Pacific." Hearing of the House International Relations Committee, Asia and the Pacific Subcommittee, 7 May 1998.
Testimony of Douglas Peterson, U.S. Ambassador to Vietnam, House Committee on Ways and Means, Subcommittee on Trade, 18 June 1998.
Statement on Status of the U.S.–Vietnam Bilateral Trade Agreement, Office of the U.S. Trade Representative, House Ways and Means Subcommittee on Trade, 18 June 1998.
"Vietnamese Intentions, Capabilities and Performance Concerning the POW/MIA Issue." Declassified portion of National Intelligence Estimate, August 1998.
Testimony of Douglas Peterson, U.S. Ambassador to Vietnam, Hearing on Extension of the Jackson Vanik Waiver for Vietnam, The Trade Subcommittee of the House Ways and Means Committee, 17 June 1999.
Testimony of Douglas Peterson, U.S. Ambassador to Vietnam, Senate Subcommittee on International Economic Policy, Exports and Trade Promotion, and Senate Subcommittee on East Asian and Pacific Affairs, 4 August 1999.
Department of State, Office of the Spokesman. "Statement by Richard Boucher: Inclusion of the Socialist Republic of Vietnam in the U.S. Humanitarian Demining Program." 14 June 2000.

INDEX

Agent Orange 99, 151, 157–159, 179, 183, 202, 203, 220
Air War College 69, 70, 118, 195, 204, 218
Albright, Madeline 150, 157–158
Amerasian children 10
American Council of Learned Societies 85
American Legion 51
Anderson, Desaix 118
Anh, Le Duc 13, 26, 112, 159
Armed Forces Research Institute of Medical Sciences (AFRIMS) 40, 154
Armed Services, views on normalization 70
Army Corps of Engineers 40, 69, 89, 213
ASEAN Regional Forum (ARF) 78, 88, 123, 156, 161
Asia Pacific Center for Strategic Studies (APCSS) 122, 161, 163–164, 196
Asia Pacific Dialogue 176
Asia Pacific Military Medical Conference 195
Asia Pacific Policy Center 176
Asian Development Bank 33
Assistant Secretary of Defense for International Security Affairs (ASD/ISA) 38, 69, 71, 154
Association of Southeast Asian Nations (ASEAN) 17, 18, 39, 76, 151, 161, 176, 184

Bader, Jeffrey 134
Baker, James 11
Bang, Le Van 4, 57, 117, 130, 146, 186, 206, 208, 221
Beijing 8; *see also* China
Beneficiary Developing Countries 79

Berger, Sandy 49, 149
Bien, Tran 98–99, 115, 132
Bilateral Trade Agreement 44, 144, 210, 215, 223, 234–235
Bin, Nguyen Dinh 119, 145–146
Bond, Christopher 51
Border Committee 154
Bung, Nguyen Thoi 47, 59, 76–78, 100, 115, 118–119, 222
Bush, George 7, 10, 18–22, 226

Ca, Tran Van 4
Cam, Nguyen Manh 14, 25, 32, 50, 52, 80, 86, 176–181, 194–195
Cam Ranh Bay 132–133, 226
Cambodia 8, 10, 11, 12, 15, 39, 42, 51
Campbell, Kurt 4, 107, 117–123, 134, 222
Capstone 202, 204, 218
Carter, Jimmy 3, 7, 8, 9
Cheney, Richard 21
Chief of Naval Operations 138
Childress, Richard 82
China 8, 9, 39, 44, 53, 55, 107, 110, 121, 125–126, 128–129, 138, 139, 143, 151, 173, 194–196, 200, 201, 205, 206, 216, 217, 223–225
Christopher, Warren 31, 50, 72, 74, 78, 80
CILHI (Central Identification Laboratory — Hawaii) 95, 209
Clinton, William 3, 23–26, 31, 36, 42–43, 45, 66–68, 98, 104, 173–174, 219–220, 225–226
Co, Tran Quang 4, 13, 26, 52
Cohen, William 176–182, 199–201, 204–209, 209–212, 216–217

287

Commander in Chief, Pacific (CINCPAC) 74, 121, 235, 145
Commando Compensation Law 161
Comprehensive POW/MIA Review 59–60, 80–82, 95–96
Cong, Vo Chi 160
"Consolidating the International Rear" 9
Consular issues 28–29
Counter Narcotics Cooperation 4

Dau, Nguyen Manh 156, 157, 166
Defense Attaché's Office (U.S.) 58, 84, 88, 118
Defense Attaché's Office (Vietnam) 88
Defense Intelligence Agency 58, 84, 102
Defense Liaison Office 58
Defense Mapping Agency 42, 69, 89
Defense policy process (U.S) 90–92, 100–102, 110–112, 112–116, 177–178, 192–193, 221, 225–228
Defense policy process (Vietnam) 69–72, 74–75, 76–78, 84–88, 108–110, 142–143, 190–193, 196–199, 221–225
Defense POW/MIA Office (DPMO) 70–71, 102–105, 127, 134, 149
Defense relations 36–42, 57–59, 69–72, 84–92, 96–98, 112–159, 164–165, 176–178, 182, 198, 201–204, 213–215, 217–220, 241–244
Defense Security Assistance Agency (DSAA) 133
Demining 1, 69, 180–181, 188, 211, 213, 220
Department of Defense 39, 59, 126
Deputy Assistant Secretary of Defense for Asian and Pacific Affairs (DASD/AP) 3, 20, 71
Deputy Assistant Secretary of Defense for POW/MIA Affairs (DASD/POW-MIA) 4, 96
Deputy Chief of Mission, Embassy of Vietnam 4
Disaster assistance 1
Dole, Robert 64, 68
Domestic dimensions of normalization (U.S.) 23–26, 32, 38–39, 52–54, 70–71, 80–84, 126–127, 180–181, 238–241
Domestic dimensions of normalization (Vietnam) 23–27, 54–55, 67–68, 75, 83–84, 105–108, 187–188, 196–199, 238–241
Dornan, Robert 82–83, 102–105

"E Ring" 3

"East Asia Strategy Review" 88
Embargo 7, 11, 15–16, 21, 25, 30–31, 32–33, 36–37, 42, 45
Engineering and Civic Action Projects 154
Environmental issues 211–212, 218
Export-Import Bank (EXIM) 44, 80, 91–92, 149, 171
External Relations Department (Ministry of National Defense) 77–78, 117–123, 129–160, 163–164, 185, 190–193, 199–200, 201–204, 213–215, 217–221, 228–229
External Relations Department (Vietnamese Communist Party Central Committee) 86, 119

"Flyout" 170
Foote, Virginia 4
Ford, Carl 21, 81–82
Foreign Assistance Act 49
Foreign Operations Appropriations Act 49
Foreign policy priorities 16–18
Frozen assets 36

General Agreement on Tariffs and Trade (GATT) 33, 79
General Political Department (Ministry of National Defense 23, 29, 36, 44, 201
General System of Preferences 44, 79
Giao, Nguyen Ngoc 4
Gilman, Benjamin 205
Gober, Hershel 4, 28, 46–49, 60–62

Ha, Hong 85–88
Hanh, Tran 1, 153, 161, 169, 173, 175, 181–184, 195, 242, 243
Harken, Tom 64
Harter, Dennis 4
"Healing the Wounds of War" 8
Helms, Jesse 205
Hendon, Bill 62–64
Ho Chi Minh Mausoleum 206
Hoat, Doan Viet 177
House Committee on National Security 107
House International Relations Committee 65
House Military Personnel Sub-Committee 82, 104
House of Representatives 9, 82, 175
Human rights 29, 36, 41, 44, 78
Humanitarian assistance 40–42, 69, 71, 89–90, 180–181, 197–198, 208–209, 215

Hung, Nguyen Manh 4, 169

Intellectual property rights 44
International Conference on Kampuchea 10
International Financial Institutions (IFI) 9, 15, 24, 30, 33, 44
International Monetary Fund 19, 21, 27, 33
International Munitions List 235–236
International Security Affairs (ISA) 20, 37, 38, 69, 74, 127–129, 136–137, 164–165, 176–178, 182, 198, 201–204, 213–215, 217–220, 228–229, 229–234

Jackson, Karl 2
Jackson-Vanik Amendment 44, 79, 91, 94, 111, 144, 161, 169, 170, 171, 174
Joint Interagency Task Force-West (JIATF-West) 171, 172
Joint POW/MIA Field Operations 14, 24, 44, 46
Joint Staff 3, 5, 35, 69, 129–130, 148
Joint Task force Full Accounting (JTFFA) 24, 26, 33, 40, 42, 46–49, 57, 63, 65, 74–75, 80, 89, 90, 102–105, 206
Jones, Robert 4

Kerry, John 20, 22, 26–27, 50–51, 56, 64
Khai, Phan Van 31, 160, 209
Khoan, Vu 155–157
Khue, Doan 13, 118, 119–120, 137, 151
Kien, Pham Duc 4
Kiet, Vo Van 32, 44, 51, 60, 64, 98, 159, 160
Kosovo 196, 199, 200, 205
Kozyrev, Andre 30
Kramer, Franklin 134, 145–146, 155–157

Lake, Anthony 58, 110–112
Lang, Trinh Xuan 105
Laos 9, 22, 25, 27–28, 45, 50
Larson, Charles 74
Last Known Alive Discrepancy Cases 14, 28
Liaison Office 29, 40, 43–44, 45, 48, 55–57, 80
Lich, Dao Trong 172
Linh, Nguyen Van 159
Live Sighting Investigation 25, 28, 34, 46, 56, 63
Lord, Winston 25, 28–30, 32, 46–49, 60–62, 95
Luong, Tran Duc 209

Macke, R.C. 74

Mai, Le 11, 29, 31, 58–59, 64, 75, 98–100
McCain, John 27, 51, 56, 61, 64
McNamara, Robert 61
Medical assistance 1, 69
Military historians 69, 89
Military Law Division (Ministry of National Defense) 83
Military sales 235–236
Military Strategy Institute (Ministry of National Defense) 195
Minh, Phan The 142
Ministry of Foreign Affairs 13, 23, 26, 34, 43–44, 49, 67, 105–108, 142, 201, 221
Ministry of Interior 13, 34, 46–47, 61, 83
Ministry of Labor, War Invalids, and Social Affairs 47
Ministry of National Defense 3, 13, 28, 34, 61, 76–78, 191–194, 201, 221–225, 234
Moscow 8, 26
Most Favored Nations Trading Status (MFN) 3, 36, 44, 59, 68, 78–79, 144, 180, 189
Muoi, Do 12, 13, 16, 25, 26, 29, 45–46, 46–49, 51, 56–57, 60–62, 86–87, 98, 109, 157–158, 159
Murkowski, Frank 25
Muskie, Edmund 25

National Assembly 3, 13, 26, 142, 144
National Defense Academy (Vietnam) 206
National Defense Authorization Act 51, 59, 65, 81
National Defense University (U.S.) 69, 118, 161, 202
National League of POW/MIA Families 42–43, 46–49, 51–52, 97, 104
National Security Council 71, 80, 92, 101, 227
Negotiating 229–234
Ngo, Bui Thien 28–29, 46–47
Nhu, Bui Trong 182
Nien, Nguyen Duy 32, 209
Normalization 3, 7, 8, 19, 23, 24, 29, 36, 55–57, 66–68, 72–75, 76–78, 238–241
North Atlantic Treaty Organization (NATO) 200
Nye, Joseph 85–88

O'Dowd, Edward 3, 4, 156, 157
Office of the Assistant Secretary of Defense for Special Operations and Low Intensity Conflict 71

Office of the Prime Minister 34
Orderly Departure Program 10
Overseas Private Investment Corporation (OPIC) 79, 91–92
Pacific Command (PACOM) 3–5, 35, 57–58, 90, 148, 202
Paris Agreement (Cambodia) 11, 15, 40
Perry, William 74, 137
Peterson, Douglas "Pete" 151, 185
Phieu, Le Kha 109, 159, 194–196
Phong, Nguyen Xuan 4, 59
Pike, Douglas 6
Presidential Commission 9
Presidential Delegation 24–25, 27, 28–30, 46–49, 60–62, 66, 80–81, 88, 97–100
Presidential Emissary 4, 11, 25, 26, 43, 118
Prisoner of War/Missing in Action (POW/MIA) 9–10, 15, 19–20, 23, 25–27, 30–31, 32–33, 35, 42, 50, 51–53, 56–57, 60–62, 62–64, 66–68, 72–75, 82–83, 90, 98–99, 111, 140–141, 149, 180–181, 184, 189–190, 207–209, 216–217, 225–226, 234
Property claims 36, 43, 79

Quang, Tran Van 26, 45
Quang, Vo Dinh 4, 131, 146, 151–152, 166, 167, 172, 173, 186, 208
Que, Pham Van 4, 158

Reagan, Ronald 10, 43
Reeducation camps 10
Refugees 7, 111, 150, 179
Remittances 10
Reparations 9
"Roadmap" 11–12, 14–16, 19–20, 24–25, 38, 56, 127
Robb, Chuck 29
Rohrbacher, Dana 205
Roth, Stanley 4
Rumsfeld, Donald 1

Science and Technology Institute (Ministry of National Defense) 167–168
Search and Rescue 1, 172, 203, 211, 213
Secretary of Defense 176–181, 184–188, 199–201, 204–209, 209–212, 216–217
Senate 63, 174
Senate Select Committee on POW/MIA Affairs 22, 25
Shelton, Charles 50
Ship visit 2, 132–133, 141, 161, 203, 212, 213, 219

Sino-Vietnamese Rapproachment 15
Slocombe, Walter 37, 81, 96–97, 101–102, 116, 148, 152–153
Smith, Robert 22, 51, 59, 64, 67, 68, 105, 149
Social Policy Department (Ministry of National Defense) 165, 197, 201, 228
Solomon, Richard 11
South China Sea 78, 118
Southeast Asia 8, 38, 41, 53
Sovereignty 2, 11, 18, 36
Soviet Military Intelligence Documents 26, 30, 149
Soviet Union 8, 19, 60
Special National Intelligence Estimate (SNIE) 102–105
Special Remains Cases 50, 60–61
State Department 9, 24, 28–29, 40, 47–48, 64, 68, 71, 84, 128, 133, 149, 174, 226–228, 235–236

Tan, Vu 115–116, 129–130, 134–137, 163–164, 185, 200, 206, 214–215
Task Force on Pacific Security 138–139
Thach, Nguyen Co 11, 12, 20, 28
Thomas, Craig 105
Thong, Ha Huy 4, 112–116, 121–122, 158
Tra, Pham Van 1, 2, 186, 200
Trading with the Enemy Act 30, 33, 36–37
Tran, Le Minh 4
Turley, William 5

Under Secretary of Defense for Policy 37, 81, 96–97, 101–102, 116, 148, 152–153
United Nations Development Program (UNDP) 40
United Nations Transitional Authority in Cambodia 11
United States Army Center of Military History 41
United States Army Pacific (USARPAC) 215
United States Marine Corps (USMC) 70, 215
United States–Russian Joint Commission on POW/MIAs 60
United States Trade and Development Agency 79–80

Van, Nguyen Ngoc 195
Vessey, John W., Jr. 4, 11, 25, 26, 40
Veterans of Foreign Wars (VFW) 56, 58–59

Vienna Convention on Consular Relations 44, 55–56
Vietnam Office for Seeking Missing Personnel (VNOSMP) 22, 26, 34, 60–61, 117, 237
Vietnam Veterans Association 45
Vietnamese Communist Party 4, 12–13, 14–15, 16–18, 32–33, 56, 93–94, 108–110
Vietnam's Missing in Action (MIAs) 135, 162, 165–166, 182, 201, 203, 210, 220

Wold, James 46–49, 50, 60–62, 95–96

Wolfowitz, Paul 21
Woodcock, Leonard 9
World Bank 33
World Food Program 40
World Health Organization 40
World Trade Organization 44
"Wounds of War" 214

Yeltsin, Boris 60

Zasloff, Joseph 5

www.ingramcontent.com/pod-product-compliance
Ingram Content Group UK Ltd.
Pitfield, Milton Keynes, MK11 3LW, UK
UKHW041927140426
5217IPUK00014B/352